Cold War at 30,000 Feet

Jeffrey A. Engel

Cold War at 30,000 Feet

The Anglo-American Fight for
Aviation Supremacy

Harvard University Press

Cambridge, Massachusetts, and London, England   2007

Library of Congress Cataloging-in-Publication Data

Engel, Jeffrey A.
  Cold War at 30,000 feet : the Anglo-American fight for aviation supremacy / Jeffrey A. Engel.
    p.   cm.
  Includes bibliographical references and index.
  ISBN-13: 978-0-674-02461-8 (alk. paper)
  ISBN-10: 0-674-02461-3 (alk. paper)
    1. United States—Foreign relations—Great Britain. 2. Great Britain—Foreign relations—
United States.   3. Technology and international affairs—History—20th century.
4. Aeronautics—Technological innovations—History—20th century. 5. Aircraft industry—
Political aspects—United States—History—20th century. 6. Aircraft industry—Political
aspects—Great Britain—History—20th century. 7. United States—Foreign economic
relations—Communist countries. 8. Great Britain—Foreign economic realtions—Communist
countries. 9. Cold War. 10. United States—Foreign relations—1945–1989. I. Title II. Title:
Cold war at thirty thousand feet.
  E183.8.G7E49 2007
  338.4′762913340973—dc22   2006049667

For Katie
M.T.T.C.T.

Contents

Illustrations follow page 158.

Preface

This is not the study I set out to write. I thought the story of British and American aviation diplomacy would be a tale of export promotion capable of demonstrating the economic impact of foreign policy decisions on communities. Because during the Cold War aviation was—as it remains today— an industry important enough to garner the attention of presidents and prime ministers alike, I thought a study of government efforts on its behalf would entail following money's well-worn path of influence to the promised land of sales, jobs, and power.

I realized after two days in the archives that I had an entirely different story on my hands. Aviation diplomacy during the Cold War was not a matter of export promotion, I discovered, but of export control. This was not a story of policymakers forcing open closed foreign markets or acting as international guides for corporations seeking prosperity. Instead, Western governments focused on containing and controlling the strategically valuable (and potentially quite profitable) aviation technologies those corporations produced in order to keep them from communist hands, just like Olympus once sought to keep fire from mankind. This was no simple process, because for policymakers the imperatives of security and sales were often at odds. Corporations on both sides of the Atlantic Ocean sought to sell their wares far and wide, even beyond the iron curtain, with little consideration for the long-term consequences if communists acquired their best technologies. Time and again, corporate leaders—even those with government or military experience—acted out of concern only for their bottom line, seeking buyers wherever they could find them. Government officials in London and Washington therefore frequently had to restrain sales efforts lest overexuberant exporters tip the Cold War's delicate strategic balance toward their enemies; yet even the most hawkish strategists realized that Western corporations needed to be profitable if they were to be helpful in the Cold War fight. Rigid restraints on sales would keep communists from gaining Western technologies, this was true; but such restraints, if too tight, risked suffocating the jet aviation industry in its infancy. Reducing limitations on sales to a bare minimum, meanwhile, might produce great short-term profits, but might equally endanger Western security by allowing communist states or agents easy access to the best technologies the West had to offer.

This story was not about export promotion so much as it was about the troubled search these governments on both sides of the Atlantic endured in the hope of finding a safe middle path between unbridled sales and suffocating technological security. It reveals the constant interplay between the history of aviation with its soaring achievements and milestone moments, and the more mundane, though no less important, daily diplomacy required to get the planes and missiles of the modern age into the hands of consumers and soldiers who so desperately longed to enter the jet age. In short, a close look at aviation diplomacy reveals policymakers balancing sales and security in an effort to control the entrance of strategically valuable technologies into the Cold War marketplace.

Policymakers on both sides of the Atlantic faced the same balancing act and the same communist enemies. But they employed different scales and different standards unique to their own national experience. Indeed, each brought to this problem not only analyses of their nation's needs but also a sense of moral certainty whose history provides valuable insights for our own day. American leaders, intoxicated by their own power after 1945 yet fearful of a world made dangerously intimate by the advent of intercontinental aviation, judged allies solely by whether they conformed to American security concerns. Demanding unquestioned obedience, they failed to listen when their allies spoke, and failed to hear their concerns. Their British counterparts, impoverished by two world wars yet lured by prospects of future power through aviation, also failed to sufficiently consider others' worldviews. In particular, anxious for their aviation mastery to provide Britain with profit and great-power status, they failed to sufficiently recognize Washington's own anxiety over its newfound hegemonic role in a world in which America was, for the first time in modern history, within range of enemy attack. Leaders in London and Washington persisted in believing that their own policies not only provided the strategically correct middle path between sales and security but were morally correct as well. When their policies clashed, as they did with alarming frequency, this combination of strategic thinking and moral certainty nearly poisoned their long-standing special relationship built on common values, language, history, and enemies. Their mutual fear of the communist world frequently helped smooth over such difficulties, but underlying their most fundamental arguments was their inability to agree upon just how dangerous that communist threat was in the first place.

Though it seems an increasingly disfavored view as I write this note, this history of the frequently bitter clashes between two intimate allies in search of a mutually acceptable balance between profits and security shows that while power is the international system's ultimate trump card, even superpowers need allies. Even more than they need the troops and supplies that allies might offer, the strongest of nations need to heed the advice of their allies as well. They need to listen as much as to lead. Power is an intoxicant, and wise counsel its best antidote. But before wise counsel can be heeded, it must be acknowledged. Neither country in this story sufficiently acknowledged its partner's needs or sufficiently respected the other's worldview. Within this dance of strategy and certainty, the dynamics of commerce and security must be understood in their proper order and sequence. Each nation's aviation security program grew out of that nation's particular financial situation and geopolitical outlook, a calculus of the country's capabilities that ultimately reflected its worldview—which required little explanation within the one government but appeared strange when viewed by the government across the Atlantic. Leaders in both countries could count columns of numbers just as proficiently. They could each read ledgers and maps. What they failed to do, however, even in the midst of disputes, was to fully appreciate that each believed that not only prudence, but also providence, was on their side. The pages that follow show the way disputes over aviation nearly ruptured the Anglo-American special relationship, that bedrock of the Western effort against global Communism. It shows the strains inherent in even the closest of international relationships, and the intoxicating power of power.

Cold War at 30,000 Feet

Introduction

This is a story about power. Power enough to shape nations and the world. It is an examination of the bitter battles fought by British and American officials over the proper maintenance of the international system following the horrors of World War II, and ultimately of their contest to see which nation would lead the Western crusade against global Communism during the ensuing Cold War. The contest would determine which nation was best equipped to lead the world in its long search for stability, peace, and prosperity in the second half of the twentieth century. The competitors were not always in conflict. Rarely have two allies worked more closely than the United States and the United Kingdom, bonded by a common language, political tradition, and the burdens of combating common enemies. Yet with a fervor rarely appreciated owing to their frequent and public displays of intimacy, behind closed doors they fought bitterly—not only for their different visions of their "special relationship," in which the two nations famously operated as a tighter partnership than either capital enjoyed with any other nation, but more dramatically for their different versions of the future.

American policymakers presumed that the mantle of Western leadership was theirs for the taking after World War II, owing to their unmatched resources and prosperity in a world filled with rubble. They considered leadership their right also by virtue of their unmatched devotion to the creation of a new world order, a Pax Americana built upon the intertwined foundations of liberal trade and cooperative security, mutually guaranteed by a preponderance of American wealth and military might unmatched since the height of the Roman Empire. The United States in 1945 wielded the world's mightiest air force and navy, and the best-trained and best-equipped army. It also monopolized the shattering new power of the atomic bomb, coupled with a demonstrated willingness to use it. So too was America's economic power without peer. Major industrial centers throughout Europe and Asia lay destroyed by war's end, allowing New York to replace London as global financial capital. A stunning half of the world's economic activity occurred in or with the United States, a figure never equaled by one country before or since. The American standard of living had even managed to improve during the war while nearly every other people suffered. By 1945 the United States claimed more miles of paved roads, more telephones, more electrical power, and even more toilets per capita than any other nation. Rome in its heyday epitomized power without precedent or peer. But Rome never had it so good.[1]

Much like their imperial predecessors, American strategists believed their own success provided a model for the world. "American experience is the key to the future," *Life*'s publisher Henry Luce declared, calling for the start of a new American century. Its successes must be replicated and exported, he continued, because as the beneficiary of a clearly superior political and economic system, "America must be the older brother of nations in the brotherhood of man." In a world beset by so much death and destruction, the conservative Luce was not alone in seeing his country as civilization's last hope. Secretary of State Cordell Hull preached that nations needed only to give up their flawed ways and ancient biases, which seemingly led inexorably to war, in favor of the American example in order to make a new peaceful age a reality. Europe's day was over. American "principles and policies are so beneficial and appealing to the sense of justice, of right and of the well-being of free peoples everywhere," Hull argued, that if universally adopted, "in the course of a few years the entire international machinery should be working fairly satisfactorily." This "power to begin the world over again" had been a popular American vision since before Thomas Paine first composed the phrase in 1776. Paine's contemporaries held universal acceptance of an American model to be only a far-off prophecy. A century and a half later his compatriots finally wielded the opportunity to transform that dream into reality. American power could be "the one stabilizing influence" in a ravaged world, Washington insider John J. McCloy argued, strong enough to "bring this world into some semblance of balance again." Failure to heed Washington's siren call in an atomic world, however, when cities could disappear in a fiery instant, might prove the end of civilization's last and only chance.[2]

British policymakers did not disagree with these American goals. They too wanted a safe and prosperous world. They too feared the unchecked atom.

Having fought twice in a generation to save their own vision of Western civilization—indeed, having led the international system as banker and policeman for centuries—they merely objected to their country's playing only a supporting role in this American-led world. They also longed for time to renew their war-torn nation, rebuild homes and factories, and revitalize their tired economy. In short, they wanted to return to the kind of prosperity America now enjoyed, though without what they considered the harsher elements of America's more conservative free market. British postwar leaders longed in particular for the opportunity to create a new Britain that was more equitable and just, as their reward for wartime sacrifices. In contrast to American promises of a liberty born anew in the new world, they called their vision for a revitalized United Kingdom a "New Jerusalem." Its construction would be no easy task. A hundred thousand British homes had been destroyed since 1939 by enemy attack. Nearly half a million British soldiers had died in battle, and even more would carry their wounds the remainder of their days. Thousands of civilians had suffered the same fate. Even for those lucky enough to avoid physical harm, rationing for food and other necessities seemed to one diplomat "at siege levels" as late as 1946. Rationing would last until the mid-1950s. On a macro level, total British foreign debt equaled three times current reserves by war's end. The country was broke. In human terms, no one in Britain remained unaffected by the war. Britannia had been victorious, London's *Economist* noted in 1945, yet "our present needs are the direct consequence of the fact that we fought earlier, that we fought longest and that we fought hardest." Victory was worth these sacrifices. But the future such a victory wrought did not look promising.[3]

The future did not look hopeless, either. Even at that moment of national exhaustion, British policymakers from across the political spectrum refused to provide Washington with carte blanche to lead the Western community as it saw fit, and not just for reasons of pride. They strove instead for parity within Atlantic relations for two main reasons. First, because British strategists believed their nation needed to retain its great-power status and elevated position within the international system in order to promote the kind of long-term prosperity required to pay for their expensive New Jerusalem at home. And second, because increasingly as the Cold War heated up, London's strategists believed that Washington's vigorous, almost Manichean, persecution of all things communist threatened to undermine the world's long search for peace. Global Communism was a dangerous menace, to be sure. It simply was not in their eyes as dangerous as Americans thought, and many feared that American remedies to the communist scourge might prove as dangerous as the disease itself.

British policymakers helped convince their American counterparts of Moscow's dangerous intent before a rabid anticommunism became fashionable in Washington, though they soon became terrified of the results. The Americans responded to the red menace with the fervor often found in recent converts. "The people in the United States" appeared "more frightened of the danger of the Soviet Union than they were in England," King George VI lamented to a ranking American diplomat in May 1950. "While they [the British] were very much closer to the danger," the Americans "seemed to feel it more." This might have seemed but a curious paradox in safer times. But given the "typically violent" rhetoric of American senators and the rigidity of the American political universe on the communist issue, he continued, this paradox threatened to undermine Washington's willingness to compromise with the Soviets on a lasting peace. American fear of Communism specifically, and of international disharmony more broadly, the King believed, led to mental and thereby to diplomatic inflexibility. He wondered if policymakers "in the United States really understood the situation in Europe" at all.[4]

King George did not make policy, of course, yet his words highlight a predominant British—and to an even greater extent European—fear throughout the Cold War that American hawkishness and conviction, if not tempered, were potentially dangerous. Nuclear weapons made such fears all the more gripping. Europe lay naked between tensed Soviet and American armies, and for the first half of the Cold War at least, the tip of the American atomic spear resided not in the United States but rather on British soil. "We must not forget that by creating the American atomic base in East Anglia," Winston Churchill declared in 1951, "we have made ourselves the target, and perhaps the bull's eye, of a Soviet attack." British leaders believed they could ill afford to let Washington learn at its own pace the benefits of restraint and coexistence, and the lesson that appeasement, while potentially inglorious, was still far better than Armageddon.[5]

British policymakers believed their country had a vital role to play for peace that far surpassed giving unwavering support to Washington's anticommunist fight, and that playing this role demanded independent power. "We regard ourselves as one of the powers most vital to the peace of the world," Foreign Secretary Ernest Bevin told Parliament in 1948. "The very fact that we have fought so hard for liberty, and paid such a price, warrants our retaining that position, and indeed it places a duty upon us to continue to retain it." Britain had helped forge the international system following its last major restructuring in 1815. Its military power, financial resources, and international experience, and the moral authority that grew from each, had helped lead the world through the century of relative peace that followed. The time was ripe in 1945 for yet another global restructuring. "We still have our part to play," preached Bevin. In his view it was not his generation's destiny to cede international leadership to their former colony.[6]

Washington would heed British advice, however, only if it came accompanied by real strength. Only by wielding independent power of its own could Britain hope to play its desired dual role as trusted American ally and heeded American adviser. This would be no easy task, given London's poverty and problems. Yet British leaders across the political spectrum believed the Atlantic alliance would work best as a partnership of peers rather than as a lord-to-vassal relationship. A sound special relationship could only come, one of Churchill's principal advisers cautioned, "if we are able to build up our own prestige and safeguard our inherited interests in the economic as well as the political and military spheres." Parity would not be given as charity nor even as repayment for historic debts. Hegemons do not relinquish power on a whim. On the contrary, power had to be demanded, and taken. Nothing less than the future was at stake.[7]

This study of politics on the grandest scale is also a story about aviation, because airpower defined and symbolized international prestige and strength during the middle decades of the twentieth century. Planes embodied technological mastery, money, and influence, which were no less real for the difficulty in quantifying them, and were considered by leaders in America and Britain—and indeed, throughout the world—as key to their global policies. Failure to conquer this new frontier, conversely, guaranteed national decline. In the first years of the atomic age, when the split atom was purely a monopolized military tool of last resort, yet before the age of computers, aircraft offered the most cutting-edge military and commercial product for sale on the world market. Airpower unified money and might and symbolized the modern age, spawning terms like *jet-setter* to denote unparalleled sophistication. According to the 1945 speaker at the annual Wilbur Wright Lecture, considered the most important statement on aviation, aerial mastery was "a major tool of progress, capable of bringing the peoples of the world closer together and in furnishing the primary policing medium for a collective security system." Aviation is thus invaluable for understanding Anglo-American relations during the first decades of the Cold War, because while power directed the current of this Atlantic story, airpower was the visible movement on the water's surface.[8]

Leaders in both the developing and the developed world intuitively understood that whoever controlled the awesome power of flight *mattered*. Even an infantryman such as General Omar Bradley, chairman of the newly formed Joint Chiefs of Staff in the late 1940s, conceded that "airpower has become predominant" in strategic affairs. Similarly Churchill, a navy man to his marrow, was an air enthusiast without peer, one who recognized that aviation might prove Britain's salvation and sustenance in the twentieth century just as sea power had been in centuries past. "Air mastery is today the supreme expression of military power," he concluded in 1949. "Fleets and armies, however necessary and important, must accept subordinate rank."[9]

Leaders in the developing world, in particular heads of new nations decolonized at war's end, understood airpower's cachet equally as well. They saw aircraft as potential symbols of their authority at home and their legitimacy abroad, whether through the shining planes they ordered for their personal use or the (frequently unprofitable) national airlines that sprang up like wildflowers throughout the early Cold War. In either case, aircraft brought instant respectability. It is little exaggeration to say that countries established during this period required three things before they could claim true sovereignty: an army, a flag, and an airline. As Israel's communications minister proclaimed in 1949 upon El Al's inauguration, aircraft ownership meant that Israel "shall not rely on foreigners who come here when things are good and flee when the going gets tough." Airpower meant independence.[10]

British and American policymakers encouraged this equation of aviation with power and prestige, because the world's appetite for aircraft promised to fill their pockets and solidify their own central positions within the global hierarchy. Only Britain and the United States possessed viable aircraft industries immediately following the war; only these two countries wielded the manufacturing capacity, the technological know-how, and the financial resources to compete for dominance in global aircraft and airline markets. Other countries might supply one model or choose to specialize in a particular type of plane, but before development of the European consortium Airbus in the 1970s, only Britain and the United States could offer every type of plane a country or airline might need. For a full generation, theirs was a two-nation competition for global aviation dominance. To the winner went profits, prestige, and a hearty leg up in determining the future of the international system. The loser would suffer erosion of its international dreams. They left World War II as intimates and allies; yet they also left on an aerial collision course.

Truly, there could be no larger stakes. British strategists saw in aircraft sales to the developing world especially a new means of retaining their historic role as technology supplier of choice. Britain's imperial strength had historically rested largely on patterns of trade whereby London both profited from and carefully regulated technology sales to its minions and partners. With the empire in evident decline after 1945, however, strategists on both sides of the Atlantic predicted that new nations would naturally expect the United States to play this role. America's bountiful economy featured unmatched scientific achievement and production, and while British strategists struggled to rebuild their disrupted economy, American analysts recognized in their aviation industry a powerful tool for change. "Today men are carried away by something like a mysticism of the air," widely read author Matthew Josephson wrote in 1944. "We are destined to witness as many drastic changes in our way of life as were seen in the day of the new steam railroads over a century ago."[11]

America had all the advantages in this dynamic process, but British leaders were not ready to concede defeat. Washington's aviation industry was richer, larger, and more productive. British policymakers consequently put their faith in the quality of their products. Leaders in Whitehall reasoned that if foreign buyers could be convinced to buy superior British aircraft and thus to maintain their historic lines of trade with Britain even amid the difficult transition from war to peace, those same national decision-makers might subsequently be convinced to purchase a whole host of British products. A country willing to paint its flag upon the fuselage of a British plane would be a country willing to look to London, and not across the Atlantic, for cars, toasters, and all sorts of commercial ties. Planes were in this way not only symbols of the age, but traveling symbols of British achievement. If the United Kingdom could only be first to fly passengers across the Atlantic in a jet, predicted the air correspondent for the *Times* in 1948, a decade before the actual achievement, "every country in the world, and certainly every airline operator, would want to fly British . . . our prestige would soar."[12]

Prestige mattered just as much to British planners as did finances. Their country needed something extra, they reasoned, some unquantifiable political cachet to make up for its evident deficiencies at war's end. Aircraft had cachet in spades. Aviation's importance was "hard to put into words," one industry spokesman explained, but also "obvious when brought to mind." It was "the political and sentimental value to us which accrues when a foreign government or airline buys our products . . . the prestige we win when people travel in our aircraft and see them flying in our skies." With the world in flux and with the dynamics of colonial power increasingly strained by a rising tide of nationalism, it seemed vital that developing countries continue to consider the United Kingdom a source for modernity. The route structure for British Overseas Airways Corporation (BOAC, the precursor to today's British Airways) focused primarily on serving imperial outposts, even though such routes rarely turned a profit, because maintenance of colonial ties seemed vitally important to Whitehall strategists intent upon maintaining their country's historic influence. "To the extent that the countries of the Commonwealth and the rest of the Free World look to us for supplies of aircraft," Britain's secretary of state for air explained in 1952, "they will tend to be linked to us militarily and politically, and our influence in world affairs will thereby be increased." Airpower, in short, meant informal empire, a fact the Pax Americana's designers understood as well.[13]

The story of Anglo-American aviation diplomacy is not merely a tale of commerce or a study of global leadership, but equally a study of survival. Aviation changed the very nature of geography in the twentieth century, by simultaneously giving policymakers the ability to project their will throughout the globe and also bringing once far-off perils close to home. In the split atom and the long-range bomber, Americans faced for the first time a true threat to their once isolated continent. "The United States is now more vulnerable to assault than ever before," Hanson Baldwin, chief military affairs correspondent for the *New York Times* noted in 1945. "For the first time in history, we have 'live' frontiers—frontiers of the air." Enthusiasts called the airplane a harbinger of peace capable of bridging cultures and distant economies. Aviation pessimists had better rhetoric. The plane made America vulnerable, they argued. Death would travel through the air, whether on the wings of bombers or on the tips of unstoppable missiles. Even amid all the celebratory predictions of how air travel might usher in a new global community after 1945, one U.S. senator reviewed a study of *American* airpower during the war and termed flight "the greatest disaster that has ever happened to mankind."[14]

American leaders thus approached postwar aviation on two intertwined though conflicting levels. Aviation at once offered the power to make their Pax Americana a reality as an extension of American commercial and strategic might. Yet airpower simultaneously gave opponents of this vision, the Soviet Union especially, the means to destroy the United States and to undermine the Pax Americana's promise. And while British leaders had long lived within range of the enemy, this was a new feeling for Americans, who reacted with great alarm. "There are no distant places any longer," Republican presidential candidate Wendell Willkie declared in 1943 after circumnavigating the globe by plane. "The American people must grasp these new realities if they are to play their essential part in winning the war and building a world of peace and freedom." As the Cold War began, Americans at the pinnacle of their power confronted the awful prospect that future battles would be fought in the skies above their own homes. It was the Soviet Union's ability to strike at America's vital center, through airpower, that made it imposing enough to prompt a general reorganization of American society to meet this threat. Indeed, most Americans who stopped to consider the nature of the international system at war's end believed that airpower, coupled with atomic power, changed everything. One influential Senate commission concluded in 1947, when a single American bomber destroyed Hiroshima, "Militarily speaking, at that same hour the security frontiers of all nations disappeared from the map . . . and once again civilization stands vulnerable to annihilation." Rome may never have had it so good as America; yet at the peak of its power, neither were its citizens so deathly afraid.[15]

The conflicted American reaction to airpower as both salvation and threat thoroughly colored Washington's aviation policies throughout the Cold War. Fear of aerial assault fostered an unwavering commitment to aerial superiority over all potential rivals, and drove Washington to rigidly control aviation exports in an effort to limit the diffusion of aviation expertise to the communist world. Policymakers knew that technological progress could not be halted completely. Communist states would eventually develop sophisticated aircraft of their own, just as they would eventually develop their own atomic bomb. Achievement refused to be monopolized, meaning American safety could never be fully guaranteed.

Technological achievement did not have to be easy, however. American policymakers strove to limit the transfer of aeronautical know-how, whether through sales or espionage, to the communist world. They believed that the United States could guide the world, while remaining secure within it, only by staying technologically ahead of all foes and committed to an air force and an aviation manufacturing base that were large and flexible enough to transform the U.S. technological lead into strategic dominance. For America to lead the free world to victory in this global struggle between good and evil—for America even to survive—its airpower had to be predominant. "It's like in poker," the first chief of the Strategic Air Command was fond of saying, "the second-best hand wins you nothing and costs you dough."[16]

The resultant rigid series of export controls created tensions between American manufacturers and their government over the right and need to export, and fostered divisions within the special relationship when British policymakers developed far less rigid aviation policies of their own. American leaders would not sell to their communist enemy, and they did everything in their power to ensure that their allies would not sell to them either. Their Pax Americana came with strict rules, governed by unbending notions of right and wrong. To sell to the enemy was immoral; to aid the enemy's ability to do harm could not be justified; to even engage the devil that was the communist menace was in itself to contaminate one's soul. The question of commerce versus security was no question at all to American Cold War leaders: security won, hands down.

British Cold War strategists viewed such aviation questions more flexibly. Accustomed to the dangers of life within range of enemy bombers, and having understood from the outset that flight was a threat to national survival, they approached aircraft sales less out of fear than with a sense of aviation's potential. "The news is not that man can fly," newspaper magnate Lord Northcliffe pronounced in 1906 upon learning of a successful French flight, "but that England is no longer an island." Having been bombed during World War I and pummeled in World War II, British policymakers knew full well the likely result should the world come to blows again. Their country would be attacked and most likely atomized, and there was little they could do to avoid this fate, save to keep war from happening in the first place. Stemming American belligerence thus served a real purpose if extinction was the alternative. Even if it meant treating Soviet expansion with grudging tolerance or promoting détente through closer East–West relations, Britain's primary Cold War goal would be to prevent war from occurring. It was, indeed, their only logical goal. Selling planes abroad for profit and influence and manufacturing planes at home for military might offered Britain its best hope of creating the kind of force and wealth necessary to win the New Jerusalem at home, to beat back the Soviets if necessary, and to temper the

Americans whenever possible. But to do all three required a willingness to sell, even to the enemy.[17]

Thus we can see the inherent conflict over aviation embedded within the special relationship between Britain and the United States at the onset of the Cold War, as one side considered it vital to sell to survive, the other considered technological dissemination akin to treason. These most intimate of allies held incompatible worldviews, and aviation proved a particularly sensitive nerve within their special relationship because the field invited—indeed, demanded—public scrutiny. This was a field like no other. Flight has always fascinated, and planes verily demanded attention. Like all things desired, though, planes were difficult to obtain. Moving a model from the design stage to the runway required years of work. "Remember that we fought World War II with aircraft that were already developed when the Japs hit us at Pearl Harbor," the head of the Strategic Air Command wrote in 1950. "No new airplane was developed after December 1941, in time to participate in the war." Success in the air required immense investment in time and money, with no guarantee of an eventual payoff.[18]

Given the costs involved, government support was needed. No single British firm could afford such investments on their own after World War II, leading to direct government intervention in the country's aircraft industry beginning in 1942. The largest American companies were able to bear these costs at the close of the war, though not for long after. Boeing's decision in 1950 to construct its first jet airliner, the 707, for example, required an initial outlay of more than three times the company's total profits since 1945. Such financing was hardly to be taken lightly. "In this business," one of the world's preeminent aircraft designers would later lament, "you have to put the company on the line every three to four years." Unable to assume such risks on their own, British producers turned directly to the British Treasury for aid, where their pleas for government subsidies (and ultimately, government coordination) were quickly answered. Their more laissez-faire American counterparts rejected such connections, at least for civil aviation ventures, but in years to come their military sales brought in profits on a scale the British government could never hope to match. Military profits eventually offset commercial production costs, meaning that both governments ultimately subsidized aircraft production: the Pentagon indirectly, Whitehall without such convolutions. These seemingly disparate dynamics ensured that government officials at the highest levels, presidents and prime ministers alike, were involved in aviation decisions, and thus invested in their outcomes. Nothing happened in this field that was not studied, debated, and considered important.[19]

Aviation intertwined business and politics in part because its civilian and military fundamentals were themselves often indistinguishable. No other industrial product of this period so thoroughly connected public fascination, strategic significance, and commercial availability. This conjunction of influences posed a myriad of difficulties for policymakers charged with its regulation. Indeed, until the computer revolution of the 1960s, advanced aircraft were the most technologically sophisticated industrial product available for purchase on the world market. The word *purchase* is key here. Not every advanced technological product finds its way into the commercial marketplace during its moment of technological sophistication, just as not every military product offers a civilian counterpart. Aircraft did both. The limited availability of atomic power during this same period offers a useful comparison. Whereas the atomic bomb clearly marked the pinnacle of technological application at midcentury, this technology was hardly available for commercial buyers. It most certainly was not available for export. American officials held their atomic monopoly under the tightest security, concealing details of the Manhattan Project from their British and Canadian partners in direct violation of wartime agreements and from ranking members of Congress as well. The 1946 McMahon Act even made transfer of American atomic information abroad a treasonous offense punishable by death.[20]

Planes were another matter. In addition to their obvious military use, and unlike atomic power, aircraft offered a well-regulated prewar commercial market. Airlines had crossed oceans and connected countries for a generation by 1939, and wartime pundits expected commercial air travel and transport to blossom after the war. "The phenomenal role which aviation has played in the present war has stirred popular imagination as to its potentialities," the president of the Brookings Institution noted in 1944. "It is regarded as an open sesame to a new world." Indeed, while atomic power had only one real use in 1945 (though its possibilities for medicine, travel, and industry initially appeared endless), the technology required to transport passengers and cargo was essentially the same as that needed to drop bombs or strafe targets. The aerodynamics of flight did not change depending upon mission or purpose, and what civilian passengers wanted—speed and range—military planners longed for as well. The transport planes used to support Berlin during the 1948 airlift were the same models then used by airlines throughout the world, while Boeing's Stratocruiser airliner, inaugurated in 1949, used the same airframe and wings as the B-29 bombers that had firebombed Japan only four years before. Such "dual-use" goods are notoriously difficult to regulate. Claims of peaceful use can legitimize the legal purchase of items intended for military purposes, while fears of potential military use frequently cause regulators to thwart perfectly legitimate civilian purchases. Discerning when a sale was safe and when strategic, therefore, frequently led British and American policymakers into conflict, because many such conclusions were in the eye of the beholder.[21]

What made aviation technologies particularly difficult to regulate was that they were quite literally capable of flying away. The greatest fear of Cold War aviation policymakers was not that belligerent states would purchase civil airliners in order to supplement their military airlift capacity or to transform them into bombers (though these were legitimate concerns). Rather, officials feared most of all that communist states would steal aviation technologies from Western planes and incorporate them into their own models. The margin of error involved in preventing such technology transfer seemed dangerously slim. It would only take one ill-advised sale or disgruntled pilot for strategically vital information to leap into communist hands. Such fears prompted rigid security measures. Military pilots and crews were naturally subjected to background checks. Throughout the 1950s, BOAC pilots regularly faced security checks of their own. Even mechanics were screened before the company allowed them to work on jets bound for international airspace, lest their defection or disappearance behind the iron curtain prove a boon to Soviet engineering. One slipup, policymakers worried, could tip the delicate balance of power toward Moscow.

The idea that communist aviation might be advanced through a stolen machine or kidnapped technician was hardly an idle concern. Soviet engineers proved quite adept at reverse engineering Western aircraft. Moscow's first strategic bomber, the TU-4, was an exact replica of American B-29s that landed in Siberia during the last months of World War II. Soviet strategic airpower grew from that handful of samples. So it is no wonder that British and American policymakers strove to keep their best aircraft, be they civil or military, from falling into communist hands. Their choice seemed to be between technological security and defeat. "The military forces of democracy are numerically inferior to the military forces of communism," Air Force secretary and future senator Stuart Symington declared in 1949. "Therefore the military forces of democracy must attain and maintain qualitative—technological—superiority." Preventing inadvertent technology transfer seemed the first step toward maintaining that lead. London and Washington agreed on this point. Determining what constituted a strategic export, however, was another matter.[22]

Simply banning aircraft exports in order to prevent samples from falling into communist hands was hardly feasible. Fortunes were at stake, and military security frequently prompted potentially risky sales. Even the most technologically advanced British and American aircraft could be purchased for the right price or the right politics. Both countries sold or transferred their best warplanes to a wide range of allies for use against communist forces or insurgents in time of war or crisis. American officials in particular willingly ignored their own security regulations and the lax controls of some allies in order to place advanced aircraft in the hands of supportive nations. Their strategic calculus rated military security against the Soviets higher than technological security. In the early 1950s, for example, the Pentagon authorized sale of sophisticated fighters to several NATO air forces known to be infiltrated with communist spies and sympathizers, even as the State Department fought to halt sale of technologically similar machines to British and French airlines renowned for their tight security. This dichotomous policy nearly destroyed the special relationship, because it was not American manufacturers whose commercial sales Washington tried to halt, but rather British. For American strategists of the McCarthy era, military concerns trumped all. "It is necessary to assume the [security] risk implicit in the release for military purposes in support of national security objections," one American diplomat argued.[23]

Security did not dictate alone the delicate balance that was regulating aviation sales, however, because many jobs were also at stake in these decisions. Aircraft were vital to global economic growth, and whole regions of Britain and the United States relied upon their manufacture. Southern California and America's Pacific Northwest in particular found their fortunes wholly intertwined with their respective aircraft manufacturers. By the 1970s the Boeing Company alone supported more than fifty thousand subcontractors throughout the United States, giving the firm a truly national imprint. Indeed, aerospace provided nearly 8 percent of the country's total foreign trade by the height of the Cold War, while Boeing consistently ranked as America's largest exporter. As the House of Representatives Banking Committee was told in 1967, "Commercial aircraft exports represent the single most important commercial item in redressing the U.S. balance of payments and trade deficiencies." Halting Communism mattered; so too did keeping America's high-technology economy going.[24]

This book explores the struggle policymakers in both countries faced when forced to balance domestic and international concerns involving commerce and security. It also addresses these issues in two of the Cold War's distinct theaters: Europe and Asia. The Soviet Union posed the greatest threat in the European theater, and Western aviation security from 1945 until 1960 focused primarily on Moscow. Thereafter attention turned to China. British and American aviation policymakers approached each communist pillar differently. The Soviet Union was an industrial juggernaut of the first order and a military superpower, and by the 1950s it was rapidly improving its ability to produce aircraft. Keeping Western aeronautics from the blossoming Soviet air force seemed of particular importance during the Cold War's first decade, but by the time Soviet satellites orbited the earth—ahead of the first American models—London and Washington found it less vital to control the diffusion of civilian aviation know-how behind Europe's iron curtain.

Controlling technological diffusion to underdeveloped China thereafter dominated their attention, especially because American policymakers considered Beijing's communist regime particularly vulnerable to a harsh brand of economic warfare never applicable to the Soviet bloc. Leverage of this sort demanded a technological embargo, especially of advanced electronics and communications systems found aboard aircraft. Hoping to keep China underdeveloped and thus vulnerable to internal collapse, American policymakers longed for a full aerial isolation of Mao Zedong's regime. British leaders could not have disagreed more. Whereas Washington wanted China weak, London wanted it to grow in strength, believing prosperity offered the best hope for peaceful relations with the Chinese. British policymakers accordingly longed to sell China advanced aircraft, and given that Washington refused to trade with the Beijing regime under any circumstance, London hoped to monopolize the country's potentially quite vast long-term aviation marketplace as well.

Britain's decade-long efforts to sell aircraft to China, when coupled with simultaneous American efforts to thwart such plans, involved more than mere sales or a question of Cold War tactics. At stake was nothing less than leadership of the Western alliance. The lengths each side would go to, to see its vision persevere, and the risks the British in particular assumed in order to open and exploit the China market, proved astounding. They also proved ultimately detrimental to the United Kingdom's long-term commercial prospects in the region. By the early 1960s, British tactics reached a level of deceit bordering on conspiracy, reaching into the highest corridors of British power. As our story here will reveal, the British plotted to defy American export control laws in order to fly beyond China's Great Wall. Given the drastic lengths the British went to, it is somewhat ironic that Pakistan ultimately did the most to topple America's rigid aerial embargo of Beijing.

The first half of this book focuses predominantly on Anglo-American aviation diplomacy in Europe. Later chapters explore the special relationship as it played out in Asia. In London's and Washington's policies toward China we see the Atlantic divide over economic warfare most vividly; and in these divisions the special relationship faced its greatest Cold War strains. That British and American policymakers were uniquely intimate throughout this period makes their conflicts no less real. For such intimates, disagreements often look like betrayal. Although their fights occurred mostly behind closed doors, they were fiercer because of, not in spite of, their close relationship.

This Cold War story of economic warfare and engagement with the enemy begins in the midst of World War II, a time of aspiring hegemons and the emasculation of their closest allies. It reveals the way Washington and London viewed international politics through security and commercial calculations that ultimately revealed their sense of morality. By the 1970s, when Washington finally agreed to sell advanced jets to China, America's trade ideology had come to resemble Britain's of the 1940s and 1950s. Engagement became preferable to isolation and containment. The course of Anglo-American aviation diplomacy helped foster this change, though this evolution in American foreign policy had come at great cost. Churchill would have expected as much. As he darkly noted late one night in 1943, "We live in a world of wolves [Americans] and bears [Russians]. And far more important than India or the Colonies or solvency, is *the Air*."[25]

CHAPTER 1

The Arsenal of Democracy
versus British Planning

World War II was an airman's war. Infantry and tanks took the land while sailors controlled the seas. Yet observers the world over equated victory with the roar of planes and the swagger of pilots. Planes thrust the United States into the war one sunny morning at Pearl Harbor and just as suddenly ended the conflict in the swirl of dust over Hiroshima and Nagasaki four years later, and they dominated every theater of combat in between.

British and American leaders, though equal converts to airpower's importance, conceived of their governments' roles in securing postwar airpower in diametrically opposed ways. Their unique wartime experiences explain why. The British believed that government should direct airpower's use and development after the war as much as during it, and developed a coordinated national policy accordingly. This was partly because Britain's aviation industry lacked America's industrial and financial advantages, and partly because the immediate postwar years were ceded to American firms in wartime decisions that we will explore in the pages that follow. Washington approached aviation differently. Convinced through their own wartime experience that American manufacturers would dominate postwar markets without government help, and concerned that those same manufacturers would interpret assistance as interference, American leaders left their aviation firms to face the uncertainties of peace largely on their own. Some might go bankrupt without government aid, but policymakers in Washington reasoned that cutthroat competition within their country's aviation marketplace would at least produce an American victor in the world's.

These divergent industrial policies directly contributed to the Anglo-American diplomatic divide over aviation of the immediate postwar years, laying the groundwork for the way this vital industry altered the special relationship. To understand the nature of their later division over the best way to use the West's technological advantages to beat back Communism, one must first understand the lessons leaders from both nations took from their different wartime experiences. Together they beat back the Axis powers. Only one nation left the war empowered and emboldened enough to re-create the world system in its own image. The other left convinced that only a concerted national effort could withstand its powerful ally across the Atlantic.

Their aviation differences that came to the fore following World War II in fact began quietly enough in 1942, ironically at the moment of greatest Anglo-American solidarity. Victory seemed distant immediately following the stinging attack on Pearl Harbor. Privately, however, Churchill could barely contain his joy, believing the Japanese attack ensured the full American support for the war he had sought for so long. "So," he privately quipped the night of December 7, "we have won after all." Anglo-American solidarity knew no rival, he told Congress. It was "inexorable, irresistible, benignant." Triumph was inevitable with such a friendship focused on a common goal.[1]

Even those who shared Churchill's optimism knew the coming years would prove bloody, perhaps incomparably so, but leaders in both countries saw in aviation the possibility for an efficient, even merciful, means of victory. The British people had come to depend upon their air forces for nightly salvation against the onslaught of Luftwaffe bombers that swept in across the narrow Channel. Secured by their ocean moats from similar assaults, American leaders in 1942 looked to aircraft for their own victory strategy as well. They placed great faith in their country's massive industrial power, what President Franklin Roosevelt termed the "great arsenal of democracy," believing it might allow the Allies to avoid the devastating bloodletting of World War I. Roosevelt feared a repetition of that conflict's ruinous trench warfare, which had consumed a generation, and his war planners hoped to substitute new technologies and a war of mobility for the kind of bitter slogging that had previously demanded so much human sacrifice. Military leaders such as Dwight Eisenhower, George Patton, and Omar Bradley, each destined for fame in defeating Germany, had also spent the interwar years obsessed with developing a doctrine of mechanized warfare that would prove simultaneously devastating to the enemy and the salvation of American lives. Their solutions relied on machines, and lots of them. The head of the U.S. Army's War Plans Division later explained that, to enable the Allies to win the war without drastic casualties or battlefield stagnation, war planners counted on America's "advanced weapons systems" and "technical prowess and stupendous production capabilities." Churchill most assuredly agreed. "This kind [of war] will be more favorable to us than the somber mass slaughters of the Somme and Passchendaele," he told Parliament, leaving unstated his omnipresent fear that his country (and his government) could not withstand such losses. "With our national resources, our productive capacity, and the genius of our people for mass-production," Roosevelt similarly declared, the Allies would have their victory.[2]

Aircraft lay at the heart of this Anglo-American emphasis on sophisticated mass-produced military technologies. Indeed, aircraft production represented America's unique contribution to the Allied cause even before Washington entered the war. In the spring of 1940, as France fell before the German blitzkrieg, Roosevelt pledged his country would produce fifty thousand planes a year for rearmament and for the Allies. This was an awesome figure, demanding that an industry that had strained to produce two thousand planes during the whole of 1939 now churn out more than four thousand a month. The total amount of aluminum alone required to build so many planes, one presidential adviser calculated, exceeded America's entire annual production. The country might achieve FDR's goals, he concluded, provided it was willing to produce nothing else.[3]

Critics leapt to the attack. The most ambitious army and navy estimates put America's annual manufacturing capacity at a more reasonable nineteen thousand planes, though even this number would strain current resources to their breaking point. There were, moreover, only thirty thousand trained pilots in the entire United States in 1940, a discrepancy that worried airpower enthusiasts. "There is absolutely no use in having, let us say, 50,000 planes," argued Robert Lovett, soon to be named assistant secretary of war for air, "unless you have a well-trained pilots pool of say 90,000 to 100,000." Even Army Chief of Staff George Marshall, Roosevelt's most venerable military adviser, thought his commander's goal a shortsighted folly given what he considered the country's more pressing needs for rifles, barracks, boots, and trucks. In his opinion the American military could effectively manage only five thousand planes at its current strength. Anything more would be wasted for lack of manpower.[4]

Roosevelt's detractors thought only in terms of capabilities and obstacles; the president dealt in untapped possibilities. He had announced his goal of fifty thousand planes per year on his own, without consulting the military or the aviation industry, because he believed such a lofty goal would symbolically teach the necessity of planning and production in wartime on a scale far larger than anything accomplished before. The trying years to come would demand unprecedented efforts, and he believed the country had to learn to think big as a matter of routine. And nothing in 1940 captured the public's imagination like the airplane. "We must have clouds of warplanes," Roosevelt declared. They would lead to victory. Airpower carried a unique psychological cachet far beyond its material cost, he consistently preached, and as General Hap Arnold of the army's air corps loyally rephrased his president's argument, "Hitler would not be frightened·by new barracks in Wyoming."[5]

Roosevelt's visionary gamble worked. Fifty thousand planes a year seemed at first "an impossible goal," U.S. Steel chairman and future secretary of state Edward Stettinius later said. "But it caught the imagination of Americans, who had always believed they could accomplish the impossible." And accomplish it they did, producing 47,836 aircraft in 1942 and 96,318 aircraft two years later. They eventually turned out more than one plane every four minutes at peak production. When increases in average aircraft weight are factored in (weight being a better measure of aircraft complexity than total production), America's manufacturers far surpassed their president's prewar goals, as the total weight of aircraft production leapt a staggering 13,500 percent from 1939 to 1944. These were the machines that not only helped win the war but helped separate this conflict from the Great War's mass slaughter, even if FDR's "clouds of planes" transferred much of modern warfare's pain from the battlefront to civilians at home.[6]

Britain's planners also learned to think big in order to meet the needs of an industrial war, and aviation figured just as prominently in their thinking. But while American producers learned on the fly, well into the summer of 1942, during what the White House dubbed the "educational phase" of wartime production, British industrialists were already well versed in the logistical difficulties of producing sophisticated planes by the thousands amid a sapping global conflict. Even the simplest modern bomber required more than six hundred thousand mechanical components, the coordinated production of which taxed the most effective bureaucracy. More complicated still, the heavy four-engine bombers utilized by British and American air forces, such as the B-17s and Wellingtons that devastated Germany or the B-29 that did the same to Japan, employed thirty thousand distinct parts, and more than 1.5 million components overall.[7]

Production could not be haphazard if it were to succeed, though Britain's initial efforts were far from streamlined. Four separate ministries had over-seen some aspect of aviation procurement and production for the Royal Air Force (RAF) before the war, but by 1940, as the Battle of Britain began in earnest, so many hands in the production pot proved far too inefficient. The RAF fielded only 502 operational fighter aircraft at the beginning of the summer, having lost 944 aircraft (including 450 fighters) during the failed continental campaign. Germany, conversely, possessed over a thousand fighters based in France, and equal numbers of light and heavy bombers. The RAF was "cut to the bone," and aircraft production seemed "a muddle and a scandal," Churchill lamented upon taking office, and this while Luftwaffe chief Hermann Goering vowed his flyers would sweep the RAF's remnants from the skies in preparation for the Führer's planned invasion.[8]

Churchill knew Britain needed to swiftly improve its plane production if it was to survive, and with members of his own cabinet advising him to seek a negotiated peace with Hitler, he quickly took action. Less than two weeks after taking up the reins of power in May 1940, he streamlined his country's disjointed design and procurement system into a single Ministry of Aircraft Production (MAP), placing every aspect of aviation development and manufacturing under what is best understood as an aviation "czar." He gave this daunting portfolio to Lord Beaverbrook, a media magnate and loyal friend more experienced in newspapers than in manufacturing, and provided the energetic Canadian with a free hand in his choice of tactics. He demanded only results. "Everything depends upon Lord Beaverbrook's success," Churchill scolded one lethargic bureaucrat. "I earnestly trust you will see that his wishes are fully met."[9]

He would not be disappointed. The frenetic Beaverbrook stripped resources from transport, trainer, and (to a lesser extent) bomber production, focusing every effort on what one ranking airman termed "churning out the fighters." Only they could turn back Germany's Luftwaffe, thwart the Blitz, and save Britain's cities and frightened population. Only they could save lives in the short term. Despite delays caused by bombed-out factories, transportation disruptions, and the sudden need to prioritize production of spare parts in order to repair damaged aircraft already in service, the spirited (some might say dictatorial) Beaverbrook managed in a manner of weeks to increase aircraft production nearly 20 percent above the already ambitious national goals he inherited. During the crucial summer that followed, an average of 352 new fighters arrived at RAF bases each month. Germany produced only half as many over the same period. Even while suffering daily losses, the RAF grew in size by mid-September even as the Luftwaffe's declining strength and physical exhaustion forced Hitler to permanently suspend his invasion plans. The Battle of Britain was over. And although pilot bravery and new technologies such as radar must be counted as factors in this victory, one lesson stands out: Britain won primarily because while the enemy failed to replace its losses, RAF Spitfires and Hurricanes took to the air day after day.[10]

The RAF's aerial exploits received top billing in newsreels, but British policymakers and industrialists—aided not coincidentally by publicity from Beaverbrook's newspapers—gave equal credit for victory to the results-oriented Ministry of Aircraft Production. Indeed, Fighter Command suffered more from a lack of trained pilots during the summer of 1940 than it did from a paucity of aircraft, proving beyond doubt that the aircraft industry more than pulled its weight in protecting the nation. Beaverbrook's no-nonsense style proved the necessary jump-start the industry needed. "He was essentially a privateer," one MAP planner later conceded, "who did not in the least mind a little piracy if it served some immediate need at the expense of another department" and who believed that "MAP was entitled to an overriding priority."[11]

Historians have typically proved less generous. They claim Beaverbrook had the good fortune to inherit a well-organized production effort already on the upswing by the spring of 1940, the result of three-plus years of intense government preparation for war, and that his efforts added little more than a mindset of determined success to already well-conceived plans. RAF Marshal Sir John Slessor later added, "It would indeed have been a surprising achievement for the Archangel Gabriel to make any real improvement in the supply and repair of aircraft in less than three weeks."[12]

This charge is as true as it is shortsighted. Aircraft production was indeed primed for impressive results in the early summer of 1940, and Beaverbrook held no personal affection for planning, preferring to use his portfolio's high-priority status to solve last-minute problems quickly. Yet more important than the argument over who deserved credit for winning the Battle of Britain is the permanent imprint Beaverbrook's tenure left on British aviation. His damn-the-obstacles attitude eventually became a fabled model of centralized bureaucratic power, proof positive that although power might eventually corrupt, it could also produce impressive results along the way. His MAP in fact relied more upon planning than any other British wartime institution, but it was his ability to make planning work through ruthless determination that left the broadest mark on British aviation for the generation to come. By 1941, with the crisis past, Beaverbrook moved to a new post at Churchill's request. Fifteen years later, when one minister demanded the authority to direct his department with an iron hand, the MAP in the 1940s was the model to which he turned, arguing that "such powers a Beaverbrook in war-time would have."[13]

That all things were possible through determination and planning was the spirit of wartime Britain more broadly. This was the era of the New Jerusalem, when policymakers (particularly on the left) considered the conflict an opportunity to create the postwar society they had always sought. "War is a fearful thing, destructive and bestial," proclaimed Evan Durbin, a Labour leader and member of Parliament in 1942, "but it does free men's minds. Now is the time, when men's minds are free, to build our life anew." Armed with a legacy of resilience fostered in memories of the Blitz, the British public and their intellectual leaders left the war with a deep faith in their ability to accomplish the impossible. The *Daily Mirror* editorialized in June 1945, "We can make, as if by miracle, tanks, aircraft, battleships, pipelines, harbours!" Anything was possible in the future, even remaking society itself, so long as Britain showed "the same energy, the same brain power, the same spirit by means of which we made the fearful energies of war." This progressive legacy was arguably stronger in aircraft production than anywhere else. "It was a period of great euphoria," recalled Peter Masefield, Britain's wartime aviation attaché in Washington and later a leading industry figure. "Our Spitfires and Lancasters had won the war," he said, adding, "We had a great industry which believed that it was going to be able to turn swords into plowshares."[14]

The early 1940s was a time for swords, however, and Churchill continued to make the Ministry of Aircraft Production, always under public scrutiny, one of his most prized portfolios following Beaverbrook's departure. This was neither an easy nor a plum job. Luftwaffe bombing did not end after 1940, it increased in ferocity. Forgoing their costly daytime assaults, German bombers screamed nightly toward London, Coventry, or Dover. Bombing by the limited visibility of moonlight ensured that population centers, being most easily located in the dark, were targeted first. Coventry lost seventy thousand homes in one night alone. At least five hundred civilians died in that attack, with untold more burned and wounded in the firestorm that followed. This threat to home and hearth made aircraft production therefore seem "the most important thing in the whole war effort," one of Beaverbrook's successors later recalled.[15]

Such damage fundamentally shaped Britain's collective wartime memory and its national experience with the airplane. More than fifty-eight thousand British civilians lost their lives to enemy bombs during the war, a figure greater than total American military losses suffered in either the Korean War or the Vietnam War. Only five American civilians died as a result of bombs dropped on the U.S. mainland during World War II, and these fell from high-altitude Japanese balloons launched into the prevailing westward jet stream. Conversely, more than a hundred thousand tons of explosives fell on British soil. Even Buckingham Palace and Parliament were bombed. Franklin Roosevelt picked aircraft as a rallying symbol for his nation, but aviation meant something very real across the Atlantic. Minister of Aircraft Production Lord Brabazon later wrote, "Our very existence depended on whether we could get those few extra fighters up in the air."[16]

The effect such bombing had upon the British people and their leadership, and upon their subsequent postwar actions, cannot be underestimated, though neither can it be considered unprecedented. Airpower superseded the Royal Navy's long-standing strategic influence by December 1941, when the pride of the Pacific fleet, the battleship *Prince of Wales* and the battlecruiser *Repulse,* slid beneath the waves following two hours of unhindered Japanese air attacks. Commissioned only months before, the *Prince of Wales* embodied the pinnacle of British naval engineering and had the honor of transporting Churchill to his historic meeting with Roosevelt where the two leaders signed their Atlantic Charter outlining their common war aims. It cost the Japanese only three planes to send the ship to its grave, leaving Churchill unable to "remember any naval blow so heavy or so painful." More than Pearl Harbor, this defeat convinced even the staunchest naval advocate that the airplane's day had truly arrived. "The outstanding and vital lesson of the last war is that air power is the dominant factor in this modern world," Lord Tedder, chief of staff of the Royal Air Force, concluded in 1949. "Though the methods of exercising it will change, it will remain the dominant factor as long as power determines the fate of nations." The wartime lesson for British policymakers could not have been clearer: to survive and be powerful after the war, they would need airpower yet again.[17]

The British public already knew this lesson all too well, as any tourist taking the scenic walk along the Thames from St. Paul's Cathedral to Parliament can plainly see. Upon entering the city's medieval boundaries, one soon passes an obelisk rising above the trees, permanently "borrowed" from ancient Egypt. Two weighty replicas of the pharaoh's sphinx lie alongside as protectors, fashioned from massive blocks of steel and stone, monuments as much to Britain's industrial age as to its colonial past. One beast proudly bears the scars of duty in the form of jagged wounds received, a small placard notifies the curious, from the piercing shrapnel of German bombs.

But unlike what the tourist might expect, those bombs were not from the Blitz. They were dropped by lumbering airships during World War I, their shrapnel ripping inch-long scars into the sphinx's steel sides, deeply cutting into its solid concrete foundations. Palm-size holes remain. Metal propelled with such force would have made mincemeat out of any person caught in their path. Those scars remain today unrepaired, permanent reminders that Britain's vulnerability to aerial assault came long before the trials of the 1940s.

Such vulnerability infused British society with fear, and fundamentally altered the country's politics and culture. H. G. Wells's 1908 *War in the Air,* for example, envisioned London burned to the ground by future aerial assailants, while novelist Harold F. Wyatt prophesied a year later that his countrymen would be "doomed helplessly to gaze into the skies while fleets which they are powerless to reach pass over their heads." The result: "We shall be torn from our pedestal of insularity" by aircraft, and "flung into the same arena in the dust of which our fellow-nations strive." Flight changed British politics as well. Only six years after the end of the Great War, Prime Minister Stanley Baldwin told Parliament, "The history of our insularity has ended, because with the advent of the airplane we are no longer an island." Eight years later he glumly admitted that aviation made defense itself impossible, for the fleet could no longer keep evil at bay. "I think it is well for the man in the street to realize that there is no power on earth that can protect him from being bombed," Baldwin said. "The bomber will always get through." Subsequent British military leaders did not disagree. The Chiefs of Staff concluded in 1936 that the first week of a German air assault would bring 150,000 casualties. "It would be the most promising way of trying to knock this country out," they concluded, causing a tidal wave of fear forgotten in later harangues against Neville Chamberlain's failed logic of appeasement. As future prime minister Harold Macmillan recalled, "We thought of air warfare in 1938 rather as people think of nuclear war today," leading even a stalwart like Churchill to sourly note, "The flying peril is not a peril from which one can fly."[18]

Churchill played as significant a role as any in the evolution of Anglo-American aviation diplomacy. He was an early convert to aviation's poten-

tial, and nothing that occurred during World War II changed his 1917 opinion that "there are only two ways left now of winning the war, and they
both begin with A. One is aeroplanes, and the other is America." His term
as prime minister only reinforced his belief that Britain's sole hope for retaining great-power status following the war lay in aerial mastery, and he
backed such vision with resources. "If it came to a choice between hampering air production or tank production," he said, "I would sacrifice the tank."
He did not expect Parliament to support a large peacetime army (and did not
know if the country could afford one anyway). "Even if they did," he told
his trusted lieutenant Anthony Eden, "I should think it wiser to put the
bulk of the money into the air which must be our chief defence." For all its
attendant costs and its sure dangers, airpower seemed cheaper than large
standing armies and offered greater opportunities for global force projection.
Aircraft had proved helpful in putting down armed rebellions in British imperial outposts and mandates during the interwar period. In 1921, prolific
aerial attacks (including the use of poison gas) on Arab villages in Iraq
spawned the Orwellian term *air policing* and offered a relatively inexpensive
way to control unruly native populations. While serving as minister for the
colonies immediately after the Great War, Churchill had authorized extensive bombing of insurgents and civilians in order to save "men, materials,
and money." The airplane became his generation's equivalent of the classic
frigates of their history books that had maintained Britain's global influence
while keeping enemies far off and at bay. Without aviation, the RAF's Marshal Slessor concluded in the late 1940s, "we would be like the Royal Navy
of Nelson's day without its line of battle" and "should sink to the level of a
third-class power."[19]

Airpower offered Churchill's wartime government the opportunity to
think in global terms whenever time permitted, but in 1940 survival was
their primary concern. And survival in the air age demanded coordination and a can-do spirit. Parts and whole aircraft were ordered up to two
years ahead of their required due date during this period, while more advanced machines were simultaneously developed for use three and four
years hence. Aircraft in service, and even those rolling off the production
line ready for flight, were concurrently in a constant state of reconfigura-
tion, as lessons learned in combat required immediate implementation in
machines bound for the front. Planners thus developed construction lines
employing more than one million workers even as their designs were re-
written almost daily. These requirements demanded constant attention to

detail, because as Lord Brabazon explained, "if a warplane is to be of service it has to arrive complete with guns, electronic devices, and all the ancillary parts so necessary for a fighting plane, otherwise it is good only for making a noise in the sky."[20]

Such careful planning ultimately paid impressive dividends. British factories produced twenty-six thousand planes in 1943. In 1938 they had produced fewer than three thousand. Such performance did not come cheap, however. By June 1943, the government's total wartime investment in aviation production topped £350 million, a figure that did not include the cost of the planes themselves, with more than £150 million of that sum spent on new factories for an ever-expanding workforce. At their wartime peak, British aviation employed some three hundred thousand skilled and unskilled workers (nearly 40 percent of them women), more than a tenfold increase above prewar payrolls. Counting every British worker whose labor contributed to aircraft production indirectly (through subcontractors or supporting fields) brought total employment organized by the MAP to 1.7 million persons, making aeronautics at its peak larger than even the vaunted coal industry. "Here was the center of gravity of the entire war effort," one noted historian has concluded. "Here then was an industrial development without parallel in British history in terms of scale, speed, and cost—and of state participation."[21]

No amount of planning or investment could completely satisfy wartime Britain's massive appetite for aircraft. Churchill demanded planes not only for defense but, as early as the fall of 1940, in order to strike back as well. "The fighters are our salvation," he said, "but the bombers alone provide the means to victory." With British factories already strained to their limits in the aftermath of the Blitz, something had to give if offensive operations were to begin in earnest.[22]

That something was transport production. Britain's expanded industry lacked the prewar infrastructure, experience, or sheer resources to simultaneously supply the RAF's burgeoning transport, bomber, and fighter requirements. Most important, British manufacturers lacked time. Sophisticated aircraft took years to move from the drawing table to the runway. The Spitfire and Lancaster were each conceived before 1939. Yet the editors of *Flight and Aircraft Engineer* (Britain's leading aviation journal) wrote in 1945, "We had not a good military transport aircraft in production or even contemplated when the war broke out." Without a true transport line in production in the war's first years, the country's stock of cargo and supply aircraft rapidly dwindled after the onset of hostilities, just as the RAF cried out for warplanes. Beaverbrook's prioritization of fighter production at the height of the Blitz provided a further obstacle. "It would have been fantastic to suggest in 1939, 1940 or 1941 the diversion of part of our aircraft production resources to developing a new transport type or even to proceed with some of the existing transport types," one Air Ministry official concluded in 1944. "The shortage of all types of military aircraft was desperate," and "Lord Beaverbrook in his term at M.A.P. laid primary emphasis on fighters, though we were also pressing ahead with the development of the bomber force." Not until July 1942 did the country first fly a transport prototype, the Avro York, whose development began in late 1939. This plane eventually served BOAC for years after the war, though it did not enter service until 1944. Britain's depleted fleet needed assistance long before then.[23]

Failure to develop efficient transport lines eventually took its toll. During the summer of 1942 the RAF reluctantly stripped its already thin bomber squadrons of nearly two hundred of its most destructive Lancasters in order to transform them into transports. The airmen long avoided this despised reduction in offensive capacity because, as one explained, "these aircraft will not be converted back to bombers and represent a dead loss to the combined bombing effort on Germany." The timing of this move could not have been worse. Churchill had only recently (and then only barely) persuaded the Soviet Union's Joseph Stalin that the nascent Anglo-American strategic bombing effort represented a significant offensive campaign against Hitler. Such attacks formed, albeit only in the air, the "second front" Stalin desperately desired, Churchill argued. Soviet leaders wanted to see troops on the ground in France, not airmen above it, but Churchill feared "a useless massacre of British troops on the channel beaches" more than Stalin's wrath. He promised instead "a devastating weight of air attack on the German cities and industries." Having little real alternative, given the presence of German troops nearly a thousand miles inside his own territory, Stalin accepted Churchill's promises and pledged not to seek a separate peace.[24]

It was only upon returning to London that Churchill realized the full depth of his country's dilemma over unmet transport needs. Unrelenting pressure from his military advisers forced him to consent to reducing his already paper-thin bomber ranks in order to meet nonoffensive needs, even though robbing Bomber Command was at best a stopgap measure. His government longed to offer proof that the RAF could give the Nazis as good as they got, but according to Slessor, they had no alternative but to defer the national call for retaliation. The needed transport aircraft "could not possibly be produced without dislocating the whole current production program," and even then new transports would not be available in less than three or perhaps even four years.[25]

The United States quickly stepped in to fill this breach, setting in motion the first domino of the subsequent Anglo-American air rivalry. Despite lagging behind in fighter production in the early 1940s (Japan, Germany, and Britain each fielded superior fighters in the war's first year), American firms led the prewar world in transport production by a staggering degree. Nearly 93 percent of global air passengers flew on Douglas DC-3s in 1939, a record for market dominance by a single type never again equaled. When Douglas's manufacturing capacity was combined with that of other U.S. producers such as Boeing or Curtis, America's total transport production far exceeded that ever envisioned in wartime Britain. Indeed, America's firms produced more transports in a single year than even the most ambitious Whitehall planner could hope to employ throughout the entire war. London's 1943 logistical estimates, for example, called for 1,076 medium and heavy transports for use throughout every theater of the war, though MAP planners held no illusion that they could meet such requirements. Yet these thousand-odd planes represented less than 15 percent of the 7,386 transport craft American firms expected to produce during that same period. Indeed, American output for 1943 far exceeded even this prediction. The transports Britain needed were produced by the United States in droves.[26]

This fateful match of British needs and American capabilities led to a 1942 aircraft production agreement between the two nations. Military planners from each country had met to coordinate production as early as 1938, when buyers from London and Paris placed orders throughout the United States for planes with which to stem Hitler's expected onslaught. These Europeans ordered more than twenty-six thousand American aircraft by 1940, largely funding the industry's initial wartime expansion. The Roosevelt administration subsequently discussed coordinating American production with British needs after the fall of France, though most of these negotiations boiled down to British pleas for whatever planes Washington felt it could spare. The March 1941 Lend-Lease Act in fact eliminated direct foreign orders, as it allocated all American production to American forces; the administration would distribute any remaining aircraft to Allied nations as it saw fit.[27]

In June 1942, however, more than three months before the first American combat troops landed in North Africa, Anglo-American joint planning

sessions entered a new phase. British officials offered to forgo transport production throughout the remainder of the war provided American firms supplied transports for the entire Allied cause. Programs such as the York would
continue (at a low priority), but British negotiators pledged not to develop
any new transport lines until Hitler's defeat. That fateful day would come
far sooner, they reasoned, if their firms concentrated on the bombers and
fighters at which they excelled and for which there was endless need. "It
would be a mistake to start transport production de novo while basic capacity already existed in America," one British airman explained.[28]

Whitehall's dramatic proposal took the Americans by surprise. They had
traveled to London expecting the usual urgent British requests for planes of
all types, not a complete British withdrawal from the transport field. They
quickly agreed to Whitehall's plan, however, and signed what later came to
be known as the Arnold-Powers agreement, whereby, according to RAF analysts, "as a long term policy we were led to rely on America for transports
whilst we concentrated on medium and heavy bombers." To be precise,
London did not *abandon* transport efforts entirely in favor of American supplies. Rather, by forgoing the development of *new* transport lines, the British
simply agreed to formalize a situation that already existed. "We were in no
position to embark on the production of any of this class in the U.K. at this
advanced stage," Slessor explained, and in the interest of maximizing offensive power (and thereby shortening the war), "it was thus agreed that we
should in the main have to rely upon American air transports."[29]

The accord paid immediate dividends. Freed from the burden of transport production, Britain's aircraft manufacturers made 1943 their most productive year of the war. Total bomber and fighter output for those twelve
months exceeded one hundred times their entire prewar capacity. America's
manufacturers stepped up their aircraft production after 1942 as well, with
results that were indisputably impressive. The value of America's annual aircraft production skyrocketed to more than $16.7 billion by 1944 from its
1939 total of $250 million, as the industry as a whole leapt from forty-third
to first on the list of the country's most valuable sectors. Douglas Aviation
alone was the country's fourth-largest corporation in 1944.[30]

Washington paid for most of this growth. Investment in aviation manufacturing totaled $3.721 billion from 1940 to 1944, of which only $293 million came from private funds or from aviation companies themselves. The
remaining 92 percent came from the federal government, which offered lucrative cost-plus contracts (wherein manufacturers received payment for

their cost of production plus an additional predetermined profit) as a particular enticement to manufacturers. Every effort was made to rapidly ramp up production, the Army's official history concluded, "by harnessing the profit motive," leading Undersecretary of War Robert Patterson to sardonically quip, "Never were so many provided with so much."[31]

Despite the obvious benefits of government investment, credit for America's impressive transport output belongs primarily to prewar efforts. Each of the three most popular American models (the C-46, C-47, and C-54) was well into production before the attack on Pearl Harbor, and there was simply no substitute for time in the production of large aircraft. Indeed, America's aircraft manufacturers proved so successful that Washington planners began scaling down production after November 1943 when it became clear that they would have sufficient aircraft to win the war. "They ground airframes out like sausages," Lovett recalled. "We were producing so many planes and so many pilots that we had to cut back five months before we embarked on the greatest military amphibious landing the world had ever seen."[32]

Some additional numbers reveal the full depth of this bounty. American manufacturers produced more than 10,000 C-47s during the war, the military version of the popular Douglas DC-3 first flown in 1935. More than 1,200 such planes served with RAF units before 1945, where they joined other American models such as the Curtis C-46 Commando (first produced in 1940 with 3,330 to follow) and the Douglas C-54 Skymaster (which first flew in 1939, followed by 1,242 others). The behemoth Skymaster would later gain fame as workhorse of the 1948 Berlin airlift. In short, success begat success. American firms had led the world in transport production before the war. Wartime orders only lengthened their lead.[33]

The 1942 Arnold-Powers agreement did more than just rationalize Anglo-American wartime aircraft production; it also placed American producers in an overwhelmingly advantageous position for postwar civil aviation dominance. Planners on each side of the Atlantic knew that without a large transport model in production during the war, British firms would leave the conflict well behind their American rivals in the initial battle for postwar markets. London's offer to forgo transport production therefore surprised the Americans because, as Churchill's advisers warned, halting transport production in 1942 meant that it would be at least the late 1940s, perhaps the early 1950s, before Britain would again be able to ply the skies with a competitive homegrown aircraft. "It is out of the question for Great Britain to compete in civil aviation for at least five years after the war," the Air Ministry's Sir Roy Fedden concluded in 1943, and he was certainly not alone in this assessment. British planners took to calling American dominance in the immediate postwar years "inevitable" following the Arnold-Powers accord, no matter what future course they pursued. Wartime necessities offered little choice. To win an efficient war of machines rather than lives, British leaders knew they had to capitalize on the Allies' greatest advantage: America's industrial might.[34]

American industry might prove the savior of lives, but it also truly frightened British policymakers as they pondered the postwar world. No matter the extent of Whitehall coordination, exhortation from Beaverbrook, or support from Churchill, not only was America's aviation industry more productive than Britain's in terms of sheer capacity, but individual American companies were universally more efficient as well. American firms were generally larger, and thus benefited from the advantages of economies of scale. At the height of the war a single firm such as Consolidated (producer of B-24 Liberator bombers) employed a design staff as large as that engaged by Britain's entire aircraft industry. Boeing, Douglas, Curtis, and the like all produced on a larger scale in the 1940s than their British counterparts did, and the more planes they produced, the more efficiently they produced each one. At a time when British firms largely employed a craftswork mentality in aircraft construction, building machines in relatively small batches generally of fewer than one hundred, American firms grew massive and more modern, employing line-production techniques originally developed for the auto industry.[35]

Size mattered in this industry, and mass production paid immediate dividends. According to a 1944 Whitehall study, individual American firms were 75 percent more efficient than their British counterparts, predominantly because of longer assembly lines. The Ford Motor Company, for example, strictly an automobile producer before the war, by 1943 possessed a mammoth B-24 factory at Willow Run, Michigan, with an annual output greater than half of Germany's entire aviation industry. The plant boasted as its main assembly hall the largest room ever built, and by 1944, a massive bomber rolled off its assembly line every 63 minutes. To their great frustration, company officials never met their ultimate goal of one bomber per hour. "Bring the Germans and the Japs in to see it," Ford's production chief boasted, "hell, they'll blow their brains out." Overall, American factories doubled their daily output per worker from 1941 to 1944, to more than twice the efficiency rate found in Germany and four times that of Japan.

British companies simply were not structured to match this level of productivity. One British official's visit to Vickers at the height of the war revealed not only significant labor-management antagonism, but incredibly, "no system of line production throughout the whole organization." The largely handcrafted British planes were qualitatively among the best in the world; there simply were never enough of them.[36]

American producers seemed to hold every advantage in the expected battle for mastery of postwar markets, yet Churchill's wartime government refused to write off their long-term participation in this prestigious field without a fight. The industry had come to represent too much of Britain's progress during the war—the investments, the employment, the planning— to allow it to merely crumble at the prospect of American competition. Aviation supported nearly 8 percent of British workers by 1943, and while government planners predicted that postwar employment in the industry would level out at approximately 115,000 workers from the wartime peak of 300,000, this figure was still larger than British aviation's size at any point from 1919 to 1938. "It was not in the national interest to allow a first rate aircraft manufacturer to go bust," the supply minister later proclaimed. But how was Britain ever to counter either America's greater productivity or its experience in transport production? The Americans were bigger and richer, and they had transport aircraft already under production for the initial postwar years. Even if the future rested on control of the air, even if Britain's great-power status demanded aerial prowess, how could the country hope to compete? More importantly, how would London manage to withstand American encroachments and present an alternative to the Pax Americana if it could not even maintain a foothold in the single most important field of all?[37]

The Brabazon Plan

This was the dilemma posed to a blue-ribbon commission of British aviators and policymakers only weeks after the 1942 Arnold-Powers agreement. Their answer, which embodied the lesson that planning, quality, and determination were the three most important ingredients to successful aircraft production, shaped British aviation for the next quarter century. Named after its chairman, former MAP minister Lord Moore-Brabazon, the Committee confronted the difficult task of proposing aircraft models that would somehow break through the expected American postwar dominance and thus ensure for Britain a future place in the air. Specifically, they were told to find some way of beating the Americans in the commercial competition sure to follow Germany and Japan's defeat.[38]

Two months of fact-finding and debate produced an answer. The committee determined that Britain's future success lay not in beating American competition with superior volume—such a victory was probably not possible—but rather in beating American models to market through superior technology. The Brabazon planners knew that their machines, even if they were of equal quality, were unlikely to triumph in direct competition against those built by Boeing or Douglas. America's manufacturers could outproduce and then outsell any competitor through price cuts only they could afford, leaving the British aircraft industry with the depressing knowledge that on a level playing field, they would surely lose.

The Brabazon committee had no intention of competing on a level field. They concluded that if their country was ever to capture global aircraft markets, British manufacturers would have to beat American firms to market with advanced machines so technologically masterful that buyers would eagerly pay a premium for British quality. That the committee would fall back upon the quality of their engineering was hardly surprising. British firms had long substituted sophisticated designs for production prowess (in legend if not in fact), as their Spitfires and Lancasters, each arguably the war's best plane of its class, made up in advanced engineering for what they lacked in numbers. While American firms relied upon teams of designers and line-production techniques to build their planes en masse, British firms placed their faith in the genius of individual "designer-heroes" and the skill of trained craftsmen. Let Boeing or Douglas churn out planes like sausages, the Brabazon committee argued. British firms would produce filet mignon.[39]

British engines held particular promise. Rolls Royce, for instance, repeatedly produced piston engines considered among the best in the Allied camp, and more than one American airframe benefited from its coupling with a British power source. North American Aviation's P-51 Mustang "rose from the mediocre" to become "the best fighter in the world," according to one analyst, after being fitted with Rolls's powerful Merlin engine. Britain's technological lead over the United States was even greater in turbines, more commonly known as jets. Englishman Frank Whittle had invented the world's first working jet engine before the war (simultaneously with, but separately from, Germany's Hans von Ohain), and under his guidance the RAF began employing jet aircraft to intercept German V-1 buzz bombs over

England in 1944. Some jet-powered Gloster Meteor units even deployed to the Continent in the war's final months, though they never squared off against the Reich's first jet fighters. In all, by the war's end more than thirty thousand British workers (one-tenth of the country's aviation workforce) were engaged solely in developing this futuristic propulsion system, prompting one worried American diplomat to cable home about the extraordinary "magnitude of the British effort."[40]

America's jet development lagged considerably behind, despite the contributions of several visiting British technical teams and constant prodding from American officials such as Hap Arnold and Vannevar Bush, director of the Office of Scientific Research and Development. Bush believed American firms lacked the incentive to innovate. Secure with their guaranteed contracts, he lamented, "the [American] engine people did not do a thing on that subject [jets] or on any other unusual engine" to match Britain's wartime lead. Whatever reinvestments the companies made from their wartime profits (after paying dividends to stockholders) were usually spent on improving productivity or enhancing current models, rather than engineering radical new technologies. With the planes that would dominate wartime skies and postwar markets already in production, Bush believed American firms seemed content merely to enjoy their lead. After spending the war years as head of aircraft development and procurement for the Army Air Force, General Oliver Echols agreed, noting, "It has always been apparent they [American manufacturers] are not interested in the general progress of the art."[41]

The Brabazon planners, who feared American postwar competition as early as 1942, knew their only hope for success would lie in extensive Whitehall planning and financial backing for advanced technologies such as jets. It mattered little to Whitehall which firm led Britain into the new aviation age, only that Britain itself succeeded in the air. Theirs was a national approach. Whitehall would have to direct and to some extent subsume the autonomy of individual British firms for the survival of all. The initial postwar years seemed already lost. The Americans would surely dominate global markets through 1950, with their lead ensured by the Arnold-Powers accord. Surplus wartime models were expected to glut the immediate postwar market, in any event. At least, concluded Richard Clarkson, one of Britain's leading aerodynamicists, "We in the civil aviation field will indeed be lucky in the postwar era in not having to meet German as well as American competition." The Brabazon committee proposed transforming bombers and transports left over from the war into a "stop-gap" fleet capable of maintaining a British presence in foreign markets until more advanced models became ready. Such planes would also forestall the necessity of spending valuable hard-currency reserves on American aircraft for Britain's own airlines. "The prospects of our aircraft industry securing their fair share of the world market for civil aviation will be poor enough in the immediate postwar years," MAP minister Stafford Cripps explained in 1944. These "interim" types could at least sustain Britain's needs during "the time entailed in bringing most of the Brabazon types, of which we have commenced design, to the stage of commercial production."[42]

Future models, those "Brabazon types," would bring Britain to the front of the world's aviation stage and secure the country's massive wartime investment and jobs for tens of thousands of aviation workers. The key to the entire Brabazon program was to force American firms to play catch-up. Once entrenched in a battle of technology and quality rather than of brute productive capacity, Britain's share of the market would be ensured. Among the planes they proposed were a mammoth thirteen-ton propeller-driven craft, named the "Brabazon" in honor of the committee chairman, designed to cross the Atlantic in either direction without refueling. The committee also proposed a more technologically daring medium-range carrier employing a new turboprop engine, and the world's first pure jet airliner. This turboprop craft would become the Vickers Viscount, the most successful of all British postwar commercial models. The jet they envisioned became the Comet. Both would play important roles in the Cold War aviation diplomacy to follow.

The Brabazon committee ultimately offered five projected models (which became nine distinct planes), capable of providing international customers with a family of British planes superior to any American model then flying:

Type 1: A long-range transatlantic piston-engined airliner, larger than any existing American type (Bristol Brabazon resulted)

Type 2: A medium-range aircraft (the turboprop Viscount resulted with great commercial success, along with the less successful Airspeed Ambassador and Armstrong Whitworth Apollo)

Type 3: A medium-long-range aircraft suitable for British empire routes (the Avro 693 and Tudor II)

Type 4: A fast jet-propelled transatlantic mail airplane (the De Havilland Comet)

Type 5: A small feeder aircraft (the Miles Marathon and the De Havilland Dove)

Churchill's cabinet made the Brabazon recommendations official policy in February 1943, committing future governments to the aviation industry on an unprecedented peacetime scale. As the supply minister explained, they broke with the prewar laissez-faire tradition toward aircraft production by accepting "financial responsibility for the initiation of a programme of civil aviation upon a basis adequate to provide a minimum number of essential types of aircraft in the immediate postwar world." The cabinet was willing to pay dearly to maintain British civil aviation in the postwar world "on a scale and quality in keeping with our world position," in the hope that such investments would be repaid many times over during successive decades. Profits from military sales, especially of advanced jet fighters and engines, they reasoned, might soften this financial blow. They also assumed responsibility for promoting British sales overseas, a commitment that would ultimately lead to direct competition, not only with American firms, but with their government as well.[43]

The competition for postwar aerial mastery therefore began in earnest for the British in 1942, when Brabazon planners applied the lessons of the Beaverbrook period that planning and energy could overcome any deficit. They imbibed the wartime need for discretion as well. Initial implementation of the Brabazon plan, which had been enthusiastically received throughout the government after 1943, was of necessity undertaken with the highest degree of secrecy. Conditions on American Lend-Lease aid explicitly forbade the use of wartime material for civilian postwar goals. Thus, while the government rhetorically embraced a postwar future in the air, its preparations demanded caution. "The time is ripe for action," the supply minister wrote in October 1944. "We should, of course, have to proceed cautiously at first in order not to alarm American susceptibilities."[44]

The discretion required to forestall American investigators meant that Britain's firms could not devote their full attention to postwar transports until the close of hostilities, though the Air Ministry repeatedly tried to circumvent such restrictions. In the fall of 1944, for example, Whitehall asked Washington to reclassify sections of the Lend-Lease Act so that British companies might begin civilian production after Germany's surrender (anticipated by Christmas) instead of waiting until the Japanese surrender expected sometime later. American policymakers rejected such pleas out of hand. They too recognized that the postwar competition for aviation markets was likely to be a two-nation affair, and suspected that the British aimed to limit America's expected postwar lead. "This was pure gold," wrote Assistant Secretary of State Adolf Berle, the former New Dealer who coordinated Roosevelt's aviation policymaking. "The British have been sticking out for a right to enter the air business on a preferred basis, because of their war handicap"; and, he added, "what is worse, apparently the [military] cutback and [subsequent] civilian plane production would be done with American money." Berle told Undersecretary of State Sumner Wells that the result of accepting London's proposal would be "British aviation, developed after VE-Day but while we are still at war with Japan, at a time when we could not develop ours, and paid for with American money." The idea seemed scarcely worth entertaining. "I told [Lord Robert] Swinton [head of the British delegation to the 1944 Chicago Aviation Conference] bluntly that this was an impossible situation and that I wanted nothing of it." The price of American assistance in 1942 had been an industry-wide delay in transport production. With postwar dominance in this crucial field in their sights, Washington was not about to let British aviation off the hook.[45]

The Roosevelt administration's refusal to loosen its restraints upon British production was hardly unexpected, but even this delay could not keep London policymakers from believing their machines would ultimately dominate global markets. Following the close of hostilities, the ministers of supply and aviation jointly stated the result of wartime agreements: "We devoted our efforts to bombers and fighters while the Americans were developing their military transport aircraft, and we cannot retrieve what has inevitably been lost." They added, however, "We can ensure that there is no repetition of the existing state of affairs" through "a vigorous and farsighted policy" for "new British aircraft which can lead the world." 1950 was their target date, the time when the Brabazon models would first be ready for export. At that time, London's civil air attaché in Washington, Peter Masefield, predicted, "We will have planes the equal of any in the world," and American models would become obsolescent. "Galatians Chapter 6, verse 9 applies," he reminded wavering colleagues, referring to the King James Bible's promise that "in due season we shall reap, if we do not lose heart." Britain would eventually reap its due rewards because its planes would be better and its industry united, just as during the Blitz when determination and planning had beaten back seemingly impossible odds. Victory would come in all good time, provided, of course, that no further obstacles were placed in their way.[46]

Arsenal of Free Enterprise

The United States took a diametrically opposite approach to postwar aviation planning. Whereas Britain's government left World War II with a coherent national strategy for well into the next decade, America's aviation program was disjointed, unorganized, and ill supported. And this was exactly as both industry and the government wanted it. As Adolf Berle's passion suggests, American strategists longed to control peacetime aviation markets as much as the British did, and as we have seen, they were not above using strong-arm tactics to ensure their ultimate success. Berle and his colleagues yearned for aviation dominance, because they too believed it was key to future global affairs. As Welch Pogue, chairman of FDR's Civil Aviation Authority explained to all who would listen, airpower was to the modern world what maritime travel and commerce had been for centuries before. Airpower had the potential to spread American power even farther than the sea, however. Water had limitations of coasts and rivers, but "the oceans of the air lap at every border."[47]

The American public got the point and learned a new geographic vocabulary of the air age throughout the war. In 1944, for example, the House of Representatives' Commerce Committee adorned its hearing room with a Rockwell Kent mural entitled *On Earth Peace,* its central theme of a bustling economy dominated by aircraft soaring to the earth's four corners. "In the postwar years we will see the broad modern highway crowded with peacetime traffic," Kent explained, with "streamlined airplanes headed not only to the far corners of the United States but to the distant cities of the world as well." The economic benefits of the Pax Americana, in other words, would arrive on wings.[48]

The New York Museum of Modern Art reinforced the connection between aviation and the future with its 1943 installation "Airways to Peace." The exhibit featured an eleven-foot-high polar map of the world, designed to introduce viewers to the previously unknown possibilities of a productive Northern Hemisphere (home to 98 percent of global industrial activity) linked as never before by air. "This is the half-sphere in which the major portions of the world's national resources, technical skill, and financial strength are found," one scholar wrote. Heretofore divided by impassable ice and snow, the region—which geographers had never before even considered a single region—could now be fully exploited for the first time through the power of the plane. "There are no distant places any longer," Republican standard-bearer Wendell Willkie intoned as author of the exhibit's text, because "the world is small and the world is one." Willkie gladly assumed the role of airpower's ambassador to the American people following his circumnavigation of the globe on a goodwill visit to American troops. His 1943 best-selling chronicle of his travels, *One World,* offered controversial plans for global governance and international security, but one insistent message: the future belonged to those who could fly. "The American people must grasp these new realities," Willkie proclaimed, "if they are to play their essential part in winning the war and building a world of peace and freedom."[49]

Despite near-universal recognition of aviation's postwar potential, the United States never developed a coordinated national program for sustaining its wartime dominance in transport aircraft following the close of hostilities. The reasons why are as important as they are clear. For one thing, coordination seemed unnecessary. American planners did not doubt for a moment their nation's aviation dominance at war's end. They knew this from 1941, and nothing that occurred during the war altered that opinion. Humbled France made an unlikely candidate for serious competition in the immediate postwar years; defeated Germany and Japan would not pose much commercial threat; and Soviet factories never produced an effective large transport or bomber throughout the entire conflict. Because only Britain stood in the way of complete American market dominance, Roosevelt's aviation planners viewed the postwar world as their oyster, one that would produce its treasure with little further government agitation. "The only possible effect of this war would be that the United States would emerge with an imperial power greater than the world has ever seen," Berle recorded in 1944. It would wield more money, more influence, greater industrial capacity, and a more powerful military than any other nation, and "has at the moment substantially the *only* supply of transport planes and of immediate productive facilities to manufacture the newer types of such planes." American dominance seemed inevitable. Churchill privately conceded this fact to Commonwealth diplomats in 1943, saying that immediately after the war "the United Kingdom had no intention of attempting to compete on an equal basis with the U.S.A. in this field." They "could not do so," having "neither the population nor the resources" to contend, at least until the 1950s.[50]

With their aerial dominance so assured that even their competitors admitted likely defeat, FDR's aviation policymakers devoted the bulk of their efforts to ensuring American access to international markets and routes. Following in the tradition of Secretary of State John Hay's turn-of-the-century "fair field and no favor" call for open markets capable of sustaining hyperproductive American manufacturers, and in keeping with Secretary of State Cordell Hull's repeated calls for reductions in trade barriers, Berle's office led wartime efforts toward a substantial liberalization of the rules regulating international air commerce. Free-trade ideologies often flow from the country most able to profit from unfettered commerce, and in this FDR's policymakers were no different. The Americans trumpeted an "open skies" approach, whereby nations would agree to allow airlines of any nationality to carry passengers and cargo unheeded by borders or protectionist restrictions. The airways of the world were "a highway given by nature to all men," Berle argued; "American interests [would be] short-sighted as not to see that the doctrine of free air is their plainest road to superiority." Leaders such as Berle were not ideologically averse to directing industry from above. They simply believed American dominance made such direction unnecessary. Just as his British counterparts recognized their eventual defeat on a level playing field and developed a coordinated national policy accordingly, American planners realized that those same parameters, if not impeded, virtually guaranteed their victory. The more nations and firms requiring aircraft and the more routes to fly, they reasoned, the greater the profits that would flow to the world's dominant aircraft supplier.[51]

Even the lesson of wartime coordination's positive benefits did little to convince American policymakers of the need for postwar planning. The National Advisory Committee for Aeronautics, headed by famed aeroengineer Jerome Hunsaker, advised manufacturers on technical matters throughout the war and served as the government's primary clearinghouse for aviation ideas. Yet it held no mandate to demand that American manufacturers heed its advice. Private coordination proved equally toothless, though several of the country's larger aircraft manufacturers did voluntarily coordinate production for the sake of wartime efficiency. In April 1942, eight major West Coast manufacturers formed the Aircraft War Production Council (AWPC) in order to share resources and solutions to common problems.

Boeing joined the following year, and in 1944 the AWPC united with East Coast manufacturers to form a National Aircraft War Production Council. These groups eased wartime shortages and shared manufacturing ideas, but none made any headway in coordinating a postwar plan of action. Despite calls from the Senate's Special Committee to Investigate the National Defense Program (known as the Truman committee after its chairman) for an aircraft production czar, no American Beaverbrook was ever appointed.[52]

Washington never formed a separate air department because America never faced the dire shortages and needs that confronted Britain in 1940. Neither did the United States ever face an uphill battle for postwar superiority; American policymakers believed they would dominate without centralized planning. Many believed the government had already done its part in securing postwar aviation dominance through wartime investments. As part of the national reconversion process from wartime to peacetime production, firms purchased for pennies on the dollar facilities built with government funds during the war. Surely the knowledge gained in producing planes on the government's dime operated as an indirect subsidy. Such was the case of Boeing's postwar production of its commercial Stratoliner, an airliner built with the same wings, airframe, and engines as the B-29. The bomber cost millions to develop at taxpayer expense; Boeing's commercial division incorporated its designs for free. "Throughout the war we encouraged the aircraft manufacturers to develop air transports of larger and larger size," one Pentagon official explained in 1947, "knowing full well that with many of them their interests were principally in the prospect for commercial sales in a postwar period. It was, in fact, a Government subsidy . . . and I believe it was money well spent." As a practical matter, many American policymakers believed they had provided American aviation with a head start in the pursuit of global dominance through investments and the open-skies policy. It was up to the manufacturers themselves to win the race.[53]

This laissez-faire approach suited the country's largest aircraft manufacturers, who were by and large ideologically opposed to government direction. Centralized planning in peacetime reeked of the kind of authoritarian future many believed they fought against during the war. They epitomized the national consensus by war's end (produced by a combination of selective amnesia and faith) that free enterprise had won the war in spite of, not because of, government interventions in the marketplace. The aviation industry was particularly rife with critics of Roosevelt's New Deal even before the wartime buildup, especially as the foremost American aircraft firms were used to going it alone. The industry's leaders of this era were largely the same tinkerers-turned-businessmen who had founded their companies when flight was more a dangerous lark than a business, and who had then nursed their ailing firms through the Great Depression. These were not men who appreciated advice from government bureaucrats. As a group, they were mavericks, averse to collaboration. Robert Gross of Lockheed and Boeing's Bill Allen were alone among the heads of the country's largest aircraft companies in having a background more in business than in flight, and only Gross willingly accepted government aid as a helpful addition to his company's bottom line. "Your industry is the choicest collection of cutthroat competitors in the country," Secretary of the Navy James Forrestal complained after the war. "Maybe it's because pioneers still manage it."[54]

CEO-founders like Glenn Martin, Donald Douglas, and Jack Northrup (whose companies bore their names) put away their competitive spirit just long enough to unite for the war effort, though none believed the government had any right or reason to direct postwar competition—especially as each dreamed of dominating postwar markets on his own. Martin explained, "If our country can revert back to good old democracy and free enterprise [at war's end] and not become a social state or communist, I think everybody will have a job and can grow and prosper in the after-the-war period." The majority of America's aviation manufacturers felt they had suffered the government in order to win the war, salving their indignation with the Pentagon's cost-plus contracts and capital investments. But the peacetime belonged to them alone. They even feared the direct subsidies provided to offset the costs of transitioning from military to commercial production after the war, because, as *Aviation Week* editorialized, the "industry could not perpetually expect more millions without some sacrifices" in autonomy. Boeing's Bill Boeing put this idea most succinctly. "If the government pays for it," he constantly preached, "you'll lose control over it."[55]

America's aircraftmakers need not have worried about government intervention; hardly a soul in the Roosevelt administration had any intention of controlling their aviation juggernaut. Wartime regulations explicitly forbade the use of military contracts for research or production of commercial models, though as we have seen, Pentagon planners realized that experience gained in military production would not be forgotten when it came time for civilian designs. This rule seemed particularly galling to Martin after the war, when the expected postwar commercial boom failed to materialize. Industry enthusiasts predicted flush times, believing the tens of thousands of young pilots trained during the war would return home longing for planes of their own. It was not to be, leaving firms like Martin's with excess inventory and payrolls they could not hope to meet. In 1946 Martin attempted to escape blame for his company's paltry postwar earnings by explaining, "We were not permitted to do any engineering or research work of any kind on post-war business or designs of any description, except war designs." Though the industry seemed invincible on paper, it was in reality a paper tiger. Civilian production required far leaner manufacturing techniques than the massive "damn the costs" wartime approach. "We did not utilize our engineering forces during the war in preparation for peacetime aircraft designs," Martin lamented. "So when VJ day came we found ourselves suddenly without any designs on the shelf and no way to keep our people busy." That day of cele-bration dawned darkly for the country's planemakers. "While the problems of the war were great and the pressure upon airplane manufacturers to pro-duce was incessant," Robert Gross confided to a friend, "we knew we would get paid for whatever we built. Today we are almost entirely on our own."[56]

Most aviation leaders abandoned their opposition to government support soon after the realities of their sagging postwar market set in. One is hard-pressed to find critics of government aid in the Cold War aerospace industry. This sea change of thinking came quickly, though acceptance of government contracts should not be interpreted as an industry-wide acceptance of gov-ernment direction over commercial production. In 1944 Martin and his colleagues railed against encroaching socialism resulting from government aid. By 1947, however, America's primary aircraft manufacturers had suf-fered one of the worst periods in the industry's tumultuous history. Eight of the nation's twelve principal aircraft manufacturers hemorrhaged cash, as net sales dropped a precipitous 91.5 percent from its 1944 wartime peak. Douglas's sales alone in 1945 were larger than the industry's total for 1946, leading Donald Douglas to conclude that the future appeared "as dark as the inside of a boot." Still, he and his fellow planemakers resisted direct gov-ernment intervention lest it lead to loss of private control. Instead, they wanted new contracts for the planes deemed necessary to beat back the So-viet threat. As *Fortune* described the situation after the war, "Both govern-ment and industry have been desperately afraid that someone will come out in open meeting with the word 'nationalization,'" despite Gross's concession that "the situation in the aircraft industry today is pretty grim."[57]

What form that government support would take, however, remained to be seen. No Beaverbrook for America was on the horizon. With an eye toward continued solvency for individual firms, Pentagon planners doled out resources for the planes and missiles thought necessary for national defense as the Cold War blossomed. Yet not a dime of government money went directly to sponsoring airliner production. It did not need to, given that the country's more successful manufacturers were well versed in the dynamics of applying military lessons to commercial planes. Whether they would prove able to compete with the planned Brabazon models, especially as the leading American firms considered each other to be greater commercial threats than the British, remained an open question. What was sure to all, especially after a single plane brought devastation to an entire city in August 1945, was that aviation mattered now more than ever.

Homeland Security

Americans by 1945 were wealthy, powerful, and eager to direct the world and prove that it was possible to be prosperous without government supervision of the economy. They were also deathly afraid. American policymakers refused to allow their aviation industry to disintegrate after the war, despite their ideological aversion to interference in the marketplace, because airpower seemed not only vital to their broad Pax Americana but necessary for homeland security as well. Because of ocean-leaping bombers developed during the war, America's heartland lay vulnerable to enemy attack for the first time in the nation's modern history.

The ensuing change in American thinking cannot be overstated. American leaders universally left the war convinced of airpower's utility in modern military affairs. Strategic bombing had seemed to cripple Germany and Japan—though later studies would question this conclusion—and it offered the best means of projecting power against future adversaries. Airpower appeared in important ways even more revolutionary than the atomic bomb. As Yale professor Bernard Brodie, the most influential of the first generation of atomic strategists, argued in 1946, even the "ultimate weapon" would prove useless without some means to deliver it through the air. Believing his point to their core, analysts from the Strategic Air Command (SAC), formed in 1946 to deliver America's nuclear strikes, initially measured their destructive power not so much by the size of their atomic arsenal, but rather in terms of their aircraft's range, payload capacity, and ability to deliver strikes on target. American commanders during these years received the first of their truly transcontinental bombers capable of "doing the 10–10": carrying a ten-thousand-pound bomb load ten thousand miles—range enough to reach European and Asian targets from American bases with fuel enough to return home. Ordered in 1942, such planes found special purpose in the atomic age. "The making of an atomic bomb is not so difficult as the problem of turning it out in quantity and delivering it," Omar Bradley reminded Congress in 1949. "Deliverability" was the true key to atomic power.[58]

With ocean-leaping bombers in their own arsenal, the day did not seem far off when America itself would be vulnerable to atomic attacks launched from across the oceans. Fears of such enemy air strikes were just beneath the surface after Pearl Harbor and erupted in the war's final days. News of Hiroshima and Nagasaki, though carrying hope of a quick end to the war, initially brought more trepidation than cheers. "In that terrible flash 10,000 miles away," James Reston wrote following the Hiroshima strike, "men here have seen not only the fate of Japan, but have glimpsed the future of America." In seeing a future apocalypse for their own land in pictures of mushroom clouds rising over Japan, the influential Reston was surely not alone. "We must assume that with the passage of only a little time," H. V. Kaltenborn, one of the most respected American broadcasters, told listeners the night of August 6, 1945, "an improved form of the new weapon we use today can be turned against us . . . We have created a Frankenstein!"[59]

News of the atomic bomb shook Americans to their core, but it was wartime developments in aircraft that made them feel truly vulnerable to aerial assault, and this fear at war's end, so widespread as to be universal, fundamentally changed the way Americans viewed postwar airpower. Even pessimists expected the Soviets to have their own atomic bombs by the 1950s. When Moscow controlled transcontinental bombers as well, or worse yet when Soviet scientists—perhaps aided by scientists spirited out of Nazi Germany—developed missiles against which there seemed to be no good defense, America truly would face an end to its historic insularity.

This was a change from the way Americans initially greeted the aviation age. News of aerial accomplishments filled British subjects with fear, but prompted on the other side of the Atlantic exuberant hopes for a new millennial age. "Sail forth, winged Argonauts of trackless air," one American poet wrote in 1909, yearning for the day when nations might find commonality through aerial proximity. "On sun-blessed wings, bring harbingers of peace." Charles Lindbergh became a national hero for reaching Europe in a single hop in 1926, and even airpower zealots such as General Billy Mitchell proved unable to convince their countrymen of the future dangers aviation brought. Hoping to highlight the need for a strong air corps, Mitchell warned that a future war would include "undoubtedly an [air] attack on the great [American] centers of population." As proof his squadron successfully bombed captured German battleships to the ocean floor in 1921 while journalists watched. His success backfired, however. Most newspapers interpreted the test as further proof of America's geographic security, arguing that airpower's ability to thwart naval attackers alleviated the country's need for a large standing army or navy. Americans longed to put international affairs and far-off foreign threats on the national back burner during the 1920s. Besides, as President Calvin Coolidge offhandedly remarked, "Who's gonna fight us?"[60]

World War II changed these perceptions, striking fear in the heart of most Americans. "Attacks can now come across the arctic regions, as well as across oceans, and strike deep . . . into the heart of the country," General Carl Spaatz, wartime commander of American strategic bombing, told a Senate committee in 1945. "The Pearl Harbor of a future war might well be Chicago, or Detroit, or Pittsburgh, or even Washington." Such fears, implanted by news of European cities bombed to ashes, captured and horrified public imagination during the war only to erupt in an apocalyptic panic once the dust of Hiroshima and Nagasaki began to settle. In November 1945, *Life* famously predicted a "thirty-six hour war" and featured images of Washington consumed by a giant mushroom cloud and New York left in rubble. Manhattan's only remaining occupants, the magazine suggested, would be technicians garbed in radiation gear and the two lonely lions of the city's Public Library—stone sentinels not unlike London's battle-scarred sphinx along the Thames. "Every citizen must be ready for the time when all our great cities will be reduced to radioactive shards," syndicated columnists Joseph and Stewart Alsop told readers the following year. "Your flesh *should* creep."[61]

For all their power and powerful aspirations, then, Americans entered the postwar world imbued with a fear that was pervasive enough even to dominate national symbols. Norman Rockwell's painting *Freedom from Fear*, one of his widely distributed tributes to Roosevelt's "Four Freedoms" (America's wartime promise to the world—the others being freedom from want, of speech, and of religion) depicted children being safely tucked into bed by caring parents. Nothing could have been better proof of America's bounty, save the screaming headline of their father's newspaper that read "bombings" and "horror." In Rockwell's vision of American domesticity, painted well before B-29s or atomic bombs, the airplane offered the one power capable of destroying tranquility. American children could sleep securely for now; but for how long? "Seldom, if ever, has a war ended leaving the victors with such a sense of uncertainty and fear, with such a realization that the future is obscure and that survival is not assured," concluded broadcaster Edward R. Murrow in September 1945.[62]

Aviation and atomic power explain this dramatic change in American thinking about security and the world. The two cannot be separated. Thus began what historian H. W. Brands would call the "age of vulnerability," when Americans even in the highest corridors of power felt a sense of impending doom. "The airplane robbed us of those ocean and polar barriers which for centuries were the principal safeguards of our security," Air Force Secretary Stuart Symington declared in 1949, "and every literate person in these United States knows it." Certainly President Harry Truman understood the risks, as he warned the country in his farewell address that "the war of the future would be one in which man could extinguish millions of lives at one blow, demolish the great civilizations of the world, wipe out the cultural achievements of the past—and destroy the very structure of a civilization that has been slowly and painfully built up through hundreds of generations." Not even the center of the Pax Americana could guarantee its own survival when confronted by such awful new technologies. When barbarians stared down the gates of Rome, the whole world *seemed* at an end. This time, the warriors carried atomic lances. Survival would be a curse in the aftermath of such a war, Dwight Eisenhower told audiences. "You might as well go out and shoot everyone you see and then shoot yourself."[63]

Such notions of vulnerability had all the more powerful effect because they cut against the grain of American history. The British had had nearly two generations to come to terms with their aerial vulnerability by 1945. Such fears were wholly new to Americans, and the metaphoric language used to describe the country's newfound vulnerability reveals the depths of the emotional response. Airplanes were likened to rapists who surprise and ravage their unsuspecting victims. According to SAC's first commander, they would "penetrate" American airspace like an intruder breaches a home, while *Atlantic Monthly* editors warned readers, "Our land lies naked." Symington cautioned that enemy bombers directly threatened the home every American man was taught to consider his castle, arguing that "the airplane has brought the battlefield into every man's front yard, regardless of where he lives." Airpower destroyed the nation's most cherished collective possession. "It's as plain as two and two makes four," Senate powerhouse Arthur

Vandenberg declared. He had once been a virulent isolationist. Not anymore. "There is no such thing as isolated security when the chain reaction of an atomic bomb and the range of an air pirate" can "reduce international boundaries to the impotence of pencil marks on tissue paper."[64]

Paradoxes of Power

World War II ended with a series of paradoxes that helped determine the subsequent course and tenor of the Cold War. The world's strongest country entered the peace with the greatest sense of fear and vulnerability, whereas damaged countries such as Britain were more psychologically equipped to weather dangers. The British people feared attack after the war, but they already knew the sorts of devastation aerial bombing could bring. Fear of enemy attack haunted Americans of this generation, whose nightmares ran to extremes in the absence of evidence and under the domination of dark imagination. They had no experience to draw upon, save images of Hiroshima or Nagasaki transposed onto Chicago, New York, or Washington. "No one can stop the Russians from building the bombs and planes which will give them the ability to destroy our cities and industry in a sneak attack," warned Thomas Finletter, chair of Truman's Air Policy Commission and later secretary of the air force. "We can though make it an act of national suicide for them to do it." Such logic might have been strategically valid; but it was hardly comforting.[65]

The differences in national approaches to aviation did not end with fear or experience with foreign attack. Britain lacked America's financial and manufacturing resources. But it had a plan for future dominance. American producers seemed to possess every possible advantage. They were richer and more productive, they possessed larger design staffs, and they fielded a full family of transport models already flying. They even had the world's largest aviation market within their own borders, home to half the world's daily commercial flights after 1945, as well as the Pentagon, the world's single largest purchaser of military aircraft. This was a commercial (and later a military) market British policymakers longed to crack, especially as exports seemed their one road to industrial success. "Clearly, if the British aircraft industry is to do a thriving business in civil aircraft," the supply minister wrote in 1944, "it must find markets overseas as well as at home." American aviation firms had less incentive to export in the immediate postwar years. For them, exports were the icing on the cake.[66]

Even a downturn in sales immediately after the war could not dissuade some American manufacturers or government planners from their faith in independence. "We do not want government assistance," Douglas said, "because it inevitably carries with it limitations, controls, and influences which make it more difficult to do the job the way we know it has to be done." Conservatives and liberals alike warned that the more the government controlled American life in the face of an omnipresent foreign threat, the greater the risk of a "garrison state" dedicated solely to defense at the expense of traditional American liberties. Finding the right balance between safety and tyranny kept Eisenhower awake at night through the mid-1950s. "If we let defense spending run wild," he cautioned, "you get inflation . . . then controls . . . then a garrison state . . . and then we've lost the very values we were trying to defend." Atomic and then nuclear power seemed cheaper in the long term than large standing armies. Cheaper, but undoubtedly more destructive if superpower blustering ever led to war. "We have only one real defense," General Carl Spaatz, commander of America's air force later stated: "a planned and ready offensive." Indeed, the most famous early Cold War bureaucratic battle between proponents of unlimited defense and those who wanted to hold the line on the garrison state occurred in 1949 over just what sort of offensive capabilities America should make its first priority. Truman subdued a public insurrection from disgruntled admirals, furious that SAC bombers had won priority in budgeting over their own dreams of a "supercarrier" fleet. Both the air force and the navy believed its own units were best suited to atomize Moscow at the start of any future superpower conflict. Lost in the furor of this case, to contemporary observers and later historians, was how deeply both sides believed airpower was the key to future military operations. Their dispute was not over *whether* air-based atomic assaults were best to halt Soviet aggression, but rather *what kind* of aerial platform might best deliver American might. No one questioned that aviation was the best strategic and fiscal choice, or that vigilance provided America's only means of defense. "If we fall behind technically," Strategic Air Command General George Kenny warned, "it would take so long to catch up that we would run an excellent chance of defeat."[67]

Despite the American fascination with the subject, British leaders argued surprisingly little over the potential growth of a garrison state. Unlike those in Washington, London policymakers had zero faith in their country's ability to survive the next war. They had already been bombed in two successive European conflicts, and as Prime Minister Baldwin had warned a generation before, the bomber seemed destined to get through. Moscow would surely lash out at the United Kingdom, America's "unsinkable aircraft carrier," as their first move in any war, Britain's Chiefs of Staff predicted in 1946, hoping "to bring about the early elimination of the UK from the war by all means at her disposal, especially by air attack, piloted aircraft, robots and flying bombs." Such strikes would eventually be atomic and would bring greater devastation than anything suffered before. Britain's special relationship made it a special target, a fate depicted in George Orwell's nightmarish novel *1984,* first published in 1949. He summed up Britain's sole future purpose in its designation as "Airstrip One" for a power (undoubtedly America) across the ocean. This was a price of allegiance to America that British leaders feared most of all.

Yet a desperate sense of the inevitable also clarified the strategic thinking of many British policymakers, who believed survival in an atomic world demanded a Britain strong enough to mediate between the sparring superpowers. True British security would come only through *independent* strength. Moscow was not to be trusted, but if war would inevitably lead to Britain's complete destruction, then London could not afford to place its fate solely in Washington's hands either. Each superpower jab and spar left Britain, in the middle, at risk of feeling their atomic punches. Neither could therefore be allowed to interfere with the technological vision of such New Jerusalem programs like the Brabazon plan. Britain had to be first to market to win, Britain had to sell, because it had to be strong enough to temper its allies and its adversaries alike. That it would never regain great-power status without prosperity was clear to all; that it could not do so without aerial mastery appeared equally true. Because Britain was doomed in any future war, in other words, its leaders believed they had to prevent such a war from ever occurring. To do so and thus to survive, they needed aviation, because only a prosperous and technologically advanced nation capable of competing in this most fundamental of markets could possibly be strong enough to withstand American advances and ward off Soviet ones. Nothing could be allowed to stop them.[68]

The two nations' distinct wartime experiences with aviation led directly to their conflicts in years to come. Though industrially and geographically disadvantaged, the British possessed in their government an active guide the Americans lacked, one willing to offer both hope and sustenance. This was a government willing to fight to make that vision a reality. For the Americans, commercial dominance seemed best ensured by clearing the way for their corporations' inevitable victory. Military dominance, conversely, demanded strict vigilance to make sure that no foreign power ever gained the ability to make America's apocalyptic visions of enemy assault a reality. American striking power had to remain without peer, no matter the cost. And woe be the ally that jeopardized American security, especially if their reason was a search for geopolitical parity. The Pax Americana needed allies to succeed; it did not need true and equal partners. The central paradox of this entire story is that these true partners in the postwar world were themselves competitors for the kind of aerial dominance that exemplified and was in fact the most powerful commodity of all: power itself.

CHAPTER 2

Selling Jets to Stalin

As predicted in 1942, American firms dominated postwar commercial aviation. They sold more than a thousand transport planes to foreign and domestic customers in 1945. British sales totaled less than two hundred for the whole of 1945 and 1946. Having jolted Churchill's conservatives from power, the newly formed Labour government of Prime Minister Clement Attlee inherited an aviation industry vital to national security and international prominence but faced with a difficult uphill climb. There would be no change of course despite a different hand at the helm, however, as Labour accepted the Brabazon program without revision. Attlee and his advisers were as enthralled with aviation as their predecessors, and they had participated in the wartime coalition that developed this plan in the first place. Such intimacy did not preclude using the Arnold-Powers accord for political cover when Britain's interim aircraft failed, as predicted, to equal American designs. "The reason for our relative backwardness in the production of civil aircraft is that the British aircraft industry was required during the war to concentrate on military types and has not yet had time to produce new types of aircraft," the secretary of state for dominion affairs lamented in 1947. "The American aircraft industry was not placed in this position during the war," and thus "has a considerable head start on us."[1]

Britain needed revenues far before the Brabazon models would be ready for market in the early 1950s. Having emptied its treasury to pay for a second global war for survival in a generation, the country now confronted what economist John Maynard Keynes termed a "financial Dunkirk." Its balance of payments deficit was more than three times the available currency reserves; its total foreign debts surpassed £3 billion by the time Japan formally surrendered (VJ-day); and the land that had once financed a global empire was now deeply in debt to its former colonies and creditors (mainly

American) around the world. The new government needed a fresh influx of funds to redress this imbalance and to fund its hallmark New Jerusalem expansion of the social welfare state. Attlee knew Labour would not remain in power for long if it failed to deliver on its most important campaign promises. His political advisers accordingly called for increased social spending, but economists like Keynes warned that the country also needed to fund an unprecedented shift from wartime to peacetime production, including a massive industrial modernization program, if British producers were to remain internationally competitive. "We can sell anything we can produce," he concluded, "our problem is to reconvert industry quick enough . . . to have the exports [to sell]."[2]

Britain needed economic aid, and its prosperous partner across the Atlantic seemed the most obvious source. Whereas London's financial resources had drained away during the war, American finances boomed. By 1945 New York had superseded London as the globe's primary private banking center, and the U.S. government's gold reserves at Fort Knox reached almost two-thirds the world's known total. Keynes consequently led a negotiating team to Washington during the summer of 1945 in hope of tapping such wealth, with the particular goal of securing absolution of wartime debts and a direct reconstruction grant in the neighborhood of $5 billion. He received less than he had hoped for. American officials offered sympathy for Britain's wartime sacrifices, but little more, and offered a low-interest loan instead of a grant. More importantly, they demanded significant concessions as a condition for any aid, including future convertibility of sterling with the dollar and the eventual dismantling of the Imperial Preference System that favored trade within the empire. Easy convertibility and free trade were the economic hallmarks of the Pax Americana, and American strategists considered dismantlement of London's closed "sterling bloc" a vital prerequisite to global market integration. There would never again be as propitious a time to impose a new financial order upon friend and foe alike, Truman's financial strategists advised. "It would be unwise even to supply the fund as credit," Assistant Secretary of State Will Clayton argued, "without laying down conditions that would insure a sound advance towards our postwar objectives."[3]

Such demands rankled in London, where the empire remained an emotional issue, and where many believed the country had already delivered its down payment for help through nearly six years of blood and sweat. Fighting the Americans on every point pushed Keynes to the brink of exhaustion. But he also understood. "In this country [the U.S.] where it is a moral duty and not merely a self-regarding act to make any money which the traffic will bear and law allow," he privately explained to the chancellor of the exchequer, "some imitation of a normal banking transaction is necessary if the moral principles of the country are not to be affronted." Britain had no choice but to accept America's hard bargain, he reasoned. If not from Washington, then "where, on earth, is all that money going to come from?"[4]

A massive influx of revenue from increased exports seemed the only thing capable of financing British needs without permanently resorting to American aid and the ensuing reduction in economic sovereignty. This hardly seemed an easy solution. Keynes calculated that British exports would need to increase by an astounding 50 percent *per year* into the 1950s simply to feed its population and pay its short-term foreign debt, with nothing remaining for industrial modernization. His hypothetical figures demanded a nearly 100 percent jump over prewar trading levels simply for the country to break even, making the calculation little more than a "pipe dream" useful only to "cheer ourselves up" with the promise that their fate lay in their own hands. A less successful export drive seemed more likely, followed by years of financial hardship accompanied by increasing social unrest and a decline in British global power. The situation, Board of Trade president Hugh Dalton concluded, looked "pretty bleak."[5]

Potentially lucrative aviation sales offered one answer to this hazardous financial future. Yet few international buyers seemed interested in the country's inferior interim transport models, and there simply was not time to wait for the expected profits from the Brabazon models. Britain's military aircraft and state-of-the-art jet engines, arguably the world's best, were another matter, and offered Attlee's policymakers an irresistible revenue source when they needed it most. "We know that the USA are well ahead on production of civil aircraft," one Air Ministry official concluded in early 1946, "but it is our lead in jet engines of all types that gives us solid hope" for immediate sale and profits. Exporting jet technology to eager military buyers offered potential long-term commercial benefits as well. Whitehall strategists reasoned that government buyers would naturally gravitate toward British civil aircraft in the future when equipping their nationalized airlines if they were pleased with their initial military purchases. "We can expect that orders for military and civil aircraft will tend to go together," Board of Trade president Stafford Cripps (Dalton's successor) later reminded Attlee. Cripps believed the government should immediately sell, without restraint, its military jets, which were at that time the world's best, in order to help balance the national books but also to facilitate future civil sales. "I think we should make the strongest possible bid in the aircraft field," he said, "which in the future is as likely to be as important to us as the naval field has been in the past."[6]

The Air Ministry moved quickly after VJ-day along just this path by dramatically reducing its wartime export controls. By the close of 1945, the cash-strapped Attlee government had made the cream of Britain's jet technology available to the world. Planes and engines formerly considered too sensitive to export during the war (too sensitive even for the release of technical information to allies) were placed on the so-called "Open List" for immediate sale abroad. This list was literally a published record of the British equipment available to foreign buyers. Such a listing meant that "the jet aero engines produced by Messrs. Rolls Royce, which are beyond a doubt the most advanced in the world today," could be exported with only a minimum of government oversight, the undersecretary of supply explained. Previous regulations forbade such sales without express Whitehall approval. These new rules allowed sale even of Britain's most sophisticated equipment, including Rolls's Nene and Derwent jet engines, with a minimum of government oversight and with the presumption of government consent in any sale a British firm could secure. These were among the world's most advanced pieces of military hardware. A Derwent-driven jet set the world speed record the following year (topping 500 mph in level flight), for example, while *Flight and Aircraft Engineer* dubbed the more sophisticated Nene "the world's most powerful engine."[7]

This was an unusual liberalization of technology controls. Modern industrial states are typically loath to export their most advanced military equipment even during peacetime, preferring instead to retain sole use of sophisticated weaponry for their own forces or for trusted allies. They are typically even more hesitant to arm potential adversaries with equipment superior to that employed by their own forces, no matter what potential profits are at stake. There are clear strategic reasons for wanting to field the best-equipped forces, especially for nations such as Britain that rely upon technology rather than manpower for military prowess, and politicians typically fear the wrath of their constituents when sending soldiers into battle with inferior equipment. Yet the Open List expansion raised just that prospect. While some British squadrons were in the process of refitting with jet-powered aircraft by the close of 1945, the vast majority relied on the same piston-driven machines used to win the war. The Air Ministry's liberalization therefore offered foreign buyers the opportunity to acquire and deploy British jets ahead of some of Britain's own squadrons. Still, nary a voice in Whitehall objected to this unusual promotion of military sales in the fall of 1945. It was a silence they would come to regret.

The same could not be said of Washington. Even after the cessation of hostilities, American policymakers forbade the unhindered export of advanced military aircraft until two full years after such machines had been retired from the country's frontline forces. This is the way states typically guard their most prized military equipment. Washington was so intent upon securing the best available equipment for its own forces that it did not permit the private export of frontline aircraft until its own squadrons had been completely upgraded with new models. The government might approve sales of advanced equipment to close allies in limited cases and for specific political purposes, but as a general rule the Pentagon hoped that export controls would help ensure that American pilots never faced similarly equipped foes. When American firms sold military-quality aircraft or engines abroad after the war, they did so only under their government's direction.[8]

Whitehall's Open List consequently promised foreign buyers unfettered access to premier military technology of the kind Washington's planners would never have accepted, though this is not to say that British exports went entirely unregulated after VJ-day. Technically, the government retained the authority to forbid any undesirable sale. Modern states require export licenses for all goods ranging from gunnysacks to machine guns, though naturally it is far easier to procure a license for civilian goods than for top-of-the-line military equipment. In a pinch, Board of Trade officials argued, they could halt any suspicious sale in its tracks by refusing to grant such a license. Up until the very moment foreign buyers accepted possession of British goods, they reasoned, any sale could be squelched. The Open List expansion therefore did not wholly eliminate government control over British exports, but was instead a symbolic authorization encouraging British aircraft manufacturers to consider applications for export license as mere formalities.[9]

The Labour government put British technological know-how on the trading block as well. The Open List featured not only finished aircraft and engines, but also manufacturing licenses for jet production. For an up-front price plus royalties on every subsequent model produced, Rolls and other companies were authorized to sell foreign producers detailed instructions for producing their own British-designed jet engines. This decision was in many ways even more significant than the green light given to sales of completed models, for sophisticated technologies such as engines are notoriously difficult to reverse engineer and duplicate. Even if technicians understood how such an engine worked, production of its component parts often required metallurgical skill and equipment far beyond the capabilities of most industrial states at the time. The purchase of a manufacturing license, on the other hand, left little to the imagination, as British producers offered to sell foreign buyers not only the know-how but also the unique machinery required to put their newly purchased knowledge to quick use. In essence all a foreign power interested in producing engines had to supply was factory space, start-up capital, and raw materials. For the right price, British companies would do the rest.[10]

British ministers knew that such widespread foreign sales diluted their technological lead, and that technological monopolies, once discarded, were never regained. Yet they concurrently believed that even if such sales enhanced the technological sophistication of foreign air forces, they would do little harm to Britain's overall superiority because no other power would be capable of matching Britain's prowess for advancing the field. Their country could sell its best today and arm foreigners with impunity, they reasoned, because Britain's superior producers would continue to develop increasingly sophisticated machines at a faster clip than any potential military or commercial foe. So long as the designer heroes who had developed the engines and aircraft that had helped win the war remained ahead of their foreign rivals, as they surely would, then Britain had nothing to fear in the future from exuberant sales of today's best models. Moreover, the chances for conflict in the next few years seemed slim. Europe's appetite for war appeared to be sated for at least a decade, Attlee's policymakers concluded in late 1945, and most developing countries were only making their first embryonic strides into the air age—a step typically made with piston technology rather than more expensive jets—making it look unlikely that the RAF would engage in battle against sophisticated jet-equipped forces anywhere in the world until 1957 at the earliest. British forces were expected to have far more advanced planes than those powered by Nenes or Derwents by the midpoint of the next decade. "Messrs Rolls Royce are confident that they will, in fact, be able to keep several steps ahead of any country to which they sell the right to manufacture under license," the undersecretary of supply wrote Attlee. "This is why the Air Ministry did not worry about selling its best warplanes abroad," from a military standpoint, and why Rolls's executives "do not object, from commercial competitive reasons, to giving the information and facilities for making their existing jet engines to foreign countries" such as France or Switzerland, each considered likely buyers of British jets. The war-ravaged Soviets posed a strategic threat, though not, most Whitehall analysts believed, until the end of the 1950s. But even if Moscow gained access to a British engine, Attlee's policymakers considered Stalin's engineers too poorly trained to know what to do with it.[11]

Driven by financial necessity and justified by hubris, the Open List expansion exemplified the tendency among British policymakers to view the battle for aviation dominance as a zero-sum competition with the United States. With Germany and Japan in ruins, France rebuilding, and the Soviets no real commercial threat at all, America seemed the only potential aviation rival on the horizon. The number of international buyers, conversely, appeared finite. With few states capable of supporting multiple airlines, and with so many aviation decisions made by national leaders, British victories in foreign markets seemed to entail exclusion of future American products from that market, just as American victories would hinder Britain's manufacturers. Once a foreign market was painted on a global map in the crimson of imperial Britain or American blue, it seemed likely to remain that color for years to come.

British policymakers therefore believed they had to win markets without delay, not only to forestall an otherwise inevitable American monopoly over individual markets, but also in preparation for the full exploitation of the Brabazon lead in the next decade. Their lead in jet production was not expected to remain unchallenged by any of America's premier engine makers, and in the next few years Attlee's policymakers fully expected the commercially minded American government to authorize its own manufacturers to seek out foreign buyers with increasing zeal. Thus the Open List expansion was made not only to gain much-needed credits, but also to squeeze American competition from global markets before Washington could bring its industrial advantages to bear. "A complete prohibition on the negotiations of licenses to manufacture these [jet] engines with other countries would be a serious blow to our commercial interests," the supply minister explained in early 1946, adding, "We have a real lead in this field which would almost certainly pass, in that case, into American hands." After all, Whitehall analysts had "no expectations that the Americans will prohibit their manufacturers from giving other nations licenses to manufacture as and when the Americans develop their own engines."[12]

Charged with the image of American competition nipping at their heels,

British firms wasted little time in using the Open List to establish a lead in jet sales throughout the world. By the spring of 1946, London's manufacturers had signed contracts with France, Chiang Kai-shek's China, Canada, and Switzerland for the purchase and manufacture of jets and engines. E. W. Hives, Rolls Royce's managing director, told Cripps that such sales were the harbinger of future success. He added, "You will see that we are contributing to your policy of expanding the exports from this country." Such optimism ultimately proved shortsighted, because Whitehall's policymakers misjudged their liberal export policy on three levels. In the coming years foreign states and the Soviet Union in particular would shock London with their ability to reproduce British equipment; war would come far sooner than 1957; and exuberant military exports would frequently cause more diplomatic trouble than the export credits seemed worth.[13]

Attlee's advisers were right to fear that American producers would put commercial pressure on their government's export restraints. Despite dominating the postwar market for civil aircraft, the United States had aviation problems of its own in 1945. Surplus military transports abounded after the war, and cheerful predictions of airlines—and even individual consumers—indulging in peacetime buying sprees quickly proved overly optimistic. When coupled with the natural decline in military spending at war's end, the weak demand for new commercial craft meant that America's aircraft manufacturers lost money in 1946 at a torrential pace, driving investors before them. "The industry is still held too erratic by Wall Street analysts to merit long-term investment considerations," *Automotive and Aviation Industries* reported, and aviation stock prices reacted accordingly. Boeing's stock lost 37 percent of its value in 1946; Convair, 53 percent; Curtiss-Wright, 50 percent; Douglas, 34 percent; Lockheed, 58 percent. Such numbers made even the most vigorous opponents of government assistance ponder whether, in the words of Lockheed's Robert Gross, "the aircraft industry needs substantial government support." To *Fortune*'s editors, the sharp drop suggested nothing less than that "the aircraft industry cannot satisfactorily exist in a pure, competitive, unsubsidized, 'free-market' economy."[14]

Rather than seek direct government subsidies or increases in military spending—those arguments were still a few years away for most manufacturers—some American firms instead lobbied for the sort of liberalized export controls enjoyed by their British competitors. During the early spring of 1946, for example, Curtiss-Wright began negotiations with both Nationalist China and the Soviet Union for the sale of engines and aircraft, despite expectations that government restrictions would complicate such exports. Rolls Royce already had a firm contract with those same Chinese buyers. A Curtiss-Wright representative therefore met with State Department officials in March seeking permission to compete in this potentially lucrative market, armed with his personal guarantee that the firm sought to export only machines that were "all obsolescent and of commercial rather than military type." His company wanted to sell finished engines to the Chinese, and to sell Moscow the same type of manufacturing license Rolls Royce was then offering its own customers, albeit for piston rather than jet engines. If Washington truly wanted a prosperous but laissez-faire aviation industry, he explained, then American firms had to compete for markets far and wide, even behind the iron curtain. State Department officials viewed this plan with much "hesitation" (diplomatic code for deep disapproval). They could not endorse selling engines to the Soviets, given the tenuous state of East-West relations, and no matter what London allowed Rolls Royce to do, American sales to the troubled Chinese Nationalists were tightly coordinated with the administration's broader China policy.[15]

As Whitehall predicted, commercial pressure to ease restrictions grew when money became tight. Washington withstood such pleas for the moment. Fearing foreign aviation advances, the Truman administration rejected Curtiss-Wright's plans for both China and the Soviets, and eventually moved to stifle Britain's aerial proliferation as well. Halting American companies was easy. It was done with one letter to the company, promising rejection of any application for an export license for sale to either country. Keeping British companies from trolling such markets would prove far more difficult. The initial Anglo-American Cold War clash over aviation, the first of many to come, occurred in neither China nor the Soviet Union, but instead over South America, where policymakers on both sides of the Atlantic first realized that aviation disputes portended larger commercial and security confrontations to follow.

The First Clash

Just as British and American policymakers believed aircraft sales could help win international allies and customers, so too did they believe that careful regulation of such sales, and in turn the carefully regulated dissemination of aviation technologies, could foster international change. Their policies toward Argentina prove this point. The country was a favorite refuge of escaped Nazis, and in October 1945, British and American diplomats jointly adopted an unofficial arms embargo until Juan Peron's government fully accounted for its links to accused war criminals. Because neither Washington nor London sought to codify their embargo formally in law or to fully define its parameters, their accord became known as the "Gentleman's Agreement." Each sought flexibility, because more than simply capturing runaway Germans was at stake. The Truman administration in particular hoped to delay formalization of a joint Anglo-American arms policy for Argentina until it had finalized its own broader plans to uniformly supply military equipment throughout Latin America. This plan for "standardization" of the region's armed forces was a favorite of General George Marshall, who believed imposition of a single military norm would forestall dangerous and expensive arms races among its varied countries, while enhancing hemispheric defense. If all Latin American militaries used similar equipment, he believed, and especially if American equipment became their uniform choice, Washington could more easily arm its southern allies in times of crisis and regulate Latin American arms purchases in times of peace.[16]

Britain had other plans for the region. Its firms had long exported arms throughout Latin America, and given the omnipresent need for exports, Foreign Secretary Ernest Bevin did not want American suppliers to win what he called a "monopoly of the trade in arms with the Latin American countries" under the guise of a benevolent standardization plan. His government desired instead to keep the region open to naval and aircraft exports from Europe, especially because anti-American Argentina was among the few international buyers willing to purchase Britain's "interim" transports and airliners. Hoping to secure a foothold in this blossoming market, the cabinet consequently authorized civil transport exports to Argentina's national airline in late 1945 despite the existing arms embargo, aided by a particularly liberal interpretation of the Gentleman's Agreement that claimed airliners were not military machinery. At least, the Air Ministry argued, this was not an airliner's intended purpose. For what would surely not be the last time, American diplomats objected to British aviation sophistry. Even civilian transports could be used to ferry soldiers or war material, the State Department claimed, and additions to a country's airlift capacity, no matter under what guise, automatically aided its military capabilities. Believing the sale violated the Gentleman's Agreement, the Truman administration requested its immediate reversal.[17]

Washington's objection elicited an angry response in London. Particularly incensed, Bevin employed every bit of his linguistic training as a former dockyard organizer in a protest to American officials in late March 1946. His Majesty's government was insulted by the charge that civil sales violated the Gentleman's Agreement, Bevin fumed, and its manufacturers would most certainly continue to ply their civilian wares throughout South America without any interference from the United States. Aviation exports were a matter taken most seriously in Whitehall, he warned, which is why he yearned to stress that the Monroe Doctrine did not apply to commercial sales.[18]

Britain did not want to disrupt the unity of Anglo-American policies toward the region generally or Argentina in particular, Bevin continued, his tone softening. Thus while export of the planes in question would continue unhindered, he told the American representatives, future "proposals to export both military and civil aircraft to S[outh] America" would require his personal approval. Washington could have his word that there would be no subsequent blurring of the line between military and civilian sales, for he would personally oversee any future aircraft sales to the region. Britain needed to "avoid conflict with the United States" while Congress debated Keynes's much-needed loan package, he later explained to Attlee, no matter how distasteful American policy appeared.[19]

Attlee took a more cynical view. He saw the worst in Washington's protests, believing them a thinly veiled attack upon Britain's commercial interests. Even as America's strict interpretation of the Gentleman's Agreement hindered Britain's sales efforts in the region, the Pentagon continued to plow steadily forward with its standardization plans. Given that the British planes in question were airliners and not military craft—the argument that all aircraft were inherently dual-use proved lost on Attlee—and the Pentagon's presumption that their suppliers would win future standardization contracts, Attlee concluded that the Americans clearly "wish to preserve the South American market for themselves." "I fully appreciate the need for caution on the subject of military planes," he railed to Bevin, but added, "I wonder how far we should allow ourselves to be inhibited in the case of civil planes by what appears to be mere commercial rivalry on the part of the U.S.?" He had always presumed that commercial considerations would ultimately drive Washington's export and aviation policies. This flap over sales to Argentina merely confirmed his suspicions.[20]

Attlee had little patience for American diplomacy by the spring of 1946, and his anger over these sales must be understood as the consequence of months of difficult negotiations with the Truman administration over what he perceived to be Washington's initial hegemonic steps. Unabashed free traders such as the State Department's Clayton and Treasury Secretary Fred Vinson proved ruthless in their loan negotiations with Keynes, especially in their blanket disregard for Britain's system of colonial preference. London's capitulation to most American concessions—as Keynes had argued, what choice did they have?—prompted a brief anti-American backlash in Parliament. Having been attacked by those on the right for not hewing close enough to Washington's lead, Attlee now found himself ridiculed for having given the Americans too much in exchange for too little. Buffeted from all sides, he was moreover frustrated by the slow pace of negotiations on a general European settlement with the increasingly recalcitrant Soviets. Adding insult to injury, American politicians throughout the political spectrum regularly scored political points at home by publicly twisting the lion's tail over Britain's efforts to retain its formal empire. Keynes had worked his battered body to exhaustion to secure the loan (and was in his final weeks during this dispute over Argentina), yet caustic congressmen ungraciously charged that the loan appeared "part of the Lord Keynes and American New Deal plan for a world-wide WPA project that will lower our American standard of living." Another representative vowed never to "vote for one dollar [for British aid] to take food out of the mouths of my people."[21]

Attlee even then had a proposal on his desk to ration bread in the United Kingdom for the first time due to lack of supplies and currency. While he left to Truman the thorny issue of securing safe passage of the loan through Congress, the beleaguered prime minister surely did not appreciate either Washington's Anglophobic air or the audacity of congressional objections to helping British industry recover at the same time as the State Department tried to thwart what he considered to be legitimate British efforts to export and thus stand on its own two feet. American protests over sales efforts in Argentina therefore touched a particularly raw nerve. "The US are so very keen on 'non-discrimination' as practiced by other people," he complained to Bevin, "that they should surely not attempt to keep us out of the South American market by diplomatic pressure. I am sure you will agree with this, and also that the South American market for aircraft is likely to be valuable to us."[22]

It now fell to Bevin to restrain his frustrated prime minister. Bevin felt equally scorned by the darker elements of American politics and diplomacy after less than a year in office, but he knew well that the first priority of any twentieth-century British foreign secretary was to maintain good relations with Washington no matter how trying the circumstances. "They did, it is true," he answered Attlee, "attempt to dissuade us from selling civilian aircraft to Argentina" by arguing that "even civilian aircraft might add to the Argentine war potential." Yet he considered the matter closed. He had given his word that he would oversee future aircraft sales to the region, and he believed this assurance alone should make Washington retreat from its rigid initial protests. "Every effort is being made by this department to promote the sale of aircraft in South America," Bevin assured his boss.[23]

The matter may have appeared over to Bevin, but it was not soon forgotten. The lesson taken in Whitehall from this brief Anglo-American flap would color subsequent aviation disputes. The Americans appeared unwilling to concede even this one market to British manufacturers, despite their great wealth, leading Bevin and Attlee to conclude that Washington also viewed the international competition for aircraft markets as a zero-sum game. British producers could not afford to relax against such competitors for even a moment. More importantly, the Americans appeared willing to manipulate security arguments in order to ensure their own commercial triumph, and to use diplomacy to win what their producers could not. Future aviation conflicts would have to be judged most carefully, Attlee warned, because Washington would apparently use any argument, even a rigid interpretation of a purposefully vague embargo, to capture aviation markets. Argentina would yet again prove a bur in the side of amiable Anglo-American relations. Soon, however, British leaders would have more profound aviation worries.

Selling Jets to Stalin

Only weeks after the initial Argentina dispute, Rolls Royce's wide-ranging sales efforts netted a far more complicated customer than Juan Peron. The company had made the most of the Air Ministry's policies promoting international sales, even securing a firm contract for an engine sale to the same Nationalist Chinese buyers Washington refused to allow its own manufacturers to sell to. "We find [they] are very nice people to deal with," confided one Rolls manager in a note to Board of Trade president Cripps. Save for occasional hiccups over Latin America, all appeared to be going smoothly for Britain's aircraft export program.[24]

Then suddenly and without even preliminary negotiations, in late May

1946 the Soviet Union made Rolls an official offer for several of the company's best jet engines, including Nenes and Derwents, and for a manufacturing license to mass-produce British engines of their own. With visions of locking up Soviet Russia's vast aviation market for years to come, Rolls immediately sought Whitehall's assurance that "in spite of the fact that the engines had been placed on the 'open list,' there was really no objection to negotiating such a contract with the Soviet government." Having apparently read at least one newspaper since the war's end, Rolls's managers recognized that all was not well in East-West relations. "We hope," the company wrote Cripps, "that politics will not prevent us [from] executing this order!"[25]

Politics would do just that. Despite all their planning and rhetoric of aviation as a symbol of New Jerusalem rationality and progress, Whitehall apparently had not considered that placing engines on the trading block meant potentially offering them to the communist bloc. When the Air Ministry first evaluated the potential for technological diffusion through its liberal export policy, it considered the implications of sales made to friendly or neutral nations with embryonic aircraft industries, countries that would need five years or more to duplicate British machines. Providing engines to Geneva or even to Buenos Aires was one thing. Helping to bring the Kremlin's air force up to Britain's technological level through direct sales was far more troubling. Moscow posed Britain's only real strategic threat on the horizon, and the Kremlin directed a massive, if arguably second-rate, aircraft industry that made up for in determination what it lacked in industrial expertise. Soviet engineers might prove unable to develop their own jet engines from scratch, but if provided with a manufacturing license from Rolls, the effort required to construct a technologically advanced air force might prove shockingly small.

The Soviet bid prompted a tidal wave of previously unvoiced concerns over the full implications of the Open List expansion that concluded in a fundamental reassessment of British technology sales. As Arthur Woodburn, the Supply Ministry's parliamentary secretary, explained, "It is only recently, and largely as a direct result of the Russian dilemma that we have begun to realize the necessity of distinction, on security grounds, between the sale of finished products and of the manufacturing rights in them." Distinguishing between the two had not been necessary during the war. Britain freely offered its aviation technology to American manufacturers, but most countries were too concerned with their immediate safety to request the ability to build aircraft on their own. Most wanted deliveries of completed aircraft instead, and of course, as British firms did not trade with the Axis powers at all during the war, Whitehall had long since stopped worrying about exporting its manufacturing secrets to potential enemies. In the rush for exports after Germany's surrender (VE-day), however, such issues failed to receive their proper attention. "The importance of this is brought out by the estimates that the Russians are at present five years behind us on gas turbines," Woodburn wrote. "The sale of finished Nene and Derwent engines might reduce our lead to three years," while "the sale of manufacturing rights might reduce it to as little as one year." In other words, the Rolls export might allow the Kremlin's planes to be equal to Whitehall's by 1947.[26]

The proposed Rolls sale risked providing Moscow with the superior air force. By the close of 1947 the RAF would not even have enough Nenes or Derwents to outfit all of its own squadrons. Current plans called for Rolls to continue production of both engines for the British military until 1949, while the RAF intended to use warplanes driven by these engines until the midpoint of the next decade. Only then would more-advanced models be ready for military service. Only ten of the RAF's twenty-four squadrons would be outfitted with jets by 1948, which, the Air Ministry calculated with horror, would be a year *after* the Soviets might begin fielding their own Nene- or Derwent-powered jet squadrons if this Rolls deal went through. Terrifying visions of British propeller-driven aircraft encountering Soviet Nene-powered fighters—or worse, of Soviet jets streaking across the Channel—fully drove home the dangerous implications of the proposed Rolls sale. British analysts also were troubled by the financial sums necessary to outfit Britain's defenses with jets ahead of schedule simply to counter an increased Soviet threat. They calculated that if the sale of Britain's best engines to Moscow were approved, it would erode the West's lead in this vital field by up to three years; sale of a manufacturing license would virtually eliminate it. In either scenario, the costs of countering Soviet advances made through British sales far exceeded even Rolls's most optimistic revenue projections. In the final analysis, such a sale made to improve Britain's finances and security would be destructive of both.[27]

None of these options held much allure in the Air Ministry, which in June 1946 convened a meeting of officials gathered from throughout Whitehall's various offices to consider the ramifications of the Soviet sale and to determine if any of the attending ministries objected to the deal. "After a good deal of discussion," the undersecretary of supply informed Attlee, "it was decided that there was such an objection." A manufacturing license "would give the Russians too much relative advantage," the group concluded, since the sale would "save the Russians several years in the development" of similar engines. Sale of the engines themselves would save the Russians "about half that period," yet the group authorized Rolls to continue their negotiations for completed engines. While such a sale was not ideal from a strict security standpoint, they felt little choice but to allow engines placed on the Open List to remain available for sale. National reputation was at stake in these negotiations as much as national security, and refusal to export engines as advertised would prove a serious black eye to the industry. Rolls learned at the end of May that they could continue engine sales to the Russians for the time being, but that sale of a manufacturing license was forbidden.[28]

If Attlee's advisers, by their own admission, had considered the strategic implications of unimpeded aviation sales only superficially before the Soviet request, they quickly made up for lost time. Policymakers throughout the government responded to word of the proposed sale with a torrent of critiques of the Air Ministry's previously liberal policy. The military's chiefs of staff completely opposed selling engines to the Soviets. If access to a British engine advanced Soviet war-fighting capacity even one day, they argued, not even the most pressing economic considerations could justify such a sale. Attlee's diplomats offered a different concern. The Foreign Office agreed with the military's concern over placing a price on British military security, but also objected to the potential loss of international credibility if engines and aircraft previously declared available for sale to all were suddenly made available only to some. The Russians were fearful enough of Western intentions without the Air Ministry giving them actual evidence of discrimination. "If the deputy chiefs of staff do not want engines sold," one British diplomat argued, "they must in my opinion put them back on the secret list." The Board of Trade, which was locked in difficult negotiations for timber from the Soviet trade delegation in London, took a different tack. Its representatives argued that nothing should be done to upset the Kremlin while Britain faced a dire housing shortage that only imported wood could resolve. The government would stand or fall based primarily on its ability to fulfill the promises of the New Jerusalem, they reasoned, not on its ability to keep aviation technology from Moscow. Aviation might be Britain's future; but its elections would hinge on housing.[29]

Taking a cue from this debate over engine sales to the Kremlin, other British policymakers began questioning the broader implications of widespread aircraft exports. Offering the Soviets the best of British technology seemed an obvious security risk, but from the Supply Ministry came the reminder that other Rolls customers were hardly paragons of virtue. Even without a direct sale, the Soviets could easily gather information on British jets from agents in China, France, or any number of countries in line for Rolls's products. "I feel we are in danger of getting the worst of both worlds," the undersecretary cautioned Attlee. The prohibition on selling a manufacturing license to Moscow was bound to infuriate the Soviets. At the same time, he noted,

> I am convinced that if we allow Messrs Rolls Royce to go through with their contracts for the manufacture of engines under license in China and in France (and in future elsewhere) we shall, in fact, be giving the information and the industrial know-how to the Soviet Union in an indirect way. In the case of China, nothing, I am sure, would be easier for the Russians than to place their agents in a Chinese factory, with access to all the technical information which we give to the Chinese. I think we must face the fact that the same position is true in regard to the French contract with Hispano Suiza. Many French technicians are Communist Party members, and the present head of the French Ministry of Armaments and War Production is a Communist.[30]

No matter who the buyer, save of course trustworthy partners such as the United States and old-dominion countries such as Australia or South Africa, the sale of an export license abroad was, in his opinion, bound to diminish Britain's technological lead over the Soviet Union. Communists in every country were linked by an international committee, or so it appeared in 1946, and a communist agent in an aircraft factory therefore seemed the equivalent of an information pipeline to the Kremlin. "It has been suggested that we should make representations to the French government asking them to take steps to stop the know-how or engines going to the Russians," one British diplomat noted, adding, "This seems simple enough till one remembers that Mr. Tillon, the Minister of Armaments is a Communist!" No matter how patriotic they seemed, communists simply could not be trusted. "Thus the real effect of our present policy" of forbidding sale of a license to the Soviets, the undersecretary of supply concluded, "is that we are discriminating sharply, but ineffectively against the Russians, increasing (if that is possible!) their suspicion of us, while allowing them, in fact, access to the information we seek to withhold."[31]

Even if the initial Open List expansion appears a case in which exuberance trumped prudence, the Attlee government ultimately proved willing to heed good advice. Faced with a torrent of opposition, in July 1946, Board of Trade president Cripps canceled indefinitely Rolls's authorization to pursue the Soviet sale. The government needed more time to consider the implications of its aviation sales policies in a broader context as well as the specific consequences of exports to Moscow. Rolls received the harsh news August 1, when Cripps scribbled tersely to the company's managing director that while he was "interested to read about your export efforts . . . I am very sorry that the Russian order cannot go through at the moment."[32]

Rolls was undoubtedly disappointed at this news, going so far as to ask for a letter to show the Soviets stating that canceling the engine negotiations was not the company's idea. Whereas Rolls's executives feared potential damage to their reputation, the Kremlin's negotiators in London were furious over what they considered a direct insult to their nation. The head of the Soviet trade delegation told Cripps (a man American sources described as "personally sympathetic with the Soviets and very anxious to conclude trade agreements with them") that "he was at a loss to understand why we refused them [Rolls] to export them [Nenes and Derwents] to other countries." Though syntactically taxing, he had a point. Britain appeared to be discriminating against the Soviets in this arena, largely because Britain *was* in fact discriminating against the Soviets in this arena. But when the Soviet delegate threatened to halt negotiations for wheat and timber if Britain refused the jet sale, his objection helped rebolster Cripps, who renewed his push for approval of the engine sale despite his colleagues' objections.[33]

Further debate ultimately produced two distinct schools of thought within Whitehall on the wisdom of the sale. On the one hand were those policymakers, generally those wearing RAF uniforms, who considered export of Britain's best aviation technology directly to the Soviets far too dangerous a security risk to approve. After months of fruitless negotiations with the Soviets over the fate of Germany (among other great-power disputes), Bevin also opposed the sale, and naturally much of the Foreign Office followed his lead. "It would be improper to give away knowledge which should be withheld on security grounds in return for commercial advantages," one British diplomat argued. Balancing sales versus security was, at best, morally questionable. A second, larger group of policymakers concluded that the theoretical security risks inherent in this (and any) sale paled in comparison to Britain's serious financial difficulties. With American competition expected just around the corner, and with Washington seemingly intent upon challenging for every international aircraft market, cash-strapped London simply could not afford to unilaterally relinquish any potential buyer, no matter how small and no matter what the risks involved. Food rationing in Britain continued to escalate in 1946, and the country had only recently emerged from the harshest winter in memory. Bread went on the ration lists for the first time in June, a step the wartime government had been loath to take for fear of damaging public morale, and one Attlee avoided until the end. With the harsh reality of how long it would take Britain to climb back to prosperity slowly overtaking public euphoria over winning the war, popular support for his government continued to ebb.[34]

Policymakers in favor of consummating the Soviet jet deal recognized the government's impending political difficulties as proof of a crucial truth: despite the common theme throughout the literatures of the world espousing the virtues of poverty and the righteousness of the meek, in the world of international politics, morality is the privilege of the powerful and rich. Mounting debts meant Britain had little choice but to sell to the Soviets. As the Soviet trade delegate had made perfectly clear, Moscow would interpret refusal to sell engines already available on the Open List as an insulting admission of Britain's true sentiments toward the Soviet Union. The small but growing Anglo-Soviet trade would undoubtedly suffer as a result. So too would Anglo-Soviet relations generally, to say nothing of the reputation of British aviation. "Here is a field in which we lead the world and in which we may expect a very valuable export trade," Cripps argued. "If we stifle it, do we not risk hampering the firms whose research is producing such remarkable results?"[35]

Ultimately, it was Clement Attlee's decision to make, and he ruled that finances and diplomacy trumped security. He considered it entirely futile to treat the Soviet request as though the Nene and Derwent remained on the secret list, given that Rolls had already exported these engines to other nations. "Clearly the engines could be procured elsewhere as a prototype if the Russians wanted to manufacture," he concluded. More importantly, Attlee did not want to force an outright break with the Soviet Union over this issue. He instead determined that while the deal offered a small theoretical risk, his country's need for housing and cheap raw materials was indisputable, and moreover that access to British engines did not guarantee Russia's ability to reproduce the machines. In his view, Soviet engineers were unlikely to master the advanced science and techniques required to copy (let alone improve) British designs. They certainly were unlikely to best subsequent British models. In the final analysis, Attlee believed that Britain's technical prowess and its aviation supremacy, which had been hard-won through investment and was the present generation's birthright, put his country permanently ahead of the Russians. What concerned him most was ensuring that his country's housing shortage did not remain permanent as well. Attlee therefore personally approved the sale on September 26, 1946. "I can see no good reason for withholding them [the engines] from the USSR," he concluded, "whereas their refusal will only cause trouble and suspicion."[36]

Attlee's decision to approve direct engine sales to Moscow despite objections from within his own government established the precedent for British aviation that commerce trumped security. He ruled against sale of a manufacturing license to the Soviets in order to placate his military advisers, but informed Cripps that Rolls could export ten Nene and Derwent engines (twenty engines total) to the Soviets. The company began preparations for their immediate shipment upon hearing the news, lest the government change its mind yet again. Attlee did nothing to discourage Rolls's additional sales of manufacturing licenses abroad, even to an increasingly chaotic China, though he did instruct the company to remind foreign buyers of the necessity of proper security safeguards for British high technology. The Foreign Office offered no real guidance to its consulates abroad as to what constituted appropriate measures for securing such information, however, primarily because Whitehall had little notion of what constituted worthwhile security controls for engines in the first place. To at least one anonymous diplomat, this omission was unlikely to have much effect in any event. "Chinese security is so universally bad that a request of this sort is almost certainly useless," he scribbled on his copy of the appeal to Chiang's government for better engine security, "but I suppose we can ask anything."[37]

Rolls had good reason to move quickly on the Soviet export, because there remained one more player whose voice had yet to be heard in this debate: the United States government. Less than a week after Attlee gave final approval for the sale, Bevin cabled home from the foreign ministers conference in Paris a new set of objections to the Soviet sale. Secretary of State James Byrnes had cornered him before one session to object to Britain's proposed sale of World War II surplus aircraft to Czechoslovakia. It seemed unwise to aid a potential enemy, Byrnes advised, and to add the fuel of arms to an already smoldering East-West fire over central Europe. He had no idea how prescient his objection was. If Washington fretted over transfer of piston-driven Spitfires to the Western-leaning but precariously placed Czechs, Bevin told Attlee, imagine Byrnes's reaction to news that Britain was about to sell advanced jets to the heart of the budding Soviet empire. "The American attitude, as expressed to me by Mr. Byrnes, is worrying," Bevin wrote. "In view of his strong opposition of the sale of relatively out of date equipment [to the Czechs], he is likely to react very strongly when he hears that we are selling jet engines to the Soviet Union."[38]

Bevin therefore implored Attlee to once more reverse his decision on the Rolls sale and, more fundamentally, to authorize a full reassessment of Britain's trade in strategic and technologically advanced goods, given the steady deterioration of East-West relations. "I think the whole question of supplying the Soviet government with valuable war material and generally with machinery and equipment vital for building up Russia's war potential should be examined," he advised. And if the crumbling international scene stabilized or came into greater clarity during the months it would take to complete such an examination, so much the better. Given Byrnes's concern, and those of Britain's own military, he considered it better to be right than hasty.

Bevin's objections are instructive, not only for understanding Britain's regulation of strategic technologies, but also for the light they shed on London's view of the special relationship during this period. Specifically, his warning demonstrates that despite the importance of aviation exports in the postwar years, and despite lingering acrimony over the difficult loan negotiations the previous year, Anglo-American relations remained the Foreign Office's primary concern. Whitehall's ministers might deem exports to Russia acceptable by British standards, but Byrnes's aside in Paris reminded Bevin that Washington's reaction demanded as much consideration as the Air Ministry's or the Board of Trade's. "I am anxious not to get completely out of step with the Americans in this matter," he concluded.

Yet as Bevin was the first to point out, seeking commonality with the Americans in a technological field in which only Washington and London could lay claim to world leadership meant synchronizing their policies. It would do little good for Britain to restrict its own producers for security reasons if American firms then filled the void with similarly dangerous goods. Not only was it in Britain's interest to keep American objections to a minimum for the sake of bilateral relations, but more importantly, the interests of the entire Western community could be served only by complete coordination with the United States to ensure that neither country imposed a dangerous level of export control. A race to the bottom in this arena would only help the Kremlin. "We should re-examine the whole question of the sale of aircraft to foreign powers," he concluded, "[and] coordinate our policy with the United States government."[39]

Such coordination would not begin for over a year. Despite Byrnes's concern over British sales to Czechoslovakia, Washington in fact had little idea of the potential trouble brewing over jet sales to the Soviets. On the contrary, American sources had yet to learn of Rolls's pending sale, and thus Byrnes was apparently truly concerned with the Czech sale on its own merits. Whitehall officials had read Nenes and Derwents into the secretary's admonition about Spitfires, but Bevin's predictions of America's angry response to such sales would prove prescient.

Before news broke of the explosive sale, and before Bevin could approach Washington for a synchronization of policies, the Kremlin further upped the ante in this high-stakes game. Prior to receiving their first shipment from Rolls, Soviet officials applied for yet another round of engines and for samples of completed aircraft as well, including three each of Britain's top-of-the-line Vampire bomber and Meteor fighter (a plane one Defense Ministry official termed "the best aircraft of its type in the world today").[40]

Moscow's request for finished aircraft seemed to demonstrate what British analysts had always feared: that the Soviets were after British know-how and technology. Some in Whitehall had hoped that the Kremlin's initial order of twenty-odd engines augured future sales of all types of industrial equipment to the Soviets, but this second Soviet request, being so small and yet so specific, dashed these hopes. Access to completed planes would reveal the integration of propulsion and flight systems and thereby simplify the task of reverse engineering. "The Russian request for a few jet aircraft was clearly designed to obtain technical information from the examination of these aircraft," determined the Air Ministry, whose officials were hardly enthusiastic about making life easier for Soviet technicians. "The supply of these aircraft will give the Russians tactical knowledge of the latest RAF front-line fighters," Secretary of State for Air P. J. Noel-Baker warned Attlee. "What is more important, it may reduce the technical lead which we have over the Russians in this field by from 18 months to two years." Moreover,

Since the Meteors will be an RAF front-line fighter for some four years, we might well be faced at the end of that period with Russian interceptor aircraft equal to those of the RAF. We have been watching with ever-increasing uneasiness the growth of the Soviet Air Force and the steps being taken to modernize it. We cannot help contrasting its size with the present very reduced strength of the RAF and our small aircraft production programme. Previously we had been able to feel that we could answer Russian numbers in the air with superior British quality, but this possibility is seriously reduced by our giving the Russians some of our own jet aircraft.[41]

Fearing the complete loss of Britain's technological superiority in the air, the Air Ministry objected to this new sale. They had done so once before, only to be overruled by Attlee after repeated lobbying on the part of Cripps, who, in the words of one official, "took up the matter personally." This time, however, the Air Ministry came prepared to counter the argument that direct sales to Russia offered little additional risk of technological diffusion because information on British machines could already be garnered from third parties. Use of information gathered by communist agents in France or China was bound to be a time-consuming process, they argued. And as policymakers had been reduced to discussing the development of Russian jets in terms of months (they had believed their lead to be more than five years at the start of this process), every moment mattered. "The longer we can delay the supply," Noel-Baker argued, "the less is the risk of the Russians catching us up."[42]

Daunted by the RAF's universal condemnation of the deal and fearful of a similar reaction from Washington, but still unwilling to formally rebuke the Soviets or forsake their invaluable raw materials, Attlee once more chose a middle course. He approved export of yet more engines to Moscow in the summer of 1947 (bringing total British engine commitments to fifty-five), but withheld approval for sale of completed aircraft until the Soviets agreed to offer "equivalent" technology in return. "Equivalent" did not mean financial value equivalent to that of Britain's jet engines, but instead meant technology of equivalent worth to the producing country. The Kremlin would get Britain's best, in other words, only if it released its best technology in return. Attlee presumed that Stalin's well-known penchant for secrecy made it highly unlikely that he would approve open technological reciprocity, and he thus believed this condition would either cause the Russians to rescind their request or at least stall the negotiations for months, if not longer. Bevin wholly disagreed. "How mad we are!" he exclaimed in one meeting, to even consider risking Anglo-American relations and indeed British security merely for profit. How foolish, moreover, to place in Stalin's hands the decision to export a most prized British weapon. His pleas ultimately fell upon deaf ears, however, and the sale went through.[43]

In 1946 and again in 1947, therefore, Britain's government exported copies of their country's most advanced jet engines to their greatest strategic rival. They deliberately chose commerce over security, though with the hope that further Anglo-Soviet trade of such a prized commodity might improve the international climate and thereby improve security. After reconsidering the implications of their sale, they did so again. In the final analysis, British policymakers concluded they needed sales to keep ahead of the Americans, even at some risk to Anglo-American relations, and they felt no driving need to thwart technology transfer to the Soviets, maintaining a belief, despite warnings to the contrary, that British technology would ultimately remain supreme. Such estimations would prove tragically wrong.

Washington's Response and Renewed Tensions over Argentina

If it appeared to British ministers that Soviet acquisition of jet technology was inevitable no matter how many fingers policymakers might place in the dike of international technological advancement, the same pessimism did not yet infect Washington. News of Britain's impending jet export to the Soviet Union, therefore, produced many an Anglophobic reaction across the Atlantic. Even those American officials who presumed that the Kremlin would one day develop jets of its own did not expect that their closest ally would help in this quest. "American service reaction both in the navy and the army has been distinctly unfavorable to the sale of jet engines to Russia," the RAF's military attaché cabled home in June 1947. "These jet engines are thought by the Americans to be better than anything Russians (or indeed Americans) have at present," and thus officials believed the sale "constitute[s] an important and objectionable potential addition to Russian military capabilities." American fury at the decision seemed far from abating even a month later. "Several generals [including Curtis LeMay] tonight deplored our selling jets to Russia," he cabled.[44]

American officials balked at the strategic implications of Soviet acquisition of jet technology, but they found far more troubling the fact that the British had deemed it wise to export military equipment to the Russians in the first place. Their initial shock over news of the sale eventually prompted a deeper melancholy over the future of Anglo-American relations. If the British were willing to arm the Russians due to some financial difficulties, then how reliable could London truly be as a long-term ally? LeMay admitted the sales made him "mistrust the tendencies" of the British government, especially if London continued to rank commercial gain ahead of security. "It is the feared tendency rather than the facts which engender suspicion in military circles," the RAF delegate concluded, for in Washington, Britain was "being regarded as becoming a second Sweden," a country willing to pay for promises of peace. Britain had always seemed reliable, but now Americans feared that Britain would "give in to adversity and become nondescript like France."[45]

The decision to sell jets to Stalin, coupled with renewed tensions over sales to Argentina in the spring and summer of 1947, seemed in Washington sure signs that Attlee's government lacked moral backbone. Little progress had been made toward development of a unified export policy for Juan Peron's government following the first minor clash over export of airliners in the spring of 1946. British policymakers still hoped to make Latin America broadly, and Argentina specifically, a prime destination for their aviation exports, despite Secretary of War Robert Patterson's ominous statement in July 1946 that Washington's "100% standardization" goal included exclusion of suppliers from "outside the hemisphere." Most Whitehall analysts discounted Washington's benevolent rhetoric that standardization would lead to peaceful relations without the scourge of wasteful arms sales, believing instead that American policymakers at heart desired a captive Latin American market. "The USA have long been pursuing the monopoly of the trade in arms with the Latin American countries," Bevin reminded Attlee in March 1947, "our traditional share in which we need to preserve mainly for reasons of finance and home employment." Cripps fully agreed with Bevin's assessment, especially with potentially fruitful markets such as Argentina still open for the taking. "In our present financial situation we cannot afford to forgo any valuable hard currency orders," especially for "the aircraft field." Bevin formally notified the State Department in January 1947 of Britain's decision to abrogate the Gentleman's Agreement, though there was no specific deal with the Argentines in the works. "There may be a row with America over this," he remarked to Attlee, especially as standardization was a pet project for Marshall (now secretary of state). "I am ready to face it,"

Bevin said, "for we must earn hard currency where we can, and the American attitude on this question is quite unreasonable."[46]

As would often be the case, while policymakers debated an important decision and parsed the language of their exchanges, sales teams on the ground effectively made their decision for them. In early 1947, agents of several British aircraft firms, acting without supervision from either the Board of Trade or Britain's embassy, concluded agreements with the Argentines for export of 380 Meteor fighters, 20 Meteor trainers, and 30 Lincoln heavy bombers. These totals stunned officials in London, who had expected neither a formal agreement for military planes so soon, nor for the contract to be so large. Bevin had only recently informed Washington of his government's decision to abrogate the Gentleman's Agreement, and he feared that news of the Argentine deal immediately after his private assurances to Washington would make it appear that perfidious Albion had the sale in the works the entire time. Though potentially embarrassing on the diplomatic stage, the signed contract at least eliminated any chance of reconsideration of Whitehall's tough stand. As one of Bevin's aides remarked, it "forced our hand." Bevin chose not to inform Washington of the deal until its details could be completed, a four-month process that saw the final sale whittled down to a more reasonable 100 Gloster Meteor fighters, of which 20 were trainers. Negotiations for the 30 Lincoln bombers remained nearly finished, though still under discussion. The first of the jet-powered Meteors would leave Britain by June, Bevin told Marshall, with the remainder to be shipped over the next two years.[47]

Marshall took the news far worse than Whitehall expected. He knew Britain's move left for dead the Gentleman's Agreement, and with it his own plans to use standardization as inoculation against a Latin American arms race. "This came as a decided shock to me," he wrote Bevin. Despite Bevin's disclosure that London would no longer support their joint embargo, he said, "I had no (repeat no) idea from our talks with Lord Inverchapel [Britain's ambassador in Washington] that you contemplated supplying so dramatic a weapon which is sure to create consternation in the relations of the American republics with one another and upset the relations of all of us with Argentina." For Marshall, this "dramatic British intervention" struck a "heavy blow." His choice of the word *intervention* should not be overlooked here. It suggests Marshall's belief that the British had no right to sell in what he considered Washington's natural domain, a subtle hint that despite his sincere desire to avoid spurious arms spending throughout Latin America, perhaps London's assessment of America's broader commercial goals in the region were not far off the mark.[48]

To Marshall, Whitehall's unilateral decision was appalling and dangerous, no matter how great its export needs. "The introduction of jet fighters into South American armaments may be inevitable," he reminded Bevin, "but for your government to do it without consultation with us, when we are trying both to help you and to work out a system through the Inter-American Defense Board for avoiding an arms race in South America, disappoints me and will undoubtedly shock American opinion." By mentioning American efforts to "help," Marshall clearly implied that aid might not be so freely given in the future to countries, like Britain, that continued to defy Washington's plans. He clearly was not above threatening his longtime ally.[49]

Neither Bevin nor Attlee was particularly surprised by Marshall's anger, given frustration of his beloved standardization plans, or by this blunt linkage of exports and aid. What truly disturbed them and their principal advisers was his dramatic reaction to the inclusion of jet technology in the sale. "I have always been nervous about this sale of jet airplanes to South America," Bevin told the prime minister; this new technology carried important political and emotional overtones capable of blinding American policymakers to what he considered the logic and necessity of Britain's commercial policies. Jets were new, after all, and even though Marshall claimed to understand that "all modern fighting aircraft were bound to be jet propelled," he apparently was not prepared to believe that day had come. "The very word 'jet' had, in the imagination of the American people a dramatic tang about it which was inescapable," Marshall explained to Lord Inverchapel. Their export was sure to garner attention far in excess of sales of piston-driven planes, and the publicity of such sales to Argentina and the Soviet Union would make it hard for Washington to remain uninvolved.[50]

Just as the Brabazon planners had hoped, and as proponents of the Open List expansion desired, jets changed the rules of the Anglo-American aviation competition. Unexpectedly, however, they did so primarily by raising Washington's ire. Marshall's warning struck a particular nerve in London, where the future value of jet aircraft seemed so obvious that policymakers came to doubt the sincerity of Marshall's "shock" over a jet export to Buenos Aires. His reaction seemed completely out of touch with British realities, and particularly suspicious given his well-established military expertise. How, they asked themselves, could America's greatest living military expert, whom Truman trusted explicitly, prove so outdated in this perception of modern military equipment? His (to their minds) wholly inexplicable security objections only reinforced Whitehall's preconceived notion that Washington's aircraft diplomacy was driven primarily by commercial motivations. The cabinet concluded that any policymaker of Marshall's stature who doubted the future importance of jets, or who doubted that foreign states seeking to rearm would want to do so with jets, was either lying, inept, or driven by an ulterior motive. And Marshall was neither inept nor a liar. Attlee's cabinet concluded that "no government now wishing to acquire new fighter aircraft would think of buying anything but jet models," and therefore that because America was "about two years behind us in the production of jet aircraft," Marshall's "attitude was probably influenced by the fact that United States firms were not in a position to compete with us in tendering the supply of fighter aircraft." When viewed with any distance, they continued, "it was difficult to resist the conclusion that the attitude of the US government in this matter was determined by a desire to establish a monopoly in the supply of armaments to the South American countries." America's security objections in this way seemed mere veils for more sinister commercial motivations, leading Bevin to tutor the five-star General Marshall: "I am assured that any country wishing to equip its airforce today would want jet types."[51]

Britain's aircraft sales to Argentina troubled Anglo-American relations even as the two allies struggled to come to terms with the more strategically imposing British jet sales to the Soviet Union, and the repetitive nature of each nation's arguments ultimately reinforced preconceived notions of the other's broader foreign policies. To Washington, the British seemed determined to sell their aviation wares no matter what the political or military fallout might be. They had sold jet engines to the Soviets despite the obvious risks to Western security, and they had sold jet aircraft to the Argentines in direct violation of the Gentleman's Agreement and seemingly without concern for Latin American stability. These moves imperiled Anglo-American intimacy, because as one British diplomat cabled home, top American officials feared the sales "may be evidence of policy to trade arms (irrespective of whether we are dealing with potential aggressors) for commercial advantage." Marshall found London's actions particularly disconcerting because he believed they offered ammunition to isolationists, Anglophobes, and foreign policy critics at the very moment when his State Department was locked in a desperate struggle to gain congressional approval for the European Recovery Program, known even then as the Marshall Plan. Britain's jet sales made him therefore "keenly disappointed," he told Inverchapel. "Throughout the war," Inverchapel wrote home, "one of his chiefest preoccupations had been to deprive our [Britain's] numerous enemies in this country of any tangible pretext to embitter public opinion," but "now it looked as though he [Marshall] would have to begin all over again." Public reaction to news of jet sales to Buenos Aires and Moscow in particular "would be fierce and sustained," Inverchapel continued, especially because "the reaction of normal Americans would be painfully and indignantly to contrast the granting of credits to us with a gesture on our part which was highly distasteful to the United States government." In short, news of Britain's sales would give the "ever-watchful enemies" of strong Anglo-American relations "some such poison as this to hang their hat on."[52]

Worse yet from Washington's perspective, jet sales to the Soviet Union posed a direct national security threat. In the late summer of 1947, Secretary of Defense James Forrestal commissioned a study by the Air Intelligence Division to consider the strategic implications of Whitehall's aviation exports. Their primary conclusion, not surprisingly, was that the sales to Argentina and the Soviets exhibited a dangerous trend. "It appears that the British government has placed economic factors ahead of any present or future military implications which might be involved," Forrestal's analysts warned.

Their words resonated throughout Washington. Secretary of the Air Force Stuart Symington, later one of the Cold War's most hawkish senators, turned this charge into a series of withering private attacks against London's intransigence. The Soviet sale "illuminates a distinct British philosophy, not just an engine sale," he wrote Forrestal, since "if the British sell to the Russians at all . . . ultimately the latter are bound to get the best British thinking." Willingness to offer the best of Western military technology to the West's greatest enemy seemed to him hardly the mark of a trustworthy ally. It seemed instead akin to treason against the Western cause, and a direct challenge to American leadership.[53]

Britain's export decisions struck the Pentagon's analysts as militarily unwise as well. Britain needed exports to prosper, that was true, but it also needed a technologically advanced air force if it were to survive a Soviet attack. "This continued sale of jet aircraft and engines depletes the available number that could be used to strengthen the defensive capability of the Royal Air Force in the event of hostilities," the Pentagon group warned, making it "therefore doubtful if the UK could be preserved as an advanced air base." Because virtually every one of Washington's war plans began with the premise that American bombers would strike Soviet units in Europe and the Soviet Union itself from bases in the United Kingdom, the potential sacrifice of air superiority over the UK as a consequence of these sales called into question the central tenet of any strategy for defense of Europe. What use was an Orwellian "Airstrip One" if it could not itself be defended, they asked, and how foolish was it to sell the enemy the key to one's own destruction?[54]

Britain's jet export policies therefore seemed morally questionable to rabidly anticommunist Cold Warriors like LeMay; they seemed a dangerous precedent to hawks like Symington; they were risky and disruptive in Marshall's eyes; and they appeared downright foolhardy, if not dangerous, to the Pentagon's war planners. This was a four-of-a-kind that proponents of intimate Anglo-American relations simply did not need. By the fall of 1947, when erroneous rumors of a British export of completed jet fighters to the Soviet Union surfaced in Washington, Marshall could stand no more. Warnings from military officers and his own protests to Bevin and Inverchapel seemed to have done little to retard Whitehall's dangerous export policies. So he decided the time had come to lay out his administration's objections, and its threats, with a bluntness not even the most purposefully oblivious British decision maker could miss.

Taming the Lion

Marshall entrusted this vital message to Undersecretary of State Robert Lovett, a devoted lieutenant he trusted like few others. On October 31, 1947, Lovett summoned Lord Inverchapel to his office, where the ambassador also found Averell Harriman, the ubiquitous American diplomat and Truman's commerce secretary who had only recently returned to Washington following a stint as ambassador in London. The two Americans wasted little time in laying out their government's anger. "They complained bitterly of continuing sales of jet engines and aircraft to [the] Russians," Inverchapel cabled home. Lovett spoke from a "secret intelligence report" (most likely Forrestal's study), which he claimed contained concrete evidence that Britain was exporting not only engines on the Open List, such as the Nene and Derwent and completed jet aircraft, but even more advanced engines not yet publicly available for export even to the United States. They "refused to believe that our sales to Russia did not include any engines or aircraft on [the] secret list," Inverchapel explained, "and in any case were most dissatisfied with sales of war equipment of that kind to Russia."[55]

The discussion quickly turned from accusations to threats. "I told him frankly that his government should have in mind the fact that our armed forces feel that the British procedure was not only unwise but unnecessary," Lovett later recounted to Symington. "It also showed a surprising lack of co-operation which might have very far-reaching results in other matters affecting the relationship of our two governments," he told the ambassador. This is not the way diplomats typically speak to one another, and neither Harriman nor Lovett could ever be called Anglophobic. Yet such was their anger that they used phrases like *far-reaching results,* terms that are rarely employed by diplomats because of the serious consequences they imply. If London persisted, they warned, it might soon have to find itself a new benefactor.[56]

Such threats had their desired effect. Within weeks the Attlee government publicly rescinded its prior commitment to its liberal Open List. On November 10, Bevin reassured America's ambassador in London that whatever information the United States possessed of aircraft sales to the Soviets was indeed erroneous, and that his government had no plans to ship completed planes or even additional engines to Moscow. It planned instead to remove its most advanced engines from the Open List without delay, lest additional undesirable requests for Rolls's products arise in the future. It would further subject all future buyers to a policy of strict reciprocity, wherein Britain would export its advanced technologies (such as jets) only to countries willing to share their own most advanced products. As these restraints would be applied generally, they suggested impartiality, though in truth the policy of strict technological reciprocity was clearly devised with the Soviet bloc in mind. France and Australia seemed likely to share their strategic technology openly with the British in exchange for advanced products like Rolls Royce engines, but hardly a soul in Whitehall believed Stalin's government would do the same. One RAF leader doubted the Soviets had anything London might consider "worth-while" as a technology trade in the first place, let alone anything the Kremlin might reveal to prying Western eyes. Strict reciprocity thus seemed to Attlee's advisers the best of all possible worlds. It provided a mechanism for halting further aviation exports to the Soviets without hindering Anglo-Soviet relations; it pleased Attlee's security hawks while satisfying his diplomatic doves; and it appeased Washington.[57]

Of greatest significance, Bevin concluded his mea culpa by expressing a desire to meet personally with Marshall to remove any lingering American doubts concerning the reliability of Britain's future export policies. The two men met face-to-face a fortnight later, and Bevin continued his pleas for understanding. "The jet engines which had been acquired by the Soviet Union were . . . all almost obsolescent types," Bevin offered, using the term *obsolescent* loosely, considering his own warning to Attlee but months before that Nene and Derwent exports threatened British technological superiority. Even though such engines were outdated, he continued, his government had finally come to realize that "even the possession of obsolescent types might enable the Russians to learn of developments of which they were unaware." Not only would such technology be placed back on the secret list, but Britain's aviation manufacturers would no longer be allowed to export any plane "without specific government authority." The cabinet, in other words, would wield an iron grip over subsequent exports, ensuring that the buck stopped at Clement Attlee's desk. The era of unscrutinized aeronautical exports was officially at an end. Marshall, the British memorandum of the conversation recorded, "noted this situation with satisfaction." Though it had taken months, his diplomacy had seemed to work. Britain had seemed to buckle under American pressure.[58]

Marshall left this meeting convinced that his months of cajoling had finally constrained Britain's export zeal, though the same conclusion cannot necessarily be drawn from British sources. It is true that Britain officially altered its export policies following Lovett and Harriman's strong-arm diplomacy. It is also true that Bevin personally guaranteed a more American-like export strategy only weeks after receiving official word of Washington's displeasure. Yet this chronology does not prove whether America's tactics forced the change in Britain's policy, or whether Bevin's personal diplomacy was merely an attempt to profit from decisions already reached in Whitehall. As we have seen, though they were enthusiastic for exports, policymakers throughout Attlee's government had become increasingly uneasy with technological diffusion to the Soviets and as a result had already barred the export of completed aircraft. Bevin himself had long been a closet critic of exuberant aircraft sales. Indeed, one full month before his meeting with Marshall, and nearly three weeks before the Lovett/Harriman diplomatic double-team, an interdepartmental committee he headed had determined to enforce strict reciprocity on any future sales to the Soviets. Even after the Truman administration's explicit threats, therefore, the Attlee government only offered Washington exactly what it had already internally decided before such threats were ever made. British leaders subsequently used the pretext of American protests as a timely excuse to announce this change of policy, in order to assure Washington of their commitment to the special relationship. Neither Attlee nor Bevin was above taking international credit for a policy enacted solely for national reasons.[59]

The Attlee government therefore offered to sacrifice on the altar of Anglo-American unity only that which it had already decided to discard, while American policymakers (being unaware of Whitehall's internal discussions) believed their diplomatic pressure had prompted Britain's dramatic policy change. The near-term result was the same: Britain left 1947 with a stricter export control regime than it had begun the year with, one more in line with American desires. The long-term consequences of this diplomacy, however, proved more significant. Content in the belief that strong-arm tactics forced Britain's hand, Washington would prove increasingly likely to use threats and *faits accomplis* to win British acceptance of America's increasingly rigid line on aviation exports in the years to come. The lesson men like Forrestal, Symington, Lovett, and even Marshall took from these initial aviation disputes was that Britain, though inherently untrustworthy when issues of money were at stake, at least could be forced into doing the right thing, especially if threats involving great sums of money were involved.

British leaders took a far different lesson from these affairs. Convinced that their American counterparts used the language of security to mask commercially driven policies, London came to discount Washington's arguments for a more restrictive export line based on security or technological diffusion. They believed instead that American policymakers viewed the aviation world in an equivalent zero-sum manner. Despite American claims to the contrary, in the years that followed Attlee would believe only that Washington acted in its own commercial interest when it came to issues of aircraft security and sales. Cash-strapped Britain surely did. He certainly did. And he expected no less from Washington. This pattern of Anglo-American aviation diplomacy that would rule the field for the subsequent two decades was therefore well established only two years after World War II. It was a pattern of competition infused with misunderstanding, with each side painting its own value system upon the other.

Neither side realized the depth of their misunderstanding in 1947, though each was eager to repair any temporary breaches in their mutually important relationship. Having announced more restrictive export controls in order to salve American irritations, Whitehall spent the remainder of the year working to prove its fidelity. As Bevin and his cadre well knew, Britain would not long survive, and surely would not prosper, without American aid, and such aid would be stymied if the majority of policymakers along the Potomac began to doubt Britain's reliability as an ally, as LeMay and Symington already had. With the promise of Marshall Plan dollars in the air, British diplomats and military leaders from the foreign secretary down through the chain of command repeatedly sought to reassure their American counterparts of London's reliability broadly, and more specifically of the foolproof security of their new policy of strict technological reciprocity. They repeated these lines like a mantra. With East-West relations in steady decline, they promised, further jet sales to the Soviets were most certainly not in the cards. Britain could once more be trusted. "The milk is spilt," Lord Tedder, marshal of the RAF, wrote privately to his American counterpart, General Carl Spaatz, in December 1947. "I am sure you will agree that it would be a tragedy if any such doubts were to affect our joint collaboration in the future." Spaatz accepted this explanation with grace, though he added a final warning "that the establishment of the subsequent requirement of strict reciprocity in future negotiations with the Soviets in jet equipment will preclude any future sales."[60]

Rapprochement and the formulation of a joint Anglo-American export policy would not be as easy to achieve as the accord between these two airmen, however, especially since their subordinates would not so easily forget the disputes of 1946 and 1947. "I hoped the Air Ministry would be able to let us consult with the Americans before any [future agreement with Communist states]," the RAF's ranking officer in Washington told Admiral Thomas Inglis, head of the U.S. Navy's Office of Naval Intelligence. To alleviate American anxieties, Whitehall vowed in January 1948 to "consult" with Washington "before authorizing any aircraft or engine sale" across the iron curtain. The United States would thereafter have the opportunity to voice its concerns before Britain consummated the deal, even though one RAF marshal said that it was "of course unlikely that any further release [for the Soviets] will be agreed" to by the cabinet itself. Disputes over Argentina and Russia had shown the need for consultations, he said, because nothing should be allowed to come between such intimate allies.[61]

Inglis responded with an angry poke. "He didn't much like the reciprocal idea," his British counterpart reported home, which "seemed to leave the door open" for future trade with communists. Moreover Britain's promise to "consult" before making a potentially dangerous sale did not mean London would heed Washington's advice. This was a door he believed "should be firmly shut." To his mind, Britain's very willingness to consider future high-technology sales, even with reciprocity thrown in as a face-saving measure, made it untrustworthy. Britain, it appeared, had learned nothing from its prior mistakes. It had not planned to sell to the Soviets when it liberalized the Open List, but the sale took on a life of its own. It had not planned to institute a dangerous arms race in Latin America, but it surely had not been put off by the prospect that its aircraft sales might do just that. Now it left open the slim possibility of further direct sales to communists provided they met British security demands, and further audaciously couched this policy of appeasement behind language of "consultation" with Washington. To Inglis, perfidious Albion simply could not be trusted. Nuanced policies offered dangers of their own, he cautioned. It was better to be forthright in opposing Communism, unwavering and therefore unchallenged, like Washington. The future of Anglo-American relations would not be easy, this RAF general recorded, since Inglis "and his kind have a strong influence. They tend to believe that continued assistance to the British comes out of misplaced sentiment and that we have ceased to exist as an effective partner of war."[62]

In the end, American security hawks such as Inglis were right to be wary of British assurances. For all of its pledges of a stricter security line, London never relinquished its freedom to sell as it saw fit. Indeed, the Attlee government steadfastly rejected repeated State Department overtures for the construction of an explicit joint aviation export policy during the first half of 1948. This is not surprising. Britain's leaders considered their sovereign rights (including their right to trade as they saw fit) no less sacred than Washington's and refused any suggestion that the preponderance of American power demanded their subservience. Aircraft and technological exports were critical to their perception of Britain's independence and great-power status. Thus, despite Bevin's musings early in 1946 on the wisdom of a joint export regime, his advisers decided they did not want to forsake their freedom of action or curtail their journey to prosperity to suit Washington's whims.

Bevin ultimately concluded at the end of these first two years of bitter Cold War diplomacy that a well-defined aviation policy gave Washington too much power. American support was vital to his international plans and indeed to his nation's survival, but Bevin had no desire to turn his country into a vassal state of the new Rome. Washington's protests over previous exports, in particular those to Argentina, suggested to British leaders that the United States had, first and foremost, its own commercial needs in mind when forming its aviation regulations. Surely, Attlee's advisers reasoned, the

Truman administration had not bothered to consider Britain's commercial requirements when it had condemned Rolls's sales to the Soviets solely on security grounds. It had only considered its own security, not the needs of its allies. Britain's needs, predictably if unfortunately, ranked a distant second when Washington prioritized, though sometimes when viewed from London, it was hard to tell when money or the military was calling the shots in the Truman administration's aviation diplomacy. By promising to consult the Americans before any future sale, but by refusing to bend to Washington's desire to set guidelines for future sales ahead of time, Whitehall hoped to walk a fine line with the United States: a line seemingly rigid enough to placate American fears, yet flexible enough to withstand American control. "The fact that our overall strategy is similar need not and should not require either party to tie its hands so far in advance in regard to detailed tactics," one British diplomat concluded.[63]

Flexible policies offered risks of their own, and Britain's desire to walk the tightrope between sales and security offered risks none had anticipated. In 1946, for example, while debates concerning engine sales to the Soviets raged, ministry officials had told Rolls Royce to forestall transfer of technological information and a manufacturing license for Nenes to the Chinese until the security issues at hand could be resolved. Even Whitehall proponents of exuberant exports conceded that Chiang's government was hardly a safe protector of British expertise. "The Chinese government's security arrangements left much to be desired," one Ministry of Supply official wrote, and "it was therefore decided that R[olls] R[oyce] should be asked to delay the supply of information to the Chinese government for as long as possible." Rolls's agents repeatedly asked ministers to reassess their decision in the following months, each time receiving different instructions as to which information the company could and could not transfer. Each time, the Air Ministry approved different technical information, though it consistently forbade transfer of any classified manufacturing data.[64]

Rolls apparently misunderstood its instructions. A routine review of the company's export programs in March 1948 revealed that restricted technical data, including classified manufacturing plans for the Nene, were in fact delivered to the Chinese in 1946, despite instructions that they should not be. With the government's aviation export policies in constant flux during this period, the company argued in its own defense, it was little wonder such messages had been jumbled. Internally, Britain's policymakers commiserated with Rolls's plight, believing that blame for the confusion was partly their own. No security policy could be foolproof if developed on an ad hoc basis, they argued, and flexible policies in particular invited misapplication. Whitehall's official response to Rolls was far less benevolent. "We have expressed our strong disapproval and annoyance to directors of the firm," the Supply Ministry informed the Foreign Office, and "they have offered their regrets and assurances that the lapse was due to a misunderstanding." Given that the Soviets already had their own Nenes and Derwents by this time, the security loss was thought to be minimal. More importantly, however, the case highlighted the risks of a sliding security policy. If British officials needed any more reason to lay down a more explicit export policy, at least for their own manufacturers, it was to be soon in coming. It was one thing for London to deal with angry American diplomats; it was quite another to confront the American public.[65]

CHAPTER 3

Death by Nene

The Cold War threatened to erupt into an atomic war during the 1948 Berlin blockade. Soviet troops surrounded the beleaguered city first in April, for eleven days, and then again in June. Their siege ultimately lasted more than ten months. Roads were closed and railways blocked, leaving nearly three million people hostage to Moscow's will with less than a month's supply of food and six weeks of coal. This was an act of war designed to drive the Western powers from Europe's heart, and both superpowers girded for battle. "How long do you intend to keep it up?" a top American official asked his Soviet counterpart. "Until you drop your plans for a West German government," came the reply. President Harry Truman's response: "We stay in Berlin, period." His commanders in Germany urged dispatch of an armored column to Berlin's rescue, even if they needed to fight their way there. Truman instead ordered two squadrons of B-29 bombers, the type used for atomic strikes, to their forward-deployed bases in Britain, within range of Moscow. The atomic war so many feared seemed dangerously close. It was not, however, as close as it first appeared. Unbeknownst to the world, the American bombers arrived without their atomic cargo. The planes had not yet even been modified to carry atomic bombs, as Truman's nascent air force did not yet have the equipment necessary to make good on his atomic threats. Yet for those unaware of these top-secret deficiencies, in particular the Kremlin, their presence offered a foreboding message. For the first time since Nagasaki, the atomic sword appeared to lie unsheathed.[1]

Cooler heads, and American airpower, eventually prevailed. An unprecedented airlift involving more than two hundred thousand flights of food and supplies broke the Kremlin's grip on the city. "Operation Vittles" proved so successful that the average caloric intake of West Berliners increased during the siege. The Pentagon fattened up during the crisis as well. Aviation enthusiasts capitalized on the East-West tensions to win congressional approval for a massive air force expansion. Less than a year removed from the epic National Security Act that reorganized the nation's defense and intelligence agencies in response to the growing Soviet threat, the Pentagon's budget for warplanes ballooned more than 57 percent during the airlift's first months. By 1949, orders for military aircraft far exceeded the total spent on commercial machines, creating for manufacturers a revenue stream that lasted until the end of the Cold War. Firms like Boeing and Douglas thereafter had the luxury of pursuing commercial buyers while blanketed by the security of Pentagon contracts.

The Berlin crisis left its mark in Europe as well. The Continent remained thereafter split down the middle, seemingly destined for conflict. Neither superpower would budge on the German question, and in Berlin especially they settled in for what promised to be a long and tense stay. Their differences appeared increasingly irreconcilable, though no one knew when to expect the next flash point of international conflict. Moscow's detonation of its first atomic device the following year made the world all the more tense, as analysts on both sides of the iron curtain warned that if the Cold War ever did turn hot, it might be impossible to survive.

Asia seemed a likely East-West skirmish point. Mao Zedong's communist cadre drove Chiang Kai-shek's regime from the Chinese mainland in 1949, declaring a People's Republic in its place. Many American strategists expected Moscow—the titular head of what they believed to be an international communist conspiracy—to use Beijing as a springboard from which to spread its influence throughout the region. "The Soviet Union possesses a position of domination in China," Secretary of State Dean Acheson warned in May 1950, "which it is using to threaten Indochina, push in Malaya, stir up trouble in the Philippines, and now to start trouble in Indonesia." His advisers believed the red menace to be forever searching for its next victim, a worldview that led strategists to interpret North Korea's surprise strike at South Korea in the summer of 1950 as the first move of an orchestrated international plan for global dominance. For the policymakers who had just drafted National Security Council Document 68 (NSC-68), the militaristic blueprint for America's indefinite stand against global Communism defined as defense of Western civilization, the question was not whether the enemy would strike, but where and when. "We are now in a mortal conflict," Robert Lovett said. "We are in a war worse than we have ever experienced. It is not a cold war. It is a hot war. The only difference is that death comes more slowly and in a different fashion."[2]

This was the broad setting in which three distinct aviation conflicts contributed to the deterioration of Anglo-American relations during the late 1940s and early 1950s. Anticommunist tension escalated to a fever pitch in Washington by the end of Truman's term, culminating in witch hunts orchestrated by Senator Joseph McCarthy and his band of red-baiters. Such public machinations increasingly led Americans to view the world in Manichean terms of allies and enemies. At the same time, Britain's aviation policies seemed to threaten American security while benefiting the communists. American strategists knew they needed Britain's partnership, and British bases in particular, to thwart Moscow's advances. But to Cold War hawks like Curtis LeMay or Stuart Symington, London's aviation program demonstrated Britain's failings as a reliable ally. They hoped to reform what they considered to be Britain's more perfidious tendencies, and were not above using their economic leverage to gain results.

America's rabid anticommunism, exemplified by Washington's zeal for aviation security, suggested to many in London an American inflexibility as much a threat to peace as Soviet expansionism. This perception reinforced for many British strategists the belief that their country needed to create its own center of power if it was going to survive the superpower conflict. Surely Prime Minister Clement Attlee had reached this conclusion by 1948, when he argued for "power and influence equal to that of the United States of America and the USSR." The United Kingdom and the United States were intimately close during this period, as they were throughout the Cold War. They shared funds, secrets, and military planning. Their futures were intertwined. Their contradictory aviation policies, however, prove their perspectives were not.[3]

The first of this period's aviation strains occurred during the tense initial days of the Berlin crisis, when news of Rolls Royce's jet sales to Moscow first broke in the American press. It could not have come at a worse time for the Truman administration, which had only recently won passage of the massive European aid package known as the Marshall Plan. The fight for congressional approval had not been easy, primarily because fiscal conservatives vigorously opposed what was projected to be the largest foreign aid program in American history. Hesitant legislators ultimately agreed to fund European reconstruction only in twelve-month intervals, with future funding available only after Western Europe proved its ability to put American dollars to good use in support of American policies. In the final hard-fought deal, the administration would have its money, and the Europeans their aid, but legislators retained the ability to cut off any ally that did not live up to their standards.[4]

This was hardly the moment the administration wanted Americans to question the reliability of their closest European partner, but on April 24 newspapers throughout the country began detailing Rolls's dealings with the Soviets. "Tell us more about the jets," the *Washington Times Herald* demanded. With Berlin under siege and atomic bombers on their way to England, "few stories of greater importance to Americans are in circulation at the present time." The British embassy's explanations—that the engines were obsolete, that no completed aircraft had been shipped, and so on— seemed "coy" when measured against such threats, the newspaper's editors concluded, especially when "one of the conditions of the Marshall Plan is that no beneficiary is knowingly to let possible military assets trickle through to Russia." And, the editorial continued, "if late model jet engines and aircraft are not military assets, then Ernie Bevin is a monkey's uncle."[5]

Syndicated versions of this editorial ran throughout the country, accompanied by a stark cartoon picturing British trucks crossing into Eastern Europe with labels reading "Engines for USSR," "Machinery for USSR," and "Supplies for USSR." The caption: "What's wrong with this picture?" This question raged throughout Capitol Hill. "All day long my telephone has been rattling with indignant inquiries from Congress," Robert Lovett complained to Ambassador Inverchapel. Months after he and Averell Harriman had objected to Britain's engine sales, here was the issue in the fore yet again, this time with potentially dramatic political consequences. Lovett demanded that the Attlee government "consider what ammunition this incident would furnish members of Congress who were opposed to ERP [the European Recovery Program—the Marshall Plan]," especially in the midst of the present crisis. If a Soviet jet were to down an American transport plane on its way to Berlin, the damage to Anglo-American relations might prove irreparable. "It would be immaterial to the American public whether or not the jet planes the Soviets actually used were those supplied by the British; the effect on public opinion would be the same." The chairmen of the House and Senate appropriations committees had called to warn that the administration "would receive no money under ERP to send steel or any other supplies to the British to make planes and other armament which they [the Soviets] could use against us," Lovett told the ambassador. "In their present mood," he said, "I was sure they meant what they said." In short, Britain seemed on the verge of losing the aid it had just won, Lovett lamented, because news of its jet sales to Moscow filled every American paper. As he succinctly put it, "All hell was bucking on the hill."[6]

Aircraft exports had already been in the news far too much for the administration's liking by the time the Rolls story broke. In March 1948 the *New York Times* reported with particular incredulity that Soviet-bound ships in New York's harbor contained surplus B-24 engines contracted through a private firm. The administration had not yet authorized their sale to the Soviets; but neither had it formally disallowed the export, either. These piston-driven engines were hardly technological rivals of Rolls Royce jets, but the image of Western manufacturers providing aerial support to the country that threatened Berlin struck a sensitive nerve with the American people nonetheless. Truman decided to put the issue away for good. He signed Executive Proclamation 2776 on March 27, giving his administration complete control over all aviation exports. Washington thereafter considered aeronautical equipment of any size or ilk as strategic materials, not just military or large machines as had previously been the case. Export of even the smallest crop duster consequently required administrative approval and acquisition of a rigorously protected export license. In contrast to Britain's policy following the Open List debacle that sought to control only military aircraft while retaining maximum export flexibility, the Truman administration put the world on notice that it considered aircraft of any sort unlikely to gain easy export approval. Successive administrations would retain this distinction throughout the Cold War. Where London sought flexibility, Washington demanded control.[7]

Three months later the administration upped its anticommunist aviation policies yet again with adoption of NSC-15. Proclamation 2776 was only a stopgap measure for controlling exports until a permanent solution to the problem of aviation relations with the communist world could be devised. Issues of air travel and transport remained unresolved as well. Truman's formal approval of NSC-15 in July brought the country's aviation policies in line with its broader containment doctrine, which was designed to cut off the communist world from the free world while limiting its expansion, by installing an overarching plan for restraining and to a lesser extent destabilizing Soviet-bloc civil aeronautics. This policy entailed two primary thrusts. First, it called for aviation containment, including abolition of East-West air routes until the Soviet Union granted reciprocal landing and service rights to

American and other Western carriers. Second, and more importantly from the perspective of technology controls, NSC-15 also called for the complete prohibition of aviation exports to the Soviet bloc. Proclamation 2776 had already made aircraft de facto strategic materials. NSC-15 turned this policy of strict regulation of aircraft exports into an aeronautical embargo of the communist world. It even forbade export of spare parts to communist states, with the express intent of crippling satellite airlines reliant upon surplus American transports. If such controls were "rigidly enforced," the NSC argued, these airlines would find it increasingly difficult to fly. Internal air operations throughout the Soviet bloc would thereafter begin to suffer, placing Moscow under increasing pressure from its satellites to seek some form of aeronautical détente if only to gain access to Western equipment. America and its allies needed a better system for controlling the flow of aeronautics across the iron curtain, Truman's advisers concluded; but others besides the United States had a say in the matter.[8]

Aerial Containment

NSC-15 and its successors formed the basis for America's aviation policies toward the communist world for decades, though it was also a significant bone of contention in Anglo-American relations. During World War II, American policymakers initially favored open travel and contact throughout the wider world, including the Soviet Union. FDR's advisers thought that air routes could foster between far-flung nations a solidarity of the kind normally shared only by countries with a common border. This optimism is best understood as the opposite side of the coin from the more widespread postwar American fears regarding aviation. New technologies are often simultaneously greeted as harbingers of potential utopias and damnations, though even aviation enthusiasts realized that a new Pax Americana of the air could develop only if governments first opened their borders to international flights and travelers. "No greater tragedy could befall the world," Adolph Berle warned in 1944, "than to repeat in the air the grim and bloody history which tormented the world some centuries ago when the denial of equal opportunity for intercourse made the sea a battleground instead of a highway."[9]

Washington consequently led wartime efforts toward an international aviation standard based upon unfettered access, a policy dubbed "open skies." In 1944 the Americans gathered representatives of forty-four nations in Chicago in the hope of hammering out what Berle called "the doctrine of free air," but it was not to be. British diplomats rejected Berle's overtures, believing his utopian rhetoric belied an American intent to dominate global air travel, given the fact that in an unrestrained system natural advantages accrued to the richest and largest carriers (which were American at war's end). Believing Britain needed trade barriers to protect its home market and empire, Churchill's government instead favored regional aviation cartels. Pan Am director Juan Trippe, a consummate insider never known as an advocate of unfettered competition whenever favorable terms were available, agreed with Whitehall. BOAC and Pan Am even signed a secret route-sharing agreement in 1943, hoping to present the Roosevelt administration with cartel service imposed as a *fait accompli*. Trippe acted without White House approval, leading historian Alan Dobson to the conclusion that "British and American policies on the commercial side of aviation were totally at odds with each other."[10]

The British were right to be wary. Though American policymakers were zealous believers in the power of open skies to promote peaceful international relations, they also believed that those policies would ultimately lead to American dominance. Unrestrained competition, the chairman of Roosevelt's Civil Aviation Authority advised in 1943, would release "the technical and business proficiency of the United States," ensuring American "supremacy in the field of international air transport." Americans expected to dominate any level playing field, and as Berle penned in his diary, "American interests [would be] short-sighted not to see that the doctrine of free air is their plainest road to superiority." Washington was also not above using direct pressure, or what Churchill termed "pure blackmail," to win British submission. "We are doing our best to meet your lend-lease needs," Roosevelt reminded him following yet another British objection at the height of the 1944 Chicago conference. "We will face Congress on that subject in a few weeks and it will not be in a generous mood if it and the people feel that the United Kingdom has not agreed to a generally beneficial air agreement." Churchill refused to back down. He valued airpower too much to concede its future to Washington, and he simultaneously knew FDR was unlikely to cut off Lend-Lease so long as the war raged. His refusal to submit serves as yet another example of Anglo-American division during a period of cooperation.[11]

The Soviets also rejected "open skies" in 1944, preferring their insular system to an infusion of Western passengers and trade. Indeed, Moscow's delegation ceremoniously departed the Chicago conference before the meeting even formally commenced. The Russians seemed to Berle determined that "all operations of air routes in Soviet territories were to be carried on by Soviet planes and Soviet flyers," thereby giving Stalin complete control over who entered, who left, and who influenced his country. It was, Berle thought, "a policy of hermetically closed air," diametrically opposed to Roosevelt's vision of free transit.[12]

Repeated American attempts to pry open Soviet airspace after VE-day proved fruitless. What at first seemed to American analysts little more than typical Soviet isolationism in time became yet another sign of the Kremlin's intransigence. By July 1947, Washington's patience had worn dangerously thin. Forsaking their long-standing goal of bilateral air routes with the Soviet Union itself, George Marshall's State Department announced an "interim policy" that sought instead the more immediate goal of access to the newly formed Soviet satellites. Relations with Eastern Europe might conceivably open the Soviet Union through a side door, even though the Kremlin did not allow even satellites' airlines to overfly its territory at the time. Marshall thought it unlikely this new strategy would succeed, but he was not ready to give up on the transformative power of aerial contacts just yet. The State Department informed its London embassy, "From [the] political and economic point of view [the] restoration [of] normal commerce, communications and transportation between satellite countries and Western Europe [is] more beneficial at [this] moment than containment."[13]

Marshall's new policies would mean little if not supported by America's European allies, and Western Europe had far more immediately at stake in this issue than Washington did. Most European governments hoped to establish regular air service across the iron curtain and had planes ready to fly such routes; the Kremlin refused even to discuss air rights for American carriers. In any event, there were as yet no planes with range enough to provide direct service between the United States and the Soviet Union. These facts made Marshall's planners fear being frozen out of the region, and upon announcing the 1947 interim policy they asked Attlee's government to promise not to conclude a bilateral agreement with any Soviet satellite without first guaranteeing similar treatment for American airlines. Washington feared their exclusion might make Western Europe dependent upon the Soviet bloc for resources and trade even as the Marshall Plan was promoting the region's self-reliance. Before the communists could use air travel to divide us, American diplomats argued, the two members of the special relationship should hold closer together.[14]

As with its export policies, Whitehall had little enthusiasm for jointly coordinated civil aviation schemes, especially in an area where London had an advantage. It especially did not want Washington to thwart its efforts to open Eastern Europe to British economic penetration. Attlee's policymakers sought aviation flexibility, not the curtailment of future opportunities. After months of internal debate in the fall of 1947, primarily spent in pursuit of a reply that would be least likely to offend, London notified Washington in January 1948 that although it intended to continue "detailed consultation" over all civil aviation matters, Britain saw little need for Anglo-American coordination. "We shall of course consult the State Department before reopening negotiations with any satellite country," one British analyst noted, "but we do not feel that we should go beyond this assurance."[15]

Considering that Britain had just sold engines to the Soviet Union through its policy of flexibility, London's assurances were not particularly valued in Washington. Having been unable to secure an aviation agreement with any of the Soviet satellites by 1948, American policymakers increasingly feared unilateral British exploitation of the region and their own lack of influence behind the iron curtain. The communist coup in Czechoslovakia later that year was the backbreaking straw. American strategists interpreted the move as a clear warning of Moscow's intent to rule Europe with an iron fist, one clenched so tightly as to preclude infiltration by Western planes. "As an opening wedge [to Moscow] it had seemed important to deal with the satellites," Llewellyn Thompson, the State Department's deputy director for European affairs concluded, though he added, "It is generally considered now [after the coup] that each satellite must be treated as though it were Soviet" itself. Furthermore, given the repressive nature of the Soviet system, Thompson and his advisers could only see harm arising from access to its airspace. Communists could not be trusted, after all; and neither could those who would fly on their planes. "Commercial interests within the satellite or Russian sphere are always subordinated to political interests," one American diplomat pointed out, and thus the NSC eventually concluded that the Kremlin considered international aviation useful only for providing "speedier, and thus considerably more effective, liaison with USSR agents and Communist parties abroad." East-West air travel, in other words, had to be stopped for the sake of Western security.[16]

The British were not yet ready to take such a draconian step, in no small part because while Washington was completely shut out of Eastern Europe by 1948, Whitehall had secured a wedge into the region. Weekly flights connected London with Warsaw, and more frequent service continued to

Prague even after the coup. British executives hoped to expand this lead in the region over American carriers, especially as the Kremlin seemed intent upon punishing Pan Am and TWA for White House policies. By April 1948, when the Attlee government approved flights by the jointly owned Hungarian-Soviet airline Maszovlet from Budapest to Amsterdam via a route that overflew the British zone of occupied Germany (even as West Berlin remained cut off by Soviet troops), the Truman administration's frustration with British air contacts to the East reached a fever pitch. London acted "apparently without consultation with [the] US" despite prior pledges to do so, America's civil air attaché in Switzerland cabled home, a move that showed "distressing evidence of ineffectiveness US-UK joint air policy towards Satellites." The British government's continued approval of Polish airline LOT's flights across the British occupation zone, even after Washington had forbidden the airline to overfly the American sector, seemed further proof of Britain's willingness to subvert American policies to the detriment of American carriers and at the risk of Western security. The British apparently planned to "superimpose by unilateral action generous clearance of satellite flights over their zones[,] enabling them to bypass US zone and," the attaché argued, "leaving US holding bag."[17]

The only thing that could save American aviation opportunities in the face of these unilateral British moves, he argued, was "establishment [of a] clear determined line and simultaneous coordination of such policy" throughout the Western alliance. His colleagues stationed across Europe offered similar pleas. Washington's ambassador to Hungary appealed for a "coordinated policy and action to bar satellite access to Western Europe," especially the "immediate strengthening of [a] joint US-UK understanding." Even Dean Acheson considered a coordinated policy necessary: "It is obvious [that the] key to control of satellite flights to Western Europe . . . is zonal blockade which Dept. hopes Brit[ish] will, *in coordination with US,* keep intact."

Washington's tune on aviation relations behind the iron curtain changed in 1948 in line with the region's worsening security situation, but it cannot be ignored that the Truman administration also increasingly prioritized security considerations when evaluating aviation at the same moment as its commercial interests in the region plummeted. The British hoped regular airline service might open Eastern Europe to Western economic exploitation and influence, just as Marshall's State Department desired until the spring of 1948. Thereafter the Americans, who as yet had no commercial aviation stake in the entire region, considered those same flights to be dangerous security risks. "The immediate objective of this proposal—the confinement of Soviet and satellite aircraft to Soviet-controlled airspace," the State Department informed Attlee's government, "is of a political and security rather than a commercial or economic character." This was also what Truman's diplomats told each other. As Charles Bohlen, the State Department's chief counsel, explained to George Kennan of the policy planning staff, "I had understood that our aviation policy was motivated in very large part by security considerations."[18]

The British would have none of it. They recognized that, like with aviation exports, Washington's security arguments seemed too obviously in line with its commercial needs. The Americans claimed they wanted to isolate the Soviet bloc in order to protect Western Europe, but the only carriers their multilateral policies would harm would be British and Western European. An American-style aerial containment of Eastern Europe would mainly protect American airlines' claims to equal access. Viewing the world once more as a zero-sum game of aviation competition, Attlee's policymakers rejected Washington's security arguments primarily because they did not believe either their content or their conveyers. At the end of July 1948 the State Department delivered to London its NSC-15 program for aviation containment and embargo, along with a request for British development of a similar policy. Britain's reply did not come until October 1. Having suffered through the Nene and Derwent controversy, and having seen the damage engine sales had done to Britain's standing with the American public, Whitehall endorsed Washington's aviation embargo of the Soviet bloc. At this news the State Department breathed at least a partial sigh of relief. "The British are apparently in agreement with us [on the embargo]," Bohlen told Kennan, "and we should therefore press forward and try to implement the NSC policy on this point."[19]

British endorsement of an embargo did not prove to be much of a concession, however. Having been burned by the sale of military equipment to the Soviets once before, and with the Berlin airlift now entering its fourth month, the British had no desire to improve Soviet aviation capabilities at this time. The climate was not right for an export push behind the iron curtain when Western airpower was all that kept Berlin in the Western fold. More importantly, Whitehall had already forsaken Eastern Europe as a potential aircraft market for strictly commercial reasons. The region was awash in surplus World War II planes, one cabinet committee determined in April

1947, and these would more than satisfy satellite traffic in the immediate future. Furthermore, none of these countries possessed enough hard currency to purchase British planes. "However desirable to establish the general thesis that the supply of civil aviation equipment to the satellites should be treated as a bargaining counter for securing satisfactory civil aviation agreements with them," Attlee's cabinet concluded, the market simply did not support such aspirations. "They would be unable to pay and we could not give them credit." Britain therefore gave up little in agreeing to America's embargo demands eight months later, though this did not stop British diplomats from claiming credit for matching America's security ideals. The Foreign Office "would welcome further consultation with the US government" on the embargo, Washington learned in October. Though as one Air Ministry report made clear, explicit agreement was hardly necessary, because a de facto aviation embargo "is already largely enforced by the UK."[20]

Mutual accord would not come so easily on NSC-15's containment doctrine. The British believed they possessed genuine civil aviation opportunities behind the iron curtain, and many of Attlee's advisers believed the opportunities for widespread East-West trade and contacts far outweighed any threat from globe-trotting Soviet agents. The two allies therefore reached an impasse on issues of security and travel. Cutting off contact "would have a most depressing effect on the better disposed elements in both Czechoslovakia and Poland," the Foreign Office argued, if Western governments "deliberately embarked on a policy of cutting down the opportunities for intercourse which these [air] services give." In a time of growing tension, "it would be politic to maintain, and whenever possible to improve, such lines of contact as exist between Western Europe and the satellite countries." As for Washington's concern that regular flights aided communist infiltrators, Attlee's Defense Ministry countered that Soviet embassy staffs in all the Western capitals surely posed a far greater risk. Whatever benefits the communists gained by easy travel hardly seemed worth forsaking half of Europe.[21]

Once more, British commercial calculations lay in direct opposition to American security concerns. Attlee's hope of improved contacts through trade had undergirded his support for the Rolls Royce sales in 1946, and nearly two years later his government still hoped for continued civil air service between Europe's divided halves. London consequently rejected Washington's vision of rigid containment. Policymakers in both countries desired reciprocal aviation rights behind the iron curtain; the British were simply willing to take what they could get (even if accords temporarily favored the communists), to keep the aviation door open. As Foggy Bottom reluctantly concluded upon reviewing the British response to NSC-15, "a wide chasm separates our respective interpretations of the terms of our agreed course of action." By the spring of 1949, Britain's continued attempts to construct air routes across the iron curtain "succeeded only in confirming our increasing suspicions that the British are now unwilling, if indeed they ever were, to pay more than lip service" to aviation containment.[22]

As had been the case with jet sales to the Soviets, the mere fact that the British appeared willing to weigh the respective value of trade versus security repulsed many American policymakers. To them, halting communist expansion was a moral more than a commercial issue. It was also the paramount issue. As the acting chief of the State Department's Aviation Division wryly noted, the British "did not share the US assessment of the relative importance of the political and security factors involved" in aviation. London believed, Llewellyn Thompson explained, that "it is at least as important to have Western airlines gain access to satellite countries as to 'contain' satellite aircraft," given the "British view that air communications between the East and the West are needed in order to promote economic recovery in Europe." To many Americans, such flights were not only dangerous; they were deals with the devil.[23]

Despite being sorely disappointed over such an incautious stance, American officials knew they were unlikely to alter British policy in this matter. All of Western Europe wanted improved East-West air ties, and to toe America's rigid containment line would be for London a tacit admission that the divisions of the nascent Cold War were permanent. Most Europeans were not yet ready to face that reality in 1949. Neither were they willing to so blatantly bow to American pressures over such a public issue. One American diplomat claimed there was "not much hope of winning them over no matter how forceful our representations," even though "there was little, if any, substance to the British contention" that air contacts promoted trade across Europe. "The East and the West are doing very little business requiring air travel," Acheson's analysts concluded, but it was the hope of a better future and not the reality of the present that drove London's civil air policies.[24]

Unable to win, American policymakers chose instead to redefine their terms. In the summer of 1949, Acheson asked the Joint Chiefs of Staff (JCS) to reconsider their security objections to air travel between the regions. The secretary's advisers reasoned that the United States could still hold to a rigid security line if the threat analysis for commercial flights could be down-graded to match British thinking. The Chiefs fell in line and in less than three weeks threw out NSC-15's very foundation. While the need remained for an aviation embargo, they said, further study revealed that commercial flights posed less of a security risk than initially thought. Indeed, they now considered that the West had just as much to gain as the Soviets "in the fields of intelligence, air transport, and communications which could result to them from reciprocal civil aviation penetration." The administration pro-posed a new anticommunist aviation policy in 1950, outlined in NSC-15/3, envisioning a more "flexible" approach to the communist world. Whereas NSC-15/1 "called for only one counter measure" against the Soviets, invio-lable containment, the new policy approved of aviation agreements so long as the net benefit of the accord could be proved to benefit the West. "Our new policy," officials stationed at the American embassy in London ex-plained, "envisages the possibility that the United States and certain non-curtain states, particularly Western European states, might be able to beat the USSR and its satellites at their own game."[25]

Washington's change of course suggests a sophisticated balancing of strat-egy with the politics of the possible. Unlike in the case of jet fighter exports to the Kremlin, East-West civil aviation accords appeared too ambiguous for the United States to stake out a rigid diplomatic position. In revising their policy, the Americans made sure they did not lose face or inadvertently pro-vide the impression that commerce was in fact more vital than security. "The adoption of this additional tactic should not be construed to mean that we have 'relaxed' or 'softened' our previous severely restrictive policy," the American legation in London warned. Containment was easy: no air travel, ever. Washington's new policy instead required adroit vigilance, therefore any notion that the United States had softened its position was "without sound foundation." It "would be illogical for us to embrace an 'easier' pol-icy," they continued, "in the face of a reaffirmation of the seriousness of the security threat with which we are still confronted." America's new policy was not easier, Truman's diplomats explained at great length; it was only wiser.[26]

London won this round when Washington lowered its expectations for aerial containment, but victory was not without cost. The Attlee govern-ment's rejection of American security concerns in favor of commercial op-portunities, that same rejection seen in the Soviet jet sale, left its mark among America's most influential policymakers. As Acting Secretary of State

James Webb reluctantly concluded, "British opposition appears to be based on the fact that they do not share our assessment of the security and political factors involved." This was steadily becoming a pattern. In civil aviation as in aviation exports, London's vision of security differed from Washington's. This was an unpleasant fact the Americans would not soon forget.[27]

Twisting the Lion's Tail over China

Anglo-American disagreements over aviation behind the iron curtain were largely conducted with the quiet of diplomatic discussions, but their wide divide would soon erupt into the public domain again. Their joint anticommunist aircraft embargo, initially designed for Eastern Europe, was first put to the test in revolutionary China. The country with the largest population in the world fell into the communist camp in October 1949. The event altered geopolitics around the globe, though London and Washington approached future relations with Mao's government quite differently. On December 15, the Attlee government officially recognized the new government (effective in January), arguing that the security of Hong Kong, Britain's vital but vulnerable colony on China's southeastern coast, and any future hope of positive relations with Beijing, demanded recognition of the obvious fact of Mao's power. Whitehall's decision reflected the logic of its East-West travel policies: that policymakers had to deal with the world as they found it rather than pine for the world they desired. Once again, Britain's Cold War preference was for engagement over strict containment's policies of exclusion. "If we are not to drive Communist China into the arms of Moscow we must do our utmost to maintain Western contacts," Bevin said. The West's "best hope," he believed, lay in "keeping a foot in the door."[28]

American policymakers took a far different tack toward Mao's China, deciding somewhat paradoxically (and only after intense internal debate) that their best hope for improving future relations with China lay in driving the shattered country directly into the waiting arms of the Soviets. Acheson in particular believed that Moscow's tendency to bully its allies, coupled with the Soviet Union's paucity of financial resources, would in time convince Beijing that rapprochement with the West offered its only means of future success. After decades of fighting American-supported forces, Mao had no intention of becoming an American ally in 1949. But by pushing China even further away, in part by denying the communist government the legitimacy of formal recognition, the Truman administration hoped to lay the groundwork for its eventual return to the Western fold. It might take a quarter century or longer, Ambassador Lewis Douglas explained to Bevin, but "a new communist government in China could be more forcibly convinced of its dependence on Western economic assistance and normal economic and financial relationships by withholding such assistance and only granting help in consideration for specific concessions." This was international tough-love. China's communists would "have to learn these facts the hard way," Acheson blustered, that the Soviet Union "had little to offer, that Soviet friendship is always one-sided, that China will lose much more than it will gain by such association, [and] that it will receive no assistance from US as long as it is a satellite of the USSR."[29]

Diplomatic recognition was more than a formality, and Washington's refusal to confer upon Mao's government this distinction carried immediate consequences for Anglo-American aviation relations. International law and custom consider nationalized assets the property of a people, not their rulers, and officially recognized governments therefore gain access to the holdings (and debts) of the previous regime. One such asset Mao's government desperately sought upon assuming power was the fleet of airliners and transports previously operated by the Nationalist regime. China sponsored two major airlines from the 1930s onward, the China National Aviation Corporation (CNAC) and the Central Air Transport Corporation (CAT). Both were headquartered in Hong Kong by 1949, their routine service having retreated from communist-held areas since 1945. The latter, CAT, was backed with American money, and when Mao declared the People's Republic, eighty-three of its aircraft, primarily wartime surplus models such as C-46s, DC-4s, and DC-3s, remained in the British colony. There they awaited their fate, not so much planes without a country as planes whose national identity remained unclear in the chaotic aftermath of the civil war.[30]

They would not have long to wait. Less than a month after declaration of the People's Republic in Beijing, the general managers of both airlines defected to the communists with twelve valuable planes. Rumors swirled throughout Hong Kong that the remainder of the airlines' pilots would soon do the same, taking with them one of Asia's largest transport fleets. Airline employees and local residents loyal to Mao's government stormed the remaining aircraft a week after the first defection, vowing to remain until the British government recognized Beijing's legal right to the planes. They pledged to fly the fleet to the communists at the first available moment, a defection that to some would have posed a dire threat to the Nationalist government in exile on the island of Formosa. "We felt," recalled Whiting Willauer, CAT's American director, "if [the communists] got those transport planes and put them together with Red paratroops, considering the chaos which existed on Formosa at the time, it would have been a pushover for the Reds to have taken Formosa."[31]

With his partner Claire Chennault, who had famously directed America's Flying Tigers squadrons against the Japanese a few years before, Willauer sprang to the defense of the remaining planes. The two men met with Nationalist leader Chiang Kai-shek only days after the initial defection of pilots and aircraft to the communists, and persuaded Chiang to transfer ownership of the remaining planes to their private airline. If Americans owned the planes instead of the Nationalist government, they reasoned, Mao's regime would have no legal claim to the machines as the property of the Chinese people. Even if the Beijing government was formally recognized by the British (as appeared increasingly likely by November), it could not claim planes owned by an American company. The machines could be saved, and Formosa's defenses thereby bolstered, merely by the transfer of titles.[32]

Willauer and Chennault's purchase of the Nationalist fleet would soon draw the United States government into this quagmire. Founded in 1946, CAT was private but by no means neutral in China's civil war. By 1948 it was a mainstay of Nationalist air operations, flying soldiers and supplies throughout the country in addition to its irregular commercial service. The airline's transports even dropped rudimentary bombs on communist positions and ferried thousands of Chiang loyalists to Formosa. CAT also had a long-standing relationship with America's Central Intelligence Agency and its predecessor, the Office of Strategic Services. Chennault and Willauer enthusiastically offered their planes for innumerable clandestine American missions throughout China's civil war, and the two men called upon their contacts in Washington once ownership of the Nationalists' former airline came into question. Their plan to save the planes demanded what Willauer termed "the strongest co-operation and support" from the British and American governments. The former, whose laws reigned supreme in Hong Kong, would need to honor their ownership in the colony's courts. American diplomatic pressure was presumed necessary to ensure London did so. Before committing their own dollars into the controversy over the disputed transport fleet in Hong Kong, Chennault and Willauer first secured promises, at least from the CIA, of American support in the controversy sure to follow. According to one CAT official, such support was not only "wholeheartedly offered," it was "promised as a necessary condition of the operation being undertaken at all." Indeed, if CAT's rapaciously anticommunist owners are to be believed, the CIA even helped fund their initial purchase of the planes.[33]

The Truman administration had every reason to support any move to keep the airplanes from the communists. The NSC considered any addition to Beijing's airlift capacity a direct threat to Western security, and though initially directed at the Soviet bloc, versions of NSC-15 approved in 1950 broadened America's aviation embargo and containment doctrines to include China. Denying Beijing modern aircraft meant more than merely fulfillment of a logical sequence expanding containment to new communist states. The State Department firmly believed that Mao's expansionistic regime had its eyes on Formosa as well as on lands to the south. As the deputy director of the Office of South Asian Affairs explained, an airline provided an "instrument of Chinese infiltration" throughout the continent. Denying Beijing a ready-made fleet therefore seemed the easiest way to thwart the revolution's expansionary tendencies. Clark Clifford, one of Truman's closest aides, even likened the airline's strategic importance to that of the British fleet during World War II. The disputed planes could "solve his [Mao's] air transportation problem," he told Truman, allowing Mao "to consolidate his economic and military gains of the past year." Chennault, never one to miss a dramatic military analogy, told the White House his flotilla offered the functional equivalent of the "French fleet at Oran which the British felt compelled to destroy" during the last war. If it could not remain in Western hands, he argued, it must not be allowed to fall to the communists. Powerful allies on Capitol Hill, including Representative Mike Mansfield of Montana, agreed and pressured Truman to do everything in his power to prevent the loss of this military asset.[34]

Truman needed little prodding. In December 1949, he authorized his Civil Aviation Authority (CAA) to issue registration cards for the aircraft, giving his government's seal of approval to CAT's possession of the fleet. CAA registration made these planes legal property of the American company, at least in Washington's eyes. Almost simultaneously, Mao's government registered with Hong Kong's colonial government as the fleet's legal title holder. Naturally, both could not be owners of the same planes, and authorities in the British colony impounded the entire fleet until its courts could determine true ownership. Preliminary hearings were scheduled for January 1950, with an initial ruling expected soon after.[35]

Washington hoped the case might never get that far, though thwarting Hong Kong's Colonial Court would require British aid. In December the State Department formally asked London to take "extraordinary measures . . . to prevent the aircraft from falling into the hands of the Communists." The request was not specific, though Washington left little doubt that it hoped the Attlee government would, for the sake of the free world, circumvent legal channels and release the planes to CAT's custody before the courts ever heard the case. Less subtle pressure was also applied. In the weeks that followed, the American chargé d'affaires in London, Julius Holmes, and William Donovan, the former chief of the Office of Strategic Services, made their own personal pleas to the British government, conveying Washington's "strong" desire that the planes remain in Western hands. To argue his case in person, Donovan traveled to Hong Kong, where he promptly caused a minor diplomatic incident by marching into the colonial governor's office to demand the immediate release of the planes while, in the governor's words, "thumping the table, metaphorically if not physically." He reminded the governor that "if it had not been for the United States Britain would have lost the war," a charge unlikely to win favor in the Dominions. Such actions may explain why Donovan's reputation was built on clandestine rather than diplomatic service.[36]

More importantly, if less bombastically, Donovan also threatened a sharp reduction in Marshall Plan aid if the British did not safeguard the planes. He would not be the last to use this threat, which by all appearances was hardly an idle one. Accompanying the former spymaster was Karl Rankin, the United States consul general for Hong Kong and Washington's chief diplomat in the colony. Technically, according to one British diplomat back in London, Donovan's words therefore "must be regarded as having an official character." Livid career Foreign Office diplomats lobbied for a formal complaint to the State Department over this interference, as Donovan was a private citizen despite his pedigree. Cooler heads eventually prevailed in Whitehall. Yet Donovan's message, even if impolitely delivered, represented a powerful vein of thinking in Washington, where hearings for another year of Marshall Plan appropriations were soon to begin on Capitol Hill. The real price of American aid, it seemed, was constant American reminders that aid could be withdrawn. With each such threat, London was reminded why it had to regain the strength to be independent. Donovan's warning, in any event, had its intended effect. "The Americans feel so strongly" about the matter, one diplomat warned, "that a surrender of the aircraft to the Communists could have a very serious effect on Anglo-American relations with incalculable consequences." Alliances had been broken over less, and China remained a particularly sensitive topic for the American people and their government at the end of 1949.[37]

Attlee's government found itself in a tight spot. Most of the prime minister's advisers cautioned against allowing the planes to fall to the communists, yet they also worried that any overtly anticommunist move could jeopardize Hong Kong. Whitehall had recently pledged to support NSC-15's anticommunist aviation embargo, though to be specific, Britain had only formally pledged to embargo aircraft from communists in Europe. Legally therefore it was unclear whether Attlee's government had pledged to halt the transfer of Western aircraft to Beijing; it was clear, however, that such an embargo was well within the spirit, if not the letter, of Britain's promises. "Whatever the legal aspects of the case might be," one of Foreign Secretary Bevin's chief advisers cautioned, "we are under an obligation . . . to prevent any satellite power obtaining strategic materials such as aircraft; and with regard to China[,] assurances had been given to the United States already that we would prevent strategic materials being made available." The Truman administration viewed aircraft of any type as a strategic commodity, and allowing Beijing to take possession of the disputed transport fleet was likely to touch a raw nerve with American leaders who already doubted Britain's anticommunist zeal. "Both our countries had been engaged for some time past in trying to persuade European countries to deny [communists] supplies in the same way as we were doing," Washington's minister in London said. "They would not understand it if [Britain] allowed those seventy planes to go to China."[38]

Whatever diplomatic obligations British policymakers believed they had toward Washington, they felt a similar, if not stronger, commitment to their own legal system. The case was already before Hong Kong's courts, and Bevin's legal counselor advised allowing the litigation to run its course. Strictly speaking, he could not even determine if the anticommunist aviation embargo applied in this case. The planes, after all, might not be London's to control. Even though Britain's acceptance of the air embargo was "fully applicable to sales of aircraft over which we had executive control," technically this "could not mean that we should refuse to hand over to a communist government property that by a decision of a court proved to be legally theirs." He continued, "It must be remembered that we are concerned here, with an attempt by the communists, not to purchase civil aircraft, but to recover civil aircraft which may prove legally to belong to them," adding, "There is a considerable difference between preventing aircraft from being sold to the communists, and denying to them aircraft which prove to be legally theirs." Such sophistry aside, Bevin recognized that Washington "expects us to act in the spirit rather than the letter of the embargo," no matter who technically owned the planes.[39]

The question of CAT's fleet ultimately devolved into a quagmire that brought to light vital differences in British and American attitudes toward the growing Cold War in Asia. Truman's principal advisers generally found it easy to justify denying the planes to the communists. Their vigorous Cold War worldview demanded as much. The Americans prioritized security over all other considerations, as they had in their previous arguments over jet engine security and East-West transit. They did the same by pressuring Britain to take "extraordinary measures" to rescue the fleet from communist hands. In this case, they valued security even above the law, believing that providing Beijing with a modern air fleet was hardly consistent with Acheson's policy of nonrecognition.

Whitehall held no great love for Mao's brand of Communism, but Washington's view of the world in Manichean terms and choice of a temporary expediency over lasting respect for the rule of law seemed to British minds both dangerous and downright hypocritical. The American hard-line stance on the disputed planes seemed dangerous because angering Beijing imperiled Hong Kong; hypocritical because the free world the Americans fought to defend was itself predicated upon that very rule of law that men like Chennault and Donovan seemed all too ready to discard when it was inconvenient. Attlee's advisers might have savored the irony of the situation, had it not been so frustrating. CAT's owners sought protection through Hong Kong's courts for what they considered their property. They simultaneously urged London to void the legal process under way in those same courts, should Beijing's claim be upheld. The Americans appeared willing to forsake their own fundamental beliefs to save a few planes ten thousand miles from their shores, leaving many in Whitehall to wonder what freedoms they would willingly discard if their own security were at stake. "The Americans, more than any other people in the world, traditionally respect the inviolability of legal proceedings," one of Bevin's counselors railed. "It is therefore intolerable that the United States Government should with one voice admit the correctness of our attitude [in respecting the court's rulings] and with another threaten us if we abide by our principles."[40]

For Attlee, trained as a lawyer, the decision was clear. The rule of law was inviolable. "The Prime Minister was shocked at any suggestion that we should seek to transfer [the planes] without process of justice in Hong Kong," his secretary noted during the first week of 1950. He subsequently told Churchill (as a courtesy to the opposition leader) that while his government was "fully sympathetic to the American desire to obtain these aircraft and above all, to their desire that they should not fall into Communist hands, it would be improper and undesirable for us to frustrate the normal course of law." Attlee personally hoped Hong Kong's courts might rule in America's favor. But he refused to influence their decision. It might take the courts a year or more to render their final decision, he reasoned (and hoped), during which time an amicable solution might be found to this seemingly intractable problem.[41]

Attlee would not be so lucky, as Beijing and Washington each threatened to define their relations with Britain upon the outcome of this affair. China's foreign minister, Zhou Enlai, told Western reporters the planes were a "sacred property right" of the Chinese people that "no one is allowed to encroach upon or damage." His vice-minister for foreign affairs warned that one British-owned warehouse in Shanghai would burn to the ground for each aircraft the courts handed over to the Americans. Washington offered similar, if less fiery, warnings. Consul general Rankin, now free of Donovan, reminded Hong Kong officials that his government considered the planes American property no matter what the courts might decide. At home, Acheson's State Department suffered attacks from angry congressmen who once more balked at sending American dollars across the Atlantic to allies who were not even trustworthy enough to protect American assets abroad. Acheson had better "twist the lion's tail and twist it hard," Senator Lester Hill of Alabama blustered, "because I assure you, if it should come up that the planes are turned over to the communists, there will be a hue and cry up here [on Capitol Hill]." Hill promised a wave of protest in such an event that "will probably have very serious implications in terms of any aid you may have planned to give to England." The future of the Marshall Plan itself, he warned, rested on London making the right decision over the fate of these planes.[42]

No amount of tail twisting in London could influence the opinions of colonial courts when Attlee refused to intervene. On February 20, 1950, fourteen weeks after Chennault and Willauer first purchased the planes from Chiang, Hong Kong's jurists ruled the planes belonged to the communists.

Importantly, they did so without any influence from London. The British government had extended de facto, if not de jure, recognition of the Beijing regime while the planes were still owned by Chiang's airlines, the court reasoned. Therefore the Nationalists had no right to sell property that was already the legal possession of the country's new government. Put simply, when Mao declared his People's Republic and when London informally treated it as the legitimate guardian of the Chinese people, the planes became Chinese property no matter whose names appeared on their registration cards. The courts ordered the planes transferred to Beijing's control as soon as possible (many needed repairs before flying) and authorized shipments of CAT's aviation stores without delay.[43]

American policymakers were livid at the news. Acheson told a hastily assembled news conference how he had "vigorously protested" the decision to authorities in both London and Hong Kong, though regrettably to no avail. Senator William Knowland, a Californian Republican and leader of the pro-Chiang China bloc in Congress, fumed from the senate floor that release of the aircraft was "one of the greatest blows to the non-communist world that has been delivered in that part of the world." He believed the United States should make it clear that "Britain can no longer expect assistance from us to help to stop communism in Europe while the British government, by their recognition of the communist regime and by this latest action of turning over 71 planes, actually accelerate the spread of communism in Asia."[44]

Already under attack from conservative and even moderate Republican legislators for what they perceived as lax China policies, Acheson took such warnings to heart. "Some congressmen were talking in terms of opposing MAP [Mutual Aid Program] shipments and ECA [Economic Cooperation Administration—the Marshall Plan] assistance to Britain unless this problem were resolved," he warned Britain's ambassador. Congressional conservatives even threatened to slash his department's funding unless it could bend Britain to its will. These attacks were "only the beginning," and, he added, "this subject would become even hotter" if the British did not find some way to save the planes from communist hands. Perhaps the Hong Kong government "had not been made sufficiently aware by London of the importance of the larger issues involved, including [for] US-UK relations," he hinted.[45]

American diplomats and politicians had threatened to slash Britain's aid before, as when Rolls Royce sold its jet engines to Moscow and when Whitehall authorized Vickers to sell its fighter jets to Buenos Aires. On each occasion the

State Department's bark proved worse than its bite. Though on each occasion the Attlee government altered its policies in a way Washington favored, in neither instance was this change made out of fear for American reprisals. This time, however, Whitehall appeared to listen. The devaluation of sterling against the dollar the year before, and the pound's precipitous drop in open trading, had once more driven home Britain's financial precariousness. To Downing Street's further dismay, Labour's postwar promises of prosperity were beginning to ring hollow. Housing, the celebrated centerpiece of the New Jerusalem's social promise, cost four times what it had in 1939. The pesky dollar gap—Western Europe's inability to gain through normal trade the hard-currency dollars it needed—seemed unsolvable and utterly "baffling" to Sir Stafford Cripps, chancellor of the exchequer, whose futile efforts to combat the problem resulted only in his personal exhaustion and a lengthy sanatorium stay. Rationing of food and scarce supplies continued, and nearly five years into Labour's rule the average weekly allotment for an Englishman amounted to what one historian has described as "less than a pound of meat, one and half—one and a half—ounces of cheese, six ounces of butter and margarine, one ounce cooking fat, half a pound of sugar, two pints of milk and one solitary egg." Churchill thought this a fine portion, until his advisers reminded him it was food for a week, not for a day as he had thought. As a means of comparison, the above amount roughly approximates what a typical Manhattan restaurant diner would consume on an average Saturday night at the close of the twentieth century.[46]

Finances were forever at the fore of British strategic thinking in the spring of 1950. Their country could not be truly sovereign or offer an effective alternative to the Pax Americana if it was not financially strong; and it had made little progress in developing the economic structures necessary to wean itself from American aid. "My eyes were steadily fixed every week and every month on the 1st July 1952," Ambassador Oliver Franks wrote home in March 1950, "the date at which we should no longer be in receipt of extraordinary assistance under the ERP and when we had to be in a position to balance our international accounts." Once American transfusions stopped, he lamented, fulfilling the government's domestic agenda would be that much harder. Britain could never meet this politically vital goal if American aid ended prematurely. He further noted, "[As for] our legitimate ambition to play our part as a world power, to suggest that we could play it without continuous reference to our economic position in the middle of 1952 was absurd." Washington held all the cards, he glumly concluded. Its leaders could "look on the foreign scene with all the freedom that comes from the possession of a very strong and a very prosperous economy." The British, conversely, "were bound to count the cost" of any foreign policy decision, and were less free and thus less than sovereign as a result.[47]

Ironically this same Whitehall preoccupation with finances, which gave Washington tremendous leverage in their relationship, infuriated American policymakers to no end. Acheson's policymakers knew the British listened to their complaints over the CAT and other aviation matters—and in so many others—only because of Washington's financial aid. This made sense, after all, for it was part of America's strategy to gain influence through wealth and the promise of prosperity. Yet at the same time this dynamic, when dealing with their closest ally in issues involving their harshest enemy, seemed wrong. At stake in the CAT affair were matters of morality and security, not finances or commerce, and American officials believed the British should know better than to confuse the two. The State Department's Bureau of European Affairs, for example, advised Acheson at the height of the CAT crisis that "the UK should be persuaded" to "adopt a *broader* approach to many of the type[s] [of] problems it has, increasingly, been treating from a narrow 'dollars and cents' point of view." The bureau's head, Assistant Secretary of State George Perkins, privately added that the British were "obsessed by the feeling that they must cut their overseas and defense expenses, sterling as well as dollar expenses, so as to save every possible penny." They consequently "put undue weight on the financial aspects of their foreign policy." Assistant Secretary of State for Far Eastern Affairs Dean Rusk fully agreed, noting that "the limits of foreign policy action by the British seem to be determined by what could pass through a fine treasury screen." London's chief diplomatic characteristic was therefore "penny-pinching" and an attendant tendency to grouse and grumble when brave moral stands were in order. Even if the British did eventually heed Washington's warnings and accept its advice, Rusk concluded, they did so for the wrong reasons. Allies who acted for the wrong reasons might not ultimately prove trustworthy in times of crisis, or when Washington was not holding a sword of Damocles over their heads.[48]

The broader complaints of these American strategists notwithstanding, in this case, Britain's financial straits worked to Washington's advantage. On May 10, after months of American lobbying and a series of progressively disheartened cabinet debates, Attlee reversed his previous pledge not to intervene in Hong Kong's judicial process, and he overruled the colony's courts.

Overruled only slightly, that is. The cabinet ordered a halt to transfers of the planes and equipment to the Chinese until the question of ownership had been decided "by full processes of law," that is, until all avenues for appeal by both sides had been exhausted, including the litigants' final right of a hearing in London's Privy Council. As such appeals would require at least another two years to adjudicate, the order significantly delayed any final decision in the matter. Moreover, it ensured that the final ruling would be made in London rather than Hong Kong, where geostrategic interests might outweigh local ones. This decision violated legal precedent. According to Sir Alexander Grantham, Hong Kong's colonial governor, Attlee "overrode the law as it stood and in effect made a new law" with the clear purpose, no matter what Whitehall's official line, to "pass the planes to the Americans." For all of the prime minister's personal invocations of the sanctity of law, such niceties ranked second behind access to dollars.[49]

Mao's government reacted furiously to the ruling, which it termed "a demonstration of a most unfriendly attitude towards the Chinese People's Republic." Mao personally threatened that any delay in transferring the planes would disrupt London's tenuous diplomatic foothold with his government. In response to these charges that the aircraft dispute might poison Sino-British relations, Bevin rose in the House of Commons to lecture Beijing's new leaders on what he considered proper behavior for dignified states. "It is not for a Foreign Secretary of this country to determine whether these planes have been sold legally," he said. "What we have done is to make arrangements for the process of law to be carried out properly, and we stand or fall by whatever are the decisions of the courts. But this is a separate and distinct thing altogether from the establishment of diplomatic relations. My message to the Chinese government is that I would not imitate these bad practices from elsewhere," a thinly veiled reference to Moscow. The nascent Chinese government had much to learn about great-power relations, Bevin argued, and it could do far better than to imitate its new patron.[50]

Bevin's admonition might have served just as well for Washington, which remained unsatisfied with London's handling of the dispute. Attlee's decision was clearly a blow to Beijing's interests, yet it was not the clear-cut victory the Americans sought. The Truman administration sought clarity and an unequivocal stand against Communism in all forms, while Attlee's government purposefully walked a fine line between angering its Atlantic partner and upsetting its budding Asian adversary. "In this way," the *New York Times* concluded, "government circles see the only hope of steering between the Scylla of increased United States resentment and the Charybdis of Chinese Communist anger." A wire report the following day claiming the Soviets had recently moved jet fighters to Chinese airfields did little to help London's case in the United States.[51]

Attlee's policy of delay therefore did little to satisfy America's most vocally anticommunist politicians, several of whom suggested that Acheson should further exploit America's financial leverage. He had better "take every necessary diplomatic and economic step" to frustrate Britain's "deliberate attempt to appease the Chinese reds," Republican Senator Harry Cain of Washington publicly declared. The early 1950s seemed to them a time for action rather than temperance, and Britain's refusal to rule on behalf of American interests in the case only bolstered those who argued that London did not fully appreciate the true nature of the communist threat in Asia. "The large number of transport planes involved would be a powerful addition to the war making potential of the Communists," Cain said. "How can a [friendly] nation justify handing 40 [sic] airplanes to our enemies at this time?"[52]

Willauer and Chennault lost every legal appeal of their case over the subsequent eighteen months, save for the final one. Each Hong Kong court that reviewed the case ruled in Beijing's favor. Chief Justice Sir Gerald Howe of the colony's Supreme Court even lambasted CAT's initial purchase of the planes as not a sale made in good faith, but rather as a mere "device" intended only to keep the planes from communist hands. By the time the case reached the Privy Council in July 1952, however, all pretense of British indecision in Asia had long since crumbled beneath the weight of the Korean War. "Don't let's fall out with the United States for the sake of China," newly reinstalled Prime Minister Winston Churchill wrote his foreign secretary, Anthony Eden. This message was apparently passed along to the Privy Council, which ruled in the summer of 1952 that the planes belonged, once and for all, to the Americans. This decision was reached on the basis, not of law, but rather of politics, and even then only after a final bout of wrangling between the British and American governments and CAT's increasingly fatigued owners. Just prior to the Privy Council's hearing of the case, and as a precondition to their ruling, Chennault and Willauer agreed to remove the planes from Asia rather than give them to the Nationalists on Taiwan, lest this final insult enrage Beijing. The two men further promised not to remove the planes from Hong Kong before Beijing's National Day in October, lest their departure inflame pro-communist forces throughout the colony.[53]

This last condition would be harder to meet than would appear at first blush. Two years without proper maintenance had rendered most of the machines unflyable. In yet another break with precedent, the White House consequently authorized their removal aboard the escort carrier *Cape Esperance*. American law expressly forbade the navy from transporting privately owned aircraft, but following personal lobbying from Texas Senator Lyndon Johnson, Truman ordered the planes loaded aboard the carrier under the cover of darkness. Cold War necessities transformed laws into little more than technicalities for the men who ran and supported CAT. As Chennault reminded Johnson, "The technicality that they are unavoidably private property on a Navy ship can be faced after they are gotten off. An overriding public interest is the preclusive denial of their physical possession to the Chinese Communists." Their safe return to the United States offered, in Chennault's biased view, "the first defeat the Communists had suffered in the Far East." Jurisprudence had been defeated long before.[54]

CAT's planes never entered communist possession, though the controversy they raised clearly affected the special relationship. In denying CAT's fleet to the Chinese, the Attlee government ultimately decided in Washington's favor. In taking nearly two years to reach this decision, however, British policymakers were forced to endure repeated attacks by American legislators, ridicule by American pundits, and threats by American diplomats. All these groups believed the case should have been decided at the end of 1949, not at the close of 1952. In American politics at the height of the Korean War and the apex of Joseph McCarthy's power, Cold War calculations mattered most. Policymakers and pundits alike expected the largest recipient of American aid to be a staunch supporter of its global policies. America's mission in the world, Acheson declared, was to "stop the spread of communism." And he warned Attlee, if the free world was forced to "surrender in the Far East, especially if this results from the actions of our Allies, [the] American people will be against help in the West to those who brought about the collapse." Americans "demand" that Britain's anticommunism "be vigorous everywhere," just like their own, Acheson warned. The CAT affair revealed to many Americans what many of Truman's advisers already believed: the British were less a staunch ally than previously thought. Once again, planes were the source of conflict.[55]

The Nene's Unexpected Arrival

Britain's aviation policies appeared perfidious to many Americans in the late 1940s. By 1950, those policies proved deadly. On November 1, six months into the Korean War, the first Soviet-built jet fighters, flying North Korean colors, appeared above the battlefield. Recovery of the downed MiG-15 planes would later prove what Western analysts feared: they employed exact replicas of the Nene engine Britain had exported to the Soviets in 1946.

Soviet engineers had been far more successful at reproducing British technology than anyone in London had anticipated. They took less than two years to do what the Air Ministry expected would take five, as Soviet planes powered by Nene replicas first flew in late 1948, only eighteen months after the first Rolls Royce engines arrived on communist soil. Soviet frontline units began receiving production models by the close of 1949, in numbers that far exceeded Whitehall's wildest expectations. By 1950, British agents reported that the planes were pouring out of Russian factories at a rate of two hundred per month. America's top fighter of the Korean War, the F-86 Sabre, trickled off its assembly line at the height of the conflict at but two planes a week.[56]

British policymakers grudgingly gave credit where credit was due, and ultimately (at least internally) accepted their share of the blame. "The speed with which the Russians exploited the Nene engine as the power unit for the MiG-15 has been remarkable," the Air Ministry concluded in 1952. "In 2.5 years from the receipt of the Nene engine a high performance fighter, powered by this engine, was being produced in quantity." No one expected Soviet prowess in the air to come so quickly, leading some British analysts—especially those who had disparaged Russian technological capabilities—to credit scientists and designs pilfered after the war. "The Russians had devoted considerable resources" to the problem, Attlee's chief of the air staff concluded, and "had the advantage of the services of German designers." The Soviets would never have advanced so quickly in this field without the help of British engines to study, that much was clear. The Soviet engine developed directly from Nene copies, the RD-45F, provided more than twice the power and thrust offered by the Soviet's previous best engine. "Undoubtedly," he continued, the "sale to Russia of the RR jet engines" was a "contributing factor" to their rapid success. The Rolls export had done what Bevin and others had most feared: it allowed the Soviets to catch up.[57]

Whitehall received the Soviet achievement with grudging respect; in the skies above Korea, however, the sight of MiG squadrons had a more chilling effect. The Soviet-built planes outclassed anything the RAF could throw against them. The impoverished Labour government had decided in the late 1940s to develop state-of-the-art machines for deployment in the mid-

1950s rather than to spend precious funds on first-generation fighters which would have been available far sooner. Consequently, British fighters were entirely outmatched by Russian-made MiGs. It took time to produce any new warplane, even in the midst of an international crisis, and thus, beleaguered RAF pilots expected little help any time soon. "This aircraft (MiG-15) is appreciably superior in performance not only to any fighter aircraft now in production in this country, but to any British type of fighter likely to be available . . . [even] in 1953," Britain's defense minister reluctantly concluded.[58]

British policymakers immediately confronted this deadly threat by justifying their previous decisions. "It may at first seem deplorable that the Russians should have been able since the war to develop and produce an aircraft so much superior to anything we have here," the defense minister informed the cabinet, "especially since this is an industrial field in which we have always been supreme." Yet this was the unfortunate outcome of Britain's decision to concentrate "on the really big advances in aero-dynamic design and engine development which would enable us to have a commanding lead" over the Soviets by 1957, when an East-West war seemed more likely. The supply minister agreed, and drew his response to Attlee not only from the same logic, but seemingly from the same thesaurus as well. "It is certainly disquieting that the Russians, profiting by the sale to them in 1946 and 1947 of RR Derwent and Nene engines, should have been able to produce an aircraft as good as the MiG-15," he wrote Attlee. "It would have been possible for us to have had something similar in production [by 1950]," "had we not decided, in view of the limited resources available, to concentrate on something representing a bigger advance." Britain would not field a squadron capable of matching the MiG until 1953. Indeed, the RAF was so ill prepared for the Korean conflict that it suffered from shortages of supplies and ammunition until well into 1951. "We are producing in one month enough ammunition for one sortie by two squadrons," the secretary of state for air for Churchill's new government warned the cabinet that November. Even when Britain's new fighters joined the fray, he said, "we shall be short of the guns, ammunition, and rockets they need to fight with."[59]

American warplanes initially fared little better against the speedy MiG-15. The Soviet fighter bested any propeller-driven American fighter brought to battle in the fall of 1950 (after United Nations fliers had virtually eliminated North Korea's air force in the war's first months) and outpaced the country's first-generation F-80 Shooting Star and F-84 Thunderstreak jets. As the U.S. Air Force's official history of the war dourly concluded, "The Soviet fighter's performance rendered obsolete every American plane in the Far East. The Russian fighter hopelessly outclassed the [piston-driven P-51] Mustang, whose pilots had no hope for survival when attacked by a MiG except to keep turning inside, to hit the deck, and to head for home as fast as possible." In level flight the MiG was fully 100 miles an hour faster than the F-80C and, air force historians reported, "it could climb away from the old Shooting Star as if it were anchored in the sky." The MiGs proved most devastating against Western bombers. Designed more as a bomber interceptor than a dogfighter, the planes frequently made short work of lumbering B-29 Superfortresses whenever given the chance. *New York Times* military analyst Hanson Baldwin told readers that when "MiGs break through our fighter screen to get within gun range, a B-29 [is] shot down or damaged nearly every time." In "one famous raid" jumped by Soviet-built MiGs, "eight out of eight was the score—three B-29s lost, the rest cracked up in landing or ditched or badly damaged." Such losses hindered the air force's strategic bombing campaign, which its leaders promised would crush North Korea's will to fight, and in this way the MiG not only took American lives in the air but helped prolong the war at untold cost. One Marine pilot put his fears of MiGs to verse, to the tune of "On Top of Old Smokey,"[60]

> On Top of old Ping Pong, all covered with flak
> I lost my poor wingman, he'll never come back.
> Though flying is pleasure, and crashing is grief
> A quick-triggered Commie, is worse than a thief
> A thief will just rob you, and take all you save
> A quick-triggered Commie, will lead to the grave.[61]

The only American fighter capable of matching the MiG-15 was the F-86 Sabre, though this comparison—itself an endless debate among aviation historians—is unfair. The F-86 was a dogfighter, the MiG a bomber interceptor. The former protected its pilot with heavy armor and safety equipment; the latter used speed as its best defense and flew almost stripped of protective equipment. The MiGs carried heavier, 20-mm cannons but an inadequate gun sight; the Sabres employed an advanced firing system but inadequate machine guns. Indeed, when American test pilots who flew a captured MiG after the war listed the equipment they would have added to the plane, the total weight of their additions, according to one air force general, would have produced a machine "just as heavy as an F-86 and [that] would fly the same way." Most importantly, the two planes performed best at different altitudes: the MiG above 35,000 feet, the F-86 below 35,000. Each was superior in its own realm. "I could make ace in a day flying a MiG just by picking off stragglers trying to come and get me" at 50,000 feet, one American who did make ace during the war later commented.[62]

Regardless of which plane was better, one fact remains indisputable: without Rolls Royce's exports, Western pilots might have had their run of the Korean peninsula. Because of them, no Western pilot could ever feel secure that his plane was the best in the sky, a sentiment repeatedly passed to the American public throughout 1951. "A jet fighter is no better than its engine," Captain James Jabara, the country's first jet ace, said during a press tour of the United States in June, adding that, compared to his Sabre, "the MiG has a better engine." The disparity was, he said, simply "disgusting." Later that month another air force ace on a similar public relations tour made strikingly similar offhand remarks about the MiG's prowess and powerful engine. "We need something better than we've got," he told reporters. Even Air Force Chief General Hoyt Vandenberg submitted to the pressure of congressional query when he told senators in May 1951 that the Soviets "have a jet engine in the MiG-15 that is superior to any jet engine that we have today." To the *New York Times,* Soviet aviation prowess was troubling. "Aviation had its birth in this country, but our pilots cannot fly on reputation." Americans had to face the "unpleasant fact," Air Force Secretary Thomas Finletter admitted in January 1951, that "we're not the only one who can build these things." By September 1951, the Soviets would have more than five hundred MiG-15s in theater; the Americans would have only ninety F-86s.[63]

British and American policymakers were under no illusions as to the MiG's origins. They all firmly believed (though absolute proof would come only through study of a captured MiG) the plane employed Rolls Royce technology. Each wanted to keep that information secret as long as possible, as both knew the Attlee government would face a political and public relations nightmare once proof of the MiG-Nene connection hit the press. By April 1951, those storm clouds seemed about to break. Republican congressman Clarence Brown of Ohio took to the House floor to chastise London by stating as fact what many already believed, that Rolls had sold Moscow the secrets of the MiG. This was the moment London feared, but as one British diplomat noted, Brown's attack went "off half-cock." The congressman charged that the remains of a downed MiG recovered by UN forces proved its British pedigree. Yet as both the British embassy and the Pentagon quickly pointed out, no such plane had been recovered. Ironically, Brown did not know at the time how close he came to being right. "We were able to stamp pretty effectively on Mr. Brown's effort," despite the truth of his charge, Britain's embassy in Washington cabled home, but "what the press does not know . . . is that an engine was, in fact, retrieved something like a matter of hours after Mr. Brown's revelation!" The possibility of the verified story breaking that summer was, Britain's diplomats concluded, "a very real one," since the recovered engine did prove to be "an improved and modified version of the Nene."[64]

Whitehall feared for the worst once this news could be verified. "We expect a first class row about this in the United States," the Foreign Office warned. "If the Russian propagandists knew their job, they would shortly announce that the engine which powers the MiG-15 is developed from the Nenes and Derwents which we sold in 1947," one British diplomat wrote. In preparation for the expected firestorm of American protests, Whitehall distributed to its overseas embassies a history of the case, since forewarned was forearmed. Clearly the British were at fault for this development, London told its representatives, though perhaps not so much to blame. "It is easy in the present state of international relations to point to security risks which are obvious now but were not so in 1946/47. There was no war in Korea nor any special reason to expect one. Chiang Kai-shek was the government of China and Mao Tse-Tung was a communist rebel . . . Czechoslovakia was an independent democratic republic and the high-tide of communism seemed to have passed." Domestically, the Foreign Office continued, "we had to earn the scarce hard currencies," for "without this we could not feed our people." Britain's only hope lay in exporting whenever possible. "Having led the world with jet engines at the end of the war, we not only felt able to take the earliest models off the secret list, but felt, and rightly, that they were a good asset for earning foreign currency and paying our way again in the world."[65]

This justification mattered little on Capitol Hill, but in the end the "row" over the Nene proved less an issue than Whitehall had feared. The Pentagon had no desire to thwart Anglo-American relations during a war, and its leaders did their best to minimize the impact of the British export when testifying before Congress. When asked by the Senate Armed Forces Committee if he had "any knowledge as to whether or not the Russians built this engine that is in these MiGs, or do we think it is an improvement of the British jet engine," General Vandenberg defused the issue as best he could. Yes, the Soviet engine outclassed anything America could throw into combat, but the engine was "a very marked improvement of the almost obsolescent jet engine that was sold to the Russians several years ago." His message was clear: the British were at fault for selling the engine, but the blame attached should not be great, as the Nene was outdated even at the time of the sale. The MiG was "made and developed in Russia," he said, "possibly with the help of German technicians."[66]

Vandenberg stretched the truth to help the special relationship. The Nene may have been outdated in 1951, but it was most certainly state-of-the-art four years earlier when exported to Moscow. In public, he and other American officials minimized the affair; in private, they viewed the matter gravely. The United States had protested Britain's engine sales to the Soviets, and now those warnings proved all too prescient. The United States wanted a more rigid aviation embargo and containment program for halting Soviet expansion throughout Western Europe, but the British resisted Washington's plans to string an aerial net between Europe's divided halves. Even the goodwill generated by Britain's easy acceptance of NSC-15's aviation embargo of the Soviet bloc, an acceptance made only after reaching the conclusion that the region offered few prospects for aircraft sales, was overshadowed by Whitehall's apparent willingness to hand CAT's transport fleet over to the Chinese communists. Taken together, these events made American analysts realize that the special relationship did not equal a complete partnership in aviation security, and now American pilots and bomber crews lay dead because of Britain's failings. The British had repeatedly valued commerce over safety, trade over defense, and flexibility over rigidity when dealing with communists, and to American minds the free world was weaker for it. This was not the stuff of proper allies.

Had each of these three contentious issues—civil aviation containment, the CAT planes, and the MiG—occurred individually, they might have constituted little more than a hiccup in the long history of Anglo-American solidarity. But because they occurred contemporaneously and so soon after the disputed sales to Argentina and the Soviet Union, they combined to foster serious doubts in the two capitals over each other's larger Cold War policies. Their overall effect was realization on both sides of the Atlantic that the special relationship was not as intimate as many would like. One British diplomat noted in the summer of 1951 after reviewing the history of the Nene,

"It is unfortunately clear from the papers that at the time the Americans were much more worried than we were about giving secrets away to the Russians." Washington valued technological security far more than London did, though the Americans, of course, he said, "did not have our export worries."[67]

CHAPTER 4

Comet Dreams

Britain won the race to jets. In 1952, a decade after the Brabazon committee's initial vision for Britain's aviation future, De Havilland Aviation introduced its innovative Comet, the world's first commercial jet airliner. Sleek, fast, and a full five years ahead of any similar American model, the plane promised to revolutionize air travel and monopolize aircraft markets for years to come, bringing the prominence and prosperity Winston Churchill's cabinet deemed vital if their country was ever to reassert an independent foreign policy. It is no exaggeration to say that British leaders projected their nation's very future upon the Comet's success and the technological lead it represented.

There remained only one catch: Comet sales threatened American security. Future models set for export in 1954 incorporated advanced engines more powerful than anything then available to the Soviet air force. With engines like these, British and American analysts independently calculated, Moscow's bombers would gain for the first time the range and payload capacity to launch atomic strikes throughout the continental United States. Wary of repeating the mistakes of the Nene and of inflaming Washington's well-known fears of enemy attack, and thereby faced with the hard choice between their closest ally and their most important export, Churchill's cabinet faced a decisive moment. The special relationship hung in the balance.

Poverty hung ominously over their every deliberation. Years of Marshall Plan aid had done little to solve Britain's perennial financial woes, and the military Keynesianism of NSC-68 and the Korean War that proved a boon to America's postwar economy only drove the United Kingdom further into debt. The country's foreign trade deficit reached $940 million for the last quarter of 1951 alone, and the cabinet expected Britain's total foreign debt to exceed $2.1 billion by the following December, a sum equal to three times

Britain's currency reserves. Such lingering debt strained policymakers and inevitably took its toll on Britain's fatigued population, who continued to carry ration cards for certain foodstuffs nearly seven years after Hitler's defeat, while the government continued to ration industrial supplies like rubber and steel. Piles of rubble still dotted random street corners throughout London as vivid reminders of the Blitz and the costs of victory. At seven years after the war, lamented Paymaster General Lord Cherwell, "still we were not in sight of economic equilibrium." In the spring of 1952 Anthony Eden even forbade ministers to travel to the United States unless on official business, because, as he explained to Churchill, with the country stalled by tight currency restrictions, "there could be question as to where the dollars would have come from, since even if Ministers stay with friends, some expense is inevitable for tips, etc." This was what Britain had come to: the country that had once financed a global empire could no longer even afford to tip.[1]

Britain's continued need for American financial assistance pained the new government. Newly returned to power, Conservatives longed to make good on what Attlee and Bevin had promised but never truly delivered: the reassertion of international independence. Churchill had personal motives as well, believing he might serve as a bridge between the two sparring superpowers. Washington and London agreed on the goal of limiting Moscow's aggression. Yet the two frequently disagreed on the best tactics for achieving that goal. Just as their predecessors had believed, Churchill's cadre calculated that their country would gain an equal voice in the special relationship and a position of true leadership of the West only by cutting their umbilical cord of American aid; they knew just as surely that they lacked the financial security to openly break with the United States just yet. "If the Americans have to go on paying the piper," the Foreign Office's Robin Cecil argued, "they will call the tune (e.g. the tendency to attach more strings to military and economic aid)." More than a year into the Korean War, British strategists had become increasingly wary of America's zeal for the Cold War fight and increasingly aware that Washington questioned their commitment to that cause. The Americans showed "impatience with the more cautious British approach to . . . containment of Communism in the Far East, European Integration, etc.," Cecil continued. "This contrasts with British anxiety that impetuous 'all or nothing' tendencies in the United States will prematurely expose this country to the first onslaught of Communist aggression." This difference of approach had contributed to the previous decade's aviation disputes. It now made policymakers in both countries realize to their dismay that the world viewed from the Thames looked far different from how it looked viewed from the Potomac.[2]

Prosperity therefore underlay everything Churchill's new government desired. Prosperity would allow them to roll back those parts of the Labour's New Jerusalem they found offensive or unwise, while prosperity allowed the luxury of a more assertive foreign policy, especially vis-à-vis Washington. "The maintenance of our economic independence is vital to a healthy Anglo-American relationship," said Ambassador Roger Makins. "We must strive in every way to avoid again becoming dependent [on American support]." The answer seemed simple enough, but this omnipresent British conflation of prosperity and power offered a cruel paradox. Churchill's strategists wanted free from American commitments. Yet they simultaneously recognized that the skyrocketing cost of maintaining a top spot in Washington's hierarchy of allies—a role considered vital to Britain's chance at eventual economic revitalization, given Washington's open wallet and penchant for propping up the sagging British pound—was itself a bar to prosperity. It was a classic case of needing to spend money to make money, and postwar Britain did not have extra money to spare. To prove it was a worthwhile ally in order to receive special consideration, Whitehall spent precious funds demanded at home on expensive endeavors overseas. British troops patrolled international trouble spots in Germany, Trieste, Hong Kong, and the Middle East, and the Union Jack flew above naval vessels in the Indian Ocean, in the Mediterranean, and off the coast of China. These commitments were vital to maintaining British prestige and security, and both Labour and Conservative strategists believed they were fundamental elements of their country's continued great-power aspirations; but these commitments were also assumed in no small part so as to remain in Washington's good graces as a peerless ally. No other country assumed such far-flung burdens; no other country assumed so many burdens the Americans would otherwise have to bear.[3]

The costs involved in such far-flung missions strained Britain's battered economy to the breaking point. Total British military expenses had been only 6.5 percent of GNP in 1949, yet this portion skyrocketed to 18 percent by 1951, an increase that cannot wholly be explained by the Korean War. Few of Churchill's policymakers believed their tired public would stand this level of international commitment for long. Domestic spending was already stripped thin, Foreign Secretary Eden later admitted, making it "impossible to go on cutting home consumption and imports essential to the life and continued strength of the community while still retaining public support for the defense programme at its present level." Without economic recovery of the kind promised in the 1951 election campaign, the new government would be forced to slash spending, rolling back those parts of the New Jerusalem the public had grown to love, and slashing Britain's full-fledged commitment to the global anticommunist fight. Gone in such an eventuality, Churchill knew, would be Britain's remaining claim to great-power status, and its special place as America's closest ally. He traveled to Washington in January 1952, his first foreign trip upon returning to power, in search of further aid and hoping for Truman's blessing in reducing Britain's global military presence. He longed for a summit of equals. Ambassador Makins saw the mission for what it truly was. "However we try to disguise it," he said, "we are back in the breadline for a third time in six years."[4]

While Whitehall counted its pennies, times were better in America. The country enjoyed prosperity and international power on a scale not seen in recent memory, and arguably never before seen in human history. Following NSC-68's global blueprint, the Pentagon pumped more than $53 billion into the American and international economies in 1952, and annual military spending, which had totaled only $14 billion in 1949, would remain near the $40 billion mark for the remainder of the decade. This Keynesian spending whisked away any hint of economic downturn during Truman's final years of office, making fears of a return to the depression of the 1930s a thing of the past. America's real GNP surpassed its wartime peak in 1950, never again to recede below that level. The exceptional recessionary hiccup notwithstanding, the American economy soared through the 1950s, as the country's 6 percent of the world's population produced 25 percent of the world's goods and services. Home ownership soared, America's cities began bursting at the seams into new suburbs and housing complexes, and the country's largest baby boom in history was in full bloom.[5]

These were prosperous years for the country's aircraft producers as well. By 1951, Boeing enjoyed what historian Eugene Rogers termed the "happy time" in the corporation's life. Profits were up; investors were content; and the Pentagon's expanding budget was largely to thank. William Allen, Boeing's longtime chairman, penned in his diary two months into the Korean War, "Operations have improved greatly . . . Out of debt with money in the bank. Now have large backlog of orders." Times were good in America. And there were no piles of rubble left over from enemy bombers as far as the eye could see.[6]

Still American international policymakers relied upon British support. Strategists rarely like to go it alone. Washington counted on Britain's global reach to extend the Cold War fight into areas where American might was thin, such as the Middle East and South Asia, and looked to British participation for broad political support as well. Allies with global interests, global visions, a Security Council veto, and a sense of historic global mission along with a far-flung air force and navy capable of backing it up were hard to come by. "The UK is the one country outside of France (which we are directly supporting in Indochina) that plays an important military role outside its own immediate geographic area," John Ohly, a coordinator with America's Mutual Security Assistance Program, noted just prior to Churchill's 1952 visit. "We depend" on the British, he said, "to carry out military responsibilities that are vital to our whole security position." Even Rome had allies, after all.[7]

The United States and the United Kingdom thus enjoyed and endured a mutually dependent relationship by 1952, though each wanted more than the other was prepared to give. Washington demanded unquestioned British support for its Cold War policies, yet Churchill left his summit with Truman with only the $300 million in new military aid agreed upon before the conference began. No less disappointing, he failed to secure formalization of the unique Anglo-American tie of the kind that would have allowed him to retreat from his country's expensive global commitments without jeopardizing its standing among American geostrategists. Britain would have to be satisfied with its assured place as first among equals, Truman told him. To formalize their special relationship would politically weaken Washington's commitments to others. Because the British remained literally and figuratively in Washington's debt, Truman considered the meeting with Churchill a success. The negotiations left a far more lasting mark across the Atlantic. Truman's seeming indifference to Britain's unique needs—or rather, the president's unwillingness to recognize that Britain's needs were any more pressing than those of America's other close allies—eliminated any lingering doubts among Churchill's leading advisers over the wisdom of striving for diplomatic autonomy. Siding with the Americans on their terms was driving Britain to bankruptcy while doing little to make Britain safe from nuclear war, Eden concluded. As he revealed to the cabinet upon his return to London, the frustrating talks left him with "a renewed conviction of our need to do everything possible to re-establish our economic and financial independence." This would remain his overarching foreign policy goal, both as foreign secretary and later as head of his country, a conviction with vital consequences for his government's pursuit of airpower both military and civilian.[8]

One might argue that this strain in Atlantic relations, which culminated in the European unilateralism of the 1956 Suez crisis and in Eden's fall from power, was an inevitable consequence of Washington's refusal to treat London by a different standard than its other allies. In 1952, however, Eden and the majority of Churchill's advisers believed the key to British autonomy lay more in prosperity and thus in autonomous power than in independent reassertions of empire. "In their discussions on the balance of payments the Cabinet were all the time deeply conscious that the real remedy to our problem is an increase in exports," Eden informed Churchill. Particularly appealing, he later explained to Makins, were the country's "engineering exports," which cost little in terms of raw-material imports but capitalized on the country's technological expertise. Anyone could make steel, he argued. Its production was no longer the mark of a great power. The real secret to British prosperity would be mastery of high technology, and its ability to sell.[9]

Technological exports, that is, like aircraft. The seven years since VE-day had done little to dispel Whitehall's fascination with airpower, and given Britain's broad rearmament spurred by the Korean War, Churchill's government inherited an aviation program at its highest production since 1944. The RAF and its sister services more than doubled the value of their orders from 1950 to 1952, with nearly a fifth of the national military budget allotted for aviation. Employment throughout the industry nearly doubled as well, leaping from 150,000 to nearly 270,000 in but twenty-four months. These figures made Britain's aviation industry the free world's second largest, behind only America's. In terms of quality, some argued it was Britain that led the way.[10]

The year 1952 was to be the year Britain laid its claim to undisputed world leadership in aviation, especially in the commercial arena, with the introduction of two planes envisioned by the Brabazon committee a decade before. De Havilland introduced the Comet, the world's first pure-jet airliner, while Vickers stood poised to market its improved Viscount, the first mass-produced turboprop airliner, which had debuted in 1950 and which officials hoped would dominate medium-range sales by mid-decade. Churchill's ministers believed these planes offered their country's best chance of breaking America's stranglehold on global aviation markets. "The airlines of the world have to replace large numbers of civilian aircraft within the next two or three years," the Foreign Office told its overseas missions, "and as most of the aircraft which are to be replaced were made in the United States, the natural tendency is for airlines to continue to buy United States aircraft." If Britain was ever to achieve aviation success, 1952 had to be the time. "At the moment we have a technological lead over the Americans, but we cannot expect to keep it for long. It is therefore most important to get as many foreign airlines as possible committed during the next year or so to re-equipping with British aircraft."[11]

The Comet itself seemed capable of retrieving a glorious imperial past and was considered throughout Britain a proud symbol of resurgence after the hardships of war. *Flight* magazine depicted a Comet on a dusty airstrip somewhere in the darkest regions of far-off Africa. Gold-adorned women draped in native garb and naked babies, caricatured with exaggerated lips and features, gaze with wide eyes upon the sleek silver jet. Under the hot African sun, the image suggested, modernity met not so much savagery but rather backwardness. The Comet, conversely, represented modernity. Streams of light focus the viewer's eye on the plane as though the airplane itself was the source of the illumination. Dark-skinned men patrol around the craft offering varied forms of maintenance, their work overseen by the sole Caucasian figure, a uniformed pilot. He alone controls the technology, and with his arm pointing in a universal symbol of instruction, the message is clear: through such technology, Britain would retain its historic role as regulator of progress and civilization. "To the extent that the countries of the Commonwealth and the rest of the Free World look to us for supplies of aircraft (and of the electronics and other equipment that goes with them)," Supply Minister Duncan Sandys reminded the cabinet, "they will tend to be linked to us militarily and politically, and our influence in world affairs will thereby be increased."[12]

The Comet was a modern-day Prometheus, and a powerful geopolitical lever. No nation outfitted with British aircraft, British strategists reasoned, could ever easily forsake London's will, lest they turn off the spigot of technologically advanced spare parts. The power to supply was both weighty and long-lasting as well. Yet this power was by no means assured in 1952, despite Britain's technological lead. British ministers ever concerned with launching an independent course apart from American influence knew that their opportunity for influence abroad could easily vanish if American producers ever resumed their lead. "If our aircraft industry is not sustained by export orders," Sandys warned, "it will not be able, qualitatively, to meet all our own needs, and we shall have to resign ourselves indefinitely to dependence on America." It was in 1952, therefore, that the fruits of the Brabazon program were finally ripe for the picking, and the questions of technological superiority, finance, and great-power status that had driven British aviation policy since 1942, all came to a head. "Over the next few years the UK has an opportunity, which may not occur [again], of developing aircraft manufacture as one of our major export industries," Sandys said. "On whether we grasp this opportunity and so establish firmly an industry of the utmost strategic and economic importance, our future as a great nation may to no small extent depend."[13]

American competition was the only thing standing in their way. This fact led Churchill's policymakers to adopt their predecessors' view of aviation competition as a zero-sum game, meaning that considerations of beating American firms permeated their every aviation decision. When the RAF sought to thwart a sale of twelve Vampire jet fighters to Venezuela in January 1952, claiming that their use by NATO should be prioritized over the commercial or political advantages of consummating the sale, Eden personally lobbied for the deal, arguing that it should not be considered in financial or military terms or even with regard to Anglo-Venezuelan relations. On the contrary, he sought their export primarily as part of the Anglo-American competition for aviation dominance. "If we forgo this sale, we shall lose a hard won foothold in a market hitherto dominated by the U.S.," he pleaded. Board of Trade president Peter Thorneycroft agreed, writing that British aviation must be forever vigilant toward its principal rival. "Our exporters have had to contend with the strongest United States competition in Venezuela"; "if the Venezuelan government are disappointed in their desire to complete their force of Vampire aircraft, they will turn to the US as a source of supply." Markets lost to their primary competitor were unlikely to be regained.[14]

Churchill's government thus entered 1952 intent upon bringing the Brabazon program to fruition, though fully aware that their technological lead alone did not guarantee commercial success. International sales failed to meet British expectations during the first months of 1952. It was well known that the revamped Viscount and innovative Comet would fly sometime that year, though the exact moment of the latter's first commercial flights (and first exports) remained shrouded in mystery. Sales slowed in anticipation, leaving ministers pondering how to jump-start their stagnating industry. "Maybe we expected by now to be further ahead than we are," the Ministry of Civil Aviation's E. S. Wilson glumly concluded. "Our new turbine aircraft are not yet in service; America still has a pretty strong grip on the market; some operators are still flying on the cheap without the will or the substance to buy new aircraft."[15]

Industry observers considered government restrictions at least partly to blame for this lethargy. Export constraints remained intense and prohibitive since the Nene debacle, and the Korean War prompted the Attlee government to place aviation production almost entirely under the direction of military planners. In 1950, policymakers forbade export of any aviation material until the RAF could certify that the equipment would not be better used for rearmament, and military demands forced the cancellation of numerous commercial contracts, some only weeks before delivery. Whitehall had exhorted the country's manufacturers, one policymaker conceded, to "go all-out for exports" from 1945 on, "then came Korea." Few jets or jet engines promised to civilian buyers made it past the military's requisition officers, and the Society of British Aircraft Companies formally complained that its members had been accused of unpatriotic behavior when pursuing international sales despite the government's rhetoric that exports were as much a national priority as defense. In April, for example, an irate De Havilland salesman cabled the Air Ministry that his efforts to sell Chipmunk military aircraft to Jordan were squelched by delays in securing an export license. And Chipmunks were merely propeller-driven trainers. If outdated machines were held up by government restrictions, he wondered, how would they ever be able to crack American dominance with technologically advanced jet and turboprop airliners? Worse yet, De Havilland's salesmen reported that their efforts to sell Comets in Venezuela were hopelessly stalled until the government approved the still-pending Vampire sale. Despite Eden's prodding, the Air Ministry refused to "promise any definite date of delivery," and De Havilland's senior officials concluded, to their great frustration, that such indecision on a relatively minor transaction was about to thwart a potentially far more lucrative Comet deal. The year 1952 could prove to be "a most important landmark," E. S. Wilson, of the Air Ministry, conceded, but only if the government enabled firms to capitalize on their technological lead. Armed with the advanced planes they had always sought and that the government had spent years and countless millions supporting, companies needed "some assurances, [that] short of actual war, there will be as little interference as possible with such contracts as may be entered into with HMG's approval in any new export drive."[16]

Such complaints found sympathetic ears in the cabinet. Churchill directed a meeting in May 1952, just as Attlee had in 1945, to consider reductions in aviation export controls so that manufacturers might better exploit commercial opportunities. Unlike in the optimistic first months after Hitler's defeat, however, gaining blanket approval for exuberant aircraft sales would not be so easy this time round. East-West tensions seemed far starker, years of Anglo-American divisions over aircraft sales and travel continued to resurface at inconvenient times, and Western diplomats in the Coordinating Committee for Multilateral Export Controls (COCOM; the free world's regulatory body for strategic trade controls) had formally banned direct aircraft sales to communist states the previous year. Ministers worried in particular about American objections following the Nene and the tendency among Capitol Hill Anglophobes to criticize any British endeavor that did not directly aid Western security. "Publicity [of any export liberalization] has got to be handled very carefully," Britain's deputy supply secretary pleaded. "We do not want American off-shore help to be jeopardized because the British government appears to be going over from the production of military aircraft to the production of civil aircraft, with the object of capturing the world market from the Americans." Of course, that was exactly Britain's goal. The scenario of 1952 was in many ways the same as in 1945: Britain needed export revenues and it had superior aviation equipment to sell. For many, its future as a great power, and its future free from American control, seemed to hinge on the result of these decisions and these sales. This time, at least, the cabinet stopped to consider Washington's reaction.[17]

Briefly Collaring the Market

While ministers weighed liberalized restrictions against Washington's expected reaction, the country's most visible symbol of aviation dominance and the promise of a better tomorrow took to the air. On May 2, BOAC began scheduled passenger service aboard its innovative Comet, the world's first jetliner for civilian use. The plane promised to revolutionize air travel. Flying at well over 400 miles per hour at a time when most passenger aircraft cruised closer to 180 mph, the Comet nearly halved the time required to travel its maiden voyage from London to Johannesburg, which BOAC's first flight completed, with several stops, in a breathless twenty-three hours. With speed like this, the airline's chairman Sir Miles Thomas quipped, "New Yorkers will be able to take a swim in Bermuda and dry themselves at home."[18]

Comet passengers looked forward to unparalleled speed and comfort. The

Comet's jet engines offered a smooth ride for its thirty-six first-class passengers nearly twenty thousand feet above the turbulent skies that so often made transit on a propeller-driven craft seem like a ride on a roller coaster. "No passenger who rides in the quiet, vibrationless cabin of a plane driven by a spinning turbine will ever again spend a shilling to ride in the most perfectly silenced plane driven by a reciprocating engine," announced jet inventor Sir Frank Whittle after his first Comet flight. No doubt De Havilland's salesmen hoped Whittle was right, and the plane's first commercial flight generated a level of public excitement rarely seen for a scheduled airline trip. Thousands gathered in the cool mist of an English morning to see the Comet's departure, and more than twenty thousand spectators witnessed the plane's arrival at Johannesburg's Palmieterfontein field. Those who dawdled nearly missed the show. The Comet arrived at the end of its 6,274-mile journey three full minutes ahead of schedule, and the sheepish pilots reported having to make wide sweeping turns down the whole length of Africa so as to avoid arriving *too far* in advance of their planned arrival. "We fly on schedule," they proudly explained.[19]

The Comet's most impressive feature was not its speed or comfort but the pace with which it entered production. Aided by abundant government support, less than four years passed from the war's end until the first Comet test-flight. When Comets began carrying passengers three years later, the most advanced American jet airliners existed only as penciled sketches on drawing boards. Indeed, it was only after BOAC announced the date of its historical maiden voyage that Boeing's William Allen formally committed to producing a Comet rival, a task demanding years of intense work and an unprecedented financial commitment. Allen labored over his decision. Aviation's future undoubtedly belonged to jets, but with so many airlines still in the red from paying off their initial postwar purchases of piston-driven aircraft, industry observers wondered if De Havilland's move wasn't premature. The British needed to run risks to beat American competition and to beat back fears of national poverty, but with profits streaming in from military orders, firms like Boeing were not quite so pressed. Donald Douglas, for one, preferred to wait, allowing BOAC and De Havilland to iron out the bugs inevitable with any new breed of transport before committing to jet airliner production. "In our business the race is not always to the swiftest nor the first to start," he claimed. "There may be some distinction in being the first to build a jet transport. It is our ambition at Douglas to build the best and most successful."[20]

Political and commercial pressure ultimately pushed American companies into the fray. Britain's jets "will pose a severe competitive threat to our international airlines and transport aircraft manufacturers," Truman's civil aviation adviser, C. F. Horne, warned. "This country has no comparable aircraft of its own." The president urged American firms to develop their own jet designs, though it ultimately took government money to prompt Boeing's final decision to enter the commercial jet age. The Pentagon promised to purchase jet tankers (KC-135s, designed to refuel jet bombers) purposefully similar to the company's proposed jetliner, thus easing Boeing's exorbitant development costs. Boeing's commercial division employed the tanker's fuselage and wing designs, and much of the avionics, each developed at government expense, in their first airliner prototypes. "We looked at the prototype requirements of both the commercial jetliner and the military tanker throughout," Ed Wells, one of Boeing's chief designers, later admitted. Aiding commercial production through military contracts allowed government and business alike to maintain the façade that neither endorsed direct subsidies for commercial aviation; the truth was that Boeing forged ahead, at a profit, with its jetliner production, safe in the knowledge that the Pentagon would pick up much of the tab.[21]

Even with subtle government support, it would take five years for the first American jets to be ready for sale, prompting some American analysts to take the Comet's success, on the heels of unexpected Soviet advances such as the MiG-15, as an occasion to reassess their nation's role as the world's preeminent aircraft manufacturer. America's aviation dominance "is seriously threatened by the British," John Stuart of the *New York Times* wrote after BOAC's first Comet flight. This was a serious matter, one that "goes far beyond the loss of passengers to friendly rivals," since "the American manufacturer has supplied practically all the airlines of the world with their postwar planes and engines, except for those behind the Iron Curtain." If American firms did not offer a technological challenge to the British, and soon, "this whole American business abroad will whither." Faced for the first time with genuine international competition, American aviation analysts began to fear British progress and aerial prowess. Before, they had thought in terms of companies and markets: would Boeing win, or perhaps Douglas or Consolidated? Whichever firm won, surely it would be American. The Comet forced them to think, not in terms of companies, but rather in terms of nations. "Whether we like it or not, the British are giving the U.S. a drubbing in jet transport," Wayne Parrish, *Aviation Week*'s influential editor argued. "So here we are, with blueprints by the thousands, with all the reasons in the world for not rushing into jet transport, while the Comet is doing the impossible. The Comet should not be flying in scheduled service today. The Comet should not be sold to Venezuela or Japan or Canadian Pacific or Air France. It can't be produced in quantity. But the Comet is all of these things."[22]

While American critics fumed and fussed, throughout Britain the plane was cause for celebration. Headlines blasted news of the plane's maiden voyage, as Whitehall policymakers began salivating for the export credits they expected to follow. Comets "hold the field," Sandys told an excited cabinet. "If we make the most of our opportunities there is no reason why we should not capture a large part of the world market from the Americans." With planes like these, "we may not only get orders which airlines all over the world want to place," predicted Lord Swinton, minister for materials, before the House of Lords, "we may have collared the market for a generation." The upper chamber of Britain's Parliament, a body known for its sedate and august proceedings and thus not typically given to exuberant exhibitions, responded with an outburst of huzzahs, the waving of hats, and congratulations for all. Global aviation demand might exceed "a thousand million pounds" in the next decade, British European Airways chairman Peter Masefield declared, with Comets naturally composing a large part of that total. After years of searching for prosperity, Swinton concluded, the Comet offered "one of the greatest chances we have ever had."[23]

Just as Churchill's cabinet had hoped, the plane immediately reenergized their sagging aviation industry. The "wait and see" attitude one analyst noted at the start of 1952 ended in a heartbeat as British manufacturers scrambled to claim their own small piece of the Comet's glory. Advertisements adorned with pictures of the sleek craft filled nearly every page of *Flight* magazine following the Comet's first commercial voyage, each noting that the sponsoring company had produced the handles, blankets, wires, or widgets that made jet travel possible. Each was a contributor to modernity and to Britain's place in the sun. Northern Aluminum provided alloys; Terry's Springs their featured line; British Insulated Callender's Cables wired the electrical services; Godfrey and Partners ventilated passenger air; Tubes Limited offered the engine's "centrifugal shaft"; and the list goes on. James Booth and Company, at least, owned up to their obvious attempt to garner stature from connection to the world's first commercial jet flight with an ad featuring a soaring Comet and the simple message: "We're in it, too."[24]

And just as predicted, airlines lined up to purchase these innovative craft, believing public demand for jet travel would eventually prove insatiable. Air France and Canadian Pacific Airlines followed BOAC's lead and ordered an entire fleet. Juan Trippe even defied pressure from America's aircraft manufacturers and placed an order for Pan Am, giving De Havilland what seemed a vital breakthrough in the lucrative American market. De Havilland was eventually forced to hastily construct new guest quarters at their main plant to accommodate the rash of airline officials all bent on securing their place in the queue for future models. "Never before had Hatfield been a tourist site," one company official gleefully recalled. A year later, with fifty-six Comets on order and more in the offing, *Fortune* dubbed 1953 the "Year of the Coronation and the Comet." Of course the planes were not yet built nor were the profits collected, but with the Comet in service, the Brabazon gamble seemed finally ready to pay off.[25]

The Comet's success guaranteed victory for those in Whitehall who had argued that eased export restrictions, coupled with enhanced government assistance, would lead the British aviation industry to fulfill its promise. In the heady weeks following the first Comet flight, De Havilland received a virtual green light to seek out buyers wherever they could be found. Approval for an export license for a Comet 1 could be considered merely pro forma, Philip de Zulueta, a ranking diplomat, told the company. "The only countries to which we do not wish aircraft to be sold are those in the Soviet Bloc (including of course China)," he said. As they had since 1947, the cabinet retained final approval over any aircraft export, but with the Treasury preparing to declare the trade deficit the country's highest priority, de Zulueta explained that De Havilland should consider government consent a mere formality. "Provided therefore the aircraft are not sold to a communist country and you are satisfied that re-sale to such a country is not contemplated," he said, "we are not concerned who the buyer is."[26]

The cabinet went even further in support of Comet sales in October by giving aircraft production broadly, and Comet and Viscount manufacturing specifically, "super-priority" designation—a category ensuring that scarce raw materials and labor would go first to aircraft construction. Building Comets and Viscounts thus officially became a principal national security concern. "Our technical lead in large jet airliners is due in large measure to the fact that the government has financed the development of the new types," Sandys reminded his colleagues, "and it is vitally important that in the critical three or four years ahead, this assistance should continue." Aircraft exports then totaled more than £40 million a year, and "if we can further stimulate development and production there is no reason why this figure should not in due course be doubled." As with all aviation matters, American competition figured prominently in the decision. "The American civil aircraft manufacturers are becoming increasingly alive to the challenge from Britain and are intensifying their efforts to shorten the technical lead which our industry has established," Secretary of State for Air William Sidney argued. "If we are not to lose the advantage we now possess, everything possible must be done to accelerate production and so advance the delivery dates which can be offered."[27]

By the close of 1952, therefore, a year of financial worry for British policymakers fearful for their country's place in the world and for their role within Washington's vast pantheon of allies, Britain's future looked suddenly bright. It had won the race to jets, and its policymakers and planemakers alike seemed poised to reap the fruits of their labor. Global commitments remained, the Soviets and Chinese were no less threatening, and the Americans appeared no less bent upon unbridled leadership in their anticommunist crusade, but a new dawn seemed ready to break. The Comet offered profits, prestige, and most importantly, validation for the sacrifices of the decade-long Brabazon program with its belief that planning and technological excellence could combine to overcome the enormous resources available to American manufacturers. The Comet seemed validation, in the end, of British aspirations, making what happened next all the more troubling.

The History of the Nene Engines Should Not Be Repeated

Before the Comet could save the country, Churchill's government had to confront the plane's dangerous security implications. The first Comets used Ghost engines manufactured by De Havilland's own engine branch. These were civil versions of the Goblins that drove the RAF's Vampire bombers, one of Britain's first postwar jets, and offered approximately 3,500 pounds of thrust from a centrifugal design similar to that of the contemporary Nenes and Derwents. Though powerful and battle-tested—both the MiG-15 and the F-86 employed this design—centrifugal engines were no longer considered state-of-the-art by 1952. Most analysts believed instead that axial-flow models held more promise, owing to a design that relied less on engine width and weight than on length, and thereby offering greater growth potential for airframe designers. Increasingly powerful axial-flow engines would fit easily inside previously designed wings, for example, whereas centrifugal

models—wherein the air was spun to produce thrust—required larger aper-
tures and thus redesigned wings in order to achieve greater power. Aerodynamicists hated redesigning planes piecemeal, an expensive practice fraught
with danger. Though axial-flow designs were more complicated and expensive on their own, they were the clear choice for the consistently larger craft
then under consideration. In short, they were the key to jet aviation's future, including for machines designed to traverse oceans.[28]

De Havilland's engineers planned to grow their Comet in successively
larger models throughout the 1950s, and naturally sought the advantages
offered by axial-flow engines. The Comet 2, set for sale in 1954 but already
undergoing flight tests by the time its predecessor (a Comet 1) flew to Johannesburg, was the first to incorporate this new engine design. It used four
Rolls Royce Avon 2 engines, the civilian equivalent of the power source
for many of the RAF's most impressive warplanes, including the Canberra
bomber, the first jet to cross the Atlantic in a single hop. Engines like these
allowed Comet 2s to offer greater range and speed than their predecessors,
and by 1956 BOAC and De Havilland hoped such Comets might even travel
nonstop across the Atlantic, the airline industry's holy grail of profitability.[29]

Therein lay the problem, for an engine capable of powering a commercial
jet across the wide Atlantic was an engine of tremendous military importance. In fact, the Avons designed for the Comet 2 were more powerful than
anything the Soviet Union could then put in the air. This civilian combination of a Comet powered by Rolls Royce Avons was therefore more capable
than Moscow's best bomber, a point immediately grasped by analysts in the
United States and the United Kingdom. For all their success in centrifugal types, such as their copied British Nene, Soviet engineers had by 1952
proved unable to duplicate their achievements with axial-flow technology.
Their failure placed severe constraints on the Red air force's most powerful
bombers, restricting their strategic capabilities. Even if launched from re-
mote Siberian bases, their farthest-ranging centrifugal-powered jet lacked
the ability to reach targets within the continental United States. Moscow's
longer-ranging propeller models could, in theory, reach America from these
isolated outposts, and Pentagon officials calculated that Soviet TU-4 models
(copied from the B-29) sent on one-way missions could, theoretically, strike
as far as South Carolina. Few thoughtful observers on either side of the iron
curtain considered suicide flights from ice-bound airstrips a profitable means
of attack, however, and the TU-4's slow speed and sluggish maneuverability
offered slim chance for success against America's air defenses. American

crews had learned to their great regret over Korea that propeller-driven heavy bombers flying without fighter support suffered mightily at the hands of spirited jet defenders. As the CIA concluded in April 1950, "If there are doubts about the ability of the [propeller driven] B-36 to deliver the atom bomb against the USSR, how much greater the doubts that the Soviet B-29 could deliver it successfully against an effective and alert US defense." The CIA subsequently concluded that propeller-driven bombers were inadequate for Moscow's long-term strategic needs, as were the Kremlin's centrifugal-powered jets and embryonic missiles.[30]

Soviet jet-powered bombers capable of streaking across the North Pole toward targets throughout the continental United States, however, posed just the sort of strategic threat to hearth and home American policymakers had always feared. Despite rampant fears of atomic attack after 1945, Americans remained safe behind their ocean moats by the close of the Korean War. The best the Soviets could guarantee in an atomic exchange, their fiery rhetoric aside, was to level Paris, London, or Tokyo. Such devastation would give pause to any American official, but without the ability to strike Washington the Soviets lacked the full political and psychological use of their atomic trump card. Russian development of an axial-flow bomber, however, would bring America's heartland under the threat of enemy attack for the first time in modern history.

The Comet, or more specifically, inadvertent diffusion of axial-flow technology as a result of Comet flights, risked making that American fear a reality, thereby altering the Cold War's delicate strategic balance. In May 1952, while most of Britain celebrated the Comet's achievements, RAF and Air Ministry officials met to sort through their latest intelligence reports on Soviet air capabilities. Their judgment proved simultaneously reassuring and troubling. "Russian attempts to produce axial-flow engines of better than 6,000 lb. indicates that they are experiencing difficulty in achieving specific weights, specific consumptions, and specific thrusts," the Air Ministry concluded, noting that the Soviet engines were in no way "comparable with engines at present under development in this country." This was the reassuring part. The West was ahead and likely to stay that way, given that the Russians appeared better at reproducing Western technology than at creating their own. It would take the shock of Sputnik later that decade to change that opinion.[31]

Not all the news was so reassuring. British analysts concluded the Soviets might easily catch up to Western standards if, like they did with the

Nene, they acquired advanced Western designs. This was the troubling part. "The knowledge which the Russians would gain if they acquired engines of these types or full information about them and their manufacture technique would enable them to overcome technical difficulties which were at present holding up the development of high-thrust engines for bombers," Britain's Defense Ministry concluded. If given an engine to copy, the Soviets would undoubtedly prove able to reproduce even the most advanced British engine, a realization that led Defense Minister Sir Harold Alexander to demand the highest level of security for Britain's axial-flow engines. "The history of the Nene engines should not be repeated," he demanded.[32]

The legacy of the Nene continued to haunt Whitehall, even with a different government in power. The timing of Alexander's declaration made his fears all the more telling. Policymakers had received the Air Ministry's final report on the Attlee government's Nene sale only two days before these first security meetings on axial-flow aircraft in May 1952. The report's conclusions were scathing, in particular in the blame its authors placed on the previous government for British aviation deficiencies, including the RAF's poor showing against the MiG-15. "The present inferiority of the RAF in day intercept fighters" resulted directly from "the export in 1946 and 1947 to the Russians of Derwent and Nene jet engines which supplied them with the power unit needed for their advanced air frame design." This decision violated what the Air Ministry in hindsight called the fundamental "two axioms" of technology transfer: First, that, owing to the rapid technological developments inherent to the field, any aircraft in service with frontline squadrons should already have its replacement under development. "Second, that an advantage in production of any weapon should not be surrendered gratuitously to a potential opponent."[33]

The lesson British analysts took from the Nene debacle was to fear Russian reverse-engineering capabilities, and therefore to guard closely the best of Western technology while continuing to fund future developments. Ministers immediately applied this lesson to their lead in axial-flow technology. No one considered selling such engines directly to the Russians, but the potential for inadvertent technology diffusion increased every time an engine went abroad. The group therefore concluded, "We should for the time being, delay any export of our own more developed types of axial flow engines," and they imposed a six-month ban on axial-flow exports, a ruling that caused little pain to British exporters because the RAF and De Havilland had already claimed Rolls's total expected production of axial-flow types for that entire period. They expected to rescind their ban by October 1952, in time to meet anticipated demand for Comet 2s. Secretary of State for Air Sidney was quick to point out, "The Comet would in a year or two's time be powered by Avon engines," adding, "We must be very careful not to sacrifice the commercial advantage we had gained in this field." Ultimately, security mattered most when it was the only factor under consideration, but once finances entered the equation, perfect security departed.[34]

American firms produced axial-flow types, too, and Churchill's policy-makers recognized that any worthwhile security policy had to be matched by Washington. Indeed, despite experience with rigid American export controls and vigorous American complaints over more lenient British regulations, Whitehall policymakers feared the United States might yet adopt a relaxed security line in order to squeeze British producers from the market. Washington might feel a particular enticement to rush American axial-flow models to market, they reasoned, if Britain's lead in this cutting-edge market proved too great for their liking. The Air Ministry thus instructed its attaché in Washington to explain to the Americans that "it was not our intention to try to put an indefinite ban on these exports" and that Britain wanted only to delay their export, because "to delay them even for a matter of months would prevent us running a real risk of the Russians finding an earlier solution to these technical problems." It was imperative that the Americans not export their own engines before that time, he was told, lest they simultaneously hinder Western security and capture British markets.[35]

The embassy was authorized to take dramatic steps to keep Washington in line, including invocation of the Burns-Templer accords. This was the collective name given to a series of Anglo-American agreements, concluded from 1948 to 1950, governing the exchange of technical information. Of greatest relevance was the January 27, 1950, agreement requiring both governments' approval before the export or distribution of any jointly developed sensitive technology such as advanced jet engines. Rumors swirled throughout Whitehall in the spring of 1952 that the Pentagon was poised to offer France a manufacturing license for British Sapphire engines then under license for manufacture in the United States. "This is a point which, if our information is correct, you will have to handle very carefully," ministers warned, "since under the terms of the Burns-Templer agreement the Americans are obliged to obtain our consent to any disclosure of our classified military information to a third country." If Washington threatened to export any British-developed engine ahead of London's own manufacturers, Burns-

Templer might be a way to veto the American deal and thereby secure Britain's lead. Discussions for this matter were tentatively scheduled for later that summer.[36]

British concerns that they might lose jet sales to American competition were telling, but premature. In 1952 the United States lacked any commercial jets, with or without advanced engines. Moreover, the Pentagon had no plans to supply NATO allies with axial-flow-driven military jets until the close of 1953 at the earliest, more than a year away. British analysts, it seems, for whom 1952 offered the culmination of all their postwar aviation dreams, imposed on their American rivals their own expectations for sales and consequently jumped the gun on engine negotiations. Ignoring a bounty of previous evidence of American security hawkishness, they incorrectly presumed that Washington would be just as driven by commercial considerations as they were. Despite their incessant complaints that American diplomats did not understand British values or Britain's worldview, in the case of engines, at least, the Churchill government proved equally incapable of seeing the world through the eyes of its closest ally. When discussions for axial-flow security began in August 1952, therefore, American officials received the first British overtures of a combined export policy not with the concern the Foreign Office anticipated, but rather with pleasure. London's proposed six-month ban on exports enhanced Western security without hindering American commercial possibilities in the least. If the British unilaterally wanted to limit their own sales, Washington was certainly going to let them. "There is therefore no difference of opinion between ourselves and the Americans," London's team reported home.[37]

Such amicability ended when the six-month ban on axial-flow exports expired. In mid-November 1952, two weeks after Dwight Eisenhower captured the presidency, British and American negotiators met again to iron out the next phase of their joint engine policy. These negotiations had a different tenor from the start. Each side agreed that a permanent ban on engine exports would prove infeasible, given expected progress in the field. John Elliott, the chief American representative, admitted that manufacturers were already pressing Washington to release advanced engines for civil designs, despite the fact that no such American plane had yet to fly. "As these engines were now becoming an essential feature of modern civil aircraft," he said, "any complete and permanent ban" on their commercial use "could not be sustained." The best each nation could hope for was instead "a procedure of delay which would enable us to keep technically ahead [of the Soviets]."[38]

Both sides recognized the need to delay export of this strategically vital technology, but they immediately disagreed over what constituted a safe interval for sales and who constituted a safe buyer. They split initially over British military sales to Yugoslavia and Sweden. The British delegation, led by Richard Powell, who would later serve as permanent secretary of the Defense Ministry, informed their American counterparts that a completed Swedish contract for axial-flow Avons required only final cabinet approval. London considered it a gesture of good faith to inform Washington before finishing the deal. Yet the Pentagon had already rejected sale to Sweden of a similar American engine (Alison's J-57), as American analysts doubted Sweden's ability to keep military secrets away from prying Soviet eyes. They thus refused to authorize for Stockholm any equipment rated above "restricted." Axial-flow engines rated "top-secret" classification. When told that British approval was only a matter of time (regardless of Washington's objections, Powell implied), Elliott offered that the State Department might, if warranted by circumstance, "press the Pentagon to agree as a special case" to limited engine sales in this case. The Swedes may have been unreliable, but at least they were not communists.[39]

The Pentagon would not prove so generous with Britain's export plans for Belgrade. American analysts celebrated Marshal Josip Tito's 1949 break from the Soviet Union and yearned for his regime's survival as a chink in Moscow's armor, but in Washington's Manichean worldview, communists of any ilk were security risks. "The US government would not contemplate the release of any classified information to Yugoslavia at present," Elliott argued. Engine sales were out. The British countered that the goodwill engendered even by discussing such a crucial sale could bolster Tito, and just as in China, it was important for the free world to maintain contacts behind the iron curtain whenever opponents to the Kremlin's monolithic rule arose. Prospects for the export were quite slim in any event, Powell continued, as Belgrade was unlikely to prove financially or technologically capable of consummating the deal. London was, in other words, merely stringing Tito along using the carrot of advanced engine sales. "For broad political and strategic reasons we feel bound to show goodwill," Powell told Elliott in private, adding that to safeguard this Western technology "we think we can rely upon the practical difficulties with which Yugoslavia would have to cope in setting up manufacturing capacity, plus our own ability to impose delay in the release of the information." London's aviation temptations thus helped keep Tito outside the Soviet orbit while offering little real risk of technological diffusion. Elliott found this strategy unwise and unnerving, considering the stakes involved in gambling with one of the West's most vital technologies. He had little to counter the British proposal, however, and their meetings concluded with the understanding that neither would finalize an engine sale without notifying the other, as Burns-Templer mandated.[40]

These first negotiations on axial-flow technology demonstrated that while the two sides remained far apart when they tried to transform their mutually accepted need for engine security into practical regulations, they would at least play to form. Their stances at the end of 1952 mimicked their previous aviation debates. The British sought to balance the difficult equation between commercial sales potential and military security, and viewed aviation as a valuable addition to their geopolitical toolbox. The American negotiating team, conversely, offered no evidence that profit or East-West relations would have any bearing on their security policies. Future American sales were far off, but the struggles of the Cold War were here and now, leading Elliott's team to argue that military requirements should reign supreme in any consideration of engine technology distribution abroad.[41]

Washington's myopic approach to aviation security, refusing even to recognize Britain's commercial considerations or British officials' belief in the validity of those considerations, frustrated London's negotiators. De Havilland had already taken orders for the Comet 2, and Rolls Royce was deep in discussion for other axial-flow exports, primarily to NATO allies. The American out-of-hand rejection of commercial sales and subsequent refusal to discuss regulations for airlines flying Comets therefore seemed to the British an ostrich's policy of burying one's head in the sand rather than admitting the reality of danger. Axial-flow sales were going to happen, and most likely soon, whether Washington believed them justified or not. British finances demanded as much. Eden explained to Ambassador Makins, "It is not our aim to concert with the United States a detailed export policy. Our economic needs differ from theirs and must be given full weight." Security considerations notwithstanding, he added, "We cannot refrain from earning foreign currency provided adequate security arrangements are made." Ultimately, Eden argued, Anglo-American commercial competition mattered more than East-West technological competition. "Our concern is to obtain agreement that on security the United States will not adopt a less stringent line than ours."[42]

Britain's policy was to walk the fine line between security from the communists and a loss of sales to the Americans, though British negotiators undoubtedly understood on which side of that line they were required to fall. The Air Ministry ominously summed up the negotiations for its team in Washington. "Originally we thought it important to carry the Americans with us because of the danger that their commercial interests might be inclined to pay less attention to security than we are. Now however the tables seem to be turned and your main task may be to reassure the Americans that our policy will achieve reasonable security safeguards." As the Comet prepared to corner the market, the crack in Anglo-American aviation solidarity that had first formed over the Nene, the CAT, and civil aviation, a division of sales versus security, began to reshape anew.[43]

Wise after the Event

The agreement reached between Powell and Elliott, that each nation would consult the other before approving any sales, lasted little more than a week. British negotiations with Tito's government were in fact far ahead of anything the Americans had been led to believe, and in the first week of December 1952, Churchill's cabinet approved the Swedish sale and gave tacit approval to the Yugoslav deal. Neither could wait for an American green light. "It is a great pity," one British diplomat said, "that the issue of licenses to Sweden and Yugoslavia was approved without any attempt to reconcile U.S. views with our own," but British priorities had to prevail. Whitehall's willingness to move ahead without further consultations with the Americans shocked Britain's own negotiating team, which feared such unilateral tactics might undermine their future efforts. "I feel sure that they [the Americans] will consider such action as taking an unwarranted security risk," Powell wrote home. "This latest development will surely appear to the Americans to be a 'volte face' on our part." If the cabinet insisted upon proceeding with the Yugoslav sale, he said, "harm will be done to our relationships here and I am afraid a feeling of suspicion and distrust is liable to develop." This decision, said Powell, was "a typical example of how in the past misunderstandings have arisen between the Americans and ourselves which have sometimes resulted in the Americans criticizing us as being 'slick operators'" concerned more with profit than with allies. Britain's policy made economic and strategic sense, he argued, but it made for poor Anglo-American relations.[44]

Powell proved right to be worried. The Americans were furious when they learned of Britain's proposed exports. The outgoing Truman administration had taken seriously Britain's proposal for a joint export policy, and a combined State and Defense Department committee had been working vigorously since the end of November to develop mutually acceptable restrictions. They expected to correlate their proposals with the British in the early spring and "were therefore amazed to hear from us that what *we* were in fact proposing was an agreed method of implementing *our* disclosure policy," Sir Steel cabled home from the British embassy. With a potentially more hawkish administration coming to power the consequences might prove severe. As Ambassador Roger Makins privately warned Eden, despite numerous personal attempts "it was not possible to get an assurance that the Americans were not going to object to our arrangements with Sweden and Yugoslavia . . . [though] our impression is that they will not." However, he continued,

> You should know that the Pentagon was very much opposed to both transactions and pressed the State Department to try to have them suspended. With our encouragement the State Department were able to resist this and to raise the question above the level of recriminations. But the Pentagon are still "worried to death" about our intentions and so to some extent are the State Department. This somewhat irrational attitude may spring from an excessive preoccupation with secrecy but it is most important to dispel it as soon as possible lest this anxiety be communicated to Congress.[45]

The American position might be "irrational," but crazed giants can prove dangerous. Churchill's government already feared the new administration's strident reputation, and Makins believed this unilateral British move might strengthen the hand of incoming foreign policy hardliners such as secretary of state designee John Foster Dulles. Eden shared his concerns, believing Dulles's reputation as a fervent anticommunist might destabilize the delicate East-West balance and further erode Anglo-American relations. "The new secretary of state would not have been my choice," he confided to Churchill. Dulles was known as a hard negotiator with a moralistic edge, and was a public advocate for a "roll back" of communist gains in Europe and Korea. He was, moreover, a strategist who demanded clear-cut support from global partners and had little patience for what he perceived as duplicitous diplomacy. After what seemed years of moralistic bullying from across the Atlantic, London's own reserve of patience for American hard-line diplomacy had worn dangerously thin. "The future of Anglo-American relations depends on their readiness to treat us reasonably as a partner," Eden told Makins. "My anxiety arises from fear that the new administration . . . will show themselves cavalier in their treatment of allies. Every time they do this they give ammunition to their enemies and embarrass their friends."[46]

Eden worried that the Americans might fail to properly consult their allies before acting, but ironically his own government's decisions on axial-flow exports beat them to the punch. The cabinet's approval of further negotiations with the Yugoslavs infuriated Washington, to the point that the Foreign Office's B. H. Heddy noted that any further exports without consultation "might be sufficient to push them [the Americans] off the deep end." This was a plunge London surely did not want Washington to take. "It is easy to be wise after the event," one British diplomat noted, adding that in terms of both security and finances "we should clearly have saved ourselves time and embarrassment by showing more frankness in Washington earlier." "In any discussion with the Americans it is important to emphasize that our economic needs differ from theirs very considerably," Supply Minister Sandys advised, "and that it is because we cannot afford to refrain from earning foreign currency for advanced types of aircraft and engines, which are one of our chief assets, that we are forced to pursue a policy of allowing exports if suitable safeguards can be arranged."[47]

The problem was, Britain had no real security policy for advanced jet engines, and American negotiators balked at any policy constructed with an eye toward maximizing profits. Having decided to allow axial-flow exports and therefore to restrain security leaks after the sale—in effect, to reduce communist access by limiting the way foreign buyers might use this technology, rather than limiting sales themselves—the Churchill government's initial formulation of suitable export restraints proved disjointed at best, driven less by cold calculation of risk than by commercial enthusiasm. Their planning failed to keep pace with prospects, and their analysis of potential pitfalls suffered as a result. Subsequent efforts to devise proper security restraints, beginning in January 1953, took months, and internal debates over engine use in time included most of Britain's major cabinet ministries and the cabinet itself. Their difficulty in formulating real-world restrictions based upon their theoretical risks of technology control frustrated engine makers and potential buyers alike. In revealing much about Britain's trade priorities in this dangerous era, they prove a historical gold mine. These issues were so sensitive, in fact, and ultimately so potentially damaging to British exporters—and the language of these documents so potentially scathing toward Britain's allies—that records detailing these negotiations remained classified until nearly a decade after the end of the Cold War.

Churchill's policymakers knew that exuberant engine exports threatened

their own defense. An RAF committee asked to consider the security implications of axial-flow exports, for example, argued that to protect the Western military dominance, "no release of axial-flow jet engines should be
made to any nation or civil airline unless our own frontline squadrons will
have been substantially re-equipped with a superior type for two years."
Their recommendation fell short of the American standard wherein exports
were banned until two years after retirement from service, but their purpose
was the same: to deny enemy forces technology then in use by Western pilots. Britain's best hope for maintaining a viable military lead over the Soviet
Air Force was to adopt not a "perfect" security policy but rather "an ideal"
one, which restricted exports to "a few countries whose security is reliable
until the engines were no longer used in our front lines, or had been com-
promised, or until the Russians had independently reached a similar state of
development."[48]

An "ideal" security policy failed to meet the country's financial needs.
Policymakers based at the Treasury favored rejection of theoretical security
risks in deference to the country's quite real financial plight. "The risk of giving away, to our detriment, valuable information to the Russians is a real
one, but very difficult to assess" and even harder to quantify, one Treasury
official wrote. "On the other hand, we can almost be certain that a generally
restrictive security policy in this field would result in a very serious economic setback to this country in the important years ahead." Time was of
the essence, his colleague agreed. "The lead which we at present enjoy over
all other competitors must, in the nature of things, be short-lived, and if we
do not exploit it to the full we shall have lost, probably for ever, a unique opportunity of capturing a fair share of the world trade in aircraft in which
hitherto the Americans have had a virtual monopoly."[49]

With the Treasury arguing for sales, the RAF establishment lobbying for
security, and Makins and others in the Foreign Office hoping only to avoid
infuriating the Americans, Churchill ordered Defense Minister Alexander
to find a compromise solution. His committee chose a middle path, offering substantial restrictions not so much on the sale of British engines but
rather on their use, especially by commercial airlines. "My colleagues and I
weighed the security risk against the country's economic advantage and
need," he reported to the cabinet, and "we concluded that safeguards could
be imposed which would reduce the security risk sufficiently to warrant the
sales of these engines or aircraft in approved cases, thus enabling us to reap
the economic advantages of our technical lead." Britain would sell its en-

gines, but would force buyers to secure the technology themselves. Their controls included five major points, premised on denying communist access to British engines through loss or espionage:

No plane powered by or carrying an axial-flow engine could fly to or over communist territory.

For the engine's first 18 months of service, all scheduled maintenance must be carried out by British technicians on British territory.

All maintenance staff assigned to the plane must be screened for security.

All spare engines sent abroad must be shipped in British vessels.

Spare engines outside the United Kingdom must be held in British territory overseas and flown to foreign territory only when essential; or when housed in a foreign country, in a British owned building or military base.[50]

Policymakers initially considered mandating that spare engines overseas be chained and locked to the floor, the key held only by a British consulate official, but eventually determined this last requirement to be somewhat excessive. Ministers planned to screen buyers carefully for their ability to safeguard this strategic technology, and it went without saying that communist sympathizers would be barred from piloting such jets or working on their service crews. This was far from a perfect security policy that would eliminate the risk of technological diffusion; but in determining that approval of the full cabinet would be required for any axial-flow export (Comets included), Churchill's government at least ensured that they would not be blindsided by any unwarranted sale. It would be far easier to stand up to American opposition, they reasoned, if they had time to prepare their defense, and if they only defended sales that truly mattered. Alexander well knew the advantages of choosing one's battleground.

The cabinet expected vigorous American opposition to these new restraints, but no amount of pressure could keep them from pursuing monopolization of this all-important market. "The government look to the export of aircraft to contribute in increasing measure to the solution of the country's balance of payments problem," Alexander's committee concluded. "In all this, the axial flow engine is the key factor." De Havilland held firm orders from abroad for twenty-five Comet 2s, priced at £525,000 apiece, and predicted that at least ten more would be sold. Orders for £750,000 axial-flow Comet 3s were predicted to top one hundred. "Business of this order is of the utmost importance to the well being of the British aircraft industry, and no less to the country's external trade," the committee determined. "Obviously, Comet sales could only be set aside for the most compelling reasons of security." As Alexander explained, "Rigid adherence to the 'ideal' security policy would be to deny the export of modern axial flow jet engines for a good many years," which would "run directly counter to our economic interests." In London's balance of commerce versus security, commerce won. It had taken months to iron out the details of this conclusion; but its eventual victory had never been in doubt.[51]

Calculated Risks Are Never Justifiable

American negotiators reacted to this new policy as angrily as expected. Churchill's cabinet appeared to be repeating the mistakes of their predecessors, and American pilots had long endured the deadly consequences of flawed British calculations of sales and security. This time, however, the security of America's homeland was at stake. "The UK apparently considers almost every jet engine as eligible for release to third countries under appropriate safeguards," Elliott concluded, even those exported to commercial users. Such exports contradicted American security ideals, whereby the only possible justification for a risky export was military necessity. "The calculated risk implicit in the release of advanced gas turbine information for civil purposes is never justifiable," he wrote. Military sales made for the purpose of enhancing security were a different matter, since "it is necessary to assume the risk implicit in the release for military purposes of advanced gas turbines to nations in support of national security objections." Washington believed it could rely upon NATO militaries to rigidly enforce engine security. It had no such faith in commercial airlines.[52]

These divisions in Anglo-American aviation control reveal much about export security in the early 1950s. They tell us even more about British and American priorities. For the British, commercial concerns from the Treasury ultimately bested repeated warnings from military officials. Comet sales posed "a serious security risk," the RAF's chief stated, yet ministers could not forsake the plane's potential contributions to prosperity and to the ensuing vigorously Anglocentric foreign policy that prosperity allowed. American policymakers, who increasingly saw the globe swathed in the encroaching red of the communist menace rather than in Britain's imperial crimson, believed military security trumped all other concerns, despite the previous administration's frequent argument—the basis of aid packages such as the

Marshall Plan—that economic stability was security's true foundation. "Security risks should only be taken on the basis of military necessity," America's diplomats argued, as they considered "release of advanced gas engines for civil operational purpose" a "great security danger." Indeed, Britain's willingness to risk this danger prompted a sense of incredulity among Washington's engine negotiators. One declared he could not "believe that the UK has adequately taken into account the fact that these civilian derivatives are virtually the same as the RA-7 and RA-14 military types, and that the compromise of these derivatives through use by foreign civil airlines or otherwise would permit the Soviets to produce in a short period of time a military engine comparable in performance to that which we would be using for considerable time in our front line aircraft." In the American mind, "any safeguards for the protection of engines in the hands of foreign civil airlines would be meaningless."[53]

The Eisenhower administration's enthusiasm for exports to NATO of similar engines as then planned for the Comet further reveals key differences in Anglo-American conceptions of security control. American officials realized such exports hardly constituted an "ideal" security policy (though Washington increasingly preferred to speak in terms of "perfect security" as negotiations wore on), but believed some risks had to be assumed in order to meet, and beat, the communist threat. In their minds, NATO deserved the best equipment the West could offer. Indeed, given Soviet manpower advantages—Warsaw Pact armies were nearly three times the size of Western militaries in Europe—NATO needed every technological advantage it could find. If denied the West's best jets because of potential security hazards, there might not be a free Western Europe left to defend. "Strict military advantages of release override the security risks involved," America's negotiating team claimed.[54]

Britain's Defense Ministry believed such military sales to NATO allies were foolhardy in the extreme, far riskier than sale to any potential Comet customer. Communist infiltration made NATO security porous at best, and British analysts predicted a "fair risk" of engine loss to the Soviets with military exports to Belgium, Switzerland, and Venezuela. Military exports to France and Yugoslavia ranked as a "definite risk," while sales to Italy, Denmark, India, and Pakistan entailed "practical certainty of loss." To give axial-flow engines to air forces from these countries would be to expect that technological secrets, or worse yet samples of the engines themselves, would almost immediately flow across the iron curtain. One anonymous London policymaker even penciled in the margin of the report that it would be safer to park a Comet on Red Square outside the Kremlin walls than to follow Washington's plan to give axial-flow warplanes to the Italians. In sum, whereas their own restraints on Comet sales aimed to minimize the risk of technological diffusion, which no realistic export policy could ever hope to eliminate entirely, Alexander's experts concluded that America's plan for supplying advanced jets to NATO "will in our opinion lead *almost inevitably* to compromise of the engines by leakage of information to the Russians."[55]

Washington's disregard for the actual security of axial-flow technology in favor of a distinction between military and commercial sales therefore struck many in Whitehall as hypocritical, malicious, or both. "The fact that the Americans are purchasing off-shore for NATO countries which we regard as a bad security risk," Sir Humphreys-Davies of the Treasury observed, "exposes the falsity of their position." Their "motives are clearly suspect. This is shown only too clearly by the fact that they are prepared to sell our latest model aircraft to NATO countries which are a bad security risk while, at the same time, taking measures on security grounds which would hamper our own efforts to open up new export markets." But while the Americans were frequently blinded by rabid anticommunism, he warned, they were hardly stupid. Their tactics might be concealing a more sinister effort to hinder Britain's commercial efforts. Britain's Comet lead threatened America's grip on global aviation markets. Security restrictions that weakened Britain's export chances, even temporarily, by extension also shortened the duration of Britain's jetliner monopoly. "Nothing would please American aviation interest more than to tie up our aircraft sales efforts in security red tape," Chancellor of the Exchequer Richard "Rab" Butler was briefed. "This might give them the breathing space they need to catch up." This appeared to one minister as "a curious coincidence of security needs with American commercial interests," because "for the first time, we lead the world in aeronautical engineering. If we are held back on security grounds, it will provide a breathing space for the Americans to catch up." In his mind, "to call upon us to forgo these exports . . . is to ask us to be heavy losers."[56]

The question of whether Washington's rigid engine policies were motivated primarily by security (as the Americans claimed) or sales (as the British suspected) plagued Whitehall. The Eisenhower administration's efforts to limit British exports served both the Pentagon's and Boeing's interests, but if this was intended or coincidental they could not say. The American concern "is no doubt prompted by genuine security anxieties," one report to the cabinet signed by Minister of Defense Alexander said, but as "American officials admit, their aircraft industry is influential and eager to restrict foreign competition." Privately, at least, American officials conceded that NATO militaries were in fact equal, if not greater, security risks compared to many potential Comet users. "From the strict security standpoint," Elliott allowed during one meeting at the Pentagon, "there did not seem to be very much difference between UK civil release plans and some of the US jet engine commitments" to NATO air forces. His military aide was quick to point out the illuminating difference. Each type of sale posed a threat; but only one was morally justifiable. Security risks were warranted, he said, only when exports were made to enhance security. Sales made merely in the pursuit of profits failed to meet that standard.[57]

Limiting British exports did work to the express advantage of America's powerful aviation firms, but only if one viewed the international competition for aircraft markets as a zero-sum game. Despite its prevalence in British circles—and the ensuing assumption that Washington saw the world the same way—this was not the predominant American mindset in 1953. Britain led the world in jet aviation, and the Comet's early success had shocked many American observers out of their warm postwar cocoon in which American technologies existed without peer. Yet Boeing and other American firms believed that the race to aviation supremacy would be a long one, and they fully intended to profit from De Havilland's and BOAC's expensive lessons in the field and to triumph in the end. Rather than urge restraints upon the British, American companies instead lobbied the Truman and Eisenhower administrations for release of advanced engines for their own commercial models, even though these would not fly for at least another three years. Despite British fears to the contrary, no available record exists that suggests Boeing or Douglas ever lobbied for limits on Comet sales. Instead, they urged that engine and export restrictions be liberalized and ultimately lifted. Axial-flow technology was vital to the success of any airliner, British or American, and the last thing American firms wanted were restraints on their own civil airliners, which were but a few years away.

Alexander, for one, believed Washington's security tactics were merely a strategy for justifying future American sales. The Americans forbade the use of axial-flow engines in civil aircraft, he reasoned, in large part because they had none. "We do know however that the United States Government is under very heavy pressure from the powerful American aircraft industry" to authorize such uses for the future, he wrote Churchill. "This may become so strong that the government will have to give way." Britain's authorization of Comet sales therefore posed "a risk that the Americans would use the continuance of our present policy as an excuse for giving way to pressure from their own aircraft industry which would in any event have been irresistible whatever British policy might have been, at the same time giving anti-British elements good material for blackening our reputation." The British were in effect doing the administration's dirty work, justifying civil sales while allowing the Eisenhower administration to take the high road on the moral question of potentially risky sales. In letting the British move first, American policymakers would therefore gain the flexible security policy that American manufacturers really wanted, while maintaining their own hawkish image. We know from American records that this was not the case, and that Eisenhower's policymakers did in fact consider the Cold War a greater priority than maximizing commercial opportunities. Though it must be admitted that Alexander's analysis offers a beautifully Machiavellian logic, its greatest utility is in demonstrating just how deeply British policymakers had internalized fears of American competition.[58]

Washington's moves to date in this affair had infuriated and frustrated British strategists, but the Eisenhower administration's next move terrified them, proving the sincerity of American fears over unbridled axial-flow exports. Believing the British incapable of properly managing technologies that threatened the American heartland, Dulles's State Department tried to force London's hand. At their August 1953 meeting with Powell's team, American officials announced they would seek imposition of the Burns-Templer accord for the distribution of technologically advanced products. As mentioned above, the agreement declared certain products, if developed with input from both countries (philosophically, if not solely for copyright purposes), a "combined field" wherein their export to a third country required the express consent of *both* governments. America's diplomats argued that jet engines, which resulted from years of Anglo-American cooperation, were just such a combined field—and their distribution was therefore subject to American approval.

This demand required that British engine exports accede to American security controls, a proposal that carried tremendous implications for the Comet program. If Burns-Templer were enacted in this case, one Defense Ministry report read, it was "virtually certain that the U.S. would not agree to our planned exports of Comets II and III to foreign countries on the planned dates." Indeed, although the American proposal failed to mention

Comet exports specifically, British policymakers devoted almost the whole of their internal discussions of the matter to this aspect of the American proposal. In one discussion the cabinet learned that the American proposal meant that "before we could sell a Comet 2 or 3, we should have to get U.S. agreement and indeed their agreement would be necessary before we could put these aircraft into service on our own British airlines."[59]

"The fiercest American competition is just around the corner," the cabinet was told, and if Washington had its way, that American competition would enter the field on a par with Britain's own producers. Burns-Templer denied each country the right to export its engines without the other's permission, but it said nothing about authorizing the integration of advanced technologies into production models awaiting foreign sale. Therefore, analysts at the Ministry of Defense concluded, because "release of information to aircraft firms for civil planning purposes would be exempt from the proposed ban," the United States government could simply allow its firms to produce axial-flow jet aircraft for domestic use "and press for our agreement to declassify an engine at a stage that suited their [export] production plans." Given America's greater production strength, "when a particular engine already in military use was agreed by both sides to be no longer 'advanced,'" they would "be able to get [it] into civil operation more quickly than we could." In sum, if Britain accepted the American proposal, its lead in aviation would disappear, taking with it all of the government's aviation-inspired hopes.

Tired of failed diplomacy, with American security on the line, and with De Havilland salesmen scouring the free world for customers, Washington simply tried to impose its will on its closest ally. This draconian measure struck a sensitive nerve in London, where it was immediately interpreted as a direct assault against the crown jewel of Britain's postwar economic program, and thus a purposeful blow to British sovereignty. Faced with the choice between their patron and their most important export, Churchill convened his cabinet for a decision that, to their minds, directly affected the future of their country. The Americans had to know how crucial we consider the Comet, ministers told each other. How else to explain their effort to curtail it except as an attempt to restrain the very power and prosperity the British hoped to gain from it? "We are at an important crossroads," Alexander concluded. "There is at present an opportunity, which is not likely to recur, to capture an important and long-term market of the type on which this country must increasingly depend."[60]

"On the other hand, our policy does involve a real security risk, and pursuit of it may lead to a decrease in U.S. cooperation in other fields." This was, he calculated, "undoubtedly the most difficult problem in the whole field of arms exports." With that, the matter lay squarely in Churchill's lap. The two sides had battled over export controls and technological diffusion, over commercial opportunities and civil flights. Each foisted its worst conception of the other upon the other's moves. Now their divisions seemed at a climax. The British seemed perfidious to the Americans, morally deficient enough to willingly trade with the communists. Now they appeared ready to freely and apparently without compunction sell inherently dangerous technologies at a time when Western security seemed at stake. They threatened to make America vulnerable to atomic attack. America's closest ally, in other words, seemed intent upon undermining American security in the extreme.

To British eyes, first Truman's and now Eisenhower's administration appeared moralistic in tone and fanatical in their anticommunist crusade, but deviously Machiavellian at heart, hiding commercial opportunities behind the veil of Cold War considerations. In truth, both sides understood the other: Washington was driven by security concerns just as commerce drove London. But at the same time each side proved unable to justify their ally's actions within their own worldview. Security mattered most to Washington and commerce triumphed in London, and neither side could ever understand why the other refused to see the world their way. The Comet affair defined Anglo-American aviation diplomacy during the early Cold War. Whether Britain would win the race to jets after all, and whether the special relationship would survive that victory, remained to be seen. Far more than just sales were at stake. "We cannot," Alexander said, "avoid facing up to the fundamental issues of principle."[61]

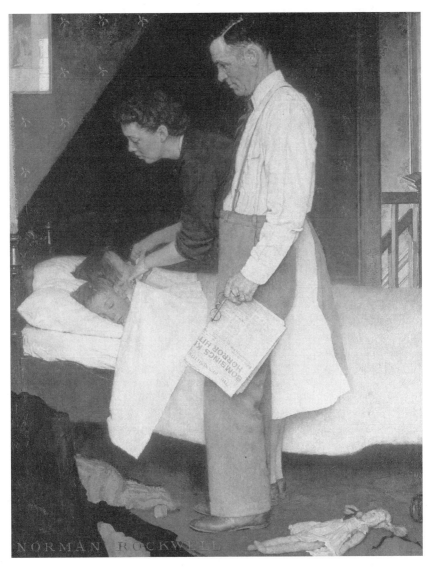

Freedom from Fear, one of Norman Rockwell's famous "Four Freedoms" images. The scene of American domestic tranquility is tempered only by the country's omnipresent fear of airpower, represented by the newspaper headlines "Bombings" and "Horror." (Printed by permission of the Norman Rockwell Family Agency, copyright ©1943 the Norman Rockwell Family Entities.)

American B-29 "Superfortress" bombers, pictured here on a bombing run during the Korean War. During the final months of World War II, American B-29s firebombed successive Japanese cities and ultimately dropped the atomic bombs on Hiroshima and Nagasaki. What such planes did to others, many Americans feared, they might one day do to the United States as well. (U.S. Air Force via National Air and Space Museum, Smithsonian Institution, SI 85-11309.)

Similarities between this Soviet-built Tupolev Tu-4 "Bull" bomber and the B-29 were not coincidental. The Soviets copied Superfortresses that crash-landed in Siberia during World War II—right down to the jerry-rigged ashtrays on the American planes—thus proving their ability to duplicate Western technology, if not to produce their own. (U.S. Air Force via National Air and Space Museum, Smithsonian Institution, SI 76-13911.)

St. Paul's Cathedral, rising from the smoke and flame of a German bombing run on London during the Battle of Britain. (A German plane is visible to the right of the main tower.) What Americans feared of airpower, the British knew all too well. (National Air and Space Museum, Smithsonian Institution, SI 85-7275.)

Chinese propagandists reveled in the success of their Soviet-built MiG-15 fighters during the Korean War. They even placed the image *(top right)* on postcards designed for public use.

Powered by copies of Britain's Nene engine, the Russian-built MiG-15 threatened Allied air superiority during the Korean War. This particular plane, pictured here on Okinawa with U.S. Air Force markings, was flown to Kimpo Air Base by a defecting North Korean pilot. A team of American pilots, including Chuck Yeager (the first man to fly faster than the speed of sound), subsequently fully tested the captured plane, proving that without its British-designed engine the plane would have been no match for American jets. (National Archives and Records Administration.)

The Vickers Viscount was one of Britain's aviation success stories during the 1950s. By 1961 its export—including its secret export of onboard American-licensed equipment in violation of Washington's export control laws—nearly brought about a new crisis in Anglo-American relations. Luckily for London, Washington never discovered the ruse. (National Air and Space Museum, Smithsonian Institution, SI 84-4447.)

Sleek, fast, and five years ahead of any American competition, the De Havilland DH-106 "Comet" was the crown jewel of Britain's postwar industrialization plans. Its export nearly brought the Anglo-American special relationship to a speedy halt. (BAE Systems Heritage—Farnborough.)

The Comet seemed to many the pinnacle of British technological achievement, and as this 1951 cover from *Flight and Aircraft Engineer* demonstrates, many within the British aviation industry believed the plane might help reestablish the country's imperial past. A full discussion of this image is offered in Chapter 4. (Reed Business Information Ltd.)

One of Boeing's most lucrative (and longest-running) ventures, the KC-135 jet tanker proved capable of keeping up with the Strategic Air Command's fastest and longest-ranging bombers. By the mid-1950s the Pentagon also allowed the company to cut costs by constructing tankers, as well as its similar 707 jet-liner, on parallel production lines. (Copyright © Boeing. Used under license.)

Similarities between this Boeing 707, shown here at its historic 1954 rollout for test flights, and the KC-135 *(top of page)* are no coincidence. Boeing engineers made their commercial venture profitable by implementing lessons learned in the tanker's construction, and by duplicating such important design components as the fuselage and wings. Britain's Royal Air Force could never dream of offering its civil manufacturers such a subsidy. (National Air and Space Museum, Smithsonian Institution, 83-16437.)

CHAPTER **5**

A Lead Lost

Britain's leaders were not about to let their long-sought aviation lead go without a fight. Neither were American leaders eager to have their closest ally jeopardize American security for the sake of profit. Washington's August 1953 proposal to have advanced axial-flow engines declared a Burns-Templer combined field received Whitehall's highest attention. Prime Minister Winston Churchill met repeatedly during October and November with a select committee, including his foreign secretary, the ministers of supply and defense, the chancellor of the exchequer, and the president of the Board of Trade, in search of some way to retain their country's freedom to export without disrupting the all-important special relationship. They could accept American demands and forgo a decade's effort that had brought British aviation to the brink of international success. Or they could reject Washington's security concerns, risking the loss of Western technological superiority and Anglo-American relations in the process. That Whitehall had promoted aviation in order to preserve its diplomatic independence made this decision particularly painful, as policymakers were left to weigh the freedom they desired against the special relationship they required. "We are faced with a clear alternative," the Defense Ministry's A. J. Edden warned. "Either we have to accept a serious security risk and possibly far-reaching repercussions on our relations with the Americans, or we have to face the loss over the next five years of the greater part of our expected exports of civil aircraft and, perhaps more important, of an opportunity (which is unlikely to recur) to establish a new, continuing and remunerative export market." In the British search for a great-power future in the air, this would be their decisive moment.[1]

At stake for the Americans was nothing less than the safety of their homes and, to their minds, the strategic balance of the Cold War. The Soviets exploded their first thermonuclear device in August 1953. They had mastered atomic energy four years before. Western intelligence services believed Soviet engineers had yet to produce efficient axial-flow engines, however, meaning that their most advanced jet bombers lacked the range to effectively reach targets throughout the continental United States. Moscow brandished a nuclear spear, in other words, but without a means of delivering it against the continental United States it lacked the full psychological and political benefits of its nuclear arsenal. Kremlin strategists yearned to level the nuclear playing field, either through improvements in their homegrown delivery systems or by repeating their Nene and B-29 reverse-engineering masterpieces. This time, of course, American bombers would not be landing inside Soviet territory, nor would Britain remake the mistake of selling engines directly to Moscow. Western analysts feared instead that Soviet agents would try to steal data on the new engines wherever they could, by infiltrating NATO bases where axial-flow military jets were housed, or by accessing axial-flow Comet 2s once they began service in 1954.[2]

To the American diplomats who demanded a halt to Comet 2 sales in August 1953, time was of the essence. Soviet engineers would eventually solve their deliverability problems, but as Eisenhower's diplomats reminded their British counterparts, they did not want careless sales to speed that moment even a single day. "Experience over the Rolls Royce Nene shows the Russians were able to produce in quantity in two years copies of the centrifugal flow engine." Especially now, John Elliott, director of the State Department's Office of Munitions Control announced, "with the revelation that the Soviets have the H-bomb, it seems to me that the most advanced means of carrying the bomb should be afforded greater protection than ever before."[3]

The restrictions advocated by the United States—functionally the demand for a veto over British jet exports—seemed to Whitehall strategists to guarantee not only loss of valuable markets but destruction of their aviation industry. "It would be a great mistake to accept the American proposal that research and development of advanced jet engines should be a combined field under the Burns-Templer agreement," Supply Minister Duncan Sandys told Churchill's advisory group, "[because] we seemed to be on the threshold of capturing the export market." To accept Washington's position would allow "the Americans time to catch up." This would mean "bankruptcy for certain aircraft firms"; it would "curtail the provision of adequate war potential which depended upon the continued prosperity of both civilian and military aircraft production"; and, said Sandys, "[It would] deny us chances of building up commonwealth air forces with types of British aircraft." Washington's proposal therefore seemed to guarantee America's victory in the zero-sum game of aviation competition, and ultimately meant "throwing away our present technical lead in this field," Alexander warned, "and the economic benefits that we hope to reap from it."[4]

For these policymakers obsessed with maintaining parity within the special relationship, Washington's proposal seemed an affront to their national sovereignty. "The decision [to export] must rest exclusively with Her Majesty's Government," Chancellor of the Exchequer Rab Butler declared, and on November 11, 1953—poignantly, Armistice Day—he and his colleagues voted unanimously to reject the American proposal. One unnamed British diplomat put the issue in the clearest terms possible. "I do not think we should acquiesce in the American assumption that they have any right to dictate to us what principles we should follow in the sale of our own aircraft," he wrote on a circulated memo. He need not have worried. Two days after the cabinet's decision, the Foreign Office officially advised De Havilland that it could continue its export drive unimpeded. "We shall continue to apply whatever safeguards and procedures can be devised to reduce the security risk," the message read, "short of frustrating exports."[5]

Churchill's advisers spent the remainder of their aviation discussions throughout the fall of 1953 divining the best method for handling Washington's expected heated response. The Eisenhower administration had never specifically described the consequences of British defiance, instead letting imagination undermine British confidence in a way specific threats never could have. Elliot repeatedly stressed the "urgency which the United States government attach[es] to this question," leading the Foreign Office to believe that the administration viewed the matter as a test case for Anglo-American security arrangements. Churchill worried rejection of American demands might poison the special relationship more broadly. There were "dangers in rejecting the Americans' proposals and in deciding to follow our own line in the export of these aircraft," he argued. "This would give them further grounds for criticizing our security." Given American sensitivities over aerial vulnerability, and Britain's recent bad press over the Nene and the CAT affair, Congress would most likely respond to news of Britain's intransigence by slashing foreign aid. Worse yet, Churchill feared, revelation of Britain's decision to jeopardize American security might even prompt a new American isolationism and "induce them to retreat from their European commitments and to pursue what they call a system of peripheral defense," leaving Europe naked before the Russians. Ambassador Roger Makins concurred, believing open defiance might ultimately disrupt the whole of Atlantic relations. "I hope that there are no misconceptions at home about the explosive nature of this issue here," he reminded the Foreign Office. "It has nothing in common with the sale of the Nene engine to the Russians," but could "very easily be represented as a repetition of it [the Nene] by persons of ill will in this country, and as a further example of our perennial disregard for security and of our readiness to subordinate anything for economic gain." He agreed the cabinet had no choice but to pursue lucrative sales wherever they arose, but added, "I must warn you there may be trouble ahead."[6]

These were prescient warnings. American policymakers reacted angrily to Britain's decision to proceed with Comet sales despite the risks involved. Yet the Pentagon continued with its plans to outfit NATO air forces with axial-flow-driven fighters beginning in the spring of 1954 (or at the same time as the first Comet 2 exports), despite the risk the exports posed of inadvertent Soviet acquisition of axial-flow technology. The Americans willingly accepted such risks, believing Western military pilots deserved the best technologies available and that allies would be more likely to fight for their own defense if properly equipped. "We want the aircraft to be flown by non-Americans to fight Russians," Najeeb Halaby, deputy assistant secretary of defense, told the Senate. American officials consequently accepted the risks of exporting for defense, even as they rejected Britain's exports for profit. "The calculated risk implicit in the release of advance gas turbine information for civil purposes is never justifiable," Elliott's team concluded, even though "it is necessary to assume the risk implicit in the release for military purpose of advanced gas turbines to nations in support of national security objectives." It was not that the military or commercial exports were more or less likely to risk Western technological superiority, it was that only military sales could be justified in Washington's Cold War universe.[7]

This American tendency to view international problems in such clear-cut moral terms fostered a split between Atlantic allies, because the British brought a different value system to bear. They valued commerce on a par with security. Indeed, they believed true security impossible without a solid economic foundation. Churchill's policymakers applied their own world-view to Washington and thus incorrectly saw crass commercialism in the State Department's sanctimonious stand. Available evidence points to the contrary. Boeing and Douglas each lobbied incessantly throughout 1953 and 1954 for a more liberal export control line, hoping to sell their own axial-flow-driven airliners before the end of the decade. The companies wanted export restraints kept to the bare minimum, even for the British, lest the precedent of government controls hinder their own pursuit of potential buyers.

Administration officials rebuffed these overtures at every turn. They truly believed that widespread axial-flow exports for commercial consumers threatened American security, and thus rigidly opposed the efforts of these powerful corporate interests. How long they could maintain this stance, once the Boeing 707 or Douglas's DC-8 were ready for market, remained a question of great concern to strategists like Elliott. In early December he privately warned Richard Powell, his British counterpart, that London's dogged pursuit of Comet sales undermined his government's ability to constrain its own firms. "If we stick to our present line" in support of vigorous advanced-engine sales, Powell consequently warned Downing Street of Elliott's fear, "the US government will feel bound to give way to the pressure which their aircraft industry is putting upon it. If this is so, there is obviously a danger that our lack of security consciousness, or whatever the right term is, may be quoted as an excuse" for a more liberal policy down the road. If Britain insisted upon a race to the bottom over aviation security, the Eisenhower administration would have no choice but to follow, and Powell believed this was a race his country would eventually lose.[8]

Despite his central role in shaping them, Elliott was not satisfied with his own government's security policies, either, which struck him as problematic bordering on hypocritical. While refraining from endorsing the export of axial-flow engines, the administration allowed Boeing and Douglas and the like to incorporate these engines into their aircraft designs, while simultaneously chiding the British for their "premature" exports of axial-flow types. He considered it naïve to believe that his government would subsequently restrain American firms from selling fully functioning jets, developed at the cost of tens of millions of dollars. To allow their development while planning for their embargo or restraint seemed to him akin to sewing dragon's teeth for a future showdown between Washington and two of its most important companies. It was not only bad policy, he repeatedly told his negotiating team, but also unwise diplomacy, giving the "impression that the US had shifted its emphasis regarding civil releases towards more liberal releases to US airliners" for the future. "If this were true," he "did not see how the US could protest UK civil releases on security grounds," especially since "from the strict security viewpoint there did not seem to be very much difference between UK civil release plans and some of the US jet engine commitments" for NATO.[9]

Elliott's military aide quickly reframed the issue in response, which was never purely about engine security or Western technological superiority. Neither was it about which types of sales would most jeopardize American homes or which nations had jets to sell. Everyone knew NATO was rife with communists, and it was only a matter of time before the Soviets attained axial-flow technology. The real question at stake in this brewing Anglo-American crisis was therefore not how to achieve the panacea of perfect security, but rather what types of sales justified their risk. The real issue was defining what actions allies would take, or would curtail, for the sake of their common cause. The Korean War had ended only months before. Red forces seemed on the move throughout the world, and demagogues saw communists around every corner at home as well. Now was the moment when Western forces had to do all they could to keep technologically ahead, and achieving victory naturally required assuming some risks. Winning the Cold War justified security risks. Winning markets did not. "These questions could only be answered by weighing military needs against security risk," he said. "On this basis, UK civil releases were not justified, whereas US military releases were on the grounds of military necessity." When Elliott complained again of his "disadvantageous [negotiating] position with the British in insisting that they desist from planning to compromise the civilian use of advanced engines when we were placing engines in the hands of foreign military establishments," his aide once more offered the same response. "The Air Force . . . did not intend to barter with the UK on the basis of the US abandoning important defense or military objectives and programming obsolete or inadequate equipment for our potential allies in order to induce the UK to refrain from committing exports of jet engines for profit." Military and commercial exports were two separate things. The first was justified; the latter was not. One was moral, the other perfidious. It was a question of values: whether one valued standing up to the communists around the world and at home as well, and whether one was willing to put a price on security. For most American policymakers, this question required no debate at all, save wonderment that the British did not see things the same way.[10]

Why Technology Does, and Does Not, Matter

Diplomats from both countries recognized the difficulties of their positions, yet neither saw fit in the coming months to temper them for the sake of allied unity. Each side believed they held the moral high ground; each thought themselves the more pragmatic as well. "Neither the Americans nor ourselves are on completely firm ground in this argument," Alexander conceded. Comet sales threatened Western security, but so too did the Pentagon's export plans. "The Americans are prepared to supply these aircraft and engines to NATO countries, such as Italy and Denmark, whose security we regard as extremely bad," and "such supplies will in our opinion lead almost inevitably to compromise of the engines by leakage of information to the Russians." His country thus faced the unfortunate predicament that pursuit of their independent line threatened their most fundamental relationship, whereas adherence to Washington's leadership risked the genuine diminishment of British security. This was not a happy predicament.[11]

Churchill, who had spent much of his career enthralled by American power and eager to pursue Britain's interests through close connection with it, sought an eleventh-hour solution. With negotiations at an impasse, but with the date of the first Comet 2 export fast approaching, he proposed taking the matter directly to Eisenhower, believing their friendship might help smooth out their governments' differences. Makins immediately scuttled this plan. To raise the matter to the level of the Oval Office ensured a decision while providing Eisenhower an opportunity to instigate a grand discussion of Britain's Cold War failings. It was "better to play the matter long," Makins instead advised, providing De Havilland time to capitalize on its lead and avoiding Eisenhower's rebukes entirely. "For us to transfer the question from the technical to the political level would indicate that we can see no solution to the problem and would merely bring the issue to a head." Such discussions would "aggravate the danger of a leak from the Pentagon, probably to one of their pet Congressmen." If the American public perceived that Britain was risking American security for the sake of sales, "the fat would then be in the fire."[12]

Despite near-constant discussion of this contentious issue throughout Whitehall, an omnipresent concern impressive not least for the government's ability to keep the affair secret for nearly a half century, British policymakers never addressed one of its central points: whether the Burns-Templer accords actually applied to this case. No government committee ever explored Washington's claim that axial-flow technology was a joint Anglo-American product. Neither did any of Eden's diplomats suggest rejecting this claim as a stalling tactic. American policymakers similarly ignored the technical merits of the question of whether engines were actually a joint Anglo-American product.

The question of joint Anglo-American ownership of this technology was not so much unimportant for the policymakers who faced this crisis, as it was to their minds irrelevant and moot. Its omission by both camps prompts two conclusions. First, diplomats are rarely technical experts. Their expertise lies more in promoting and formulating policies than in understanding high technologies. Having been told to argue that engines were or were not a joint product, they did as instructed, regardless of the technical merits of their case. Elliott never asked his team for irrefutable evidence that America's Burns-Templer claim was true. Neither did Britain's Powell ever demand such evidence from him. This omission suggests that the Burns-Templer agreements were merely the avenue American policymakers used to broach the difficult subject of engine security with their British counterparts, and that their British counterparts—who had, of course, already raised the Burns-Templer issue in 1952 when they had initially feared American restraints would be too lax—recognized the supremacy of politics in this question. Indeed, no available American document addressed whether engines were subject to Burns-Templer controls in the first place.

British sources are nearly as uninterested in this question. At least one British document, written in 1952 before the first Comet sales, described axial-flow technology as a joint Anglo-American product, concluding: "US and UK technology in this field cannot be disassociated from each other." If this document is to be believed, therefore, Washington had the right to veto such engine exports. Such details mattered hardly at all to the diplomats, though, because despite the centrality of this question to the Comet engine debates, what mattered most to the men and women charged with advocating their country's policies were issues of safety and sovereignty. Even in a case premised on technical distinctions involving thrust ratios, bomber range, airspeed, and the like, technical policies were ultimately determined by politicians and diplomats. Their tools come measured, not in pounds per square inch, but rather in worldviews, power calculations, and emotions.[13]

The Comet dispute accordingly mattered less to the technological development of British and American aviation than to the larger breakdown of trust within the Anglo-American relationship. American policymakers found in this diplomatic crisis renewed reason to doubt Britain's Cold War commitment. The affair left a far more lasting mark in British circles, where policymakers became increasingly aware that the Americans were not posturing when they advocated a harsh security line over commercial possibilities. Security really did matter to Washington more than sales, even with Boeing and Douglas primed to enter the market. This realization troubled British leaders, who perceived once more that Washington's hawkishness—as exposed yet again through Washington's risky endorsement of dangerous exports to dubious NATO allies—posed as great a long-term threat as Soviet aggression. "The main trouble with the American people at the moment is 'fear,'" Makins wrote home in March, "fear of themselves and their new responsibilities. Fear above all of what is vaguely and loosely called 'communism.'" The country seemed caught up in the fiery search for the red menace, and Makins worried the engine affair might strike a sensitive nerve in such a period of rampant McCarthyite red-baiting. "Ministers have underrated the serious effects on our relations with the United States Administration of their decision to insist on the export of these engines."[14]

Eisenhower knew well British anxieties over American anticommunism. The two countries had already squabbled over relations with China and over Washington's threat to use atomic weapons during the Korean War, and in March 1953, Eisenhower responded to Dulles's reminder that British leaders wanted to discuss "atomic issues" by noting that "what they really want to know is that we are not starting a war." Yet despite his awareness of British fears, he seemed to deepen their concern at every turn. In early February 1954, for example, with the Comet affair still unresolved, Eisenhower wrote Churchill a particularly haunting personal message. "More and more I come to the conclusion that the salvation of liberty rests upon the unremitting effort of all of us to establish a solidarity among ourselves that in major objectives and purposes will remain firm against any assault," the president wrote, and the free world must be "always faithful to our pledges." Ike did not explicitly mention jet engines in this or any other personal correspondence with Churchill. Yet the prime minister well knew that a "faithful" American partner would not endanger its allies for profit. Allies "faithful" to Eisenhower's leadership, moreover, understood the true nature of their common foe. "Our consortium must rest solidly upon a common understanding of the Russian menace," the president continued. "It is only when one allows his mind to contemplate momentarily such a disaster for the world [a communist victory] and attempts to picture an atheistic materialism in complete domination of all human life, that he fully appreciates how necessary it is to seek renewed faith and strength from his God, and sharpen up his sword for the struggle that cannot possibly be escaped."[15]

Such late-night ramblings from the world's most powerful man terrified Britain's leaders. Caught between the world's two atomic powers, London wanted peaceful coexistence and time to renew their battered economy more than the readying of weapons. Churchill immediately showed the letter to Eden, who described Eisenhower's reference to swords as the "one phrase in the letter which should not be allowed to pass unchallenged," because "taken by themselves, these words can undoubtedly be taken as meaning that President Eisenhower thinks that a war with the Soviet Union cannot be escaped and that we should build up our armaments with that in mind." This was simply not how the Cold War was viewed in Britain. "It may be that he is indulging in a general and informal 'thinking aloud,'" Eden continued, and if so the letter could safely be ignored. Even so, he suggested the following response:

> I agree especially with the grave words you use at the end of your letter about the faith which must inspire us in the struggle against atheistic materialism. I take it that you are referring there to the spiritual struggle. Otherwise your words might suggest that you believe war to be inevitable. I certainly do not think so and I am sure you do not either.

Eisenhower ultimately admitted to exaggerated rhetoric, and promised Dulles he would never again write allies so late into the night. Both leaders let the matter drop, never discussing it again.[16]

Yet Ike's sentiments left their mark. They seemed his real feelings, unvarnished by the more cautious Dulles, the kind of sentiments approaching truth that nighttime and the time to weigh important matters frequently evoked in Eisenhower. It was such conviction, seemingly rampant throughout Washington and what the British might term "righteousness," that prompted many within Churchill's government to argue that the Americans could no longer be trusted to safely lead the free world's anticommunist fight. The Comet case seemed proof of this argument. A growing chorus of British strategists concluded that Washington's refusal to consider Britain's economic needs when judging the matter alleviated Whitehall's obligation to consider American security at all. Chief among these critics was Reginald Jones, Whitehall's director of scientific intelligence. Jones had played a key role in developing the crucial radar systems that had tracked incoming German bombers during the war, and contemporary observers on both sides of the Atlantic dubbed him the "father of scientific intelligence." The Central Intelligence Agency even named a lifetime achievement award in his honor in the late 1990s, an honor they might have reconsidered had they known what advice he gave forty years before when Churchill personally asked him to review the Comet case and to chart Britain's subsequent course.[17]

From the first, Jones endorsed the cabinet's decision to proceed with Comet sales. Only Britain had jet airliners to sell in 1953, and he believed that delaying exports even for one day risked "losing a perhaps unique chance of capturing the market." This was an argument the cabinet had already heard and accepted. Jones's real contribution lay in his consideration of how Comet sales might affect Britain's future. He concluded that the Cold War itself offered three general possibilities: "armed peace, limited war of the Korean type, [or] total war." Coincidentally, American policymakers operating under Eisenhower's direct instruction and without input from their European allies had recently discerned three similar possible futures in their own top-secret "Project Solarium," so named because its deliberations began at the president's request in the White House sunroom. Yet whereas the Americans considered issues such as preemptive war and communist rollback, each predicated on Soviet or American action, Jones focused instead on Britain's secondary role in the superpower struggle. He concluded that no matter what path the global juggernauts chose, unrestrained aviation sales seemed Britain's only logical choice. "If there is to be armed peace, we should obviously proceed to sell as many civil aircraft engines as possible," since "the only danger would be if our [commercial] rivals were to copy our designs and sell them more cheaply." If the Cold War never turned hot, he reasoned, the Soviets would never find the opportunity to employ their latest military technologies. Britain would only have hurt itself if it limited sales in order to ensure technological security for a war that never occurred.[18]

Peace thus offered little reason for Britain to limit sales, but neither did war. Jones calculated that export restrictions would make little difference if the future brought limited conflicts such as the Korean War, even if Soviet forces co-opted British technology. "The outcome in Korea was not substantially altered by the intervention of the MiG-15," he concluded, since in their "hurry to get into production," the Soviets had not been able to complement the plane's powerful engine with similarly advanced avionics or armaments. "The truth must be that superiority in air warfare depends on several factors," with engines being only one. So long as Britain continued to advance all fields of aeronautics, he reasoned, Whitehall had nothing to fear from exports of one kind, and much to gain from the lucrative trade. Of course, this was the same logic of British engineering superiority that had led to the 1946 Nene sale in the first place.[19]

Neither armed peace nor limited war seemed to Jones sufficient to warrant export restraints on engines of the kind likely to kill the Comet program, and his advice turned fatalistic as he considered his third possibility, total war. Here his deductions are of the greatest use. Even in the air age, he believed geography would determine Britain's ultimate destiny as it had throughout history. Bombs fell on London in World War I and nearly destroyed Britain's cities in World War II. "If total war occurs" in the Cold War, he concluded, "we in Great Britain will probably be so violently attacked sooner or later that we shall not be able to prevent many atomic bombs from being dropped on us, whether the Russians are able to copy our latest engines or not." Destruction was inevitable no matter what engine restrictions Britain imposed, because the country already lay within the enemy's range. And if the bombs did fall, "we should henceforward have no further interest in any problem, and we might therefore just have well enjoyed the profits from selling our engines in the years left to us." This was a carpe diem of the geopolitical sort. Perched within range of even antiquated Soviet bombers, atomization seemed assured. Security restraints would therefore matter little to Britain's chances of survival (which were already nil), and would in fact hinder British prosperity for no purpose. Safeguarding against Armageddon meant little if the end result would inevitably be the same. Because safeguards would prove inconsequential for British security, its planemakers should sell all they could, while they could! In the final analysis then, no matter what the future might bring, Britain should sell without delay. Churchill's chief advisers welcomed Jones's paper, especially as it supported the conclusion they had already reached. The prime minister ordered Jones's advice widely distributed. So long as Britain's fate remained their primary concern, it provided the rationale for sales without restraint.[20]

It was only when policymakers showed concern for American security that engine restraints made sense, and they soon realized that America's sense of security might itself prove Britain's ultimate downfall. Jones and his cadre might have taken their responsibilities to safeguard American security more seriously had Washington been a more thoughtful ally, but to their mind Britain's best hope lay, not in maximizing survivability during a superpower war, but rather in ensuring a stable peace. This meant not only countering the Soviets but tempering the Americans as well. In the final analysis, sales and the long-standing promise of the Brabazon program mattered most to British policymakers, as did their recognition that British security—or lack thereof—would be unaffected by their export decisions. But these same policymakers also balked at sacrificing their prosperity and independence for the sake of an ally who seemed indifferent to their unique economic or political needs. Paradoxically, it seemed that America's sense of vulnerability—or lack thereof—most threatened British safety. Britain would be bombed in any future war. That much seemed certain. But while temporarily safe (if fearful) behind their ocean moats, America would eventually face the same fate once Soviet engineers solved their deliverability problems. Many of Churchill's advisers believed that on that day of true American vulnerability, Britain would become more secure. A truly vulnerable United States might be less bombastic in tone and less belligerent in its desire to wage the Cold War with vigor, lest their brinkmanship and bluster lead to Armageddon on American shores. It was easy to be belligerent when safe behind a wall, after all. Proximity to danger most often had a calming effect. Britain faced sure destruction in war, thus its policymakers promoted coexistence, believing there was no other sane choice. Churchill's advisers recognized Washington's fears of aerial attack, its preference for security over commerce, and America's broader tendency to see the Cold War as a crusade. They simply did not agree with any of it, and they secretly longed for Washington to experience the world just a bit more as they, Europe, and the rest of humanity forced to live on the Cold War's front lines did. "Americans, in view of their geographical position," Supply Minister Sandys remarked to a visiting French official, "had a very special interest in safe-guarding technical information which might result in increasing the range of Russian bomber aircraft." In the final analysis, Britain's best hope for saving the peace lay not in enhancing American safety, but rather in assiduously undermining it. Comet sales, and technology diffusion across the iron curtain, might ultimately make the world a safer place. Being perfidious, in other words, and favoring commerce over security in a quest for profits, was actually a strategy for survival.[21]

In yet another sign of how these two intimate allies traveled on opposite tracks in the midst of the Comet affair, while British leaders thought peace might require taking the Americans down a notch, some American leaders thought this current strain within the special relationship resulted from Britain's faltering military spirit. Perhaps the United States could loan the RAF some of its long-range B-47 bombers, Defense Secretary Charles Wilson suggested, believing the ability to strike the Soviets directly "might get their courage up." Dulles and Eisenhower agreed. Transferring such advanced bombers might prove logistically difficult, but both men sought something to buck up their major European allies, chiefly the British. "I have a certain sense of discouragement due to the fact that it is impossible to get off the ground the more dynamic and bolder policies which I felt were necessary when I took on this job," Dulles privately told C. D. Jackson, one of Eisenhower's advisers, in the spring of 1954. "At every turn we are blocked by the fact that our principal allies are not willing to take any risks." Dulles wanted allies who would risk their fortunes and even their peace to defeat global communism. "Nations, like individuals, cannot live to themselves alone," he later said, and the United States was "unsympathetic to assertions of sovereignty which do not accept the concept of social interdependence." His view of social interdependence, while laudable, was narrow. He rejected assertions of sovereignty that cut against his primary policies, the retention of American leadership chief among them, and to that end he wanted British compliance on American terms. What he found instead was a global partner willing to risk American security for the sake of profit and for the cause of creating the very type of independence—and in turn the very sort of geopolitical challenge—to American power that he wished to avoid.[22]

The Comet debate stood at a stalemate by spring of 1954, though it remained far from the public eye. Intensive classification by both nations ensured it would stay that way for nearly a half century. The Eisenhower administration proved unwilling to bring the matter to a head before the Comet 2s were ready for delivery, and unsure what course they might pursue if Britain proceeded with the sale despite their heartfelt objections. Across the Atlantic, Churchill's successful policy of delay, while anxiety-provoking in Whitehall, provided De Havilland with sufficient time to wrap up several important contracts overseas, making it increasingly unlikely that the government would ever bow to American pressures. "Things have gone too far," one British diplomat concluded, "for there to be any chance of our changing our minds about the Comet 2 for any reason likely to arise from discussions with the Americans." The issue continued to occupy Washington's diplomatic attention, though Elliott reminded his superiors that the Foreign Office's first priority "was to retain its freedom of action." With the British he appeared less understanding, implying that Eisenhower and Dulles were both losing patience with London's incessant delays over an issue they considered "one of the utmost importance in Anglo-American defense relations." Senators Stuart Symington and Styles Bridges, both hawkish anticommunists, added to Foreign Office fears in March when they embarked on a ten-day visit of Britain's aircraft factories. Whitehall believed the two sought evidence of communist infiltration. Finding little sign of the red menace they eventually cut their trip short, though not before attending a Billy Graham revival in London. This was further proof, it seemed to their hosts, of Washington's crusading brand of anticommunism. "Americans may think the time past when they need consider the feelings or difficulties of their allies," Eden complained to Makins after learning that Washington had yet again rejected British arguments for a liberal jet engine policy. "It is the conviction that this tendency becomes more pronounced every week that is creating mounting difficulties for anyone in this country who wants to maintain close Anglo-American relations."[23]

Bolts from the Blue

Everything changed on April 8, 1954. A Comet exploded in midair, only moments after departing Rome, leaving no survivors. Sadly, this was not the first such mishap. Eleven passengers and crew had died in March 1953 when a Comet failed to become airborne on takeoff. Two months later, forty-three lives were lost when a Comet disintegrated in a thunderstorm over Calcutta. Investigators concluded that the plane's overloaded tail and the violent weather contributed to its demise, just as they found similar seemingly fixable problems to blame for the March accident. Corrections were made, and Comet flights resumed. In January 1954, only six months later, another Comet exploded, again only minutes after takeoff. Thirty-five people perished. Unlike the others, this tragedy occurred in broad daylight and in perfect weather. Witnesses reported hearing three explosions, leading investigators to presume sabotage, though the similarity with the previous loss prompted the Air Ministry to ground Comets worldwide pending a complete investigation. The planes were authorized to resume flights only in March 1954, following improvements to the fuel and fire-suppression systems.[24]

The April 1954 tragedy outside Rome was therefore the fourth fatal Comet crash in little more than a year, and three seemed disturbingly similar, with the plane exploding without warning as it climbed for altitude. Painstaking research, precipitated by an unprecedented Royal Navy salvage program that retrieved the wreckage of the second downed Comet from nearly one hundred feet of water, soon blamed an unforeseen type of metal fatigue as the culprit. The pressures of jet flight had caused microscopic cracks in the metal sheeting surrounding the planes' fuselage. When these split, typically in the midst of the rapid pressure change associated with takeoff, the doomed plane imploded. There was no warning of danger. Neither was there any hope of survival.

No one had predicted this problem. Previous experience with jet aeronautics had involved military planes whose useful airborne lifespan rarely topped a thousand flying hours. Normal training might place these planes in the air for two or three hours a day. The economics of commercial flight demanded far more flight time, up to fifteen hours daily coupled with numerous stops, straining the fuselage each time the plane changed altitude and pressure. In other words, the Comets were subjected to unprecedented pressures, and they suffered for it.[25]

The Air Ministry grounded the entire fleet following the April crash. Most Comet 1s never flew commercially again. It would be nearly four more years before the next generation of redesigned Comets took to the air, with wings and fuselages designed to withstand the strains of commercial flight. In the meantime, De Havilland lost £15 million in suddenly worthless spare parts and specialized machine tools. More importantly, it lost the hard-won lead in jet aviation deemed so vital to its success. Such a crushing blow "nearly flattened the place," one employee recalled. To its credit, the firm freely offered information gleaned from the Comet disasters to other manufacturers, including Boeing and Douglas, so that their planes might avoid a similar fate. Grounded too were the axial-flow-powered Comet 2s, which employed the same tragically flawed fuselage as the original. Britain's lead in jet aviation never recovered. Writing five years later, after American jets had swept De Havilland from the market, Prime Minister Harold Macmillan's private secretary added the final blunt word. "The Comet would have been a world-beater, if it had not exploded in mid-air."[26]

The pressure of impending axial-flow Comet flights was gone by April 1954, but then, only weeks later, occurred something else with even greater consequences for the special relationship: America became a reachable target. At the climax of the Soviet Union's annual May Day military parade, after waves of tanks and troops had passed the Kremlin walls, a mammoth bomber suddenly appeared in the sky. It circled alone above the cheering crowd and assembled foreign dignitaries, joined moments later by the remainder of its squadron. Another squadron then flew by. Then another. It was a massive display of airpower, a public statement of Soviet nuclear might. Witnesses on the ground could clearly make out the plane's four rounded engines. Smuggled photos subsequently confirmed the worst. Not only did these engines appear to be axial-flow, but if the calculations derived from the grainy images proved correct, they were more powerful than the Comet 2's Avons. British and American analysts simultaneously concluded that engines like these would finally give Soviet planes the range to effectively reach targets throughout the continental United States.[27]

This later proved to be a less dramatic development than it first appeared, as the Soviet air force had in fact repeatedly flown its limited fleet of bombers over the crowd at Red Square in order to give the impression that they wielded a full fleet of such planes, when in truth they possessed merely a handful. The ruse worked, however, and thus began the infamous "bomber gap," the presumptive Western fear of Soviet strategic bomber superiority. No matter who was ahead, and no matter how large the Soviet fleet, one thing was clear to the policymakers charged with safeguarding Western aviation technology: the Soviets had caught up. "The new heavy jet bomber of the Soviet Union is in its form and in its characteristics comparable with our own B-52," Air Force Chief of Staff General Nathan Twinning admitted. "Despite our best efforts, the Reds have shown the world that they are in possession of a jet bomber of a similar type." Symington demanded from the Senate floor to know why the White House was not doing more to secure America's aerial frontiers. "If we are to survive in this dangerous world, the people must know the brutal truth about the growing military strength of the Communists," he declared. "Why have not the American people been shown pictures of the new Communist long-range jet bomber which was recently displayed over Moscow?" British analysts proved less bombastic. When asked by Alexander to comment on the potential impact of the new Soviet bomber, Vice-Marshall F. J. Fressanges scribbled hard in reply (so hard he tore a hole where pen met paper): "It *IS* Axial Flow!" No further comment seemed necessary.[28]

These twin developments, the Comet disasters and the appearance of an axial-flow Soviet bomber, dramatically altered the landscape of Anglo-American engine negotiations and demonstrated once more the fallacy that Western policymakers could defeat Soviet aerial developments by controlling their own exports. The nearly three-year exercise had been designed to keep axial-flow technology from communist hands. Now the Soviets possessed such technology of their own. The mistakes of the Nene had been avoided, yet as Alexander was briefed, "the appearance of a four-engined jet bomber in the May Day parade indicates that, by some means or other, the Russians have succeeded in producing an aircraft of a type which we had previously thought they were incapable of making."[29]

News of this new Soviet bomber did little to change the Foreign Office's negotiating strategy with Washington. Whitehall did not use its appearance as cause to cancel their ongoing negotiations with the Americans over engine security, for example. This was partly because their continuing faith in Britain's technological superiority made them believe some form of export control for advanced engines remained necessary, as it seemed inevitable that Soviet engineers would benefit from access to Western designs. What they resisted, of course, were controls of the intensity proposed by the Americans. "The appearance of the new Russian bomber has introduced a new factor" into Anglo-American engine negotiations, the Defense Ministry's Jim Honi argued, while Powell believed the bomber "very materially altered the nature of the problem" of strategic controls. He did not believe its appearance eliminated the need for Western controls, however, especially because "one cannot discount the possibility that the Russians have simply got this aircraft into the air for propaganda purposes with engines which are good enough to enable it to make show in a parade but which would be inadequate for operational purposes." So deep-seated was British disdain for Soviet technological capabilities that the official report on the engine situation given to Churchill in August 1954 refused, despite overwhelming evidence, to grant Moscow credit for its achievement. The Soviet engine "may be a native Russian design, possibly assisted by their German collaborators, but it might be a scaled-up version of one of the American engines captured in Korea." Even with pictures of the plane on their desks, Churchill's advisers still concluded, "It is impossible to say whether the Russians have so mastered axial flow 'know-how' as to have produced [such] an engine." For policymakers determined to maintain technological superiority, admitting Soviet accomplishments simply proved too much.[30]

American officials also did not consider revelation of the Soviet bomber reason to halt negotiations with the British, but for different reasons. The British believed restraints continued to be necessary in order to minimize Soviet technological progress. While Elliott's team agreed with this goal, they again proved determined to insert their own ethic of risk assessment into export decisions, hoping in the process to break once and for all Britain's penchant for independent strategic thinking. The Comet crashes pushed the question of engine exports to the back burner (it would be years before a commercial jetliner would again be ready for export), but to their minds this unfortunate and unsatisfying end to the Anglo-American dispute did little to solve the fundamental issues at stake: the British had proved willing to compromise security for profit, and willing as well to disregard Washington's leadership. Indeed, American officials believed the new Soviet bomber only buttressed their argument that military security alone justified security risks, because proof of advanced Soviet aircraft demanded even more advanced NATO machines to counter them. Such American demands for technological superiority in the Cold War, if taken to their logical conclusions, were endless. The communists were ever advancing; there could be no respite either in Western progress or vigilance. "With the very serious threat from the Soviet air developments revealed to be far ahead of earlier US evaluations," Mutual Security Director Harold Stassen wrote Secretary of Defense Charles Wilson in July, "it seems to me fundamental that the maximum encouragement of all advanced modern free world" air forces "should be a major element of US policy." The United States should plow ahead with military exports to NATO and vital allies broadly. "Less fundamental considerations," such as commercial exports, "should not be permitted to cut across this basic security objective."[31]

It was as if the negotiations of the previous two years had never occurred. "While security objectives must be accepted for compelling military reasons and to accomplish national military objectives," Elliott's team concluded in the fall of 1954, "such risks do not have to be accepted for commercial purposes and to further profit-making venture." By the close of the year, neither side proved willing or capable of altering their fundamental position. Just as in 1952, the British believed issues of sovereignty and finance demanded the freedom to export; the Americans believed Cold War military considerations trumped the search for sales.[32]

That the two sides did not change did not mean that they did not learn. The British recognized the lengths they would go to safeguard their sovereignty against incursions imposed by the special relationship, while the Americans learned the depth of their passion for security. That the Comet affair never forced a full break in Anglo-American relations was fortuitous for both nations, though it was fate, in the form of the Comet tragedies and the unexpected revelation of a Soviet axial-flow threat, that ultimately saved the special relationship. While fateful events pushed this divisive issue to the rear, by 1954 the die had already been cast. Churchill's government had decided to break with Washington, if necessary, for the sake of Comet sales and for the prosperity and independent power they promised. Despite Churchill's fear that Washington might adopt a more isolationist tone in response, and despite the cabinet's fear that Britain would no longer be America's global partner once such a break was made, they chose sovereignty over the special relationship.

Washington's rationales for imposing a rigid distinction between military and commercial exports eventually lost their saliency, but not because of any concern for the special relationship. Boeing's first 707 prototype rolled out of its production shed on May 14, 1954, two weeks after the revelation of the Soviet Union's new bomber and only a month after the final grounding of the initial Comet fleet. Like the Comet 2 and the Soviet plane, it relied on the axial-flow technology that had been the focus of these negotiations for years, employing four Pratt and Whitney JT-3 engines, a power source similar to the Avons that powered De Havilland's now-defunct Comet 2s. The American engine was a technological marvel. It was the first production engine to develop more than ten thousand pounds of thrust, and in May 1953 a North American F-100 powered by the military's version of the engine became the first production aircraft to break the sound barrier in level flight. For their effort, Pratt and Whitney garnered the Collier Trophy, the annual award given for the "greatest achievement in aviation in America." Here was a machine on the cutting edge of this strategic art. Here also was a commercial engine with clear military implications. From Whitehall's perspective, here was a machine whose existence spelled the end of Britain's technological superiority in the air.[33]

Boeing's 707 prototype used this engine when it flew its maiden flight in July 1954, and company executives planned for initial commercial sales within two years. *Time* featured the plane on its cover as a symbol of American achievement and Cold War aims, while the White House soon contracted for a 707 for Air Force One. The Soviets plowed resources into warplanes and bombers designed to kill, American commentators noted, but the free world applied its knowledge to peaceful products designed to better humankind. Boeing officials desperately wanted Washington's permission to begin full-scale production of its airliner with these engines aboard, especially because sales teams had already begun negotiations with European and Asian buyers for the first 707 exports scheduled for 1957. Yet, still troubled by the security implications of such sales, the Eisenhower administration withheld its final go-ahead. The company therefore instigated a massive lobbying campaign throughout the fall of 1954, employing both of its aviation-minded senators and a nationwide public relations effort, to have restraints on civil aircraft exports lifted as soon as possible. "Representatives of the US aircraft industry have noted with concern the restraints placed upon them by existing security restrictions," Samuel Waugh, the assistant secretary of state, wrote the secretaries of the navy and the air force. "They definitely feel that they are placed at a disadvantage when competing with British manufacturers whose government has followed a more liberal and aggressive policy than that of the US."[34]

Such lobbying worked. As the British had long feared, and indeed as Elliott had predicted, Washington liberalized its export policies once American firms had jetliners to sell. This decision was at least partly driven by the argument that American producers should not be more hamstrung by restraints than their British competitors. Even Elliott's team reluctantly recognized that "the time has arrived when American and British industry must be placed in a position to compete equally and to develop markets for jet propulsion units and to further the development of the commercial application of jet propulsion." They left no doubt as to the reason for their conversion. "The advent of the commercial application of jet propulsion has drawn closer with resulting increased pressure on the part of industry to release for commercial reasons, jet engine information that is still classified." Such a statement may as well have been written by the Ministry of Supply in 1951, but it came from the same American policymakers who only months before had railed at the British willingness to trade security for commercial gain. Soviet aeronautical developments diminished some of the need to limit all commercial exports. But the real reasons behind the change in America's export policies were the development of American commercial aircraft and Britain's refusal to toe a more rigid security line. Had London restrained its own exporters, Washington might have found strength to do the same. But without British consent, the administration instead found a politically easy justification for liberalizing restraints.[35]

Eisenhower's policymakers still strove for some means of Anglo-American control over jet sales. They proposed that each nation adopt a "phased release program based on step-by-step declassification that could be jointly prepared and concurred in by the US and the UK" to ensure that neither moved too quickly in authorizing potentially risky exports. Having no faith in British self-control, the Americans hoped to forestall dangerous British sales in the future. Internally, however, they doubted the likelihood, and even the wisdom, of bilateral controls. Whereas before they had sought to temper British sales exuberance, by the middle of the 1950s they realized that tying the two nation's export policies together could hinder American commercial designs, since experience over Burns-Templer proved that the

British would hardly let prior agreements hinder their commercial opportunities. "There seems to me to be no other alternative than for us to act unilaterally in determining our own requirements for security of engines," the Pentagon's liaison to Elliott's unit wrote, especially since the United States now needed a "release program to afford US industry equitable competitive position." Given their behavior over the past few years on this matter, he even balked at sharing further jet information with the British at all. Better RAF jets meant a more powerful NATO, but it was "essential that we examine carefully our program of exchanging information with [the] British in jet engine field to be sure it is justified by technical advantage to US and warrants obvious security risks." The British were still not to be trusted, but now that the Americans were ahead, perhaps the British were less needed as well.[36]

Victory Unclaimed and the Path Not Taken

Anglo-American negotiations over jet engine security ended less with a bang than with a whimper. The Comet crashes and subsequent grounding of the fleet kept this issue from reaching a climactic head. The British were never forced to openly break with Washington to complete their sales; neither was Washington forced to demand British compliance. Neither country subsequently believed it possible to impose its export program on the other, thus no further progress was made on this issue. Each agreed in the fall of 1954 to notify the other before exporting advanced engines, but prior notification of an impending sale was hardly the same as the veto power American negotiators had sought only months before. This pledge at least maintained the formal structure of a joint Anglo-American policy on aviation sales, because the two sides agreed to discuss the matter "periodically," or in the words of Andrew Foster, chief counselor to the American embassy in London, every "six months or so."[37]

The greatest impact of these negotiations thus lay in how they colored each side's strategic conception of the other. American officials left the affair more convinced than ever of Britain's lax security consciousness. Pentagon representatives in particular, Foster noted, "seemed convinced that we are just wasting time trying to get the British to accept our type of tight security control," since "the British are motivated as much by commercial considerations in their policy decisions" as by any concern for Western security. The lesson they drew from this affair consequently remained that "the British are almost certainly going to allow commercial considerations to have some influence on their policies towards the release of this type of information."[38]

Yet American officials relaxed their rigid distinction between commercial and military exports once Boeing's 707 (and Douglas's DC-8 soon after) took flight. Indeed, their subsequent policy of phased commercial jet sales mimicked Whitehall's, allowing sales to free-world airlines provided the jets were not used by communists. In other words, when given jetliners to sell, the Eisenhower administration adopted the very policy it had once chastised. This change lent even further credibility to the pervasive British perception that Washington's initial jet engine policy—the Burns-Templer policy couched so heavily in security terms—was merely a commercial policy in disguise. One minister had noted the "curious coincidence of security needs with American commercial interests" posed by Washington's proposals in 1953. Now that controls diminished once America had commercial planes to sell, many of his colleagues concluded that commerce had in fact been the State Department's motive all along.[39]

A logical conclusion, but incorrect. To suggest that American leaders devised their hawkish security line merely to hinder British commerce is to fundamentally underestimate the intensity of Washington's zeal for the Cold War fight. The liberalization of security restraints after the 707's appearance demonstrates Washington's interest in commerce, but the chronology of these events proves that American policymakers were more concerned with safeguarding Western technological superiority than in clearing the way for Boeing. In 1952 and 1953, when Britain had commercial planes to sell and when the Soviets appeared stymied without the influx of Western jet technology, Washington formed a security policy bent upon limiting security risks to military cases. America's line changed by 1954. But the need to safeguard this technology from the Soviets also diminished *before* Boeing and Douglas ever sought commercial exports of axial-flow jets. Appearances notwithstanding, there was no commercially driven deviousness in Washington's application of Burns-Templer in 1953. Limiting potentially dangerous commercial sales was to American minds merely the best means of ensuring Western, and especially American, security, especially given their accurate assessment that Britain's controls would not satisfy American concerns. American officials wanted to retard Britain's civil sales. But they tried to do so only because those sales, as every responsible British official agreed, posed a genuine security risk. British leaders saw hypocrisy in the evolution of Washington's arguments and downgraded their opinion of their American ally accordingly; their perception of hypocrisy demonstrates most of all their own fundamental misperception of American Cold War priorities.

Britain's willingness to place a price on American security infuriated American officials, many of whom already questioned Western Europe's commitment to the Cold War fight. London's failure to assume greater security burdens was particularly galling to American policymakers who wanted the British to accept their junior status with enthusiasm rather than disdain. "I get the impression that they would still like to take for granted the fundamentals of a special relationship which reached back to 1938–1939," Dean Rusk wrote in a personal note to Dulles in July 1954, harkening back to a period of greater parity in Atlantic affairs. "It may also be that they are reluctant to talk in fundamental terms since it would only lay bare their dependence upon a close Anglo-American tie and the necessity of paying a considerable price to maintain it." To Rusk's great frustration, Britain's reluctance to accept American leadership hindered the anticommunist fight, and perhaps more importantly, it made London the clear leader of the budding movement of resistance to American hegemony. "If some of our friends, and the neutrals, were less inclined to take us for granted and to expect us to modify our positions," he argued, "they might begin to put a little more pressure where it belongs—on communist intransigence."[40]

Rusk was preaching to the choir. Dulles returned from his intense May 1954 negotiations in Geneva over the future of Southeast Asia clearly fearful of the growing strength of his adversaries. Moscow and Beijing were stronger now than when he had entered office, and their power clearly limited his options in Southeast Asia and beyond. Yet he directed most of his anger against his allies, London in particular. Though always a "sincere believer in Anglo-American understanding," according to Ambassador Makins, Dulles suffered from a "slow burn" toward the British. "The differences between us [the U.S. and the UK] were much deeper and more serious than was generally realized," the secretary told reporters in an off-the-record session in June. "Indeed, there were more differences than points of agreement between the two countries," highlighted by a fundamental distinction in the way each gauged the communist threat. The British tended to view Washington's rigid anticommunism with "gloom and alarm," America's ambassador to Britain wrote Dulles that same month, and as "confirmation of their fears" that coexistence played no part in the Eisenhower administration's grand strategy. The dispute over engines seemed but one more sign of the growing rift between them. Believing rapprochement with the Soviets impossible and negotiations with the Chinese pointless, Washington was beginning to see military solutions to every problem to the exclusion of all other possible solutions, and even to those problems (such as how to limit diffusion of advanced aviation technologies) that seemed exacerbated by a military option (placing more advanced engines in harm's way by distributing them freely to unreliable NATO allies). American officials were consequently beginning to question allies who considered engagement with communism a potentially worthwhile endeavor, questioning not only the commitment, but also the sanity, of those who considered anything less than the strictest anticommunism.[41]

The Comet affair also demonstrated to both countries the limits of bilateral diplomacy. London's conception of aviation as a zero-sum game demanded not only technological superiority but export autonomy as well. As the latest, albeit most dramatic, in the long series of Anglo-American aviation disputes since 1945, British strategists left the Comet affair convinced that bilaterally negotiated controls with the United States simply did not fit their aviation needs. By the end of 1954 they were unwilling to give Washington the opportunity to limit British sales again. "It would be most undesirable to tie ourselves down to a rigid formula" for engine releases as the Americans suggested, the Foreign Office's negotiating team concluded in December. As it involved sales of a British product made by British workers and financed with British funds, they remarked, "we regard this as a domestic matter," one in which Britain had every right to proceed without American influence, and without American encroachments. Their patience for bilateral negotiations reached an end by 1956. "The procedure which we originally agreed [jointly notified phased releases] no longer serves any useful purpose," the British team concluded. London thereafter would "look at each case on its merits," but it would not agree to a joint export policy ahead of time.[42]

American policymakers realized the limits of bilateral diplomacy as well. Thereafter when issues of aviation control arose, as they inevitably did, the United States turned its attention with increasing frequency to COCOM, the free world's regulatory body for the anticommunist strategic embargo. The group, formed in 1949, already governed the sale and diffusion of strategically valuable Western products, and aircraft were on its list of products banned from export to the communist world. Though the Comet affair was handled as strictly an Anglo-American dispute—no other COCOM member had axial-flow engines to export, and direct Comet sales behind the

iron curtain were never contemplated—subsequent Anglo-American aviation diplomacy would lie with this group. Being unable to corral British exuberance bilaterally, Washington put its faith in multilateral controls. In doing
so, as we shall see, American diplomats in effect traded one diplomatic opponent for a dozen, and strengthened London's hand by making it the de
facto leader of the growing, though subaltern, movement within the Western community against perfunctory American leadership.

In the end these aviation crises did not sever the special relationship.
Perhaps nothing could. The differences separating the communist and free
worlds clearly outweighed those that divided London from Washington. It is
well worth remembering, however, that Churchill's government was never
forced to put into action its decision to break with Washington over the future of Comet sales. In November 1953 they pledged to export their Comets
no matter what the American reaction. They pledged to sacrifice the intimacy of the special relationship for sales and for the promise of independent
British power. Fate intervened, but this does not diminish the power of their
intent, nor of their decision to choose planes over their partner. The special
relationship was the cornerstone of British diplomacy, but the search for independent power and prosperity were the reasons Britain had a foreign policy in the first place. In the early 1950s, Britain chose its own commercial interests over American security. This is the key lesson of this entire affair.
British strategists chose the Comet over Atlantic solidarity, and took a stand
for sovereignty over subservience.

Perhaps the cruel fate that downed the Comet and awoke the West to the
Kremlin's growing technological achievements in fact aided the special relationship. Washington surely benefited from its close alliance with the United
Kingdom after the Comet affair, though the issues of relative power that
divided them remained unresolved until the last gasp of British imperial
power at Suez. In that vein we might consider that these unexpected events
of 1954, the Comet crashes and appearance of a Soviet long-range bomber,
ultimately served Britain's best interests, because the special relationship did
not break as a result of them. British leaders never gained the advantages of
independent power and prosperity they had sought when they chose to defy
Washington's will, but after 1954, when the dust from this debate cleared,
they still clearly gained from their particular place in Washington's hierarchy of allies through aid, information, and prestige. Their differences aside,
in military affairs in particular, the special relationship offered unprecedented intimacy. At the time of these Comet negotiations, we should recall,

British and American policymakers actively discussed the RAF taking control of whole squadrons of American-built B-47 bombers. This was an offer the Americans would not have made to any other nation. Churchill's cabinet ultimately determined that the costs involved in taking on these aging planes would be too great, and with thanks they declined the offer. Such a magnanimous proposal was possible only between the closest of allies, as Britain and the United States were and as they continued to be.

Intimacy does not always equal trust, however. This display of Anglo-American solidarity notwithstanding, British policymakers retained their view of aviation competition as a zero-sum game, as well as their inherent fear of the hidden motivations behind even seemingly generous American overtures. William Sidney, secretary of state for air, told Churchill that the American proposal was "generous . . . both as a political gesture and for its military value," but Supply Minister Duncan Sandys, who always had Churchill's ear, cautioned that accepting the bombers instead of developing homegrown machines "would have the most serious effects" on Britain's aircraft producers, "which are making such an important contribution to our export trade." His argument proved persuasive, and Churchill's government rejected the American offer not because they did not want the planes, but rather because they feared that acceptance of American technology would hinder their subsequent ability to produce similar machines and an autonomous nuclear deterrent in the future. To have accepted American planes in 1954 and to have made Britain's strategic strike force an American force in all but name would have placed another nail in the coffin of Britain's claims to great-power status. This they would not do.[43]

Britain won the race to jets, but victory did not bring the status or the power the Brabazon planners had promised. In pursuing its aviation dreams without regard for American security concerns, their country ultimately lost not only a valued lead in a vital field, but also a level of true intimacy with its Atlantic partner. Events perhaps did not serve either country well in the spring of 1954. The two Atlantic partners lost something vital, though impossible to quantify, as a result of their tense engine dispute. Both lost a modicum of respect for the other's opinions and worldview. Britain lost the opportunity to influence and to temper Washington's rigid Cold War stance. Washington lost the advice of the one nation, above all others, its policymakers might have found persuasive. History is often the study of the path taken. But it is also an inquiry into alternatives not pursued. By choosing to break with the Americans and by showing their hand in an effort to create a power base outside of American influence, London diminished its sway in Washington. It thereby hindered its ability to offer an effective alternative to American Cold War leadership from within the confines of the special relationship. There is an important irony to this loss of intimacy, given that leaders from both countries strove throughout this crisis to minimize any public dispute between them. They presented to the world a unified front and voiced their differences in private. Yet their subsequent meetings behind closed doors meant less and less. In pursuing policies that successive American administrations considered reckless bordering on treacherous, and in proving willing to put a price on American homeland security, the British lost their ally's ear and diminished their influence in Washington. America, in turn, lost the nearest thing it had to a brake on its foreign policy. London's pursuit of great-power autonomy and parity within Atlantic relations—a quest predicated on airpower since 1942—enabled American leaders to solidify their hard-edged Pax Americana, now devoid of the former softening effects of British advice. When their joint attention turned from Europe's aviation issues to Asia's, however, they would need to learn these lessons yet again.

CHAPTER 6

Approaching China

Anglo-American aviation relations appeared calm after the Comet, yet the two countries were never farther apart. In the late 1950s and early 1960s, both countries transitioned from controls designed to keep technologies from the Soviets to controls for China, yet divisions still ran deep over their views of trade and technology's role in waging the Cold War. Suez laid bare their divisions in 1956, prompting Anthony Eden's ouster from office, followed by a Whitehall power struggle that eventually saw Harold Macmillan installed at 10 Downing Street. Quietly in the midst of such international upheaval, their aviation industries traveled on distinctly different trajectories as well. American aviation soared by the close of the decade. In 1958 Boeing launched commercial service of its 707, America's first long-range jet airliner. With nearly eight hundred of the planes flying by 1970, *Fortune* later dubbed it "the biggest triumph in the history of the [aviation] industry." Douglas's initial jetliner, the DC-8, proved less profitable though no less important to aviation history following its 1959 launch. Together the rival machines helped usher in a new era of global travel and American aerospace dominance. Passenger traffic in the United States nearly doubled by 1961, a trend matched overseas, as popular demand for jets exceeded expectation. Ripe with profits and eager to put a stranglehold on the world's aviation markets, Boeing subsequently began production on its innovative 727, designed for lucrative (even if less celebrated) short- and medium-range routes. The company hoped to sell 250. They eventually sold more than 1,800, making the 727 the most prolific model in industry history and making Boeing one of the wealthiest of American corporations. Military sales helped the bottom line as well. The company churned out 744 B-52 bombers and a similar number of KC-135 tankers for the air force by the mid-1960s, garnering unprecedented financial resources and research through subsidized government contracts. With intercontinental missile production and contracts for space exploration also coming on line by mid-decade, American aviation's prospects looked unlimited.[1]

British aviation, on the other hand, stumbled to a disappointing finish by the close of the 1950s. The once-vaunted Comet led the way in possibilities unfulfilled. Buyers were in short supply by 1955, and only an eleventh-hour purchase of eighteen Comet 2s for the Royal Air Force, coupled with £10 million in government aid, saved De Havilland from bankruptcy. Resources spent to prolong the dying program exacted a terrible price on the rest of the industry, suffocating Whitehall's zeal for direct public financing of expensive new airliner projects. In November 1955, following an announcement that the national trade deficit had climbed above £115 million, fiscal conservatives managed to kill government support for the country's next major long-range jetliner, the Vickers V1000, arguing that the costs (and risks) of the ambitious project were best handled by industry alone. The program quickly folded as a result, leaving American planes unchallenged in their quest for market control. "All that we have not got is a pure jet aircraft capable of crossing the Atlantic non-stop in the early 1960s," explained Supply Minister Reginald Maudling, an astounding understatement given the primacy airline executives afforded transatlantic flights. British firms were free to build aircraft capable of competing in other areas, Maudling argued, but his government would not foot the bill.[2]

In the wake of the Comet, the V1000 cancellation was, to historian Derek Wood, "the point at which British airliner development really began to go wrong." Beating American planes to market had been the hallmark of Whitehall aviation policies since 1942 and the overarching creed of the Brabazon ideal. By canceling the nation's most viable long-range jet during a moment of financial desperation, Britain surrendered the field, and with it leadership in this prestigious arena. Aviation enthusiasts considered the Vickers cancellation a stab in the back for a reeling industry. "The nation turned from long-range jet aviation, canceling the V1000," the chairman of Hawker-Siddeley later said, "at precisely the moment when it was about to grow and we were ahead of everybody." Fiscal conservatives saw the Anglo-American race for market dominance differently. Whereas the first group believed the Comet would have captured sales that eventually went to the 707 and DC-8, naysayers argued that buyers would have chosen the larger and more cost-effective American planes over British models in any event. Yet each side in this unending debate missed the central point: Britain led the world in jet aviation in 1953; after the Comet, Sir George Edwards, BOAC's chairman later lamented, "We were behind all the time."[3]

Times were equally difficult for Britain's military producers, largely because of fundamental changes in London's strategic planning. Warplane construction represented 70 percent of the industry's total output at its mid-1950s high, prompting many manufacturers to consider military production their real sustenance. The defense white paper authorized by Duncan Sandys in April 1957 changed all that. He believed Britain could no longer afford to spend 10 percent of its gross national product on arms and assorted Cold War programs in order to prove its great-power status and its worth to Washington. Neither could it depend upon America's nuclear umbrella without conceding its political subordination. The country required its own nuclear deterrent if it were ever to be truly independent, Sandys argued, and it had to be cost-effective if London were not to spend itself into irrelevance. With Prime Minister Harold Macmillan's backing, he proposed a military more reliant on missiles and nuclear weapons than upon traditional (and more expensive) components such as infantry or armor. Gone by 1963 would be universal military service, battleships, and 40 percent of the country's total troop level. In their place would be the less expensive threat of massive retaliation. Britain exploded its first hydrogen bomb less than a month after the white paper's publication—proof, its leaders claimed, of their ability to retain influence at a reasonable cost through the cruel economics of mass destruction. "We must rely on the power of the nuclear deterrent," Macmillan privately conceded, "or we must throw up the sponge!"[4]

Sandys's white paper dramatically changed Britain's aviation industry, just as its creators intended. The new emphasis on missiles prompted a sharp decrease in aircraft orders, and because missile production demanded only a fraction of the labor of complex planes, industry-wide employment was expected to tumble from its postwar peak of 311,000 in 1957 to 150,000 by 1963. The number of British aviation firms would naturally shrink as well, which was again a central part of Macmillan's plan. Market-focused Tories hoped to carry into the next decade only those firms capable of competing primarily with private capital, so that any additional government subsidies might be focused only on those companies capable of truly matching the Americans. There were simply too many British firms for maximum efficiency, Macmillan's advisers believed. The Society of British Aircraft Constructors fielded thirty-one full members by mid-decade, only three less than in 1945. By contrast, twenty-three companies served America's larger military and commercial aviation market at the same point, and these were almost universally larger than their British counterparts. Rolls Royce employed 35,000 workers in its engine operations in the mid-1950s. Many American aviation firms employed that many in individual divisions, leading Whitehall policymakers to conclude that Britain's companies had to grow in size but shrink in number if they were to survive. "The government should use their power both of persuasion and of contracts to shape the industry," Supply Minister Edward Heath advised the cabinet in 1957. The plan worked. A flurry of mergers and takeovers left only a handful of consolidated British firms by 1961, though victory for government's policy dubbed "rationalization" came at tremendous human cost, as layoffs and plant closings abounded. Britain was left with fewer firms of larger size, just as Heath wanted. Yet "it was a time of great turmoil," one executive recalled, "rarely equaled in any industry."[5]

Whitehall's continued fascination with American competition drove rationalization, though a growing number of British analysts believed their structural disadvantages in this two-nation competition might simply be too awesome to overcome. American firms were the "main overseas competitor" of British companies, Heath said in justification of the government's policies. They "enjoy the natural advantage of a large domestic market and thus the prospect of a handsome return to offset the inevitably heavy outlays on research and development." Yet this was a domestic market Britain simply could not match. In January 1958, for example, intense government pressure prompted BOAC to stretch past its realistic needs to purchase the first thirty-five of Vickers's VC-10 jetliners off the assembly line. At £68 million, this was at the time the most expensive order ever for a British civil aircraft. Vickers needed these sales in order to survive until foreign buyers could be found; BOAC did not truly need the planes, however, and subsequently ran them at a loss. Later that year, again at the cabinet's prodding, British European Airways (BEA) contracted with a consortium of rationalized producers headed by De Havilland for the first twenty-five of the company's Tridents, at a cost of £39 million, in order to initiate production of the much-ballyhooed plane. The airline did not necessarily want these planes either, at least not at those quantities, but government analysts hoped these purchases would provide the manufacturers with sufficient capital to bring their machines to market without further subsidies.[6]

Such orders, finalized only after much cajoling and hand-wringing in

Whitehall, paled in comparison to those placed by American airlines. Three years *before* the initial Trident and the VC-10 contracts, Pan Am alone ordered $250 million worth of American-built jets from Boeing and Douglas. And Pan Am was only one of four American airlines larger than BEA and BOAC combined, to say nothing of the dozen additional major U.S. carriers of the period. Even when stretched beyond its useful limit through Whitehall pressure, Britain's domestic market was simply dwarfed by America's. The disparity in purchasing power for airliners paled when compared to Washington's enormous military pocketbook. The Pentagon was the world's largest single buyer of aeronautical equipment by the late 1950s, and its spending offered profits to American firms that seemed from Whitehall's perspective little more than a legal, if galling, subsidy to commercial production. From 1945 until 1957, according to Heath's advisers, the American military purchased versions of homegrown civil planes that included over 850 Boeing Stratocruisers, 400 KC-135s, 200 Douglas DC-6 series, 250 of Lockheed's Constellation series, and 300 assorted transports from Convair. "This can be contrasted," the supply minister wrote, with RAF "Transport Command's orders for 13, rising to 20 Britannia's and 13 Comets." Though biased and guilty of comparing tankers and transports like so many apples and oranges, the ministry's point remains astounding: the Pentagon ordered sixty times the number of planes the RAF ordered.[7]

British policymakers firmly believed this disparity in market and military spending underlay all of their aviation difficulties. Exports during this period were merely the icing on the cake for American manufacturers; their real sustenance came from producing for their own domestic buyers, both military and commercial. British firms, conversely, needed exports to survive, a harsh reality that made clashes with Washington over foreign markets all the more acute. This was the reason British producers believed their success required superior technology and salesmanship, and why British policymakers believed it their duty to promote aviation so vigorously: they could not hope to compete on a level playing field against American firms aided simultaneously by an unparalleled home market and unprecedented military spending. No wonder American planners could rail against subsidies as anticompetitive, Macmillan's cabinet reasoned. They were already intimately involved in their own aviation marketplace as a direct buyer. "In the United States the aircraft industry was continuing to receive considerable financial support from the government through the placing of large orders for military aircraft," Whitehall's Aircraft Industry Working Party lamented in 1957. "It would be difficult for the British aircraft industry, if left to its own resources, to compete with the United States industry." Indeed, "it was for consideration whether the British industry, even with government support, could stand up to this formidable US competition [at all]."[8]

Macmillan's aviation policymakers left the 1950s feeling undergunned, underfinanced, and despondent over having lost their prized lead in jets to the Americans following the Comet disasters. Yet not a single persuasive British politician advocated abdicating the field. They believed no less than their predecessors that prosperity demanded a vibrant aviation industry, and that no country could be truly great without the kinds of power that grew from this high-technology domain. "It is an industry of rapidly developing technique, and its progress has brought in its train accompanying advances in other fields," Heath argued in 1957, including technological advances in "metallurgy, light engineering, fuel efficiency, electronics and electrics—advances which would certainly not have been achieved without its stimulus." By one Whitehall calculation, foreign expenditures on commercial aircraft would total more than £150 million by 1970 if the aircraft industry crumbled. The cost of supplying the country's military needs with foreign (most likely American) models would prove even greater.[9]

The broader cost of abandoning aviation seemed beyond potential calculation. "It would be wrong to judge whether an aircraft industry should be retained in this country solely by economic criteria," the cabinet's aviation committee concluded. "There are other important factors such as defense and the gain to national prestige and thereby to British influence in the world from the use of British aircraft on international air routes." For a nation that considered itself a technological power, Heath argued, "by its nature it is very much the kind of industry we ought to have." It was "therefore unthinkable," the minister of aviation stated in 1959, "that we should contemplate the possibility of withdrawing from the civil transport field." Britain was not given to bow out of the competition simply because it was tough, Minister of Power Percy Mills reminded Macmillan. "We are probably as yet only on the threshold of the air age," he said. "Airlines and aircraft will [in the future] play the role filled by the shipping and the railroads of the nineteenth century—expensive and often risky to develop, but simultaneously both an economic asset and the hallmark of achievement."[10]

Rationalization and the transformation of Britain's military structure begun in the mid-1950s were each designed to promote a truly competitive aircraft industry. Beginning in 1959, the government also promised direct financial infusions, dubbed "launch aid," to rationalization's survivors in order to stimulate production of planes deemed capable of winning foreign markets. Whitehall analysts predicted global demand for commercial aircraft would exceed fifty-five hundred planes by 1970. If Britain could capture only one-quarter of those sales, they fantasized, "there would be export earnings between £150–375 millions." This money could go a long way to solving the country's ever-present financial difficulties. Policymakers pledged to couple this aid with renewed diplomatic support for producers seeking to sell overseas. Aircraft exports need "encouragement," one MP reminded Macmillan, and "though Duncan Sandys' policy of concentration [rationalization] may lead to stronger units which are better able to face a lean time and acute competition, it does not in itself bring any orders for the aircraft industry." The prime minister wholly agreed. Previous Whitehall governments considered reductions in security restraints their primary means of encouraging sales. Macmillan's government went further. The Foreign Office exhorted its far-flung representatives to help British producers sell planes and with them the aura of British technology. "American competition is growing," Foreign Secretary Selwyn Lloyd wrote in one typical missive, and "the lines on which our exports in arms and aircraft can be encouraged should be continuously explored by all concerned." British officials subsequently hosted seminars at embassies and consulates overseas; introduced sales teams and local buyers; and arranged well-publicized galas on behalf of demonstration flights of the newest British aircraft, all with the intention of besting American competition. "No effort should be spared to bring home to potential purchasers the merits of British equipment," Lloyd said. Under his watch Britain's overseas consulates became virtual field offices for the country's aircraft producers.[11]

Faced with the prospect of American aerial dominance, and chastened both by the Comet disasters and by the potentially overwhelming costs of sustaining a vast aeronautical industry at government expense, British policymakers used rationalization, the promise of launch aid, and new promises of diplomatic support to recharge their enthusiasm for aviation by the close of the 1960s. This effort led inexorably to a search for buyers behind the iron and bamboo curtains. Washington barred its own producers from plying these markets, thus they appeared open and unfettered when viewed from London. British firms struggled to compete in contested arenas. They would have no such American competition in their pursuit of communist buyers. This move toward communist markets effectively ends the first half of this

Cold War story, which was primarily a debate over safeguarding technologies from the Soviets. The battles of the next generation would focus on sales to China, America's most bitter Cold War foe and Britain's most alluring market. The debate that followed touched the very nature of the Cold War fight.

Strategic Restraints on Aviation in the 1950s

Aviation diplomacy by the late 1950s had developed into a multinational, and thus more complicated, affair than the bilateral restraints of the early Cold War. Ironically, though, it was through multilateralism that Washington ultimately gained its long-sought veto over British sales. COCOM restraints imposed in 1950 barred Western producers from selling aircraft of any sort directly to communist regimes (save for breakaway regimes such as Yugoslavia). This Korean War–era regulation inspired by the Americans began to chafe British interests by the mid-decade, though revisions to COCOM restraints required approval of the entire body. Countries were not legally bound to adhere to COCOM regulations, nor were they bound to participate in voluntary organization at all. British policymakers could have chosen simply to disregard COCOM policies in order to complete any sale, but the diplomatic consequences of rejecting a COCOM ruling seemed too daunting an option for serious Whitehall consideration throughout much of the 1950s. Unanimity was thus COCOM's norm: countries were loath to defy the organization's will, so the tradition of unanimous consent gave any member a functional veto over any disputable sale. At the same time, countries dissented only with the greatest of caution, lest they appear out of step with their closest allies.[12]

Rather than defy COCOM's prohibitions on aircraft sales behind the iron curtain, Macmillan's advisers sought to do away with the prohibitions. They presumed that the majority of COCOM members, save of course the United States, would acquiesce to any opening of communist markets for aviation. Members typically entered debate only on items their own firms produced. Thus only Washington, London, and Paris had any real stake in the body's aviation rules during this period, they being the only members capable of exporting aircraft, and the French had their own visions of selling behind the iron curtain. With most states unlikely to voice an opinion on the matter, and with Japanese delegates reflexively in favor of liberalized trade restraints of any sort, British policymakers presumed that winning COCOM approval for aircraft sales to the communists required, in practical terms, winning American approval.[13]

No one believed this would be easy. Washington had not revised its over-arching East-West aviation policies since the Truman administration, and Eisenhower's White House gave little indication during its first term that it had any interest in expanding Western aviation ties to the communists. The Americans still classified aircraft of any type as weapons of war and continued to favor aerial isolation of the Soviet bloc until Moscow showed signs of peaceful change. They also aspired to have the rest of the free world do the same.[14]

A seeming thaw in Soviet aviation policies in 1956 prompted Washington to reassess its plans. The Kremlin began negotiating to expand Aeroflot's operations throughout Western Europe in the spring of that year and opened Soviet airspace for the first time to other bloc carriers later that summer. Moscow concluded bilateral aviation agreements with seven nonbloc countries (Afghanistan, Austria, Denmark, Finland, Norway, Sweden, and Yugoslavia) by June, with the first direct East-West air service—along a Moscow-to-Copenhagen route—scheduled to begin in December 1957. These moves struck many American policymakers as proof of a new Soviet openness. More importantly, they demonstrated Western Europe's intent to penetrate the Soviet bloc with or without Washington's approval, furthering American fears that its own airlines might be frozen out of the region as Western Europe became increasingly dependent upon Soviet trade.[15]

Wary of falling behind the curve on aviation ties, Secretary of State John Foster Dulles ordered a reexamination of his country's stance on East-West air traffic. The ensuing document, NSC-5726, displayed a new willingness to fly and even to export to the Soviet sphere. Whereas the Truman administration's NSC-15/3 had sought limited communist access to Western Europe, its successor considered such flights desirable, because "reciprocal air exchanges would facilitate the expansion of East-West contacts and represent a significant breach in the Iron Curtain." The National Security Council (NSC) made no move to improve American access to Eastern Europe, however, and American leaders stubbornly waited for Moscow to initiate discussions on direct US-USSR flights. NSC-5726 only approved the *idea* of direct East-West flights, not a particular zeal for them, especially given that they appeared likely with or without American approval.[16]

European politics prompted Washington's reexamination of East-West aviation, but Soviet technological advances had the greatest influence on

NSC-5726's liberalization. Previous directives prioritized an embargo on Western aviation products. It only made sense to prohibit aircraft sales to the Soviet bloc in 1949 when the West was the region's only source of supply. But by 1956 Poland, Czechoslovakia, and Hungary joined the Soviet Union in manufacturing civil planes, prompting the NSC to conclude, "It is fully expected that by the end of 1959 Soviet civil aviation will have a substantial number of turbo-jet and/or turboprop transports in operation." American analysts considered these communist-built machines inferior to Western models, though their production displayed the bloc's limited vulnerability to Western export restraints. Incorporation of Western technologies might make these planes better, but only marginally so compared to the input of Western know-how when Soviet bloc aircraft were truly at the embryonic stage. Indeed, Moscow's success with Sputnik, the first man-made satellite, launched in October 1957, severely undermined any lingering doubt about Soviet aeronautical abilities, convincing even skeptics that the communists might prove to be good flyers. Though adopted before Sputnik shocked the world, NSC-5726 embodied a grudging acceptance of Soviet industrial development and consequently ceased to prioritize a full-bore Western aviation embargo. No one in Washington advocated selling sophisticated military aeronautics to the Soviets at this still tense point in the Cold War; the administration's new policy simply acknowledged that keeping rudimentary Western equipment designed for civilian use from Eastern Europe would do little to keep communist airliners grounded and could potentially strain allied relations. Rather than wage a rearguard action defending rigid aviation restraints against increasingly intense allied pressure, the NSC simply agreed that an iron curtain of the air was no longer worth the effort, and that a more focused regulation of truly strategic commodities would be the better investment.[17]

The changes embodied in NSC-5726 were superficial at best. Its quiet acquiescence in East-West aviation trade and ties did not extend to communist Asia, which American policymakers still considered vulnerable to a full aviation embargo and containment. Neither was it a wholesale endorsement of exports to the Soviet sphere. On the contrary, American policymakers reluctantly assented to the greater East-West aviation ties that were already a *fait accompli,* but on the issue of sales, the document stated, "The United States should consider on a case-by-case basis the sale of a reasonable amount of aviation safety equipment to the USSR and of civil aircraft and aeronautical equipment to selected European satellites." This was considered solely a preemptory conclusion, given that so far as Washington knew, none of its allies had immediate plans for direct sales to communist buyers.[18]

Exports played only a small part of the administration's new aviation policy, as the NSC devoted most of its aviation discussions to the political ramifications of East-West flights. One meeting attended by Eisenhower ignored exports entirely in favor of discussion of possible means of countering communist aerial expansion into underdeveloped nations. The Soviets were developing aerial ties throughout Africa and Asia in particular, frequently buying favor with new regimes through promises of aid for new airfields and planes, leading Eisenhower, among others, to consider aviation the vanguard of a new Soviet push for influence throughout the nonaligned world. "We should do whatever we are obliged to do in order to meet Soviet competition," the president said. Though equally wary of Soviet penetration, his advisers balked at this request. Joint Chiefs Chairman Maxwell Taylor noted that their government had neither the inclination nor perhaps even the legal authority to subsidize unprofitable aircraft sales to imperiled nations just to promote Western political interests or to parry Soviet thrusts. The administration wielded the legal authority to restrict American carriers and producers as part of its Cold War fight while supporting similar restraints for its allies. It would even distribute American-built warplanes to any nation willing to stand against Communism. But in keeping with the long-standing American fear of interference in the commercial aviation marketplace—a universally accepted façade, given the Pentagon's prolific spending—Eisenhower's principal advisers believed they could not condone direct subsidies of commercial exports even though geostrategic considerations seemed at stake. They were powerless to meet Eisenhower's request, and in the final analysis NSC-5726 proved to be more an exercise in approving the idea of expanded American sales and flights than a vibrant new promotion of such ties.[19]

British policymakers found little to endorse in Washington's new aviation policies. They noted upon receiving copies of the document that NSC-5726's vow to "consider" exports on a "case-by-case" basis was hardly an iron-clad endorsement of East-West aircraft sales, and that the statement made no mention of promoting flights by American carriers behind the iron curtain. London's position was far different. The Air Ministry endorsed what its undersecretary termed "a broad policy" to "support the export to the Sino-Soviet bloc of civil aircraft and parts." Ever seeking export profits and continually captivated by the prospects for better relations through trade, British policymakers in 1957 promised to support any aircraft export to the communist world, "provided they [the planes] do not contain classified equipment, are ordered in reasonable quantities" to ensure a profit, and "are intended for genuine civil end use." It was telling, the Foreign Office concluded, that NSC-5726's apparent endorsement of exports to the bloc failed to mention COCOM, whose consent would be a precondition of any export to the communist world. "We are at one with the Americans in thinking that this policy [NSC-15/3] needs revision," the head of the Foreign Office's economic division concluded. "We start diverging, however, when we get down to details," because for neither the first nor the last time, "generally speaking, the Americans seem far too rigid and doctrinaire in their approach."[20]

Economic Warfare

It is not surprising that British and American policymakers could not agree on a unified strategy for aviation beyond the iron curtain, because the issue of trade with the communist world divided the Atlantic community throughout the Cold War. The literature on this topic is detailed. Given our focus, its broadest themes should suffice. Put simply, the British believed in engagement through trade, while Washington consistently promoted economic containment. Just as they had during the late 1940s before the Korean War stifled most early proponents of accommodation of the communist world, successive Whitehall governments of the 1950s endorsed the expansion of trade and contact with communist regimes, not only for profit (though profit was their ultimate motivation) but also as a way to develop positive East-West relations. For hardly the first or last time, national policymakers forged an ideological justification for policies that were clearly in their material and strategic interest. In this case, British strategists calculated that communist prosperity, as an outgrowth of enhanced East-West trade, not only promoted positive political relations with bloc countries but, more importantly, also enhanced within those countries the stability required for détente. American thinkers were willing to debate and even concede aspects of this point for the Soviet Union, though their zeal to liberalize East-West trade was never as strong as in Britain. They adamantly rejected any promotion of Chinese trade and development. Washington refused to recognize the Beijing government's legitimacy even more than a decade after the communist revolution—they would not formally do so until the late 1970s—and successive administrations accordingly barred all American trade with the People's Republic. Just as they had before the Korean War, American policymakers under Eisenhower wanted China to remain weak so that its economy might crumble. And they wanted their allies to help make this happen. More to the point, successive American administrations wanted the Western community to treat its trade with the two halves of the communist world differently, with more stringent controls imposed on contact with the Chinese bloc than with the Soviet.[21]

British and American differences over trade with China came to a head in the mid-1950s over this "China differential," the name given to the two-tiered system of COCOM regulations developed during the Korean War. Though many imposed restraints, no other free-world state followed Washington's lead in halting all trade with China after 1950. Washington secured a United Nations resolution in 1951 asking members to refrain from selling arms or munitions to the People's Republic, though it could do no better than to make adherence strictly voluntary. As such, adherence was hardly widespread. The Truman administration found better success winning support for restraints from its closest allies in COCOM, where beginning in 1950 the group restrained trade with China beyond the limits imposed on Eastern European countries. While it controlled the trade of some 260 items with the Soviet bloc during 1953, the China Trade Coordinating Committee (CHINCOM, a division of COCOM responsible for regulating trade with communist Asia) controlled nearly 400 items. The 140 items available to communist regimes in Europe but not in Asia constituted the "differential."[22]

Most COCOM members favored a single standard for trade with the entire communist world following the Korean War, believing that peace demanded a resumption of trade and reasoning that a single standard would be more easily enforced. London led this charge. "Hong Kong must trade with the mainland to live," Foreign Secretary Herbert Morrison had stated in September 1951, and as the decade progressed, British policymakers increasingly came to believe their country needed that trade as well. The Bank of England's governor reported at mid-decade that currency reserves were "just above the danger mark," and when the Board of Trade simultaneously reported that British exports to Beijing totaled more than $85 million, the allure of untapped markets just a political decision away was irresistible. The first Quemoy-Matsu crisis of 1954—the shelling of Nationalist-held islands by communist forces that nearly precipitated a violent American response—stymied most British calls for an immediate resurgence of trade with the mainland. But renewed demands for access soon resurfaced. "We are a trad-ing country," Macmillan reminded Dulles only a year later, one that "simply could not live if it was denied the opportunity to trade throughout the world." Only American obduracy kept British traders from profits in China, he continued. Dulles later told Eisenhower that the prime minister had, quite uncharacteristically, become "positively angry" while attacking the American position.[23]

Britain's economic and strategic straits contributed to Macmillan's anger, as did a difficult political situation at home. The differential struck British thinkers as illogical (as goods available to one were available to all through intrabloc trade) and economically damaging at the precise moment when their faltering finances demanded new markets. Whether the Chinese would want to increase their trade with the United Kingdom remained to be seen, but this question was rarely discussed in Parliament, where growing economic uncertainty prompted calls for increased China trade from across the political spectrum. By 1956 Foreign Secretary Lloyd warned Dulles that criticism of the differential approached "flood" level in the House of Com-mons, where Washington's reputation suffered from the pervasive belief that only American anger kept British traders from pursuing sales in China. "There has been rising criticism of the United States in areas where there was unemployment," he explained, "which was ascribed rightly or wrongly, to the United States refusal to let them trade with China." In short, British interests combined to condemn the differential by the mid-1950s as costly, pointless, and proof of excessive American Cold War belligerence. It was not in Britain's best interest (as interpreted by the majority of British strategists) and was favored only in the United States. In the final analysis, it was fur-ther proof of London's weakness and its inability to defy Washington's will.[24]

The differential was as popular in Washington as it was despised in Lon-don, as American thinkers believed it demonstrated the free world's resolve in beating back further Chinese aggression in Asia. It was a public gesture the State Department believed made clear to all that China was a "pariah in the family of nations," and Eisenhower's national security team had no plans to back down one inch in this vital Cold War battleground. American policy in Asia would be "finished," Joint Chiefs Chairman Arthur Radford warned in 1955, if the United States bowed to British pressure to eliminate the differential. He believed such a move would send a signal of weakness to a region obsessed with honor, and the ensuing loss of American prestige would "require us to reorient our entire policy towards the Far East." Domestically, Chinese affairs were a third-rail issue of American politics, electric enough to kill any who dared to touch them, as influential leaders in Congress and throughout the administration's upper echelons considered the bar on trade with China's evil regime to be morally unambiguous. "We don't want to trade with the dirty s.o.b.'s," Secretary of Defense Charles Wilson explained, "nor do we want the Free World Nations to trade with them either." He told the NSC he was "completely at a loss as to how you could love the Chinese Communists and fight them at one and the same time." Privately, and only by his second term, Eisenhower wondered if increased trade might not show the Chinese people the best the West could offer (nothing symbolized Western allure better than its products, after all). Publicly, however, his administration maintained its unbending opposition to any accommodation of Beijing. "Many members of Congress want to crucify anyone who argues in favor of permitting any kind of trade between the free nations and Communist China," Eisenhower explained. He refused to martyr his administration simply to appease the British.[25]

Politics aside, American policymakers supported the differential as a fundamental weapon in their Cold War arsenal, believing that the trade restraints were justified simply because they hurt Beijing's economy. "[We] realize that it is neat and logical to have a single policy which applies to all areas and all countries," the chief economics officer at the State Department's Office of Chinese Affairs noted in 1952. "But we do not think the situation allows this tidiness at the expense of possible real gains in bringing the Chinese communists to terms, in delaying their timetable of industrial achievement, or in slowing up their possible aggressive intentions in areas in the Far East other than Korea." Eisenhower's aides wholly accepted this logic. In 1956 the NSC calculated that CHINCOM regulations cost Beijing nearly $200 million a year in the mid-1950s, mostly in extra costs required to transport goods from Soviet industrial centers that would otherwise have been more inexpensively available through Western trade. This annual burden alone was reason enough for Eisenhower to continue his support for the differential, believing this was $200 million Beijing could not subsequently use for its military or to solidify its hold on power. "In general, Britain would like to have our controls on China trade identical with those we observe with respect to the Soviets," Ike recorded in his diary in February 1956. "We, on the other hand have felt that even though the Soviets might try to ship considerable quantities of supplies to China, a much longer route and higher expense was involved for the Communists." Anything that could be done to limit Beijing's ability to upset East Asia's delicate stability was to his mind well worth doing.[26]

That the differential hurt China and symbolically demonstrated Western resolve were the two surface (and most often cited) reasons for Washington's continued support of the two-tiered trade control system. The more fundamental reason for Washington's embrace of the differential underscores a broader divide in British and American thinking about technology's role in the Cold War fight that ultimately threatened the intimacy of their special relationship: British policymakers wanted China to grow as a way of overthrowing the Maoist regime, whereas their American counterparts wanted China to crumble in order to achieve the same. Having been chastened by their experience in open warfare against Beijing, American analysts came to believe the best way to defeat Communism in Asia was to topple it from the inside by hindering Beijing's industrialization and economic modernization. They consequently favored a broad policy of economic warfare, limiting trade, hindering Chinese access to crucial materials and goods, and generally doing all in their power to make Beijing's road to prosperity treacherous and impassable. London meanwhile favored economic expansion, believing not only that trade would help Britain's bottom line, but also that trade and prosperity offered the best way to temper the communist regime.

Strict economic warfare had been Washington's initial inclination for COCOM's anti-Soviet policies at the start of the 1950s as well, but strategists within the Truman administration quickly concluded that the Soviet economy was already too industrially advanced for such a policy to have much immediate effect. During World War II, Soviet factories had produced more tanks than Germany, a sure sign of industrial power, and given that Eastern Europe derived only 1 percent of its combined gross domestic product from foreign trade at the time of COCOM's founding, Secretary of State Dean Acheson considered economic warfare unwinnable in Europe. He concluded that "the Soviet bloc economy is relatively so self-sufficient" as to be invulnerable to economic weapons, imposed from the outside, intended to foster its collapse. It might not fully prosper without Western trade, but neither would it quickly collapse. American policymakers consequently adopted narrower controls aimed only at limiting Soviet access to needed technologies or bottleneck goods, such as advanced jet engines. "The present objective of US economic warfare/defense measures is to reduce or limit the build-up of military potential within the Soviet bloc by economic means, concurrently with an effort to conserve and increase the military capabilities of the Free World," Secretary of Defense Robert Lovett explained in 1952. "[The] methods used in the attainment of this objective include, for example, the control or denial of strategic commodities, including arms, ammunition and implements of war, control or denial of transporting cargo to the bloc; control of financial transactions; [and] actions to reduce the dependence of the United States and friendly foreign governments on East-West trade." COCOM regulations subsequently embodied this emphasis on restricting Soviet military development.[27]

China was different. Whereas by 1945 the Soviet Union was an industrial power, capable of autonomous economic activity including development of Eastern Europe as a market and source for materials, postrevolution China was underindustrialized, economically weak, and dependent on foreign trade. It consequently appeared vulnerable to broad economic pressures aimed specifically at limiting its development. China's new leaders had daunting needs after 1949. They had a burgeoning population to feed, new social and political systems to impose, and the expenses of a foreign policy that was simultaneously expansionistic and reactionary, ideologically committed to East-West conflict yet ever fearful of Western encroachments. Moreover, the new government also desired power in line with their reading of Chinese history. Believing that great powers required a world-class economy, and sure that China was destined to become a global force, Mao announced soon after taking office a new program of rapid industrialization termed "rash advance" designed for just that purpose. Allocating 25.6 percent of government expenditures to economic development during 1951, he promised "three years of reconstruction and then 10 years of development," in order to produce predicted annual gains of 15 percent in heavy industry, 10 percent in handicrafts, and 5 percent in agriculture. These were awesomely ambitious figures. In return for the great sacrifices such a rapid industrialization program demanded of his people, Mao subsequently promised a "revolution in the technological field" that would allow the country to "overtake Britain in fifteen or more years." As for the United States, he said, "We will surely overtake it."[28]

The Truman administration considered such ambitions to be China's Achilles' heel. Industrialization would not prove easy for a country as vast, underdeveloped, and overpopulated as China. American policymakers consequently reasoned that failure of the new government's modernization program and the resulting widespread suffering among its people, especially after such widespread sacrifices, would undermine its credibility at home and abroad, producing a wave of discontent perhaps strong enough to topple Mao's regime. Economic failure would bring political collapse and regime change at a far smaller cost than outright warfare.

This was the fundamental reasoning behind Washington's support for the differential: Chinese trade controls were aimed not so much at hindering China's military as at frustrating its very industrialization. Pentagon analysts argued as early as 1950 that to "retard the development of the war potential of China, it will be necessary to extend the present pattern of restriction to include a variety of less advanced equipment and materials required by such a backward country" to a greater extent than the restrictions aimed at the Soviet bloc. With the CHINCOM list, which emphasized machine tools and basic industrial goods as much as military products, the goal of checking Chinese development became primary. "The China differential was not designed to strangle trade with Communist China," the Joint Chiefs reminded Secretary of Defense Wilson in 1957, especially since other countries were unwilling to adopt Washington's wholesale embargo. It did, however, "serve to retard her industrial growth."[29]

China's populace was the ultimate target of America's economic warfare strategy. American thinkers believed like a catechism that a government's fundamental responsibility was the maintenance of its population, and that a government incapable of providing its people's basic needs would eventually be discarded. Through economic warfare, they hoped to promote enough suffering among the Chinese people that they would recognize their government's failings (even if only as a consequence of prejudicial Western pressure) and revolt against it. "It is important to keep the Chinese Communist regime under economic (and other) pressures," Eisenhower's Steering Committee on East-West Trade concluded in 1957 in defense of the differential. "Such pressures add to the strains which can ultimately lead to disintegration; the Communist regime has undertaken heavy commitments, and it appears probable that it cannot under present circumstances increase its resources fast enough to cover all commitments. This kind of dilemma leads to a breakdown."[30]

Washington's passion for thwarting Chinese development spawned its break with Britain over the differential. While American strategists hoped to keep China underindustrialized, their British counterparts sought greater communist prosperity, believing economic development might soften China's anti-Western attitudes. Whereas the Americans sought to defeat Communism by burying it, the British hoped to defuse communist belligerence by remolding it in a Western image. Foreign Secretary Ernest Bevin, as we have already seen, thought trade could keep Britain's "foot in the door" in China during the tumultuous postrevolution period, thus retaining China within the community of nations. Winston Churchill took a similar stand in 1951. He told Eisenhower that "[East-West] trade means contacts and probably involves a good deal of friendly infiltration which I think would be to our advantage from every point of view." He advocated liberalizing trade across the iron curtain, limiting restraints to the bare minimum necessary to keep war material from the Sino-Soviet bloc. The Eden government even deduced by 1956 that since NATO war plans called for immediate nuclear retaliation in any future conflict with the Soviets, trade controls should be limited to nuclear materials. It mattered little if the Kremlin had the industrial potential to build tanks or planes for a war's second year if the world would be atomized by its second day. They tried to gain COCOM acceptance of this strategic rationale, but made little headway against Washington's tough-line stand on such issues.[31]

The ultimate embodiment of this British idea that communist prosperity could promote détente came in October 1957 from Board of Trade president A. D. Neale. "Is a thin or a fat communist more likely to start a war?" he asked Macmillan. It was more than a mere rhetorical question. "The more prosperous the Bloc the more powerful will their middle-class become," Neale wrote, "and it is to the professional and managerial classes that we can look to crack the monolithic philosophy of communism." Trade did not so much equal détente as lay the economic foundation for it, as trade built up the sense of contentment and well-being that would diffuse and dissipate the rhetoric of discontent so crucial to Communism's appeal. Therefore, "the more peaceful trade we can do with the Bloc the more chance we have of weakening the dictatorship of the militants." Successive British governments in the 1950s toed this line. Both Neale's and Churchill's statements in support of East-West trade were made specifically in reference to the Soviet Union, but British attitudes toward Chinese trade differed little. London wanted Chinese prosperity and therefore worked to eliminate the hated differential and promote Sino-Western trade, and not only for the short-term goal of profiting off trade with Beijing. Almost universally, British policymakers fervently believed Chinese prosperity would breed peace.[32]

The Eisenhower administration fought furiously against this British position, believing London's efforts undermined its own economic warfare plans while enhancing Beijing's potential strength. They also directly equated support for rigid trade controls with a country's reliability as a Cold War ally. When Anthony Eden threatened to unilaterally discard the differential in January 1956, American diplomats argued the logic of the differential in economic, political, and diplomatic terms. The president, however, made his final personal appeal a question of commitment, warning Eden "to decide which is more valuable, friendship in this country, or [with] somebody else." Dulles simultaneously told Macmillan that any move against the differential would create "a high degree of ill-feeling" in Washington. This was an issue in which American policymakers did not want their leadership disputed.[33]

Eden took heed of these warnings and, despite numerous aborted attempts, never mustered the political courage to withdraw Britain from CHINCOM. His weak position following the Suez debacle left him unable to withstand American pressure on something as symbolically vital as strategic trade controls. It was up to his successor to accomplish the task. Harold Macmillan informed Parliament in 1957 of his government's plans to begin respecting a single list of export controls for the entire communist world. "The commercial interests of our two countries are not at all alike," Macmillan wrote Eisenhower. America could afford its moral stands, but "we live by exports—and by exports alone." Moreover, as he had earlier explained, the world's strategic landscape looked far different if viewed from the Thames rather than the Potomac. Beijing was public enemy number one in Washington, but "it is very hard to persuade the English that the Chinese are more dangerous than the Russians." Therefore, he said, "I feel that we cannot any longer maintain the existing differential between Russian and Chinese trade." The majority of COCOM states immediately followed Britain's lead, leaving the differential for dead. By the end of 1957 only the United States maintained two sets of export controls.[34]

Understanding the nature and the intensity of these divisions over the China differential and the efficacy of economic warfare is crucial to understanding the aviation diplomacy that followed when Britain pursued aircraft sales behind the bamboo curtain. The National Security Council considered COCOM difficulties "a source of constant irritation" to the special relationship, while Lloyd termed the differential "a major source of Anglo-American differences." Ambassador Roger Makins even called the issue "more dangerous for Anglo-American relations than any single subject since the default on the World War I debts." Previous scholars have already noted the important role trade controls played in Anglo-American relations. But they have failed to give proper attention to the importance of industrialization as a component of the economic warfare strategies that were, according to Washington's chief minister to London, evidence of the "fundamentally divergent tendencies between the US and the UK in their evaluation of the importance of these controls as they affect East-West relationships."[35]

Contemporary debate over the differential illuminates the full depth of these irreconcilable positions. "Our trade with the bloc helps the liberal tendencies, in those countries, which we want to encourage," Foreign Secretary Sir Alec Douglas-Home noted, while Board of Trade president Frederick Erroll later argued that "economic warfare in peacetime is as out of date as the Zeppelin." He believed that "British public opinion resents American interference in our freedom to trade with all countries." American leaders under both Eisenhower and his successor, John Kennedy, found Britain's stand infuriating and potentially corrosive. "We have maintained, virtually in isolation, a trade posture tantamount to economic warfare" against China, a 1963 State Department briefing paper concluded. American policies toward the Soviets were different: "The United States has a very clear policy of *not* engaging in economic warfare against the Soviet Bloc." The reason for this difference in economic approaches was clear. As Secretary of State Dean Rusk explained to Congress, economic warfare was applicable only in the half of the communist world vulnerable to industrial attacks. "If the US were to relax its trade and financial controls against Communist China and North Korea to the level now applied against the Soviet Bloc generally," he said, "it would significantly increase the capacity of Communist China to overcome its economic difficulties."[36]

We now can appreciate the difficulties British leaders faced when trying to open the China market to aircraft. It had taken all of their diplomatic strength to counter America's stand on the differential, but by eliminating CHINCOM by the close of 1957, they had succeeded in securing a single standard for trade with the communist world. Thereafter, one set of regulations governed Western trade with Moscow and with Beijing, and any good exportable to Europe's communist bloc was equally available, so far as COCOM was concerned, for export to communist states in Asia. The British still did not have COCOM approval for exports of aircraft to communist states, however, despite Washington's pledge given in NSC-5726 to "consider" aircraft sales across the iron curtain. They planned to eliminate this restriction through revision of COCOM's aviation rules in the fall of 1958, as part of the body's annual list review. If London had its way, commercial aircraft would be exportable east by the close of the year.[37]

Winning Washington's acquiescence for such sales to Eastern Europe would prove difficult enough, but British planners had their sights firmly set on China's budding aviation market. Beijing had no domestic producer capable of matching British planes; American manufacturers were banned from such trade; and with the world's largest population, China's future need for aircraft seemingly knew no bounds. Indeed, unknown to Washington, a Rolls Royce sales team secretly visited Beijing in the fall of 1957 to discuss export of their turboprop Dart engine. They even fielded a Chinese request that Rolls establish an engine production facility in China itself. Only months after their Anglo-American divide over the differential, therefore, and before COCOM had even discussed loosening its restraints on aircraft sales—in other words, while any aviation sale to a communist state was still officially forbidden—the British had already made the first moves toward opening the China market. "There can be no question of RR selling aircraft engines to the Chinese at the present time," the Foreign Office's W. P. Cranston informed the company. But if COCOM's restrictions were somehow surmounted, the undersecretary for air concluded upon reviewing the Rolls request, "we should probably support an application of this kind." Thus Cranston promised the company, "We are about to discuss with the Americans and later in COCOM the revision of the strategic export controls [on aircraft]," though he warned against too great an optimism. American acquiescence was in no way assured, and no Western government had yet defied a COCOM ruling in order to complete a controversial export. Consequently, not one of the select few Whitehall officials privy to the secretive Rolls Royce effort underestimated the difficulties ahead. "Any such proposal would raise the strongest objections on the part of the Americans who are particularly sensitive about the question of exports to China, especially of aircraft," Cranston warned, noting that the Americans were especially wary of "any proposal to assist the Chinese to set up a jet air engine factory." Through great effort, British diplomats had won the right to sell equally to China as to the Soviet Union. Whether they could gain COCOM and American approval for aircraft sales, however, so as to seek profits in a market devoid of American competition and potentially capable of sustaining British aviation for years to come, remained to be seen.[38]

The Czech Ploy

By mid-decade Eisenhower's advisers grudgingly accepted the logic of liberalized air travel across Europe's iron curtain, but they continued to single out the Chinese bloc for aerial containment. Said a brief signed (though most likely not written) by Dulles in June 1956, "Our end objective vis-à-vis the USSR and its satellites from a civil aviation policy point of view remains the same as toward other countries, . . . the orderly development of air transport relations on the basis of reciprocal rights and the broadest possible freedom consistent with our national security and sound economic principles." China, however, was different. "Consistent with US unilateral restrictions on relations with the Communist Asian states, the United States should not authorize US airliners to establish services to Communist China, North Korea, or North Viet-nam," NSC-5726 stated, and "should oppose establishment of air services between other Free World countries and the three Asian Communist states."[39]

Containment would be Washington's watchword for Asia, and American strategists sought to impose a strict aerial embargo around China as well. Mao's regime needed planes to spread its uniquely belligerent brand of Communism, yet having no indigenous aviation industry of its own, it appeared more sensitive to outside economic pressures. As we have seen, forces loyal to the Nationalists absconded to Taiwan with the country's main transport fleets at the close of China's civil war, and the bulk of the country's aircraft during the early 1950s came from the Soviet bloc. By 1957, however, as the seeds of Sino-Soviet tension began to sprout, Beijing began to seek the kind of strategic independence and prestige an indigenous aviation industry could bring. American policymakers were determined to deny it to them. "The United States should (a) not sell or export to these [Asian] states civil aircraft or associated aviation equipment," the National Security Council concluded. More importantly, it should "(b) seek to prevent other Free World nations from selling or exporting to these states civil aircraft or associated aviation equipment."[40]

London's prospective sale of Rolls Royce engines to China in 1957 therefore required delicate handling, because Washington was sure to view the sale as a direct threat to its own aviation policies in Asia, and because COCOM consent required Washington's acquiescence. A direct approach to the State Department, seeking approval for sales to China, seemed pointless, the Supply Ministry's James Barnes noted, "particularly after the never-to-be-forgotten Nene affair." London thus chose a more circuitous route. In February 1958 the Foreign Office asked for COCOM approval for an export of $23,000 worth of World War II surplus DC-3 parts to Czechoslovakia. British officials reasoned that not even Washington could object to such an innocuous sale of outdated parts to one of the Soviet bloc's more pro-Western states without seeming overly belligerent to COCOM's members, especially given its recent rhetorical support of expanded aviation ties to Eastern Europe. Much was at stake with this application. With the differential now a thing of the past, COCOM approval of a sale to Eastern Europe automatically meant approval of a similar sale to China. A sale to Prague would open the route to Beijing.[41]

The Czech sale, then, was merely a ploy. China was the real goal. The application to export these parts to Prague had been languishing in Foreign Office files for over a year by the time of Britain's request to COCOM, and exports valued at a mere $23,000 rarely merited the attention of Britain's highest diplomats. Yet London raised the matter with COCOM only weeks after Rolls's request for Whitehall permission to sell engines to China, and this sale certainly captivated the Foreign Office. Macmillan's government enthusiastically (if quietly) supported Rolls's efforts in Asia. "There is something to be said for getting in on the ground floor of a new market that may soon open up so long as we concurrently conform to the rules," Cranston wrote in April 1958. His ministry advised Rolls to continue their quiet cultivation of the Chinese. British planes might no longer be the unquestioned best, but in the Brabazon spirit they could still be first.[42]

Timing alone thus offers at least a circumstantial case for the charge that London conspired to fly to Beijing via Prague. More telling is evidence from Duncan Sandys, who by 1959 headed up Macmillan's aviation portfolio. Writing of the pending Czech sale, Sandys wrote Macmillan in May 1958, "Our proposal to release from embargo aircraft which are in normal use will not be considered in COCOM until mid-June," adding, "In terms of potential trade, this is one of the most important of the changes we are proposing to COCOM." Then came the kicker. "I need not remind you of the value to the aircraft industry of access to the *Chinese* market for civil aircraft." In other words, Britain's COCOM application for aircraft sales to Czechoslovakia was really all about China. It was about using easy sales to set the precedent within COCOM for controversial ones, a tactic made possible only following elimination of the despised differential.[43]

Whitehall fully expected the Americans to take the bait. "We consider that no strategic risk is attached to this [the Czech] export," one British diplomat concluded, and consequently any American "justification for an embargo of these spare parts is ephemeral." Britain's ambassador to the United States, Harold Caccia, even cornered Douglas Dillon, undersecretary of state for economic affairs, in order to emphasize that an American objection to the sale would be seen in Europe as yet another obstinate American move of the kind that threatened COCOM's foundation. "I instanced the case of the spare parts for obsolescent Czech DC3s," Caccia reported home, "pointing out that a refusal to permit the export of something which to any reasonable man could not have the least significance on any strategic considerations, made it more difficult to retain any sort of respect for and acceptance of the controls which were really necessary." Even though American policymakers opposed any aircraft sale across the iron curtain, Europeans wanted to see that Washington was wise enough in pursuit of their larger goals to let small things pass. To Caccia's way of thinking, halting one minor sale of obsolete parts to a reasonable communist state was not worth risking Western solidarity on the trade controls that truly mattered.[44]

Whitehall should have learned by 1958 never to underestimate American inflexibility. Despite repeated British lobbying, when COCOM met to debate Britain's proposed sale to Czechoslovakia, the American representative lodged the only protest. "The US objected on the grounds that although the aircraft are civil and very old," Britain's delegation reported, "they considered that any form of aircraft and parts are a direct adjunct of the military air arm of the Sino-Soviet bloc." The NSC had envisioned releasing civil aircraft to the Soviet bloc on a case-by-case basis, but apparently not even spare parts for discarded planes were safe enough to export.[45]

Aircraft were only one of numerous relaxations to the COCOM lists proposed in the summer of 1958. France and Japan joined with Britain in leading a general charge within the body to relax East-West trade restraints, leaving only the American delegation as consistent opponents of liberalization. London's delegation argued that COCOM rules were "designed to embargo the most modern armaments . . . not industrial machinery or items which are used predominantly for civil purposes." Economic warfare, in other words, was worthwhile if directed against communist militaries, but repugnant if used to hinder development or harm civilians. Nearly every delegation save Washington's agreed. "The rest of COCOM [was] with us on most items under dispute with the US," Britain's representative concluded. Only the United States wanted to broaden the embargo. "Their stand on aircraft remains particularly uncompromising," London's team added in June. The Americans called for the continued embargo of "virtually all civil aircraft of any size," despite Europe's march toward aerial integration over the past two years. Washington's arguments in favor of strict aviation containment had succeeded in 1948, when initiated at the onset of the Berlin airlift. Their proposals for a general aviation embargo of the communist world similarly worked in 1951 at the height of the Korean War. By 1958, however, objections to the sale of outdated civilian aircraft and parts had lost all relevance outside of Washington. Most European states even backed Britain's proposal to limit COCOM restraints to solely nuclear materials and technology. Fearing destruction of COCOM itself in the face of such unanimous opposition, in August the Americans finally backed down, agreeing to a 50 percent reduction in the scope of COCOM's embargo, including sale of civil aircraft. They salvaged COCOM and passed Caccia's leadership test, though only grudgingly.[46]

Washington managed to secure one important restriction on East-West aircraft sales despite this general spirit of liberalization: that only civil aircraft, engines, or parts that had been in commercial service for at least two years could be exported to communists. Two years would surely give communist agents enough time to study machines placed in international service, and such products could thus no longer be considered to contain strategic materials worth safeguarding. Anything younger than two years would continue to be strictly controlled. COCOM retained the embargo on military aircraft and maintained the right to control sales of specific aviations and parts, even if incorporated into older aircraft. Thus a new radar system, for instance, even if loaded aboard a twenty-year-old plane, remained subject to COCOM's restraints. Such rulings seemed a significant victory for British exporters, who won the right to consummate the Czechoslovakian sale at the heart of the COCOM dispute. Indeed, when Prime Minister Macmillan was briefed on his COCOM negotiating team's results for 1958, the first item on his long catalog of exportable goods read: "most civil aircraft and civil aero engines—e.g. Viscounts."[47]

The air route to the East lay open. The year 1958 was a watershed in COCOM. British diplomats rallied European and Japanese support in their crusade against Washington's hard-line export controls, and the Eisenhower administration conceded the need for change without forsaking the international body. But the Americans had no idea what they had agreed to.

On to Asia

Rolls Royce never completed its China sale, despite these diplomatic wranglings on their behalf. Because London wanted to keep the topic as quiet as possible, the question of sales to China never directly arose during these COCOM negotiations. Washington consequently knew nothing of Rolls's secret negotiations with Beijing, believing Eastern Europe to be the real target for British exporters and the real motivation for Britain's divisive COCOM request. Washington's opposition to the Czech deal, and its general effort to keep COCOM's rules as stringent as possible throughout 1958, had the inadvertent consequence of thwarting Rolls's negotiations. COCOM approval for East-West aircraft sales came seven months after Britain's initial application for the Czech deal and thus eight months after Rolls Royce had first approached the Foreign Office for permission to sell to Beijing. By the time Whitehall gave Rolls the green light to consummate the deal, Mao's government had lost interest. "There does not seem to be any great enthusiasm on the part of the Chinese for the British aircraft industry at present," the British embassy reluctantly concluded in December 1958, despite repeated visits (some secret, some public) of British teams hawking engines, turboprop Viscounts, used Britannias, and even jet-powered Comets. "The Chinese seem more interested in collecting information than in doing any business." Given Beijing's mercurial negotiating style, no one in London assigned any particular significance to this rebuff, presuming another opportunity to sell beyond the Great Wall would arise soon enough.[48]

Rolls lost its bid to enter the China market in 1958, but Vickers pursued Beijing with vigor, believing their turboprop Viscount perfectly suited for China's nascent aviation infrastructure. The cabinet approved the company's initial negotiations, with the reminder that any export to China required Whitehall's explicit approval. Washington was more than capable of exerting bilateral pressure, even following COCOM's endorsement of any such deal. "COCOM-wise, as Viscounts are exempted from embargo, we are entitled to export them to China," one British diplomat wrote, though he warned that the case "only affects COCOM in so far as sale of Viscounts to

China could make the Americans more difficult on unrelated cases." Washington would not be pleased, after all, with news that Britain was cracking China's heretofore sealed market.[49]

Diplomatic pleas for caution lost out to more pressing economic arguments. The Board of Trade reminded the Foreign Office in August 1960, "We are anxious that this trade should be done," especially since there were "obvious advantages to selling Viscounts which are likely to be far more valuable business than all our [previous trade] for China put together for years and years." Caution remained the Foreign Office's byword of the day, however, as one British official stationed in Beijing warned that Vickers should not "draw the Chinese attention to the fact that Viscounts are off the embargo unless we were sure that we were prepared to sell them to the Chinese if they followed it up." From an international perspective, he said, they "should give the Chinese a first class opportunity to say that we were under the thumb of the Americans if we suggested that they could buy Viscounts and then refused them permission to do so because of American objections." Even with COCOM approval, in other words, Washington still might—and probably would—object to supplying Mao's government with planes. British strategists and manufacturers each wanted to sell aircraft to China by the beginning of the 1960s. They had wanted to do so three years before. What they needed was the right moment, and the will to withstand inevitable American objections.[50]

Halfway across the world, Chinese prime minister Zhou Enlai provided just such an opportunity. While flying aboard an Indian Viscount from Rangoon to Delhi in the late summer of 1961, Zhou waxed enthusiastic to his escorts about the plane and his long-standing desire to purchase similar Western machines. He compared the plane favorably with the Soviet IL-18 (of which China possessed several), and even engaged his pilot in the conversation. Zhou seemed smitten with the prospect of buying British, and his escort passed news of the incident to the Foreign Office, which quickly forwarded the information to Vickers. The company dispatched a sales team to Beijing within a week, beginning what would be months of arduous, if promising, negotiations. "The energy with which the Chinese have tackled the discussions leave no doubt of their serious interest in the possibility of buying British aircraft," the Vickers team wrote home in August 1961, using the British embassy's secure lines to send the message. The embassy itself believed a headline-grabbing aircraft sale could prompt a profitable wave of future trade in this budding market. "If this deal goes through it will mean that the first major break-through in this market has been achieved," Britain's chargé d'affaires to China said. Secret diplomacy over Prague had cleared the way, once London found the political will (and the international allies) necessary to stand up to Washington in COCOM. Whitehall policymakers surprised even themselves, however, with the lengths they would go to, to succeed in China.[51]

CHAPTER 7

The Viscount Conspiracy

Fulfilling the fears British leaders had held since World War II, by the start of the 1960s American aerial supremacy appeared poised to become a diplomatic hammer, leading to the climax of Cold War aviation relations between the two nations. The scene was primed for confrontation. "Rationalization" had left only three major British aviation firms alive by 1960, when twelve had existed only a year before. Macmillan's government wasted little time in rewarding the survivors. In February 1960, Aviation Minister Julian Amery announced "launch aid," promising timely infusions of government cash for promising civil aviation projects. Whitehall had already embarked on an unprecedented export promotion campaign to both sides of the iron curtain, buoyed by the previous decade's successful COCOM negotiations. With diplomacy, subsidies, and a chosen set of firms tempered by the fires of competition, British policymakers once more hoped to tip aviation's zero-sum game in their favor. "Our most formidable competitor is the United States," Amery declared. "Any weakening of government support would be fatal to our hopes of future success."[1]

Technology again offered one potential avenue of success. Having irretrievably lost their lead in subsonic jets to American competition by the mid-1950s, British aviation enthusiasts charged ahead with plans for a supersonic transport. As with the Brabazon models, they envisioned a plane capable of winning buyers ahead of American competition through elegant technology rather than production bulk. The exorbitant costs of producing such an advanced machine wholly on British soil ultimately led to an alliance with France and the famed Concorde. Whether unilaterally or jointly produced, supersonic flight appeared Britain's (and by extension, Europe's) only remaining chance to match the Americans in the air. "Britain has an opportunity here of gaining the leadership we so narrowly missed with the

Comet," Amery intoned, adding, "It would be wrong to leave this class of aircraft entirely to the United States." Everyone in Whitehall expected an American supersonic competitor before the end of the decade. There was never such consensus within the United States. Though initially enthusiastic, American firms ultimately found the economics of commercial supersonic flight prohibitive. Allied with the French, however, British leaders charged ahead despite the costs, believing Chancellor of the Exchequer Selwyn Lloyd's 1961 warning that to allow an American monopoly over this new technology would be to forever forsake Britain's aspirations to great-power status. They could not risk falling behind again, he cautioned, though he simultaneously warned that flagging exports and a five-year decline in Britain's share of global manufacturing limited the Treasury's ability to afford Herculean aviation projects despite the government's much-lauded promises of aid. The dilemma seemed circular: aviation was required for power, influence, and prosperity, and Britain needed to stay one step ahead of the Americans if it were to succeed; but prosperity was itself required in order to fund and support a cutting-edge aviation industry. The costs were high, Lloyd concluded, but without flight, Britain would not be able "to play a large, and indeed increasing, part in the defense of the Free World" and would lose forever its ability to offer an alternative to the Pax Americana.[2]

Just as British policymakers longed for a new push toward aviation dominance at the onset of the 1960s, a new series of events further revealed the imbalance of power within the special relationship spawned by Washington's increasing dominance of the field. In 1962, President John F. Kennedy approved sale of Hawk antiaircraft missiles to Israel, despite a prior Anglo-American pledge to forestall missile sales to the region. Intense lobbying by Israel's political backers, coupled with the lure of an untapped market, prompted the swift and unexpected change. Macmillan's fury left him nearly speechless. "I can hardly find words to express my sense of disgust and despair," he cabled Kennedy upon hearing the news. He considered the American move, coming as it did from a president for whom he felt a special closeness, a stab in the back. He threatened to retaliate by "instruct[ing] our own manufacturers to try to undersell Hawk with Bloodhound [a British alternative]," thus initiating the very Middle East arms race the two countries had long sought to avoid. Macmillan's rage eventually cooled, especially when he realized that Tel Aviv preferred to buy American. Yet Washington's unilateral decision seemed to him proof yet again of what he saw as the infuriating American ability to separate commercial and security arguments at whim whenever it suited their needs. His aerospace industry needed the sales far more, but Britain never dared break its word in order to secure them. The Americans were hardly as burdened. As Thucydides noted millennia before, strong states do as they will; weak states what they might.[3]

Macmillan had suffered from Washington's aerospace dominance before. The missile dispute over Israel was merely a minor hiccup in the special relationship. More important was the Skybolt dispute that occurred at the end of 1962. This story begins with Duncan Sandys's 1957 defense white paper and London's subsequent emphasis on pursuing cost-effective and prestigious nuclear power over more expensive traditional military forces such as ships and armies. Nuclear power soon became a crutch, however, for as Ambassador Harold Caccia advised from Washington, having slashed traditional arms, "our acceptance as a great power now rests to a large extent on our having a military nuclear program." Macmillan wholeheartedly agreed, and further believed nuclear power necessary for a healthy special relationship. Membership in the nuclear club "makes the United States pay a greater regard to our point of view," he said, which made it worth the cost.[4]

Developing the bomb proved easier than finding a credible means of delivering it. The advent of the missile age threatened obsolescence for the RAF's nuclear-capable V-Bomber almost from the moment it entered service in 1957. The plane proved too slow to elude Soviet air defenses, and too lethargic for low-level strikes below radar surveillance. Worse still, Britain's best land-based nuclear alternative, the exorbitantly expensive Blue Streak missle, required a 30-minute fueling and launch sequence at a time when a Soviet first strike would take under 15 minutes from launch to impact. Blue Streak was not a credible deterrent as a consequence, and in early 1960 Macmillan was forced to scrub the program and accept Dwight Eisenhower's pledge to provide Britain with American-made Skybolt missiles in exchange for the establishment of American submarine bases in Scotland.[5]

The deal seemed a coup for both nations. The air-launched Skybolt was cheaper and longer-ranging than the land-based Blue Streak, and its deployment as a "standoff" weapon aboard V-Bombers alleviated the need for the RAF to develop an expensive new bomber replacement. The American navy, meanwhile, gained access to valuable bases within easy sailing distance of Russia's northern coast. The deal suggested a strengthening of the special relationship based upon increased nuclear intimacy. Its details revealed a starker reality. Submarines were (along with bombers and missiles) but one leg of the American nuclear triad. Skybolt, conversely, was Britain's sole means of remaining in the nuclear game, meaning that London's celebrated independent nuclear deterrent was in fact dependent upon American technology and thus wholly subject to Washington's continued support. Britain's membership in the nuclear club was not, in this sense, independent at all, leading Macmillan to worry "[if] the Americans [are] going to let us down, and [if so] what can we do?" He had no choice but to trust Eisenhower's word that the next administration would deliver Skybolt as promised. "We are relying very heavily on you for this," he reminded Ike in October.[6]

Macmillan's faith, when unmatched by American works, brought the special relationship to the breaking point. Skybolt proved ineffective. Behind schedule and over budget, it became one of Secretary of Defense Robert McNamara's least favorite programs. Influential State Department strategists wanted it killed as well. They questioned the wisdom of London's expensive pursuit of nuclear power at a time when Washington's nuclear umbrella already covered Western Europe, and they feared that Britain's pursuit of an independent deterrent might spawn further nuclear proliferation. If London had the bomb, they reasoned, Paris would want it too, further eroding American hegemony. Faced with allies in search of strategic arms of their own, the Kennedy administration's *Basic National Security Policy* for 1961 called for "encouragement of the United Kingdom to phase out its independent strategic nuclear program." Thus buoyed by Foggy Bottom, McNamara canceled Skybolt at the end of 1962.[7]

His decision prompted a firestorm of British protests. London would lose face internationally without its publicly lauded independent deterrent, Macmillan fumed to Kennedy, and the public dismantling of his government's heralded military policy might cause his own fall from power. Surely no future British government would ever trust American promises again, prompting what he termed "a deep rift with the United States." As Defense Minister Peter Thorneycroft publicly declared, "It is American good faith that is in question."[8]

Kennedy relented before this maelstrom. Rather than resurrect Skybolt, the president (against the advice of many of his principal advisers) authorized British acquisition of the more advanced Polaris missile in its place. This conclusion appeared to be a victory for the British, who replaced a troubled and rapidly obsolescing missile system with a promising successor. Still, the brief crisis left a bitter taste for leaders from both countries, especially in London where Skybolt prompted what one witness termed "resentment

and suspicion of American intentions such as I have never experienced."
More importantly, the affair vividly illuminated Britain's subservient role
in the special relationship. As observers the world over now realized, London could not even sustain the primary symbol of its autonomy—nuclear
power—without Washington's support. It was no accident, historians of Skybolt frequently note, that Macmillan read Gibbon's *Decline and Fall of the Roman Empire* as he flew to meet Kennedy to beg for Britain's survival as a nuclear state. This was a moment when the faltering of London's global power
lay naked for all to see.[9]

Skybolt revealed Britain's aeronautical inferiority to the world, but
Macmillan's strategists had privately reached this conclusion well before the
controversy exploded into public consciousness. For them, the crisis that
erupted in the last months of 1962 actually began two years earlier, when
their prime minister rested British power upon an American-made missile,
because as they well knew, the power to supply was the power to strangle.
This was a power Whitehall had long hoped to use for its own strategic ends.
Now Washington held the cards, prompting one member of Parliament to
demand, upon hearing of the Eisenhower-Macmillan accord, that Sandys
"stop talking about this as an independent British deterrent when so much
of it is entirely American made and produced." Sandys could only answer by
stressing that there would still be a British finger on the nuclear button, no
matter where the weapon had been made, adding, "The fact that a weapon
is manufactured in a foreign country does not alter our independence of action when we have that weapon installed on our aircraft." British fingers
would not, however, control their country's nuclear assembly line, a reality
that demonstrated the country's technological dependence upon the United
States as had been feared by successive British governments since 1942. Realization of this harsh fact colored London's approach toward its dwindling
aviation opportunities.[10]

Under Macmillan, Britain's aviation future appeared hazier than ever before. Skybolt demonstrated the country's technological weakness; the Comet
was gone; the Treasury could ill afford to fund expensive new alternatives;
and the supersonic transport might never fly or be profitable. The wildly
successful Vickers Viscount, a medium-range turboprop, was nearing the
end of its production run with no promising British replacement on the
near horizon, especially as Boeing's medium-range 727 jetliner appeared
the market's consistent choice over Britain's Trident. Boeing announced initial 727 sales in 1959 to United and Eastern Airlines worth $420 million.

Meanwhile, British European Airways buckled to vigorous government pressure by ordering 115 custom-built Tridents (which airline executives believed they did not need), merely to keep the assembly line at work. Boeing eventually sold more than two thousand 727s. Additional Trident sales following the BEA purchase, conversely, barely topped 100. "As far as [aircraft] exports are concerned," Lloyd warned, "we face a big drop over the next few years."[11]

The need for aviation exports had not been this keen since 1945, thus prompting Whitehall's renewed interest in China, which seemed the answer to all that ailed Britain's faltering industry. China needed aircraft; it remained wholly off-limits to American manufacturers; and it clearly wanted Western machines following the Sino-Soviet split. "The British aircraft industry badly needs orders," Foreign Secretary Alec Douglas-Home deduced in the fall of 1961, adding, "This [the China market] is a valuable one." Beijing lacked the finances and infrastructure to sustain British aviation on its own, but the search for a British foothold in the world's most populous country was a quest for future success. China's appetite for aircraft was potentially boundless, and British analysts frequently used terms like *capture* and *monopolize* when discussing their plans for the country. They believed that a single successful sale would bring forth a torrent of future orders capable of supporting exporters for a generation. "None of us can forecast the extent of this [aircraft] market in the immediate future," the embassy in Beijing concluded in 1961, "but it is clear that the potential market could be very large and what we do now will influence future Chinese decisions."[12]

Chinese leaders were equally interested in cementing such ties. During the winter of 1960–61, their trade representatives repeatedly stated with uncharacteristic bluntness that Beijing's break with Moscow could benefit UK exporters. Sino-British trade had increased nearly 50 percent during the previous year, and Britain's embassy in Beijing reported at the start of 1961 that their contacts within Mao's government hoped this jump augured a long-term trend. "We cannot afford to ignore the existence of so large a nation whose government we have recognized," one memo for the cabinet read, "[especially because] there is a substantial market for British goods of a non-military character in China." The majority of British strategists continued to believe that Chinese economic development improved the likelihood of détente, even though their strategy directly contradicted Washington's long-favored support for brash economic warfare and political isolation, and Macmillan's cabinet yearned for any deal that might further cement ties with Beijing. Trade offered "the most constructive field of Anglo-Chinese re-lations," Board of Trade president Frederick Erroll argued, whereas restric-tions on trade "build up an atmosphere of suspicion" and "discourage ten-dencies towards a more liberal and normal regime which it must be our objective to encourage."[13]

The "fat communist" theory (that prosperous communist states would be more open to détente with the West) was alive and well in London at the very moment when Britain needed aircraft sales and Beijing sought its first Western models. American objections seemed the only potential obstacle. One British diplomat wrote in 1961, "The use of strategic controls as a mea-sure for delaying industrial development of the bloc has no place in the scheme of things. I do not think that this is a proposition that is held any-where in Whitehall (though it is certainly held across the Atlantic)." The battle to be waged for the right to sell planes to China would be a last gasp of British attempts to reach great-power status through aviation. Ironically, the only thing great about the diplomacy to follow was the level of deception re-quired.[14]

Selling to China

The Vickers team that arrived in Beijing in the summer of 1961 operated un-der a crushing burden. The future of Sino-British relations seemed to rest on their success. "If this deal goes through it will mean the first major break-through in this market," the head of the British consulate reminded them, since "the Chinese would for the first time be buying really expensive and complicated British equipment and making themselves dependent on the UK for spares and services." Failure could set back relations for years. But "if the Chinese are prepared to change their policies to the extent of buying British aircraft, the purchase, for example, of complete power stations or in-dustrial plants in the next few years will not be too difficult for them."[15]

The only thing that tempered British enthusiasm was the expectation that Washington would react with ferocity to news of an aircraft deal. It re-mained American policy to keep China as isolated as possible, and one Brit-ish policymaker lamented toward the end of Eisenhower's second term that when it came to Beijing, the Americans "might almost have been applying the criteria of 1951." Few observers expected Kennedy's team to treat China any differently. Several of the president's key advisers (including Secretary of State Dean Rusk and Assistant Secretary of State for Far Eastern Affairs

Averell Harriman) privately favored relaxation of tensions with China, but Kennedy's slim electoral victory over the impeccably anticommunist Richard Nixon precluded any softening in the new administration's Cold War stance. Kennedy "lacked a strong mandate from the American people," Rusk later wrote, and "consequently he was very cautious about selecting issues on which to do battle. And any change in China policy would have been one hell of a battle." The battles that did matter to Kennedy were with the Soviets. Improving relations with China was far less important in his global view. "I don't want to read in *The Washington Post* and *The New York Times* that the State Department is thinking about a change in China policy," he told Rusk in July 1961. The topic was simply political dynamite, as was the issue of East-West trade. His administration consequently planned no major COCOM initiatives and no loosening of American trade restraints, leading analysts at Britain's Board of Trade to predict that "COCOM has been (and may be expected to be) a running sore in Anglo-American relations."[16]

Fearing Washington's reaction, the Foreign Office and the Board of Trade each cautioned the Vickers team to keep its efforts in China as secret as possible. Although "the presence of the Vickers party in Peking will doubtless attract attention," the Foreign Office advised in August 1961, "in view of the uncertainty of the position at present and so as to not prejudice Vickers commercially we do not propose to inform the Americans for the time being." Their efforts worked. The Macmillan government followed every step of the negotiations by reading the company's mail transmitted through its embassy, but Washington would not learn of Vickers's negotiations in China until October. By this time, the sales were nearly done.[17]

The negotiations progressed with unprecedented speed. Conducting business with Mao's government was typically a tricky affair for Western firms. Beijing controlled its foreign trade with an iron hand and linked business with politics whenever possible. Chinese negotiators frequently forced European salespeople to answer for Washington's refusal to recognize their government's legitimacy, and they often required visiting trade missions to justify government policies in which they had no say and little interest. When negotiations collapsed, the disappointed foreigners often left wondering if the Chinese had sought from the start to embarrass them on an international stage. As British diplomats in Beijing noted, Chinese negotiators appeared to be playing by a different set of rules.[18]

To their surprise and delight, the Vickers team encountered no such difficulties. "The energy with which the Chinese have tackled the discussions leaves no doubt of their serious interest in the possibility of buying British aircraft," they cabled home in August. "The non-stop programme of talks over the first seven days is unprecedented so far as British business visitors are concerned, and the atmosphere in which the talks have taken place is also remarkable." Weeks into the negotiations, Chinese negotiators had yet to make a single reference to the international situation or to Sino-British relations. Beijing seemed intent upon setting up an industrial pipeline between their two countries, and it seemed interested in doing so purely on commercial terms. Prospects for a successful deal improved with each passing day. "We have, I am sure," the chargé d'affaires wrote home, "come to the most critical point to date in the promotion of Sino-British trade."[19]

Tensions across the Atlantic would soon throw up a potential roadblock. Whitehall mandated that its manufacturers adhere to all of COCOM's regulations, and the organization continued to bar shipments to communist states of planes and equipment that had been in service less than two years. With nearly a decade of international service, Viscounts seemed at first blush exportable to Beijing. Yet policymakers realized to their dismay nearly four weeks into the negotiations that the march of technological progress had created a significant COCOM hurdle. The Viscount airframes were exportable, but the radar and communications components recently installed by Vickers on new models remained subject to the multilateral embargo. Despite prodding, the Chinese refused to accept older (to their minds, inferior) equipment, arguing that their plans for international service demanded the international standard.[20]

This unexpected COCOM restraint threatened the entire deal. Vickers could not "go firm on a contract with the Chinese," the Foreign Office's E. H. Peck concluded, without the expectation of COCOM approval for the sale. British officials considered the components in question to be of negligible strategic value, having been used by Western airlines for years, and the communications equipment was already employed on flights behind the iron curtain. "Their supply will not therefore give any know-how away to the bloc," a hastily gathered group of Ministry of Aviation officials concluded, and "the release to China of small quantities of the equipment is not of strategic importance."[21]

Gaining COCOM approval, in essence American approval, for the export would not be easy. COCOM compiled two lists of goods: products barred from export to the communist world because of their military or technological value, and products whose export was quantitatively limited because of their potential role as bottlenecks to communist production. Each list was revised annually. Nations could claim an "exception" in order to export an embargoed item if denying the sale would cause material economic or political harm at home. COCOM exceptions were exceedingly rare, however, since the organization's purpose was to impose a uniform set of controls throughout the Western community, and thus the political pressures to conform to the group's will were great. Indeed, the total value of exceptions for 1959 had been less than $500,000, and none had been drawn from COCOM's list of goods considered too technologically advanced to export.[22]

States could request a COCOM exception in order to export an embargoed or controlled product, but approval was far from automatic. Any member state could object to an exception request and thereby block the export. If Germany wanted an exception in order to export an embargoed good to Hungary, for example, but Paris objected, then Bonn was expected to halt the sale in deference to French concerns. COCOM itself had no enforcement mechanism. Its guidelines were neither legally binding nor inviolable. Nothing kept Germany from completing the above hypothetical sale save fear of condemnation from its closest allies, as COCOM's rules were predicated on de facto political control. Yet such informal ties were particularly strong. No member of the group wanted to jeopardize its most important international relationships by carelessly flaunting the unanimously approved lists, just as no single member wanted to risk the group's ire by being the sole objector to an exceptional sale. Only the power of international persuasion—or coercion—forced adherence to these guidelines, for no member wanted to become a pariah within the Western community. Furthermore, because COCOM's lists were revised annually, any member wishing to export an embargoed item need only await the proper moment to suggest its release, such as when Britain secured the abolition of the China differential in 1957 and the ability to export civil aircraft a year later. Success was not guaranteed through this process, but neither was it as diplomatically risky as invoking the exception option. These factors contributed to make exception requests rare, and an exception request for truly controversial items, like the Vickers parts for the first Western aviation export to China, was almost without precedent.[23]

Vickers did not have a year to wait. Beijing's representatives, who clearly believed they held the upper hand, refused to accept anything but the most advanced components for their Viscounts. Neither would they accept a delay of delivery until the embargoed equipment passed through the embargo phase. COCOM was London's problem, they argued. Their insistence left London no choice but to ask for a COCOM exception for the embargoed Vickers parts in question or lose its dream of monopolizing the China market. This was in essence a choice of angering either Washington or Beijing. Each option carried distressing consequences. The Americans would be furious to discover Britain's efforts to open China to high-technology exports, though failure to gain Washington's approval of an exception request would leave London with the choice of toeing the line or proceeding with a sale despite American objections. Beijing would surely criticize London's inability to withstand American pressure if they chose the first path, and would be much less willing to trade in the future. Ignoring American objections, conversely, might damage the special relationship, though no one in the Foreign Office dared speculate on Washington's actual retribution. Perhaps most dramatically, rejection of an American veto might undermine COCOM itself. No country had yet forged ahead with a sale following opposition to an exception request. Macmillan's cabinet frequently complained about the intensity of the American-led strategic embargo, but they did not want to be the cause of the organization's downfall. Being predicated solely upon multilateral consent, any outright break with a collective decision risked the group's demise. These were the stark choices facing the cabinet in September 1962. Britain's future in Asia, and its waning great-power dreams, seemed to rest on decisions to be made in Washington.[24]

On October 6, the Foreign Office opted to directly ask for Washington's approval (more accurately, for Washington's promise not to block London's COCOM request), reasoning that their chances for success would plummet if the Americans first learned of the exception request during a COCOM meeting. This direct route offered at least the possibility of solving the issue behind closed doors. Jobs were at stake in this sale, jobs initially valued at £9 million. So too was prestige. More importantly, British analysts believed there was no viable strategic objection to the transfer of such outdated equipment. The radar involved "has no direct application as an airborne intercept system but offers facilities only for cloud warning, high ground avoidance, ground mapping facilities and crude measurements of drift," London advised its Washington embassy. "Its military application, therefore, is very limited," and its worldwide use ensured that the communists "have thus had ample opportunity to find out all about it." Similar communications equipment had already been shipped to the Soviet bloc to facilitate East-West flights. "In neither case, is there any real danger to giving away know-how through this transaction."[25]

Britain came clean about the impending Viscount sale on October 14, when John Rennie, commercial minister to the British embassy in Washington, met with State Department officials to request that the administration not block the sale of twelve Viscounts. His appeal did not come as a complete surprise, but neither was Washington's information on the matter completely up to date. The Americans knew as early as September 1 that China was interested in purchasing Viscounts, but Kennedy's officials had no idea that negotiations had already begun. Moreover, their sources believed Vickers hoped to sell Beijing twenty Viscounts, a total purchase far exceeding what the Americans thought the Chinese could afford. "They needed what little money they had for the purchase of food," the assistant secretary of state for economic affairs, Ed Martin, roared. Were the British financing the Chinese purchase, he demanded, and therefore funding Chinese industrialization? "The general tone of the conversation was not discouraging," Samuel Hood, minister to the British embassy in Washington, concluded. "But I would not like to hold out great hope of our securing American agreement [to a COCOM exception]."[26]

Kennedy's State Department took more than a month to respond to the British overture, which one American official admitted spawned "considerable debate" in administration circles. He advised the British not to expect a reply before mid-November, and with the Vickers team in Beijing anxiously awaiting approval for their sale, Whitehall tensions skyrocketed. "If the Chinese really want the aircraft and the sale is called off because of COCOM difficulty," one of Foreign Secretary Douglas-Home's principal advisers warned, "they will certainly do all in their power to embitter Anglo-American relations by claiming that we were prepared to do business but that, as usual, we have had to yield to American pressure." The first draft of this memorandum originally proffered "our master's voice" instead of "American pressure," indicative of the passions involved. If American pressure scuttled the sale, he continued, "we shall get the old accusations that we are merely the stooges of the Americans and, as you know this tends to strike a responsive chord among some members of Parliament." "[Under] these circumstances, we could expect an attack on COCOM in Parliament and this will almost certainly develop into an attack on the Americans."[27]

Tensions increased across the Pacific as well, where Washington's foot-dragging threatened to scuttle the deal. Further "delay in granting of an export license may result in the business being lost with consequent serious re-percussions," Vickers's representatives in Beijing reported, while embassy officials described being "seriously perturbed and embarrassed by our failure to confirm export license." After such a promising start to negotiations, they feared a thwarted deal might slam the market's door closed tighter than ever. When the State Department informed British officials on October 26 that they could not even predict when they might have a formal reply, Whitehall knew it had no choice but to proceed with a COCOM exception request without American approval. "We cannot delay any longer our re-quest for clearance," Douglas-Home telegrammed his embassies. China was too important to lose for want of an answer.[28]

Just then the story erupted in the press. "Secret Bid to Sell British Jet Liners to China," the *Daily Express* headlined for October 28. The *Daily Mail* countered with "China to Buy British Air Fleet." Citing unnamed sources, both stories offered uncannily accurate accounts of the negotiations in China. Yet both made politically damaging mistakes. For example, the *Express* accurately told readers that "for two months sales and technical experts from Britain have been shuttling to Peking and back," while to Washing-ton's surprise, the *Mail* correctly revealed that Chinese officials had secretly visited the Viscount factory in England. Each paper made sure their readers appreciated the deal's potential significance. "It could be a big breakthrough into the Chinese market that could be exploited by many of Britain's indus-tries," Angus MacPherson, the *Mail*'s aviation correspondent, wrote, "a bril-liant tail-piece to the Viscount success story." The *Express* called the sale "a spectacular export break-through."[29]

The Macmillan government thus lost the opportunity to divulge news of the sale at the moment of their choosing. Indeed, though the cabinet had already decided to proceed with the export despite the COCOM dif-ficulties, such widespread reports, including their inaccuracies, made subse-quent cancellation of the contracts a political impossibility. Each newspaper reported China would purchase twenty Viscounts, the same number con-firmed by American sources. This was not the number that Britain's em-bassy in Washington batted about each time its representatives met with American officials, however, further fueling American suspicions that Lon-don had yet to come clean on the full scope of the sale. Worse yet, the *Ex-press* erroneously reported an impending follow-up sale to Beijing of five Super VC-10s, advanced jet planes capable of international service. Ameri-can objections to the sale of outdated turboprop Viscounts would be multiplied tenfold for such advanced jets with intercontinental range. Unlike the Viscounts, these new planes were not yet eligible for export under COCOM's current rules, making it seem as though London's plans to develop China knew no bounds. "If news reports from London prove true," the *Oakland Tribune* editorialized, "Great Britain is about to be guilty of another grave disservice to the Free World for the sake of monetary profit."[30]

Such reports were incorrect, but the damage was done. "We fear that reference to VC10s will not be helpful," Britain's embassy in Washington cabled home. "In discussion with the State Department two of the points we have stressed is that the Viscounts are not of recent design, and intended for medium-range service in SE Asia." Long-range VC-10 jets were neither. Their sale would give Beijing newer technology and a greater ability to expand throughout Asia, two things the Kennedy administration sharply criticized.[31]

These public revelations constrained Kennedy's options as well. In office less than a year—during which time foreign policy debacles outnumbered successes—the new administration lacked the political capital to ignore what its public already knew. With Berlin having been divided by barbed wire less than a month before, and with communists ensconced in Cuba and multiplying in Southeast Asia, the White House could not withstand the political fallout of failure to halt the country's closest ally from aiding its deepest enemy. The Viscount case additionally threatened the administration's hard line on technology trade with China among even American companies. A week after the first press reports of the Vickers sale, the director of sales for American Airlines asked the State Department if his airline might dispose of its own used aircraft in China despite the long-standing embargo on Sino-American trade. If the British were selling there, he reasoned, his company should be allowed to as well. He received an unequivocal no in reply, but his query and the growing publicity over the case foretold an ugly trend for the White House. Kennedy's advisers split over how best to handle this diplomatic crisis in the making. The National Security Council and the State Department's economic branch both vigorously opposed the sale. To their minds, the still-operative NSC-5726 made Washington's response clear: "It is National Security Council policy that the United States should frustrate any actions in the Free World that would enhance Communist China's civil aviation capability." However, the State Department's European desk cautioned that blocking the sale could "cause considerable protest in Britain," and that any perceived "United States interference with 'legitimate' British business" would bring calls for dramatic reprisals from throughout the United Kingdom. The Pentagon, meanwhile, worried the Viscounts could enhance Chinese military capabilities, especially "if the embargoed equipment could be obtained and copied." The Commerce Department proved too divided to even render a final judgment. In sum, every involved segment of the administration opposed Britain's Viscount sale to one degree or another. None knew what to do about it. Considering the magnitude of the issue and the lack of consensus within his government, Kennedy was scheduled to make the final decision by mid-November.[32]

Time ran out as Washington debated and delayed. Vickers was prepared to sign its contract to deliver the planes that week, and preparations had been made to mark the occasion with an elaborate ceremony in Beijing. "The issue of a license is now more urgent than ever," the embassy wired home, and the Ministry of Aviation urged that Vickers be given the green light. "You expect to have an answer from the US shortly," the ministry's Andrew Peggie advised the Foreign Office, "but even if the answer does not come soon, or if it is unfavorable, I would recommend that the license be issued to Vickers in time to meet the requirements of the Chinese." After all, "it is always open to the Board of Trade to revoke the license if, at a later stage, it is decided by HMG that this is desirable and as you are aware, delivery of these aircraft is unlikely in less than eighteen months from now." This same rationale had preceded the devastating sale of Nene engines to the Soviets a generation before.[33]

The Ministry of Aviation may have been willing to treat China and Washington roughly, but it was no simple thing for Britain to authorize an export license without COCOM approval. London's COCOM delegates warned that issuing an export license *before* asking for an exception augured poorly for the group's ultimate consent. "Are we not in danger of treating COCOM a little cavalierly?" Britain's head negotiator wrote. No nation had ever ignored an exception veto, but more to the point, none had dared ask for an exception after the fact. "To issue a license even before the COCOM discussion seems to me to set a dangerous precedent," he advised. "Perhaps it is a pity we have not already made our submission."[34]

In the end, Whitehall's pursuit of American approval prior to its COCOM request, though made with the best of intentions, only drove the two countries farther apart. Kennedy's advisers recognized that London planned to make its exception request no matter the American reaction, and they did not believe the British were being entirely truthful about the sales. Their paranoia grew in relation to their inability to determine the best response. The only thing they could agree upon was their anger that Britain would consider selling China planes in the first place. On the other side of the Atlantic, just as with the Comet affair, failure to define a mutually acceptable policy with the United States, despite frank dialogue, only embittered relations. One might justifiably ask if London should have expected anything different. Could any in Whitehall truly have expected Washington, after a generation of rigid adherence to anticommunist controls for China, to do anything but reject the British request? In this light, London's request may seem little more than a fool's errand. Indeed, Ed Martin, the State Department's point man for formulating Washington's response to the British request, had been one of the initial architects of NSC-15 and the anticommunist aviation embargo a decade before. He was unlikely to suddenly warm to British sales to China in direct contradiction of a policy he had spent years defending.

The only logical explanation for London's decision to seek accommodation with the Americans over this issue outside of COCOM lies at the heart of the special relationship. A weakened Britain could not afford to anger the United States with unilateral moves. It could occasionally defy American pressure, and with sufficient warning it could resist American leadership. But it could not simply ignore the massive power across the Atlantic. Macmillan's government moved on the China differential in 1957 only after years of bilateral discussions with the Americans, and only after first securing support from the remainder of COCOM. The Americans had been furious, and the State Department despised its isolated position. But they were not surprised. In pursuing Washington's approval for the Viscounts, Whitehall again offered the Americans the choice of acceptance or isolation. And they provided time to make a reasoned decision. It is testament to the depth of their commitment to their hard line in China that the Americans did not accept this olive branch offered for the sake of Anglo-American solidarity. At the same time, Britain's pursuit of Washington's approval, despite its low probability of success, elucidates the depth of London's commitment to the special relationship. The British depended on the United States for defense, support, and even the missiles that made possible their cherished nuclear deterrent. British policymakers may not have expected Washington's approval of their Viscount export, but they had to ask for it. To have surprised America's delegation to COCOM with an unexpected request for such a controversial exception would have guaranteed their objection and poisoned Anglo-American relations. The strains of their unusually intimate and codependent relationship notwithstanding, these two nations were forever willing to discuss their problems.

The Kennedy administration finally rejected the exception request on November 9. William Burdett, the State Department's deputy assistant secretary for European affairs, told the British embassy that the White House did not have the option of acquiescing in the British sale. "Congress was currently taking an active and hostile interest in East-West trade and was receiving substantial public support," he said, and trade with China topped the agenda for the Senate's subcommittee on internal security's agenda. Such treacherous political waters meant "the Administration simply could not afford to be publicly seen to have facilitated a sale of this character."[35]

There was, Burdett added offhandedly toward the end of the meeting, "a further snag." Surely Macmillan's government was aware that the plane's communications equipment was manufactured by a British subsidiary of the American company International Telephone and Telegraph. The equipment was consequently subject to American Foreign Asset Control Regulations, and thus barred from export to China as though produced by the parent company. Special approval from the Treasury Department could legitimize the sale, but Burdett warned "the administration could not agree to this and must deny such a license." If Vickers could somehow find a way around this Treasury quandary, he appeared to think out loud, it would be "open to Her Majesty's Government to decide whether to accept in this case the unanimity rule in COCOM." If they pursued the export, "there would of course be a press and congressional outcry here, and the administration would have publicly to say that it had done all in its power to prevent the sale to China." But perhaps, he left dangling, that would be their only response.[36]

And so it began. "The implication of this is clear," Ambassador David Ormsby-Gore excitedly reported. "The administration as nearly as they dare are inviting us to overcome the US Treasury license snag and go ahead in spite of COCOM. If we take this serious step," he continued, "the Administration will, I believe, be understanding in private but critical in public. Congress and much of the press will be vociferously against us. I think we can stand up to this criticism as long as it lasts." If Burdett was to be believed, and he could not afford to be more specific, the White House was prepared to give Britain a free pass in COCOM and on the potentially touchy issue of a required Treasury license for export to China of an American-licensed good.[37]

"My advice would be to go ahead," Ormsby-Gore wrote. Rationalization had begun to take its toll on employment in the past year, and three large aircraft factories, in Portsmouth, Christchurch, and Gloucester, had closed in the preceding months. More than eight thousand aerospace workers had lost their jobs since the start of the Vickers negotiations in China. "Any orders which the aircraft industry can obtain will help avoid or delay further closures, with all the political and economic difficulties they bring," the Ministry of Aviation reminded the Foreign Office, "and just now the sale of Viscount aircraft to China would provide a most valuable stimulant for the industry." The influential aviation minister, Peter Thorneycroft, wholeheartedly agreed. "The successful completion of this business, estimated at about £10 million, is of great significance to an important sector of the British aircraft industry," he penned in a personal note to Board of Trade president Frederick Erroll. "There is a real possibility of considerable further trade developing as a result of a successful sale of Viscounts," making the sale indispensable.[38]

Though the participants to these events did not realize it at the time, they had arrived at the defining moment in the history of Anglo-American aviation relations. Successive governments had worked tirelessly to control their own exports despite American encroachments. Engines were shipped to the Soviet Union over American protests; British airliners had flown across the iron curtain despite Washington's objections; Comet orders had been taken even in the face of American threats; and the abolition of the China differential and COCOM approval for civil aircraft sales had each been achieved despite vigorous American opposition. British diplomats had, on each occasion, tempered their aviation sales in the face of American objections, but at no time had they curtailed exports entirely to fit Washington's needs. With these Viscounts exportable only with a COCOM exception, and with the Kennedy administration promising to veto any British request for one, Whitehall once more faced the decision of sales versus allied security, the choice of sovereignty versus the will of the White House. The Macmillan government could accept America's wishes and face an angry public and the disruption of its export plans. Or it could defy Washington, break with COCOM tradition, and risk its closest relations for the sake of potential profit and power.[39]

Armed with unanimous cabinet support, on November 17 Macmillan personally authorized the granting of an export license without formal COCOM approval. "The PM has seen the papers about the sale of Viscount aircraft to China," Macmillan's trusted secretary, Philip de Zulueta, told Erroll, and "he felt sure that the sale should proceed." Having long resented America's tacit control of East-West trade, Macmillan was no fan of COCOM. "Could we not consider resigning from all this [COCOM] nonsense?" he had scribbled in exasperation earlier that year, and several months later he asked Douglas-Home, "Is there really any purpose in COCOM?" We have already seen his anger over the differential, and he once even called the entire COCOM procedure "medieval," leaving his Oxbridge advisers to ponder if he meant the criticism in the metaphysical or historical sense. "I think the PM merely meant that their [American] strategic ideas are d—d old fashioned!" one eventually concluded.[40]

What infuriated Macmillan most of all about COCOM was his belief that its multilateralism was merely a façade, loosely concealing American power. Only the United States among the group's members would object to Britain's blatant defiance of the organization's precedents. None would join with London in defying America's will, however, making Washington's decisions the group's fiat merely because they were typically unopposed. "It may not be possible for Japanese to give support in present case owing to Japan's reluctance to alienate Americans at this juncture," the Tokyo embassy cabled home. Paris offered a similar line, and "against the background of the present international system," refused to back Britain's defiance of the Americans. The Germans also wished "to avoid getting out of step with the US government," the Bonn embassy reported. Reports from the remainder of COCOM states continued this trend: all thought the American position unreasonable; none was willing to stand against it. "Japan does not wish to find itself in a minority of two with the UK," Britain's embassy in Tokyo reported, while the Dutch "would join a majority in favor of delivery," but they would not stand alone with London against the Americans.[41]

Washington was out of step with its allies on this and with most East-West trade issues, but none would join Britain in standing up to what they all perceived to be America's COCOM bullying. "The Americans tend to regard strategic controls as a test of the firmness of our attitude to the Sino-Soviet bloc," one British diplomat noted, "and hence as our reliability as an ally." Few states wanted to cultivate a reputation for untrustworthiness in Washington. Given the current fate of his aviation industry and the mood of his public at home, Macmillan determined he had no choice but to accept that risk. "Whichever way the decision [in COCOM] goes," one of Douglas-Home's diplomats warned, "damage to Anglo-American relations seems unavoidable."[42]

The COCOM Debate

Export license in hand, on December 1, 1961, Vickers finally signed a contract to deliver six Viscounts to Beijing, with delivery to commence in 1963. The Foreign Office continued its plans to notify COCOM of its exception request, believing this formality would at least force Washington to veto the sale and thus demonstrate its isolated views on economic warfare. "This would be the first case in which a COCOM member government had issued a license without consulting COCOM for the export of equipment which was admittedly and undoubtedly embargoed," Britain's COCOM representative noted. But if this gross violation of precedent embarrassed the Americans, then Britain would at least gain some good from it.[43]

The only precedent that mattered to Macmillan was maintenance of Britain's sovereign right to export. He instructed Ormsby-Gore to personally inform Secretary Rusk of his decision and to convey the message that the British "regret that the United States authorities have found it necessary to object to this sale" for which, from Whitehall's perspective "the balance of advantage in this transaction lies with the West." Rusk "took the news remarkably calmly," the ambassador reported. "The only serious comment he made was that if an announcement about the sale was to be made he was very glad it would be soon and before Congress returned in January."[44]

Rusk's outward calm belied his hidden anger. He informed his ambassadors stationed in COCOM countries of the impending Viscount sale, while reminding them the "US believes strictest application [of] embargo controls justified against Chicoms [Chinese communists]." To his mind, the Viscount export exemplified the worst kind of trade: it directly hindered efforts to stanch the flow of communist subversion while aiding the communist world's development. It was, simply put, a clear betrayal. "In view of hostile and aggressive Chicom posture and manifest intent [to] employ infiltration, subversion and direct action against neighboring Free World areas," the United States "believe[s] these 15 [sic] Viscount aircraft when made fully operational with embargoed equipment could be useful in carrying out Chicom aggressive designs." The planes contained a "level of technology, specifically in terms of circuitry, production technique and prototype potential . . . superior to present Chicom capabilities," and were consequently just the sort of technology the United States wanted to keep from Chinese engineers who were "not able now [to] build such equipment without outside technical assistance and some imported components." The sale undermined

American efforts to weaken and isolate the country. "Not only is joint export control policy at issue," the NSC's Robert Komer wrote National Security Adviser McGeorge Bundy, "but also that of our attitude toward Sino-Soviet dispute."[45]

Britain submitted its request for a COCOM exception on December 4, three days after Vickers signed its contract with Beijing. The British delegation did not apologize for its break with precedent, but rather urged the group to "show its customary flexibility" in hearing London's case. "The UK aircraft industry is passing through a difficult period which has resulted in the disappearance of a number of firms and enforced mergers of others." Refusal of the Viscount order "might well cause grave effects within the industry." Less than 1 percent of the value of the Viscounts were subject to COCOM embargo, the British representative said, and denial of the export over such a small amount might give "rise to such pressures in Parliament and the press that might permanently affect the attitude which HMG is able to adopt towards COCOM."[46]

With this mild threat of withdrawal from the body hanging in the air, the British representative turned next to the potential benefits of the Viscount deal, offering a direct challenge to Washington's economic warfare program. In recognition of the shallow support for American leadership in COCOM, he offered an alternative vision for waging the Cold War and engaging the West's Cold War enemies. The sale "would have great propaganda impact in favor of the Free World." In the battle for the hearts and minds of developing countries on the Cold War's front lines, especially in Asia, China's choice of a Western supplier was an important symbolic rejection of Russian technology. The West should strive to wean Beijing and all developing nations from Soviet goods, and sale of "Viscounts would involve not only the aircraft themselves but, in succeeding years, would set in train the purchase of a broad range of Western equipment." It was imperative for détente that these avenues of contact continue to grow. "Her Majesty's Government attach great importance to being able to achieve a breakthrough of this magnitude." The free world, he concluded, must "take all possible steps to orient Chinese trade away from the Bloc and towards the West."[47]

Washington's COCOM representative was not about to let this challenge go unanswered. The "proposed export would constitute a shipment of great strategic impact," he said, "and should not be consummated." British officials were surely "in the best position to assess conditions with the UK aircraft industry," but they had apparently forgotten that COCOM exceptions were only valid when the domestic concerns were "of a nature so serious as to override the security considerations involved." The sale of a few Viscounts would have a minute impact on employment within the United Kingdom, and COCOM could not condone sale of an embargoed good on the promise of further sales to follow. More directly, the parts in question were embargoed with good reason. "The Chinese Communists would find it impossible at the present time to build" such technologies on their own. Britain's sale would "provide the Chinese Communists with strategic equipment not otherwise available to them" and aid Beijing's ability to threaten its neighbors. Baldly stated, it was wrong, and the assembled delegations should follow Washington's lead in vetoing Britain's request. "The strictest application of the embargoed controls is believed justified against the Chinese Communists at this time." Mao's government could not be appeased or bought. It could only be weakened and then defeated through unyielding Western effort.[48]

The Viscount debate in COCOM illuminated for the entire body the competing visions developed by the United States and the United Kingdom over issues of sales and security. It also gave COCOM's members a rare opportunity to choose sides. Indeed, a curious thing happened following the American presentation: nothing. No other country rose to offer an opinion, pro or con, on the British request. As promised, none rose to support London's request. However, not a single one moved to censure Britain's violation of COCOM's precedents or to endorse Washington's economic warfare regimen. No one commented on the export in question, and none broached the philosophical divide separating COCOM's two most important members. "The rest took it calmly," the British delegation later cabled home; "all this took ten minutes and we turned to other matters." Afterward the delegate from the Netherlands pulled his British colleague aside to express his government's regret over the British decision, but not so much for the export in question itself, rather only because London had decided to breach COCOM's unanimity. His government cared little about some inconsequential radar equipment, he implied, and it cared even less for Washington's draconian economic warfare plans. But multilateral consent mattered. Overall, the response in COCOM to this affair was muted, demonstrating that support for America's trade position, even when Britain was clearly in direct violation of COCOM precedents, was hardly deep. Such silence can only be interpreted as a clear American defeat.[49]

COCOM's general indifference came as a great relief to the Foreign Office in London, and reaction to Washington's expected objection can best be described as resigned acceptance. "As I have often suspected," one Ministry of Aviation official noted, "we don't seem to speak the same language as the Americans." The American delegate had described the sale as having "great strategic impact," even though, said the ministry official, "no informed person in Britain would suggest that weather radar, which had been used in civil aircraft over a considerable part of the world, and communications equipment which had been exported with the full approval of COCOM to the USSR and its satellites, could be seriously described as of great strategic impact." What the Americans really objected to was "that the export was to China."[50]

The sale proceeded despite American opposition, and COCOM did not collapse. News of the approved sale reached newspapers in mid-December, with editorial comment that ran much as would be expected. Most British observers thrilled to their future commercial prospects in China. The Chinese purchase "ranks as one of the most surprising developments of the year in civil aviation," London's *Economist* editorialized, most importantly because "whatever the motive, Pekin [sic] man seems to be behaving remarkable [sic] like Economic man." In British circles, a nation willing to engage in mutually beneficial trade was well on the path toward international acceptance, as "economic" man was perhaps the first evolutionary step on the path toward becoming a fat communist.[51]

American public reaction was far more hostile. "It is either a breakthrough by the West and a setback to the Russians," CBS's London correspondent reported home, "or else it is perfidious Albion making a shady deal behind American backs." He left little doubt that he considered it the latter. New York's Republican senator Kenneth Keating agreed. He promised to "blast" the British until they saw the folly of aiding the Chinese, while White House officials did their best to deflect congressional criticism toward London. Assistant Secretary of Commerce Jack Behrman told a House committee, "We tried very hard to stop the deal," while the American embassy in Paris took the unusual step of mentioning that the forum for American opposition had been COCOM. The secretive body typically went unmentioned in Western diplomatic circles, but with Cold War hawks up in arms the State Department sought whatever cover could be found.[52]

The administration's official response proved as subdued as Burdett had promised two months earlier. The sooner the American people forgot the issue, Kennedy's advisers decided, the sooner they would forget their own government's inability to stop the sale. Rusk told a December 9 press conference, "We were not very happy about that sale of aircraft to Communist China," but he declined further comment for the sake of Anglo-American relations. "This is one of those transactions in the commercial field which governments must decide for themselves. I think I must just let it rest at that." No one appreciated Rusk's reserve more than the British embassy. "We think that given the circumstances Mr. Rusk really went out of his way to be helpful," its officers cabled home. Indeed, the entire administration seemed intent upon putting the Viscount affair behind them. The "UK sale of Viscounts to Chicoms is now apparently water under the dam," Komer told Bundy on December 11, "but I believe we've covered ourselves sufficiently to be able to say it was over our objections."[53]

Komer spoke too soon. The Kennedy administration may have been willing to let Britain's rejection of COCOM practices slide for the sake of the special relationship, but American officials had no intention of allowing Britain to violate American laws in the process. Specifically, the administration refused to allow the American products employed on the Viscount to depart for China. It is here that the question of British sovereignty truly lay. With this sale as much as with Skybolt, policymakers on both sides of the Atlantic realized that American technological power had grown to the point that it now threatened to control Britain's foreign trade. As Burdett had warned, "There was another snag."

The Viscount Conspiracy

This would be the peak, and also the nadir, of the entire postwar history of Anglo-American aviation and diplomacy. The Viscounts as manufactured by Vickers used navigation equipment produced in the United Kingdom by Standard Telephones and Cables (STC), a subsidiary of an American company, International Telephone and Telegraph (IT&T). Under American foreign asset control laws, STC was bound to respect Washington's embargo of China wherein such an export would require explicit approval. No approval would be forthcoming, however. In COCOM the Americans wielded only moral and diplomatic power. With STC, the Americans had the law on their side. On December 14, a week after news of the sale splashed across American and British newspapers, an interdepartmental committee headed by Assistant Secretary Martin formally forbade the Treasury Department to issue a license for the American-controlled parts. The Commerce Department, which had previously allowed the Pentagon and Foggy Bottom to lead reaction to the Viscount sale, now vigorously led the charge. Its representatives urged "punitive and preventative action" against any company involved in the export, and warned against similar use of subsidiaries as a means of thwarting Washington's export controls. They even advocated blacklisting any company that participated in the sale, including "withholding of US defense and other procurement contracts from the 'offending' firm and denial of US exports to those firms." American overseas investment, especially in high-technology fields, had expanded tremendously since the 1950s. Kennedy's officials did not want to stifle growing American economic power, but neither did they want company executives to believe that by locating their manufacturing overseas, they could move physically beyond Washington's strategic control.[54]

Their resolve to hold firm did not diminish their hope to keep this latest complication of the Viscount sale from the public eye. Press reports of a blacklist or of defiance of American laws would portray American policies as being trampled by the United Kingdom, and the White House would appear weak if London managed to export the American-equipped Viscounts without Washington's consent. The only thing worse than being an international bully, after all, was failure to make the bullying stick. As Burdett concluded, "The threats of retaliation against Vickers were not idle and the more the dispute was ventilated, the less room for maneuver was left to the administration." The White House reasoned that Congress would react far more vigorously to a British transgression of American laws—which they had written and passed—than to Britain's defiance of COCOM guidelines, which were the executive's domain. Realizing that Whitehall was unlikely to forgo the sale entirely at this point, the committee urged that London be prompted to find homegrown substitutes for the equipment. On December 21, even as British policymakers celebrated their successful navigation of COCOM's treacherous waters, the American embassy in London reminded the Foreign Office that its agents would be watching the Viscount export carefully to ensure that no American goods found their way to China. Officials back in Washington simultaneously reminded IT&T's chief executives that they would be held personally responsible, and legally liable, if their subsidiary provided parts for the Beijing-bound planes. Perhaps it would be best, the company was advised (though it was more than a mere suggestion) if it suspended sales to Vickers of the communications equipment in question until the Viscounts left for China, to ensure that no wayward part "inadvertently" found its way aboard a China-bound plane.[55]

What seemed in Washington a quiet but firm application of the law caused great trepidation across the Atlantic. Try though they might, Vickers could find no suitable alternative for the communications equipment in question. No British firm could reproduce the equipment in time for export without further violating American copyrights, and Whitehall was further shocked to discover that there remained no British firm capable of producing similar equipment that was not already intertwined with an American company. Rationalization and the welcome infusion of American capital had their price. Even after the United Kingdom had defied COCOM convention, stood up to American pressure, and suffered Capitol Hill criticism, Whitehall's aviation nightmare appeared about to come true: the United States appeared to hold an effective veto over a valuable British export. Equally distressing was the realization that the Viscounts were the least American-built of all major British civil planes then on the market, using American components for less than 2 percent of their overall composition. The jet-powered Comet IV, the VC-10, and the Trident all carried a greater percentage of American-licensed parts, and nascent designs for the Concorde expected to use American goods as well. Given the complex intermingling of the two country's aviation industries, including the increasingly widespread use of outsourcing for components and avionics, it was unlikely that any future British plane would be devoid of American goods. The costs of "anglicizing" future British planes by ensuring that British firms on British soil manufactured all future parts would be prohibitive. Multilateral controls would take on a new meaning if, with the presence of a single screw, wire, or widget, Washington could demand final approval over any future British sale.[56]

In this light the once-promising Viscount sale now seemed to signal the death knell of an independent British aviation industry. "Whether or not Vickers succeed by their various expedients in defeating the American efforts to frustrate this particular sale of Viscount aircraft to China," Thorneycroft told the cabinet,

> this case raises in striking fashion certain wider issues. The China Viscounts case has thrown into sharp relief the ability of the US government, given the extent of US penetration of the British electronics industry[,] to thwart the trade policy of the British government where this is contrary to American wishes or prejudices. It has been general British policy to encourage active American capital investment in British industry. And there is not reason to doubt that, in general, it will be the wish of both the British subsidiary to prosecute as much export business as it can (within the limits set of

course by our own British export control). The difficulty arises through the ability of the US government to impose its own controls which tend to be much more restrictive than ours.[57]

China itself was at stake. "The original decision was taken to allow the sale of six Viscount aircraft and their equipment notwithstanding US opposition," Thorneycroft reminded his colleagues, because of the "possibility that the sale might serve as an introduction to a greater volume of trade with China generally." The infiltration of American business into British aviation would shortly make that decision moot. Britain needed a general policy for confronting American encroachments, such as legislation that would allow Whitehall to order its companies to defy their American parent corporations, or the ability to nationalize production when in the national good. These were issues for the future, he said. The problem at hand remained the fate of China's Viscounts.[58]

In June 1962, when Macmillan met Rusk for face-to-face meetings, this dilemma was much on the prime minister's mind. In the midst of what began as a calm discussion of the differences between Washington's and London's approach to China, Macmillan "replied vehemently that he simply did not understand American policy on China." The United States "did not even admit that China existed," a diplomatic calculus he "regarded as indefensible by any logic." Macmillan unexpectedly turned to the Viscounts. "The British do a good business with the Chinese Communists," he declared. "They had, for example, sold them fourteen [sic] Viscounts," as he emphatically reminded Rusk that "the British are an island, they live on trade."[59]

Concern for these same issues also resonated in Washington's official circles. During the first week of March, one day before Thorneycroft's presentation to Macmillan's cabinet, Lucius Battle, Rusk's executive secretary, warned National Security Adviser McGeorge Bundy of the potential implications of the Viscount issue. Any American frustration of the sale would "be a public admission that US jurisdiction extends to US subsidiaries registered in the UK," Battle said. The resulting loss of British independence would prove a political fiasco in London. British popular support of the special relationship would undoubtedly plummet if unemployment were traced to American laws. Worse yet, "according to a Foreign Office official, the STC case is especially difficult for Her Majesty's Government because STC is a large supplier to the UK government and much of their output is for defense purposes." It would therefore be "politically impossible for the UK government to permit the US government to hold a veto over a British firm supply-ing essential materials" to British armed forces, for this would be a violation of national sovereignty—and a political scandal—no government would al-low. How the British planned to handle this quandary the Americans could not say. The Viscounts were not scheduled for delivery to China until the following September, Battle concluded; thus "time and patience seem to be the British watchword of the moment."[60]

Significant global events during the final months of 1962 added particular poignancy to this issue. The Cuban missile crisis and Skybolt affair each blew a dark cloud over the special relationship in October and December, respec-tively. These were not all. The outbreak of armed conflict along the Sino-In-dian border in October 1962 seemed to validate Washington's contention that Beijing was given to unbridled aggression, and it lent particular weight to American objections to supplying China with modern transport planes. These planes would aid Beijing's ability to resupply the region in future con-flicts, Kennedy's advisers concluded. They took the fighting in the Hima-layas as an opportunity to renew their own calls for cancellation of the impending Viscount export. "It may therefore be worthwhile [to] approach [the] UK on grounds [of] political considerations as distinct from questions [of] UK and US trade controls," Ambassador David Bruce advised from Lon-don. His pleas fell on deaf ears. To every American charge that the Vis-counts would aid Chinese airlift capacity came a British response that the planes were commercial in nature, designed to be "flown on internal air civil lines." They "could not land [on] Tibet airfields" in the first place. Lon-don was determined to "play [the sale] as simple commercial deal," the State Department informed its diplomats overseas. American officials were left with no recourse but to wonder how Britain planned to surmount the difficulties of the Viscount's American parts. As late as December 1962, Bruce wrote home that there had been "no development on Viscount case." The problem is "quiescent with no mutually agreeable solution in sight."[61]

The Macmillan government had, in fact, decided on a plan, predicated less on placating America's diplomats than on deceiving them by exporting their planes to China secretly, American components and all. Endorsed in March 1962, the complicated plan went as follows. Cabinet officials first autho-rized Vickers to inform the American embassy they would not purchase any American-licensed equipment from IT&T or STC for export to China, as though the company would find other sources of supply. The cabinet next authorized British European Airways, owners of numerous Viscounts equipped with STC's components, to purchase a large quantity of the equipment from STC for their own stock. This appeared to American investigators merely a precautionary purchase, considering that the Viscount's production line was soon to close. The Ministry of Aviation then secretly purchased those spares from BEA, only to offer them (without sale) to Vickers for their Chinese-bound Viscounts. In effect, BEA and the Ministry of Aviation laundered the parts. Vickers, meanwhile, thus fulfilled the letter, if not the spirit, of their pledge not to *purchase* American equipment, since the company only *received* the equipment. Though all were complicit in the conspiracy to defy American foreign asset control laws, the Ministry of Aviation was the prime perpetrator. As Thorneycroft explained to the cabinet, "BEA have agreed to act on Vickers' behalf in this matter, provided they in turn be allowed to sell the equipment not to Vickers, but to my Department," adding, "I have authorized my department to act as an intermediary in this way."[62]

This was a dramatic and potentially devastating move. If the American press learned that Whitehall had intentionally violated American export laws in order to trade with Mao's despised regime, London's prestige within the United States would plummet. Senators like Keating would do more than merely "blast" the British. They might severely hinder ties as well. Moreover, repeated State Department reminders over the ensuing months of the importance of the issue had convinced most in Whitehall that the administration would not turn a blind eye to this circumvention of American laws, especially if word of the illegal export became public. The White House could condone secret illegalities for the sake of the special relationship; they had no space for patience once headlines blared.

Documentation illustrating the Macmillan government's subterfuge is conclusive. Cabinet and Aviation Ministry records clearly demonstrate that Thorneycroft was prepared to go ahead with this plan in March 1962, though the paper trail lacks an explicit authorization either from the cabinet as a whole or from Macmillan personally. This is not surprising, as it is not the nature of conspirators to leave detailed records. As one Aviation Ministry official wrote in February 1963 (with what might be seen as great irony) when asked for a synopsis of the government's actions to secure the Viscount parts, "There are a number of good reasons why the report should be in general terms; e.g., so that there will be no written evidence available (to prying US Congressmen) on the installation of ST and C equipment on the Viscount aircraft." By avoiding a paper trail, "it will be more difficult for the Americans to attribute the sale of the aircraft to the installation of ST and C equipment or to accuse ST and C of collusion in any form and, most importantly for COCOM relations, we should not unduly upset the US delegation by proclaiming too blatantly our ingenuity in procuring the ST and C equipment in spite of US interference."[63]

The plan worked, at least initially. Kennedy's advisers struggled throughout 1962 and 1963 to discern the origin of the communications components loaded aboard the Chinese-bound Viscounts, but failed in every attempt to discover their true nature. On March 8, 1963, for example, Assistant Secretary of State Griffith Johnson reminded Board of Trade president Erroll that American officials could find no reasonable evidence of a British attempt to find a substitute for the embargoed equipment. "I told Mr. Erroll that the US impediments had not been removed," Johnson reported to Undersecretary Ball, and "he seemed surprised and somewhat dismayed." Johnson did not believe the British could have misunderstood Washington's concern over this issue. They "could hardly have overlooked the subsequent more exhaustive discussion of the licensing issue in Mr. Burdett's statement of January 18, 1962, that under Treasury Foreign Asset Control regulations IT&T could not permit STC to deliver navigation equipment for the aircraft for China without a Treasury license." Johnson believed that unless definitive proof of Britain's innocence was found, the two countries were bound on a "collision course" with "resultant damage to Anglo-American relations" sufficient to poison the Western trade control regime and thus "throw the free world alliance into further disarray."[64]

The American search for proof of British malfeasance or innocence continued throughout 1963 with increasing vigor as the date of the Viscount export approached. "Can Embassy verify that six sets STR 34/35 VOR/ILS navigation equipment for these aircraft still not repeat not delivered by STC?" the State Department asked its representatives in London in late March. The ambassador responded the next day that his investigation showed that the equipment originally intended for the Viscounts was still in fact in STC's main warehouse. Moreover, Vickers had begun a lawsuit to recover damages from the company for a breach of contract in not delivering the equipment. British records reveal that this lawsuit was merely a ploy to throw American investigators off the track. Legal bluffs did not halt American investigators, however, who in March and April made surprise inspections of the Vickers factory in search of American components aboard the China-bound Viscounts. History does not record what they actually saw. Perhaps they failed to notice the STC equipment on board; perhaps the serial numbers had been changed; or perhaps Vickers planned to replace whatever navigation equipment was then on board the planes with STC equipment immediately before their export. Perhaps these diplomats could not discern one electrical component from another. State department records do not reveal such details; they record only what these Americans *thought* they saw. The rumors were true, they reported home. Vickers had in fact substituted obsolescent WWII surplus equipment instead of the previously planned STC goods. "It appears as though the decision not to use STC equipment was due to a Chinese requirement rather than US pressure," the Americans reported, adding that according to Vickers's representatives, the "Communist Chinese purchasing agent is proving to be a very difficult customer."[65]

This report satisfied the Kennedy administration. Whereas in April Bundy's staff argued that "there are American components on the Viscounts" and thus there remained "a still unresolved problem with regard to US export controls," by June American officials had reached a different conclusion. Treasury analysts informed their State Department colleagues that they proposed "to take no further action towards the American parent company" over the matter, since "non US-controlled navigation and pressurization equipment have been substituted for the US controlled equipment which gave rise originally to the question of Treasury licensing." The Americans would hold this line for years to come. Indeed, not a single document suggests that American officials *ever* learned of the British deception. By August 1963, as the first of the Viscounts arrived in China, Vickers dropped its lawsuit against STC, ostensibly in an effort to let bygones be bygones. Simultaneously, the U.S. embassy in London reported that a final surprise investigation revealed yet again that the six navigation sets in question remained in STC's warehouse—as of course they would be, because Vickers procured its navigation equipment from the Ministry of Aviation through BEA.[66]

The State Department continued to believe British claims that Vickers had found substitutes for the American products through the 1960s. In 1964, for example, Foggy Bottom reminded its European embassies (in a statement signed by Rusk): "The US took considerable pains over a long time to assure itself that no equipment would be incorporated in the Viscounts to China in contravention of US controls." Moreover, "according to its latest information on this matter, the US knows of no parts or equipment on the Viscounts to China which are of US origin or made under license from American firms, or that are otherwise subject to US controls." This message arrived after the Viscounts, with their American-licensed parts on board, were already in Chinese hands.[67]

This false conclusion carried significant implications. The policymakers who served under Kennedy and later Lyndon Johnson believed they had done their job so well in keeping the American parts from China that they began to worry their strenuous controls might hinder future American investments overseas. In 1964, Commerce Secretary Luther Hodges warned the Senate Foreign Relations Committee that British firms might soon limit further American investment in high-technology areas over fear of Washington's export controls, and that other countries might soon learn from their example. "Members of this committee will recall the incident of the plane that the UK wished to export to Communist China, and the problems that arose from the fact that such planes customarily contained British-made components constructed from US licensed technology," Hodges testified in 1964. American controls had worked for the Viscounts to keep American goods out of China, but

> that case was certainly an irritant in our relations with the British government, as well as for the US and foreign firms involved. Recently, representatives of some US firms that regularly license their technology to firms in friendly foreign countries have told us that some foreign concerns that they have dealt with in the past now refuse to enter into any license agreement with these US firms if they must contain special US restraints on exports to the Soviet bloc of the foreign-made products of our technology. If this sort of attitude spreads, substantial detriment to the development of free world industrial technology and the US role therein can result.[68]

The American government (incorrectly) learned from the Viscount case that their trade controls worked, but also that their trade controls could irritate foreign states in ways previously unimagined. One might even argue that American trade controls for the Viscount did work, as they vividly demonstrated the difficulties of defying American diplomacy. That Vickers secretly managed to surmount Treasury controls meant less than the fact that the Americans publicly refused to budge. Theirs was a difficult balancing act. On the one hand, American leaders did not want their actions to hinder future foreign investment; on the other hand, they wanted foreign firms to fear American resolve. Their lesson seemed to be that firm diplomacy worked. It established the rules of the game, ensuring adherence to those rules without exception.

The British, conversely, learned a lesson in paranoia. They successfully exported the embargoed American equipment to China, yet Whitehall policymakers worried incessantly throughout 1963 over Washington's possible reaction if the truth of their conspiracy came out. They wondered if the Americans already knew of the illegal export but planned to turn a blind eye for the sake of Anglo-American unity, and they worried that Rusk's State Department had laid a well-conceived trap to spring at some future date, perhaps when British aircraft sales to China next arose. The Sino-Indian conflict and Skybolt caused many in Macmillan's government to reconsider the wisdom of violating American laws so boldly. The embassy in Washington continued to repeat that the sale was purely commercial in nature, but as the Foreign Office cabled them in February 1963, "there is a weakness to this argument." The latest Air Ministry estimates concluded that the six Viscounts "would increase Chinese air-lift capacity by 15%," and "the fact that the aircraft supplied might be unsuitable for operation in forward areas is not decisive, as they would release other aircraft for these duties." It was a little late for such arguments, but nonetheless the Viscount case appeared far from over in London in 1963, and far riskier than when the contract was optimistically signed in 1961.[69]

"However one looks at this, we have put ourselves in a dangerous position," one British diplomat concluded. "The US apparently controls the licenses for some very important components in British aircraft," and "they are thus in a position to do some serious damage to our aircraft industry." He continued, "I have been very unhappy about the way we were treating the Americans from the start. We deliberately set out to deceive them, relying on the strength of Anglo-American friendship to tide us over when the truth came out." In the final analysis, "since there is US controlled equipment involved, we are still heading for trouble."[70]

Some in London wanted to come clean. Perhaps with the mistakes of the Viscount apparent to both sides, a discrete accord in future exports of jointly produced products could be developed. Proponents of this option quickly lost out. "I should be surprised if the Americans do not at least have a shrewd suspicion that we have after all managed to fit 'US-controlled' equipment to these Viscounts," the Foreign Office's H. B. McKenzie-Johnston wrote, yet "I do not see why we should go out of our way to 'confess' to the Americans before the departure of the first Viscount." He reasoned, "If the Americans are going to make a row, they will not be inhibited by a feeling that we have been courteous in telling them what we have done in advance on the delivery." Britain had pursued the sales based on cold calculations of profit and geopolitical gain. "I cannot see that we are likely to gain anything by striving after righteousness."[71]

The issue became more complicated still during the summer of 1963, when press reports began to surface that British sales teams were in Beijing to negotiate the export of BOAC's used Britannias (propeller-driven planes that dwarfed the Viscounts) and jet-powered Comet IVs. Discovery of the Viscount deception could thwart these nascent negotiations. In search of a solution the Foreign Office turned to its embassy in Washington for advice, and in so doing extended the paper trail of their earlier conspiracy. "Some of the communications and navigations equipment [aboard the Viscounts] has been supplied by Standard Telegraph and Cables, the British subsidiary of an American company," they told Ormsby-Gore in June. "Under US law, American permission for their export should have been sought. It was not, because everyone knew it would not be given for exports to China." Future British sales in the region seemed destined to stir up a hornet's nest of American inquiries. If Washington learned the truth about the Viscounts, reprisals would surely follow. "If the Americans believe that the Viscount deliveries are to be followed by deliveries of Britannias and Comets, you can be sure that they will be treated as a test case and that maximum pressure will be brought to bear on all concerned."[72]

Ormsby-Gore's reaction was heated. An intimate of the president's like no other foreign diplomat—he frequently vacationed with the Kennedy family, for example—he had been purposely kept ignorant of the Viscount deception by his superiors back in Whitehall who wanted his claims that the planes contained no American components to sound genuine. His first reaction to news of the conspiracy—and to the revelation that he had been inadvertently lying for months—was understandable fury. "I find it hard to advise on what is best to do on this matter as I have not been kept fully informed of developments since I originally warned of the inevitable difficulties which the incorporation of American equipment in this aircraft would involve." Given the intervening months, "some collision with the American authorities over this is inevitable." He proved unable to offer his government any concrete solution, though he advised against confession. "Given the Congressional attitude and after events in India, I cannot see either the State Department or the Commerce Department being able to help us." Both would "feel compelled to carry out what is the law of the US and to frustrate the supply of the further spares equipment if they can," and "they may also proceed to retaliatory actions." He recommended keeping the affair a secret. Foggy Bottom might conceal the truth (if discovered) in order to save the special relationship and its own reputation, but "some members of Congress will certainly interpret what has happened as a deliberate deception to which Her Majesty's Government have been party and will demand action."[73]

London took its ambassador's advice and never mentioned a word of the deception to the Americans. In July 1963 the first of six Viscounts began its long journey to China, with another following each month. By the following spring, China had its British planes, and Britain had its open door into China; American components were in use aboard Chinese airliners; and American officials were none the wiser.

But London's telltale heart remained. In the end, instead of opening the door to Chinese riches, the Viscount deception closed opportunities for British aviation exports to the country. British sales teams who traveled to Beijing in 1963 and after, hawking more advanced planes than the Viscounts, received the coldest of receptions from their compatriots in the Beijing embassy, and news of their progress received no warmer welcome among Britain's diplomats in the United States. Each feared the consequences of American reprisals over what London had done in order to complete the Viscount deal. As D. A. Greenhill of the Washington embassy wrote home at the end of 1963 (in a note personally approved by Ormsby-Gore), "having been misled over the Viscounts, the [American] administration will ensure that they are not caught out a second time." As for future sales of Comets or Britannias, he continued, "the Administration will undoubtedly use its influence to frustrate the deal," and "I think it is certain that the Administration would go to great lengths to ruse us off the Comet transaction." Even if unaware of the Viscount deception, he advised, the bar had been raised for future sales.[74]

"The sale of twenty Comets would be a useful development for British industry," Greenhill concluded. "But it is no good pretending that the administration are going to pass this off with a wry smile, particularly at a time when they are being accused of being too trusting of the Communists and when the situation in South Vietnam and Laos is so sensitive politically." If Britain persisted in selling even more advanced planes to an increasingly belligerent (and soon, nuclear) Beijing, and if Washington ever discovered the deception of the Viscount case, "the Administration would find themselves obliged to go to great lengths not only to prevent the delivery of Comets but to extract the prescribed penalties for the supply to China of 'American-controlled' equipment in the Viscounts." Foreign Secretary Douglas-Home agreed, telling the cabinet that while American objections over the Viscount had been fierce, "it seems certain that a fortiori they will object even more strongly to further sales of civil aircraft to China." This was a shame, because "civil aviation is a means of fostering contacts both commercial and in general with the bloc and so weakening the iron curtain," but "the United States wants to hamper the growth" of communist air fleets. "We have opposed this policy as ineffective, often counter-productive and in many ways contrary to our international obligations," but American pressure was insistent, and after the Viscounts, sure to increase. Greenhill lamented, "We have not yet seen the end of the Viscount case."[75]

Britain began the 1960s intent upon finding an independent aviation line, and more devoted than ever to their search for power through planes. As we shall see in detail in Chapter 8, it entered the second half of the decade more beholden than ever to American policy. In their deceitful effort to open the air route to China, British policymakers sowed potential seeds of their aviation demise. Britain never monopolized the China market as its leaders had hoped. They could not, because they feared Washington's reaction to subsequent sales, and because they feared especially the reach of America's financial tentacles. American investment in British aviation, and Britain's need following rationalization for electronic and other components procured through cheap and reliable providers overseas, ensured that no plane could truly be called wholly "British" by 1964. No plane carrying a "made in America" stamp on any of its components, however, was fully London's to sell as its policymakers saw fit. Britain's hope of achieving independence through aviation failed, and not only because its aviation industry lost its zero-sum game competition with the United States. It was no longer independent because the bonds of the special relationship were too strong to break, and the fear of bending those bonds too much to bear, especially after a vast conspiracy to defraud. The deceptive lengths Whitehall went to in its search for independence ultimately became ties that bind; and these ties only tightened in the year to come.

CHAPTER 8

Aviation on the New Frontier

Two Cold Wars existed by the 1960s—one in Asia, the other in Europe. While Macmillan's government struggled to preserve what was left of Britain's waning global power, Kennedy's New Frontiersmen took office in 1961 with plans for victory in Asia, Europe, and beyond. Aviation figured prominently in their plans. They considered it as much a valuable symbol of power and modernity as their predecessors had, yet they hoped to infuse their aviation policies with the same new spirit of vigor and analysis they promised for the entirety of their foreign policy endeavors. Kennedy vowed in 1961 that America would go to the moon in order to beat the Soviets in space, the Cold War's ultimate high ground. Two years later, he formally backed an American supersonic transport, lest Concorde or a Soviet entry crowd his country from this field. "It will maintain the historical United States leadership in aircraft development," he explained, and "enable this country to demonstrate the technological accomplishments which can be achieved under a democratic, free enterprise system." These endeavors would be expensive and risky, but that was part of their allure. "We cannot," he proclaimed, "permit this high cost, nor the difficulties and risks of such an ambitious program to preclude this country from participating in the logical next development of commercial aircraft." American leadership was at stake, and aviation offered power, prestige, and money: leadership's three building blocks.[1]

As with so many of the grandiose dreams developed by Kennedy's team, however, the changes to American aviation policy proved more rhetoric than substance. Kennedy's administration initially adopted without revision the guidelines in NSC-5726, from 1957, for East-West aviation constraints, including the prescription for opening the Soviet Union to American planes and influence—on Washington's terms—while keeping China isolated.

They achieved exactly the opposite. Kennedy's administration also emphasized countering communist penetration of the developing world, an emphasis in line with their broader interest in the Cold War's periphery. Their
policies would eventually bring Britain and the United States once more to
aerial loggerheads in China, but also in Pakistan, with results that would set
in motion the fundamental shift in American aviation policy necessary for
the subsequent geopolitical reorientation of the 1970s that saw the United
States finally accept the People's Republic of China into the family of nations. In pursuing with renewed vigor a traditional American line on exports
and trade in a period of international turmoil, Kennedy thus inadvertently
catalyzed the process of change to come.

Some policies remained the same, including Washington's assessment of
direct aerial relations with Moscow. American policymakers since the earliest days of the Cold War had argued for direct superpower flights once they
became in the West's best interest, though Truman and Eisenhower agreed
that such connections could be granted only after the Soviets demonstrated
a genuine desire for peaceful relations. Direct flights would be the Kremlin's
reward for good behavior, in other words, and not a bribe for good behavior
as most Western European powers advised. Washington's stand was largely
symbolic. No real iron curtain separated Europe's two halves by the 1960s,
at least not for commercial air travel. Soviet leaders had already opened
their airspace to Western planes beginning in 1957, and by 1961 a passenger
with the proper visas could travel directly between Moscow and Paris, Co-
penhagen, London, and so forth. Such flights were heavily scrutinized, but
by the 1960s they were routine as well.[2] Intercontinental travel was hardly
more difficult. If provided with the proper visas and a valid passport, a passenger, even from the Soviet bloc, could travel from any of the Western capitals to New York and beyond, unimpeded by Cold War barriers more daunting than customs agents. What they could not do was make this trip entirely
on a Soviet or American airline. This restriction troubled few travelers. Approximately fifteen thousand Americans visited the Soviet Union in 1962,
though Moscow's more restrictive rules allowed only 150 handpicked Soviet
citizens to visit the United States.[3]

Given the clear permeability of its iron curtain of the air, Washington's
rigid rejection of direct Soviet-American flights struck many in Western Europe as not only petty, but bad policy as well. British thinkers as influential as Churchill, Eden, and Macmillan firmly believed that greater contacts
across the iron curtain could improve East-West relations, and each pushed

hard for British flights to Eastern Europe, developing a philosophical justification for trade and contact in line with their economic aspirations for the region. American adherents to NSC-5726 officially believed the opposite: that improved aviation ties would strengthen the Soviet regime and thereby prolong the Cold War. The resilience of this argument had begun to weaken by the last years of the Eisenhower era, as some in the administration, frequently including the president himself, began increasingly to argue a British line behind closed doors. Their radicalism made little headway against security hawks in Eisenhower's administration, who opposed at every step changes to Washington's formal stance on aerial ties with the Soviets.[4]

Promising advances during Ike's second term forecast a wind of change. Quiet negotiations between Juan Trippe's Pan American Airways and the Soviet Union's Aeroflot in 1957 fostered an undercurrent of enthusiasm within American circles for direct superpower flights. Pan Am offered the White House a finalized deal with Trippe's powerful connections as political cover, but each time real progress beckoned, new Cold War tensions invariably intervened. The two countries agreed to reciprocal flights "in principle" in January 1958, yet they never finalized the details. Negotiations stumbled over technical issues such as Soviet acceptance of English for commercial communications over their territory, as was the international standard, and whether crew members had to be citizens of the country whose airline they flew with. American negotiators interpreted Moscow's intransigence on these seeming trivialities as part obstinacy, part ignorance, neither suggesting a genuine Soviet desire for peaceful relations. Even the hopeful "spirit of Camp David" that united Eisenhower and Soviet leader Nikita Khrushchev in 1959 fell prey to deepening distrust following the failed Paris summit of May 1960. Their nearly finalized aviation agreement fell by the wayside accordingly. The decade ended no closer to détente than it had begun, and despite having developed the rough outlines of a direct air service, the superpowers entered the 1960s far from an agreement.[5]

Kennedy's team vowed to complete the deal and began negotiating with Aeroflot from the administration's first days. Within months the two sides had initialed an agreement authorizing direct service between New York and Moscow to be jointly operated by Pan Am and Aeroflot. The Soviets yielded on multinational crews, but remained committed to the use of Russian in their airspace. Yet even with these concessions the tentative agreement was hardly a paragon of trust or of potential profitability. Neither airline predicted that a single weekly round trip would cover their costs, and neither was allowed to transport passengers or cargo beyond their initial landing point, further eroding potential profits. Nevertheless, the accord promised an important start. All that remained for flights to begin the following year was Kennedy's and Khrushchev's final approval.[6]

The Cold War intervened yet again. A bilateral air treaty "was under serious consideration when the Berlin Wall went up" in August 1961, Najeeb Halaby, head of Kennedy's Federal Aviation Administration, later observed. With the president publicly advising every citizen to "know what steps he can take without delay to protect his family in the case of [Soviet] attack," it did not seem the proper moment to allow Soviet planes, even commercial ones, access to American airspace. Washington halted aviation negotiations, and larger tensions the following year again scuttled renewed negotiations initiated by the Kremlin. "The Russians frequently and fairly insistently kept bringing it up [after the Berlin Crisis] and it became quite clear that they wanted very much to negotiate and consummate an agreement," Halaby explained. "We began seriously considering it again in the fall of '62," but the Cuban missile crisis intervened. Their hard work notwithstanding, the two countries entered 1963 officially no closer to direct air service than they had been two years earlier.[7]

Unbeknownst to Moscow, these scuttled negotiations concealed a fundamental change in American thinking on the matter. By the spring of 1963 the National Security Council and the State Department both formally required visible signs of improved superpower relations before the establishment of an air route could be approved, but theirs was a weakened position. A faction led by Halaby and Foy Kohler, ambassador to the Soviet Union, gathered adherents throughout this period to their argument that air travel could help improve Soviet-American relations. This, of course, was Whitehall's traditional stance, but whereas the British had long believed trade and contacts could promote bilateral relations, the Americans added their own unique element to this argument. "Exposure of Russians to the United States would be of great advantage to our relationship," Halaby explained, and "the possibilities of mutual understanding thereby expanded." Kohler pointed out that each weekly Aeroflot flight to New York could expose more Soviets to America than previously visited the United States in a single year. Even if only ranking Communist Party officials appeared, any opportunity to witness American generosity and power firsthand promised results. Whether they left in fear or in awe, they would realize the futility of the Soviet system and depart as advocates for East-West reconciliation.[8]

American proponents of greater East-West contact argued that democracy and capitalism were each addictive: once exposed, individuals wanted more. None within Washington dared refute this claim. Critics of formalized relations fretted that direct flights offered a symbolic acceptance of Communism. Yet not a single ranking policymaker of this period argued that direct Soviet exposure to the West might somehow undermine their cause. None argued, for example, that Soviet visitors might somehow depart *less* enthused by America than when they had arrived. That all who came to America would come to love and respect this country was an unquestioned article of faith that undergirded a broad range of policies designed to improve America's standing in the world, including assistance to foreign students and the Peace Corps. The former brought bright young minds to American shores; the latter sent America's best abroad. Each program was predicated on the proposition that to know America was to become a proselytizer for its graces.

The successive crises that scuttled promising negotiations only strengthened the resolve of the administration's proponents of a superpower aviation accord. The Berlin crisis reestablished American vulnerabilities, and many (Kennedy included) believed the world could not afford another brush with catastrophe such as occurred over Cuba. Washington and Moscow could compete in the Cold War's periphery, they tacitly concluded, but civilization could ill afford two nuclear foes who refused even the basic elements of cooperative relations. The Soviets were not going away, Halaby and Kohler argued. They had to be treated as powerful partners for peace for the sake of all. "Some say it is useless to speak of world peace or world law or world disarmament—and that it will be useless until the leaders of the Soviet Union adopt a more enlightened attitude," Kennedy declared in June 1963. "I believe we can help them do it." He did not mention aviation specifically in public, though behind closed doors the argument that engagement could cajole the Kremlin into a more liberal mindset had clearly taken hold. "Would this be a good time for us to go ahead with the air agreement with the Soviet Union?" Kennedy asked Secretary of State Dean Rusk that spring. He approved renewal of negotiations before his tragic death.[9]

No such change occurred under Kennedy's watch over aerial exports behind the iron curtain, despite NSC-5726's authorization of sales to the Soviet bloc on a "case-by-case" basis. Cold War antagonisms ran too deep for this dramatic step, and the Pentagon and Commerce Department continued to hawkishly monitor exports that might in any way improve Soviet capabili-

ties. These constraints aside, an important psychological change had occurred within American circles by 1963. The Soviet bloc still required careful
treatment, but this was a region American aviation strategists increasingly
desired to engage.[10]

The same could not be said of the Cold War beyond Europe. Kennedy's
team slowly warmed to better aviation ties across the iron curtain, yet they
fervently wished to thwart what they termed communist "penetration" of
the world's underdeveloped and postcolonial regions. This had been a particularly troubling issue for Eisenhower, though he had great difficulty making any headway on this problem. "We are witnessing a great expansion of
the Soviet and satellite airlines through the underdeveloped areas," he reminded the National Security Council in December 1957, and he warned
that failure to match Soviet generosity might significantly erode Western influence. The United States should "do whatever we are obliged to do in order to meet Soviet competition in this arena," he intoned.[11] His advisers
never found a satisfying solution to his concerns, however, because of their
ideological aversion to tampering with the marketplace. The Export-Import
Bank openly financed foreign purchases of American aircraft, but this institution only facilitated commercial sales, it did not lend monies to countries
unable to afford repayment. The Pentagon was the country's largest aeronautics customer and worked with a great variety of agencies in distributing
direct economic and military aid, but its own purchases were for defense,
strictly defined. Nowhere was there a precedent for government subsidies of
commercial aircraft for foreign states. Even if they funded international aviation grants for geopolitical purposes, Ike's National Security Council concluded, the government lacked a formal mechanism for choosing which
American manufacturers would receive orders at taxpayer expense, while
the chairman of the Civil Aeronautics Board feared "there was no legislation
or policy in existence under which we could encourage US airlines to carry
on [unprofitable] operations in underdeveloped parts of the world." Despite years of presidential pleading, by 1959 Eisenhower's Operations Coordinating Board reluctantly concluded: "There are no present programs
which call for increasing expenditures substantially . . . to cope with and to
anticipate Sino-Soviet efforts to penetrate civil aviation in the less developed
areas."[12]

Kennedy's team vowed a change in this area. Their president believed that
these "lands of the rising peoples" were pivotal to Cold War success, and
that aviation in turn offered a key to newly decolonized states and develop-

ing regions. And he believed that years of neglect had left America well behind the competition. By "seeking to exploit the strong prestige appeal that civil aviation enjoys among nationalistic elite desirous of asserting their newly acquired nationhood," the State Department's Bureau of Intelligence and Research concluded, the Soviets sought to win hearts and minds. They had to be countered, no matter the cost or legislative difficulties, because Soviet "aviation policies appear to be guided less by commercial considerations than by the desire to extend the bloc's influence in the less developed countries." Recognizing NSC-5726's failure to adequately address this pressing issue, the administration formally rescinded the document in May 1962.[13] Rusk appointed Averell Harriman, assistant secretary of state for Far Eastern affairs, to develop a replacement, though here too the response was longer on words than deeds. The Harriman committee's new aviation policy, unveiled in the summer of 1963, called yet again for "a general policy of containing Communist aviation penetration of the less-developed countries." Like NSC-5726, however, it offered no real means for doing so. Harriman's team developed no new programs by which developing countries might fund acquisition of Western aircraft, and neither did they develop the means of expanding aviation facilities within those countries. By the time the last of Britain's Viscounts flew to China in June 1963, they could only claim to be "undertaking an examination of the best means to implement or modify past policy." They wanted communist aviation kept out of the Cold War's periphery; they just did not yet know how to accomplish that goal.[14]

Harriman's committee did make one important intellectual contribution to this debate by arguing against uniform responses to communist aviation penetration. Flexibility was required instead to meet each nation's unique situation. "In the day-to-day implementation of policy, the US has reacted in most cases in equal measure to Communist civil aviation moves," they concluded. "This practice is not necessarily consistent with differences in our overall national policies with the several Communist country groupings . . . nor does it take into account the fact that Communist aviation moves may be more damaging to the Free World interests in one less-developed country than in another." Developing the broad outlines of a flexible policy remained beyond their grasp, however. More than a year after rescinding NSC-5726 because it lacked a means to counter communist incursions into underdeveloped areas, Kennedy's policymakers had little new to offer, save the realization that a blanket policy would not do.[15]

Their recognition of aviation's importance to the developing world was similar to earlier British declarations, but the fit was not exact. Kennedy's policymakers considered aircraft capable of securing geopolitical influence. Their British predecessors rarely made this argument so explicitly. As a group, Whitehall strategists were more concerned with how aviation sales could prompt formerly colonized peoples to reorient their channels of trade and supply. They believed a country willing to buy British planes would subsequently prove more willing to purchase British washing machines and cars, thereby providing London with a continuing means of influence. American thinkers more dogmatically believed that aircraft sales alone could foster geopolitical change. Newly empowered leaders willing to fly American were visibly choosing sides in the Cold War fight, they reasoned. They could consequently be counted on to think like Americans, or at least to remain loyal consumers of Western aid and aircraft lest spare parts and newer models fail to appear. Whitehall sought influence through the tether of technological supply. Their American counterparts appeared more taken by aviation's psychological impact in Africa and Asia, and they believed the Soviets shared their view. Such faith led Harriman's committee to emphasize aviation's geopolitical importance over its long-term economic or cultural impact, and in turn to react vigorously to apparent British acceptance of communist aviation advances in the years to come.

China was one such area. Kennedy's policymakers inherited from their predecessors a belief that Beijing, and not Moscow, was vulnerable to American economic warfare plans, and moreover that Mao's regime was the more belligerent. As Undersecretary of State Chester Bowles stated in the fall of 1961, Beijing was "far more dangerous, in many ways, than even the Committee of One Million [a pro-Chiang lobbying group] would have us think." The Kennedy administration therefore did nothing to change the previous decade's anti-Chinese stance regarding aviation. They sought improved ties with the Soviets and nuanced policies for countering communist penetration of the developing world, but also wanted the Chinese to remain wholly isolated from outside airlines and cut off from Western sources of supply. So wholeheartedly did Harriman's committee accept the previous administration's dual aviation policy for China and the Soviet bloc, in fact, that they included NSC-5726's statements on China word for word in their own documents: "[The] United States should (a) not sell or export to these states [China, North Korea, and North Vietnam] civil aircraft or associated aviation equipment, and (b) seek to prevent other Free world nations from selling or exporting to these states civil aircraft or associated aviation equipment or from providing to these states facilities for overhaul, refitting or major maintenance." From their perspective, Europe's Cold War was primed for aerial change; Asia's remained locked in the harshest of Manichean mindsets.[16]

These divergent policies are as much explained by the discrepancy between Soviet and Chinese aerial capabilities as by politics. Washington lacked the means to fully parry Russian aviation thrusts, but Kennedy's team believed themselves capable of stymieing Chinese expansion. The Soviets could export aircraft and technical aid; Mao's government could hardly meet its own aviation needs, let alone export aircraft to others. What Beijing could do, however, was export Maoism and promote its own international agenda through new air routes. While Soviet-American relations moved toward parity and stability by the early 1960s, many American analysts believed Beijing remained fixed at the evolutionary moment of Marxism-Leninism where the promotion of revolution abroad remained a national priority. According to Edward Rice, American consul general in Hong Kong and a recognized expert on Chinese affairs, Beijing's leaders "envisage the less developed countries as their most fruitful field for their overseas endeavors," especially given their use "as a 'poor man's' model for national development." They realized their inability to compete with Soviet or American aid, he concluded; but they had much to offer to states thirsting for international legitimacy. Aviation, sure to grab headline and demand political attention, offered "a relatively inexpensive way of appearing with the trappings of world power." Beijing might offer new states access to Chinese airports and overflight rights, for example, hoping leaders of new countries might be captivated by the prestige of acquiring bilateral air rights with so prominent a world power. Analysts like Rice believed Beijing preached a new gospel of aviation ties independent of the oppressive great powers. Just as their former colonial masters could no longer keep new nations from developing, they could not keep rising peoples from banding together. That aircraft, a symbol of modernity, offered new nations an unstoppable means of connection only reinforced Beijing's argument that world history had reached a new epoch, wherein the future belonged to those formerly at the bottom so long as they co-opted and mastered the technologies of the top.[17]

Beijing had a considerable way to go before such grandiose aerial plans could become reality. The Chinese did not enjoy any regular air service with the noncommunist world when their first Viscounts arrived in 1963. Neither did it have long-range transports capable of true worldwide service, though the Viscounts were certainly capable of reaching neighboring countries.

American policymakers vowed to keep Beijing from making headway in either department, fearing that a single crack in their aviation wall would lead to a torrent of bilateral agreements, with a subsequent "increase in Chinese prestige" their Hong Kong consulate dubbed "not inconsiderable." Britain might sell Beijing planes despite American objections; but Britain could not provide Beijing with easy access to the wider world. China's neighbors held that key.[18]

Kennedy's advisers believed they had the ability to keep China bottled up, especially because so many Asian countries depended on American aid and assistance at the onset of the 1960s. By 1963, therefore, American aviation policy toward the communist world once more split in two. And while the Kennedy administration had yet to formulate an effective response to Soviet grants of planes and aid to developing nations, save the promise of a flexible response, the New Frontiersmen knew they need not worry about similar offers from Beijing. Instead, now that China had the British-built planes necessary for launching their first international service, what Kennedy's administration worried about in Asia was halting free-world nations from accepting what Mao's government could offer: the prestige of being first to fly beyond the Great Wall.[19]

First beyond the Wall

Pakistan provided the first challenge to Washington's aerial web around China, and ultimately did as much to change American aviation policy toward Beijing in five years as London had achieved in a generation. Its contribution to this story began at the conclusion of the Viscount affair, when officials from Pakistan International Airways (PIA) notified Washington in May 1963 that they planned to sell their own aging Viscounts to make room for more sophisticated jet-powered aircraft. Boeing's latest models would be the most likely replacement, the Pakistanis hinted, but only if they were able to move their used machines. American diplomats were used to such discussions. Aircraft were so expensive and their sale so politically sensitive that they were frequently called upon to counsel foreign leaders on the matter. What the Pakistanis revealed next, however, was hardly par for the course: Beijing was their most likely buyer. Having observed Britain's efforts with great interest, PIA's leadership assumed that China would be interested in used Viscounts for spare parts or as inexpensive additions to their fleet, and that the door was now open to free-world aircraft sales to Mao's regime.[20]

As might be expected, the news perturbed Kennedy's diplomats. It seemed validation of their earlier fears that Vickers's sale spelled the end of their rigid aviation embargo. "Free World sales to CHICOM would provide latter with equipment not otherwise available to them," the State Department reminded its Karachi consulate, "which would strengthen their paramilitary and possible military capabilities." Lest such security considerations fail to move the Pakistanis, PIA was also reminded that their Viscounts contained American-built parts not permitted for re-export to China. "If such planes [are] sold to Communist China," Foggy Bottom offered in the clipped telephonic style of the day, "[it] would not be possible [to] supply such replacement or maintenance parts which might be of US origin or manufactured by [a] subsidiary or licensee of US company."[21]

Because they believed their hardball Viscount diplomacy had worked with London, American officials tried the same approach with Pakistan. Washington further instructed its diplomats, "If Pakistani officials inquire about new Viscounts for Communist China in this connection, you may say that effort being made to eliminate all US origin items from Viscounts being built for Communist China," and that the "same rule would apply for replacement and maintenance parts for these [Pakistan's] Viscounts." The United States would not condone the sale, American officials subsequently blustered. They would force PIA to remove all American parts from their China-bound Viscounts, just as they believed they had with Britain's. They could sell to Beijing if they wished, but the company should not expect to buy American afterward.[22]

Pakistani officials did not respond well to these threats, and they upped the ante in response by disclosing their plans to sell their Viscounts to China not only to make room for new Boeings, but also as a condition of the bilateral air agreement with Beijing then under negotiation. This was a daring admission. The service would be the first between China and a noncommunist nation, though such a move would be wholly in keeping with PIA's ambitious history. PIA was the first Asian airline to regularly operate jet aircraft, initiating regular jet service to London in March 1960 and then across the Atlantic to New York only fourteen months later. This was less than two years after BOAC had inaugurated nonstop jet service along this lucrative route. Ever on the vanguard, PIA even employed Pakistan's first modern computer in 1967, and the company became a vital symbol of unity for a nation divided from its inception by more than one thousand miles of frequently hostile Indian territory. As PIA's official history accurately noted, "probably never has air transport been more important to the development of a new nation than in the case of Pakistan."[23]

China thus seemed to PIA officials another milestone on their path to international prominence, and a crucial step in their ambitious plans for an inter-Asian service all the way to Japan. Tokyo had thus far proved lukewarm to the idea of granting PIA landing rights, though their reluctance did not prevent PIA's planners from calculating the potential profits of linking Japanese businesspeople and tourists with Mao's budding market. Because Tokyo had yielded to American pressures to bar direct flights to China, Japanese bound for the country were required first to fly to Hong Kong, where they would take a train or bus across the border (usually the next day), and only then catch a flight to their Chinese destination. A trip from Osaka to Shanghai, though only four hours away by air, required nearly thirty arduous hours of travel. Despite growing commercial ties with Beijing, Japanese officials were understandably reluctant to authorize any service of their own to China, lest they incur Washington's wrath.[24]

PIA's attempt to breach the Great Wall and connect Asia's two greatest markets would therefore come as no surprise to industry observers, though American officials were less impressed by the airline playing to form. On June 8, 1963, Pakistan's ambassador to the United States met with Phillip Talbot and Roger Hilsman, both senior officials at the State Department's Asian desk. The Americans bluntly laid out their opposition to PIA's proposed expansion and sale. "The proposed Pakistani-Chinese air link would represent [a] major breach of the Free World position regarding air service to and from Communist China," they said. Particularly troubling was the opportunity such an air route offered the Chinese to increase their "subversive efforts in [the] Near East and Africa." Naturally, Washington opposed the venture, which Talbot and Hilsman none-too-subtly termed "potentially harmful to [the] totality of US-Pakistani relations." A week later, America's ambassador offered to Pakistani president Ayub Khan a similar warning that left no doubt as to the potential fallout should Islamabad proceed in opening China to the West. "I put heavy weight on breach of Free World solidarity in commercial aviation field vis-à-vis Communist China," Ambassador Walter McConaughy reported home. "I told the President . . . it would ill become Pakistan as a still staunch ally to become an instrument [in] service [to] Chinese Communist purposes in the aviation field and facilitating the funneling of Chinese Communist agents through Dacca and Karachi to all parts of South Africa, Near East and Africa to do their harmful business."[25]

American officials repeated their opposition to PIA's proposed expansion in successive meetings held in Karachi and Washington. They threatened; they cajoled; and most importantly they offered the Pakistanis no reason to believe their response would in any way be flexible. Pakistani-American relations, they repeatedly warned, and with it American aid, hung in the balance.

Not everyone in the administration believed threats were the best way to handle the budding crisis. John Kenneth Galbraith, the academic turned ambassador to India, injected himself into this affair soon after Ambassador McConaughy's tough talk with President Khan. For Galbraith, whose embassy received copies of cables concerning Pakistani affairs, the administration's response seemed emblematic of larger problems then facing American diplomacy. "People involved are reacting without thought," he wrote Harriman. "There is a tactical and strategic aspect to the problem, both bad." On a practical level, Galbraith believed, Washington's opposition to PIA's venture was doomed from the start. Thus far, American officials had warned only vaguely of dramatic consequences should the Pakistanis knowingly violate American will, and they had failed to provide a detailed accounting of the losses intransigence would bring. "If we were serious," Galbraith advised, "we would deny the Pakistanis landing rights in the US, parts for the Boeings, or, for that matter, foreclose our mortgage on the planes." Foggy Bottom had entertained none of these options, thereby giving the Pakistanis no reason to think American threats were anything more than bluster. This seemed to Galbraith neither effective nor wise. "We should not repeat not give the impression to these countries, as we do now, that our requests are purely trivial," he advised. "The rule is to consider carefully what we ask for and when we ask[, to] make it stick." As it presently stood, "President Ayub kisses off McConaughy's objections, and even jokes that flights through China will help them pay for the [Boeing] planes."[26]

Galbraith believed Washington's handling of the case revealed the broader failings of his government's containment policies. The need for flexibility in countering communist aerial incursions had been one of the Harriman committee's principal reasons for rejecting NSC-5726. Yet when offered their first opportunity to enact a nuanced response to Chinese penetration of a particularly sensitive area, the State Department had fallen back on knee-jerk anticommunism. "Both in Washington and Karachi great stress has been made on the fact that the new airline would enable the Chinese to export subversive influence to the rest of Asia and Africa," he wrote. "We should not repeat not use fatuous arguments of this sort." The Chinese could already send their agents abroad via boats or even through commercial flights from Hong Kong. To think, in 1963, that Chinese subversion (which he considered real) could be quarantined simply by denying Chinese agents a direct flight to their intended destinations was to underestimate Chinese capabilities and resolve. Any operative worthy of his masters' trust would surely be capable of making a connecting flight. "Our policy should be to resist firmly their [Beijing's] military expansion and efforts to promote revolution," he argued, but "arm twisting our friends on these matters seems to me particularly offensive because it puts us in conflict with our friends and doesn't accomplish a damn thing." In short, Galbraith saw in Washington's response a retreat to prior tendencies; or as he put it, "Some people continue to think that Dulles and Admiral Radford are continuing models for our diplomacy."[27]

Galbraith's evaluation seemed out of line even by his famously curmudgeonly standards. He and Harriman had been intimate correspondents for years before joining the Kennedy team. This time, however, his caustic critiques were not addressed to Harriman alone. "I admire your pugnacious instincts but don't think that it would be a good idea to apply sanctions to Paks just at this time," Harriman responded. "I agree that they are being bloody and letting themselves be used by adroit CHICOMS, in opening up a route which may turn out to be extremely dangerous to us." Yet Harriman did not think it wise to move beyond bluster and threats to truly turning the screws on the Pakistanis. "I am old fashioned enough to believe the Paks are useful allies," he told Galbraith, "even though it is more modern to love the Indians more."[28]

Perhaps because it had been swathed in barbs, Harriman missed Galbraith's broader point. He was not arguing that Washington should sharply punish Pakistan for breaking the seal on quarantined China. On the contrary, Galbraith saw in Washington's automatic opposition to PIA's move a too-doctrinaire approach to thwarting communist expansion. The New Frontiersmen were so focused on halting communist penetration at all costs that Harriman's own aviation committee could not even consider the new avenues of diplomacy they had demanded. "I am most of all against protests which are for questionable ends and do not even accomplish those," Galbraith immediately responded. A week later he broached the matter with Rusk in yet another unsolicited cable. "While I am reluctant as ever to criticize the department," he began (a line that surely elicited laughter in Foggy

Bottom), "this is a clear example of how not to run a foreign policy." Washington's hollow threats allowed Karachi "to stage another demonstration that our words need not be taken seriously in these parts." The air quarantine on China was unlikely to thwart Beijing's subversion, just as Washington was unlikely to keep PIA from plying this potentially lucrative market, and thus the only consequences of America's rigid reaction were to embitter US-Pakistani relations, without truly halting Chinese subversion throughout Asia, while demonstrating American weakness. "I have a feeling that we see here an occasion where reaction was automatic," he concluded, "rather than subject to the penetrating analytical processes otherwise characteristic of the New Frontier."[29]

Rusk put a quick end to Galbraith's insurrection, primarily because he had his eyes on a larger prize. He realized the State Department's hardball, though ultimately conciliatory, diplomacy with Pakistan may not have been perfect for dealing with Khan's government. It was, however, perfectly in line with the administration's broader opposition to Chinese expansion, which Harriman's team believed necessary to counter wherever it arose, lest the first opening wedge become a flood of subsequent flights. Consequently, they were determined to do everything in their power to keep Pakistan from breaching that wall. On July 7, the Pakistani ambassador to the United States paid a farewell visit to Harriman (he was leaving Washington for home), and in the midst of what the State Department recorded as a "lengthy, cordial, and relaxed" meeting, the American brought up the aviation controversy yet again, this time by weighing PIA's actions on a global scale. "Khrushchev is under severe challenge from CHICOMS who are making inroads in almost every communist party in the world," Harriman said. Global peace rested upon Beijing losing this struggle for supremacy within the communist world. While dangerous, the Soviets could at least be dealt with as responsible partners. But "in this period, no member of the Free World should do anything to aid and abet" the far more dangerous Chinese, and the "proposed air link with CHICOMS was sort of action he was referring to." In short, Harriman warned, "Pakistan should be very careful in its dealing with the Chicoms and not jeopardize its relations with the Western world."[30]

Kennedy's advisers reacted strongly to Pakistan's flirtations with Beijing, but they surely were not surprised. They did not trust Pakistan's leadership, despite having granted the country millions in aid, and questioned not only their anticommunist zeal but also their commitment to stability in one of the world's most volatile regions. "The chief cloud on horizon [in Pakistani-American relations] is Pak flirtation with Chicoms," senior national security adviser Robert Komer informed the president in July. It was "silly to say latest Pak move to extend airline to Peiping [*sic*] is a straight commercial deal." The move was clearly designed—as were all Pakistani moves, in his opinion—to pressure the United States regarding India. American aid to New Delhi had increased during the six months since India's border conflict with China, and these aviation negotiations were Pakistan's way of displaying its disquiet over this development. Every time Washington moved closer to Delhi, Komer noted, Karachi turned to Moscow and Beijing. "Such moves cause real irritation," Komer reminded the president later that year, for "if Paks are justifying their China policy domestically by saying 'an enemy of my enemy is our friend,' they must grant that some sections of US opinion might say 'a friend of our enemy is our enemy too." By this playground logic, Pakistan was engaging in a dangerous game. "We intend to continue generous aid to Pakistan," Komer concluded, but only "*if* our basic relationship remains unshaken."[31]

Khan's government ultimately rebuffed Washington's repeated pressures and concluded an aviation agreement with Beijing in July 1963. Their efforts may have been geopolitical in nature, designed to strengthen ties with the adversary of their archenemy India; and the deal offered commercial benefits in its own right. One thing is sure: Khan was not dissuaded by America's strong-arm tactics. His advisers knew that Washington needed allies on China's border, regardless of those allies' proclivity for dealing with their communist neighbors. The White House validated Khan's assessment later that summer when it waged a bitter public battle against congressional attempts to cut aid to Karachi by legislators enraged by PIA's dealings with Beijing. Karachi was "being bloody," as Harriman had put it. Geography alone gave it the leverage to do so. Pakistan won this first round of aviation diplomacy with the United States, making it appear that Galbraith was right. Despite their desire to hem in the communist menace, the Kennedy administration's automated threats proved as harmless as a paper tiger.[32]

Why, then, did Washington make such bitter protests at all? Why embitter Pakistani-American relations to the degree that State Department analysts in the fall of 1963 termed them "in the lowest ebb in the history of the alliance"? The answer lies in the depth of the administration's anti-Chinese conviction. The New Frontiersmen viewed every conflict in Asia through an anticommunist lens. Political unrest in Laos and Vietnam seemed clear examples of Beijing's growing influence throughout the region, while Chinese incursions into the disputed border with India fueled fears of Mao's exuberant expansionism. Due to the administration's fundamentally anti-Chinese worldview, the New Frontier's promises of nuance and flexibility in confronting communist aviation penetration ultimately fell before an inflexible anticommunism.[33]

Britain's Viscounts were unlikely on their own to make Beijing into a world power, and Pakistani air routes into China, on their own, would probably not alter Asia's strategic balance. Instead, at stake were issues of precedent and prestige. Superficially, Beijing's search for prestige was at hand. It had the most to gain from normalizing relations beyond the communist world. Truly at stake in both these cases, however, was Washington's standing in Asia and its ability to direct the continent's peaceful development by retarding China's growth, which seemed to American strategists from Kennan to Kennedy the world's most destabilizing force. Pakistan was being "bloody" in American eyes, because its actions seemed designed to tweak American strategists at their most sensitive point. Komer reminded Kennedy, "We are in the anticommunist business." All other geopolitical goals paled by comparison. The Pakistanis may have thought they were reminding Washington of their importance in South Asia, or they may simply have lusted after the China market. Either way, Komer concluded, they surely underestimated Washington's passion for isolating Beijing. "The basic theme might be that we want to go forward with our Pak alliance," he said, "but current PAK policies risk killing the goose that lays the golden egg." Halting India was Karachi's fundamental concern, but Washington was the larger power, and thus Komer believed its concerns would ultimately drive their relationship. "What we don't see" in Pakistan's pursuit of Beijing, he concluded, "is why the Paks fail to realize they're playing with fire and hurting their own cause." Komer and those around him could see nothing in their mental map of Asia but potential routes for Chinese expansion and potential victims of Chinese aggression. Countries were bulwarks or battlements against Maoist assaults. Their internal politics paled in importance when compared to Washington's perception of their geopolitical role.[34]

By 1963 the only foreign policy goal as important to Washington as halting Chinese expansion was stabilizing relations with Moscow. The American effort in Vietnam that later seared a generation can be viewed through this lens; so too can the Kennedy administration's efforts to solidify its role as leader of the global anticommunist fight in both Cold War theaters. Soviet and American officials renewed efforts at finalizing a bilateral air link as a sign of their growing mutual respect. The previous year, Kennedy had quietly suggested to Khrushchev a joint Soviet-American air strike against Beijing's embryonic nuclear program. The Kremlin ultimately rebuffed Kennedy's overture, though not without considering it. Such a partnership would have seemed too fantastic for words but a few years before: the thought of one pillar of Communism attacking the other with help from capitalism's epicenter would have been beyond imagination. But by 1963, both Soviet and American leaders considered Beijing's zealotry the most pressing threat to world peace. Undersecretary of State George Ball said as much during his August 1963 mission to Pakistan, when he tried to heal the wounds caused by PIA's advances. "The Chinese threat was a threat to the entire subcontinent," he said, and "the defense of the subcontinent should be against a common enemy."[35]

Pakistan's blossoming aviation relationship with China demonstrated the limits of American power. Even in an area of vital importance to American strategists, massive outpourings of aid paradoxically offered little leverage. Kennedy's team believed aviation would offer them geopolitical control. A country in line with American aviation policies and flying American planes was supposed to be malleable to Washington's desires. Such would not ultimately prove to be the case. The only thing worse than a country (or a politician) for sale, Kennedy's advisers learned to their dismay, was one that would not stay bought. Geography and the New Frontiersmen's anticommunist obsession combined to put Pakistan in the driver's seat by the summer of 1963. As Khan's government would soon learn to their great regret, however, the reach of American financial and business might offered policymakers a scalpel with which to perform diplomatic surgery when the blunt hammer of diplomatic pressure proved insufficient. Pakistan cracked the Western wall around communist China. Whether PIA could subsequently procure planes capable of flying such routes without Washington's approval was another matter entirely.

Pakistani Precedent

Washington had held the power to thwart Pakistan's aerial ambitions the entire time, provided that American policymakers were willing to use it. PIA planned to employ Boeing jets on flights to China, including 720Bs acquired in 1961 and 1962, and the new 727s the airline was even then negotiating to purchase. However, such flights promised to violate American foreign asset control laws, because while flying the planes to China was technically allowed, servicing them there was not. No legislation specifically restricted use of an American-built plane once received by its purchaser. Buyers were barred from reselling their machines to communist countries, but their use was their own concern. Just as General Motors or Jaguar cannot restrict purchasers from performing any number of dangerous or illegal acts in their cars after they have left the sales lot, so too did American policymakers recognize that once bought and delivered, a plane became the buyer's responsibility. As the State Department explained in July 1963 after Japan's All Nippon Airways inquired if Washington could legally bar the airline's American-built planes from flying to China, "owners [of] such aircraft are not prohibited from flying aircraft to or through mainland China and no assurances against such use are required by United States Government" before its purchase.[36]

Whether Washington would authorize the export of planes to buyers intending to fly such routes was another matter. Officials could not keep foreign buyers from violating American laws, but they did not have to knowingly equip them to do so. This was a moral Rubicon the State and Commerce departments had yet to cross. Neither had they formally ruled on the storage of American-built spare parts in China required before any airline could provide regular service. American officials might not have been able to bar a foreign airline from flying to China in 1963, but they could make it infeasible to do so. The power to supply, spare parts in this case, was a strong power indeed. America's "embargo on exports of US origin products to mainland China would prohibit stocking of US parts, lubricants, and other supplies in that area," Foggy Bottom explained to its Tokyo embassy. No spares meant no repairs and no maintenance, and thus no way to operate commercial flights.[37]

The State Department assured Pakistan it would enforce this ban in the summer of 1963, and hinted that it would not authorize the purchase of new Boeings intended for use in China. American law said nothing about controlling an American-built plane once it left for foreign shores, nor did it require the Commerce Department to issue an export license for a sale legal on the surface but deemed detrimental to national security. At the end of July, after the PIA-Chinese aviation treaty had been announced, the airline's managing director, Nur Khan (who simultaneously held a ranking position in the country's air force), approached Ambassador McConaughy to see if

Washington could somehow be persuaded to make an exception to these export restraints. Perhaps, Khan wondered, the White House might approve storage of American-licensed spare parts and equipment in "bonded" warehouses near the Chinese airfields but under PIA's immediate control? Such parts would be used exclusively for PIA's service and would not be mingled with Chinese supplies. "I disabused him of this notion," the ambassador informed Foggy Bottom, "and made it clear to him that he could not stock US-made parts for his Boeings in Communist China without a special Treasury license, which might prove exceedingly difficult to obtain."[38]

As relations between Pakistan and the United States worsened by September, the State Department's resolve stiffened. Whereas the department's lawyers had previously vacillated over whether they could bar the export of an American plane solely due to foreknowledge of its ultimate use, they now believed the law gave them such power. This legal conclusion was passed on to Undersecretary Ball in the midst of his mission to South Asia. "Under Foreign Asset Controls regs," a departmental cable explained, "an American firm or its foreign subsidiary would be prohibited from selling spare parts to PIA if such firm or subsidiary knew or had reason to believe item would be shipped to China." Foreknowledge of a crime was, it seemed, enough to keep the sale from occurring. There would be no sale of spare parts or of new Boeings, Karachi was warned accordingly, and no special Treasury or Commerce license either. Pakistan could frustrate American wishes by flying to China, but it would not be able to do so in planes stamped "Made in the U.S.A." Ambassador Galbraith may not have approved of this decision (no record of his response exists in American archives), but surely he would have endorsed Washington making good on its threats.[39]

Washington's hard line left PIA and Khan's government scrambling for a solution. PIA officials calculated they would need to store spares worth over $190,000 in China to make their service feasible, parts that weighed nearly three tons in total. They contemplated outfitting their current fleet with self-contained "spare part kits" capable of supporting on-site maintenance, but realized the costs involved in carrying this dead weight on every China-bound flight would erode any potential profits from the route. This was the conclusion Washington hoped they would reach, but once more Karachi did the Americans one better. PIA opened negotiations with one of Boeing's principal rivals, asking for details and contracts for British-made Hawker Siddeley Tridents. If they could not buy American, their first choice, the Pakistanis would turn to British suppliers, who were all too eager to see their planes flown to China.[40]

It looked like Washington's rigid stance was going to cost Boeing its sale, and company officials complained bitterly to the State Department. "Nur Khan preferred British to American aircraft not on technical grounds," Boeing's representative in Pakistan told the embassy, "but because he felt the United States might either in the future say PIA could not use American aircraft for flights to certain countries, or that the State Department would insist that any Export-Import Bank loan financing PIA purchase of additional aircraft contain a stipulation that the plane could not be flown to certain countries such as Red China." British officials made no such demands. Indeed, once word leaked that Boeing no longer held the inside track to the PIA sale, Hawker Siddeley's agents stepped up their own sales pitch. The company offered what one salesperson for Douglas (which was not involved in the PIA competition) dubbed "incredible terms" for their Tridents, including the offer to purchase the airline's aging Viscounts for well above their market value. The company additionally rerouted a Trident then in the midst of a worldwide promotional tour, in order to show PIA Britain's bid firsthand. In a twist of fate, the Trident was piloted by John Cunningham, the De Havilland Comet's initial test pilot. He flew Pakistani dignitaries around their country and repeatedly noted that the Trident was capable of flying anywhere its owners desired without limitations. It was roomy, efficient, right for the price, and, he slyly added, it "carried a British compass."[41]

Diplomacy, rather than commerce, threatened to decide the winner of this battle for PIA's future fleet. Boeing's products were better, PIA's representative admitted during the first week of October. Nonetheless the airline would most likely buy British due to "political considerations." The potential loss infuriated Boeing's leadership, who feared news of their frustrated sale would poison future dealings throughout the region. Washington's objections to Pakistan's efforts in China were already well known. The *Washington Post* reported the story in detail, as did several Karachi newspapers, and Boeing officials believed few Asian countries (particularly newly independent ones) would be willing to buy aircraft whose use could be dictated by a government thousands of miles away. Boeing reminded the White House that its aircraft were marketed as harbingers of independence and modernity. For newly sovereign nations especially, their ownership had to be free of foreign entanglements. According to the company's Pakistani representative, Karachi officials crystallized the issue when they argued, "PIA could not afford to stop flying to Paris, for example, just because President Kennedy had a disagreement with de Gaulle."[42]

Washington ultimately caved in to this pressure when it became clear that more than just sales to Pakistan were at stake. Reports had begun filtering back from Tokyo that All Nippon Airways (ANA), Japan's second-largest carrier, would decide between 727s or Tridents for its own fleet based upon Washington's actions toward PIA. Japanese officials hoped to fly Chinese routes someday as well, and though no one could predict when such flights might begin, most presumed it would be during the expected lifespan of these planes. The American embassy in Tokyo reported home, "Though requirement here is almost entirely for Japan domestic and interport services, airlines would probably prefer [to] purchase aircraft whose utilization is not limited nor threatened to be limited by structures of US policy." Press reports over the stalled Boeing negotiations that accurately ascribed the stumbling block in the PIA deal left an impression. America's ambassador to Japan warned that reports that "US aircraft will not be permitted under any circumstances in mainland China may discourage Japanese from even considering US products."[43] ANA officials also made their thinking clear to Boeing, which immediately passed the information along to the Kennedy administration. The choices were stark. If Pakistan was allowed to fly American planes, ANA would purchase American as well. If Washington refused to license the Pakistani sale, thereby proving that owners of American planes could not fly where they chose to, the Japanese would choose to fly British.

The consequences of this decision were great, as this was no inconsequential order. PIA sought only three aircraft. Japanese airlines planned to purchase an estimated fifty jets of the 727/Trident category by the end of the decade, and both British and American salespersons predicted that whichever nation captured this market would gain the upper hand to sell hundreds more in the decade to come to other Asian airlines likely to follow Tokyo's lead. Sales for Japan alone could be worth up to $150 million by the close of the decade, and for a country that had seen passenger air miles increase nearly 20 percent since 1960, the market's future looked boundless, and entirely within Washington's control. Roger Hilsman, assistant undersecretary of state for Far Eastern affairs, informed Undersecretary Ball in December, "The Japanese All Nippon Airlines apparently is awaiting a US government decision on PIA spare parts before deciding whether to place an order with Boeing." This decision would help determine Asia's aviation future.[44]

The prospect of selling planes to Japan prompted Washington to change its tune on exports to PIA, and thus to change its policy on controls for China more broadly. In late November, Boeing submitted to the Treasury and Commerce departments an application for an export license for PIA of one 720B and three 727s, valued at nearly twenty million dollars. Company executives took the unusual step of asking the government's permission for the sale before having signed a final contract with the airline in order to provide PIA (and ANA) with proof that their negotiations could proceed unimpeded by export restraints. Even with the trauma of Kennedy's sudden death only days later, it took less than two weeks for Washington to make its decision. Despite all the bluster and threats of the previous months, Lyndon Johnson approved the sale of Boeing jets to Pakistan during the second week of December, and approved storage of American-licensed equipment for PIA's exclusive use in bonded warehouses in China as well.

When confronted with undeniable commercial pressure, Washington reversed its position and quietly ended its generation-long aviation embargo of the People's Republic of China. As Ball explained to Undersecretary of Commerce Franklin D. Roosevelt Jr., "Our approval is based on our belief that denial of the application would work an unnecessary hardship on American business in absence of any realistic prospects of advancing our foreign policy interests with respect to China." Barring the PIA order would not have stopped the airline from flying to China. It merely would have given business to the British. Unable to halt the rapid erosion of its aviation plans for the region, Washington risked achieving the worst of both worlds: losing the wall around China and losing valuable sales as well. Johnson's White House wisely chose to cut its losses.[45]

State Department documents combined with Boeing company records prove that the prospect of selling to Japan ultimately forced acceptance of the PIA exports. Ball wrote as much to America's embassies throughout Asia, noting that a "decision [to] permit storage spares and maintenance parts in Communist China will place Boeing in better competitive position with respect to possible sales of aircraft to Japan and other countries." It was clear that "one Japanese airline [is] now considering purchase Boeings for routes which may include China," and "French and British are also competing for sale of aircraft to Japan." Surely Boeing officials believed this reason behind Washington's conversion. On December 17, company president William Allen penned a personal note to Roosevelt in appreciation of the government's decision on the PIA sale. "Your expeditious handling of this matter will, I am confident, aid us greatly in our efforts to sell aircraft in the Far East," and not just to Pakistan. Three days later Allen dictated a shorter more personal note of thanks to Commerce Undersecretary Clarence Martin. "I am told that you had a good deal to do with the clearance which we recently received on an export license covering sales of aircraft and spare parts to Pakistan," Allen wrote. "As you know, this precedent will no doubt have quite an influence on our opportunity for sales to the Japanese."[46]

Washington's decision to allow the export of American planes and parts bound for use in China directly abrogated U.S. foreign asset control laws and, as Allen rightly noted, this was a precedent-setting move. Though the State Department repeatedly observed, as it did in a telegram to Karachi on December 12, that "this does not reflect change in US trade policy or civil aviation policy toward Communist China," reality proved far different. A precedent for use of American products in China had in fact been set. In 1964 PIA inaugurated its jet service to the People's Republic of China, flying a Boeing 720. In the intervening months American diplomats won the airline's acceptance of several mild restraints on the storage and use of American-licensed parts in China, but these limits were negligible compared to the larger issue at hand. Washington had made its stand against the use of American parts in China believing the future of its aviation policies in Asia was at stake. It had done so even when strategic relations with a geographically vital ally appeared to be at risk. When pushed by commercial necessity, however, including the prospect of losing a large segment of Asian sales, Washington chose profits over security, and exports over rigid anticommunism. The Johnson administration suspended a $4.3 million loan to Pakistan immediately following commencement of the PIA service to China, aid that was to have financed expansion of the Dacca airport. As a warning against future such displays of willful disregard for American wishes, however, the move was too little, too late. A quarter century of American aviation rigidity came to a close in 1963. Halting Communism's advance had been the hallmark of American aviation policy since 1945. Commercial considerations had consistently been subordinated to this larger goal. Financial might, Pentagon spending, and the presence of an unparalleled domestic market offered successive White House administrations this luxury. For all their effort spent halting British incursions into the China market, it was a minor sale to Pakistan that changed American policy.[47]

Pakistan succeeded where Britain had failed because Islamabad proved more willing than London to stand up to American pressure. The Pakistanis mattered less in Washington than the British, and they offered far less in the return of American political and economic investments than the British. But this lesser position also gave Khan's government power. The British needed the Americans as well. The Pakistanis recognized that only their geography mattered in Washington's worldview. They knew, moreover, that others would provide whatever aid and support the Americans refused to give. The Soviets would provide cash and tools; from the Chinese they would get access to an untapped market; and ultimately the British would provide the planes and technology Islamabad needed to realize its global visions. Even the Americans were unlikely to completely shut down their spigot of supply, given Pakistan's strategic location bordering both China and the Middle East.

American threats of reduced foreign investment also meant little in Islamabad. British firms bought American components for use in high-technology manufacturing and were therefore vulnerable to American constraints. Pakistan primarily purchased only finished products. So what if the Americans forbade them use of navigation equipment or widgets? The Pakistanis bought their planes whole. So long as they were allowed to fly where they wanted and when they wanted, and so long as they could service their aircraft wherever they chose, PIA cared little whose flag was stamped on the fuselage of their planes or on the avionics within. The British had to care, because they were both purchasers and integrators of American technology. The Pakistanis merely consumed Western technology. If somebody was willing to supply, and somebody always was (whether the British, the French, or even the Soviets), the customer was always right.

American aviation diplomacy came full circle in 1963 and 1964. Policymakers had begun the Cold War chiefly motivated by security fears. Security drove Washington's objections to the Nene and Derwent sales in 1946, and to Comet sales during the next decade. Security prompted vigorous American responses to aerial openings behind the iron and bamboo curtains, and helped make Washington a clear outlier in COCOM's multilateral forum. As Robert Komer, who advised National Security Adviser McGeorge Bundy, had clearly stated, security was Washington's primary concern, for even if economic power and financial leverage combined to make America strong and American leadership unassailable, in the end, successive administrations were "in the anticommunist business." By the last weeks of 1963, however, commercial concerns finally trumped rampant anticommunism.[48]

By 1963 American aviation diplomacy closely resembled Britain's, in deed if not in word. Policymakers like Kohler, Halaby, and even the president himself favored contact and trade as a method for loosening tensions with the Soviets, just as London had long advocated; American policymakers tailored their export control policies to maximize exports, just as London had long done; and ultimately, American policymakers let their Commerce Department determine their export policies, much as Britain's Board of Trade and Treasury had consistently set the pace in Whitehall during previous decades. It would not be until the 1970s that an American firm would sell its planes directly to a communist Chinese airline, but by 1964 such a development appeared inevitable. American planes could fly to Beijing following Kennedy's death. They could be supplied with American parts while there. It seemed only a matter of time before American firms might gain the profits from direct sales as well. In less than three years, therefore, the aviation containment policies Kennedy's New Frontiersmen had inherited and had pledged to uphold faded away. The Viscount broke the seal on sales; PIA opened the door on flights; and Boeing ultimately made Washington care more for the bottom line than for the moral comfort of absolute security.

Washington's export policies devised in the aftermath of the PIA case mimicked the fate of Britain's aviation export program of the 1950s in their ultimate failure as well. Despite the radical shift in American policy in December 1963, the Kennedy administration's waving of the anticommunist banner ultimately undermined Boeing's prospects of securing its 727 sale. Even with an export license in hand, PIA chose Britain's Trident, ordering three planes with delivery dates in 1965. Company officials simply did not trust American promises after a year of berating attacks. The airline eventually ordered one Boeing plane in 1964, a 720B, but only because, as PIA officials painfully admitted, Britain did not have a similar plane worth purchasing. They would have rather bought from London. In the new generation of the zero-sum game of Anglo-American aviation competition, Britain won the first hand with its Viscount conspiracy. It won the second round when it captured the right to supply PIA's future fleet, and with this contract secured the inside track on sales to Japan and throughout Asia. These would be Britain's last such victories. The sins of the past—and the threat of American diplomacy—thwarted London's hopes for a truly independent aviation future premised upon mastery in Asia.[49]

Sins of the Past

Britain failed to capture the China market, despite its initial breakthrough sale and Washington's dramatic shift of policy in 1963 widening the aerial routes into China. As noted at the close of Chapter 6, it had the planes and the desire to sell, but failed because its policymakers, saddled by the legacy of the Viscount, lacked the will to withstand American pressure. The following pages describe this dynamic in detail, and across the 1960s. Despite initial setbacks, American strategists proved surprisingly successful at keeping China largely isolated from global aviation routes and suppliers through the remainder of the decade. Not until 1969 would a noncommunist state (again, Pakistan) next sell planes to Mao's government, and by 1972, when President Richard Nixon renewed relations with China after a quarter century of isolation and embargo, Beijing could count its noncommunist aviation partners on a single hand. This was not the total isolation Washington would have preferred. But it was close.[50]

Chinese domestic policies combined with fear of American reprisals to keep the country largely isolated. Internal strife punctuated by the vicious Cultural Revolution threatened to rip the country apart at the seams, and foreign investment nearly dried up by 1968 as a result. These factors, coupled with a general lack of hard currency, made China an unlikely buyer of Western aircraft during most of Lyndon Johnson's tenure, though his administration did not welcome or seek aviation opportunities beyond the Great Wall. Increasingly occupied by their war in Vietnam, American policymakers refused to reconsider Washington's long-standing two-tiered system for economic warfare against the communist world—the pointed strategic controls for the Soviet bloc, contrasted with broader attacks against economic development throughout communist Asia. They even tried to reimpose a new China differential in 1965. COCOM would have none of it, and the effort only displayed yet again how out of step the United States remained from its closest allies on issues of Chinese trade. "Less stringent controls on exports to Eastern Europe and [the] USSR" might be acceptable, Thomas Mann, undersecretary of state for economic affairs, told COCOM. But "tight controls on exports to Communist-controlled areas of Far East are essential to Free World security." The British had long grown immune to this argument. "The use of the COCOM procedure to conduct anything in the nature of economic warfare against China would be unacceptable for us," the cabinet concluded in response. Their reason: "Our main long term hope of breaking down the isolation of China lies in an increase of her commercial contacts with the outside world." With Japanese and French aid, London beat back this American effort at reimposing the China differential. It never appeared before COCOM again.[51]

Such forceful displays at least had the effect of warning off others from challenging Washington on the issue of trade with China. The Johnson administration's successful defeat of British efforts to capitalize on their aerial lead offers a case in point. Annually from 1963 through 1966, British policymakers halted promising negotiations with Beijing for advanced and long-range planes, including sophisticated jetliners. On every occasion, fear of American reprisals, and to a lesser extent concern for Indian criticisms, prompted Whitehall to withdraw its support for such sales even as Britain's aircraft industry continued to contract. Thousands of aviation workers lost their jobs during this period. More than ten thousand took to the streets in one January 1965 protest alone, marching from London's Waterloo Station to Hyde Park Corner in a plea for work. Sales were down; jobs were being slashed; and their leaders blamed the United States. "Britain cannot afford to be driven out of every major industry by the Americans," one union spokesman said. The government responded with new promises of support for exports under the auspices of a further industry restructuring commission led by Lord Plowden. Despite these pressures and public pledges of support for overseas sales, London vetoed further aircraft deals with China whenever they arose, and lost the opportunity to monopolize the China market—and to capitalize on the Viscount lead—as a consequence.[52]

Fear of American reprisals over the Viscount explains why. The initial round of post-Viscount negotiations between British sales teams and Chinese officials, held in 1963 and 1964, best reveals this dynamic. As the first of Vickers's planes made their way to China, the two sides held tepid discussions for sales of used BOAC Britannias and new Comet IV aircraft. The former was a large four-engine turboprop, the latter a long-range jetliner. Whitehall's optimism ran high. "We know that in general the Chinese are interested in buying civil aircraft," the Foreign Office reminded its Washington embassy in January 1963, "and we, in general, are interested in selling them."[53]

Washington objected most strenuously. In service for more than two years, both planes were clear of COCOM restraints. But both carried American-licensed equipment and thus remained liable to American controls. Moreover, whereas the medium-range Viscounts might add minimally to China's internal airlift capabilities, long-range jetliners carried the real possibility of extending Beijing's reach beyond Asia. The RAF used Comets as transports, and thus it was hard for London's advocates to argue that the planes had no military value. "The sale of jet aircraft seems to represent an area in which strategic considerations are involved," a team of American diplomats informed Oliver Foster, first secretary to the British embassy in Washington, in November 1963. "If used for external operations, the possession of jet aircraft would enable the Chinese Communists to open routes which would provide opportunities for the promotion of subversion."

"Even more important," they warned, "is the nuclear question." Beijing's nascent bomb was no match for America's (or the Soviet Union's) massive nuclear arsenals, but if coupled with a credible delivery system, Asia's first nuclear threat would transform the continent's strategic landscape. China stood on the precipice of nuclear power in November 1963. What it lacked was a means of delivering it far beyond its borders, leading the Americans to argue that "if, when they attain some nuclear capability the Chinese Communists are able to point out that they possess jet aircraft and therefore a delivery capacity, they will be able to add considerably to the effectiveness of their psychological warfare." From Chinese airstrips a Comet (with a nuclear payload) could reach New Delhi, Seoul, Tokyo, or even Honolulu. Indeed, Chinese officials proudly publicized their long-term desire to employ Comet 4C's on a Shanghai-to-London route. Even discussion of such a sale to Mao's government at such a dangerous time appeared to American eyes perfidious in the extreme.[54]

Indian policymakers also objected. Chinese and Indian troops had tangled only months before in the disputed Himalayas, and New Delhi had only reluctantly consented, and then only under great pressure, to overflights by the Chinese-bound Viscounts on their delivery flights. They would not condone further sales of an even greater strategic nature. "We do hope that no one in London is under any illusions about how serious a row such a sale could cause us with the Indians," Britain's high commissioner in New Delhi cabled home. "We have got away pretty lightly with the Viscount sale," but there was a "difference in kind between that and a Comet deal—the one merely redresses the normal wastage of the Chinese civil air fleet over the past few years, while the other would provide the Chinese with an increase of over 60% in total troop airlift (and a 100% increase for sustained operations)." Even if the Chinese employed Comets for civilian use as promised, he later warned, the deal would still strike a serious blow to Britain's standing throughout South Asia. "There is something inescapably symbolic about a modern transport jet airliner," and "there is no doubt that our supplying them to China would be reflected in an immediate and deeply felt reaction both from the Government and the public."[55]

Comet or Britannia sales were therefore unpopular in Washington and in New Delhi, but such objections were not enough to force Whitehall to scuttle the deals. Instead, British imagination and fear were to blame. Whitehall policymakers had no way of knowing if their Viscount scheme had truly been successful. Perhaps, the optimistic among them thought, Washington had been duped. On the other hand, perhaps the Americans knew full well the depth of the conspiracy and merely awaited the right moment to spring a well-laid trap. The days immediately preceding a headline-grabbing airliner sale might offer just such a moment, when a harshly worded revelation that Washington knew the full Viscount story might poison a sale and thereby disrupt ever-sensitive Sino-British relations. Washington might also seek to punish any British firm involved, for as one diplomat worried, ministers "have under-estimated the pressure which would be brought to bear upon, and reprisals against, UK companies involved in the manufacture of Comets, particularly since the experience of the Viscount deal will greatly forewarn the Americans, and our conduct in this deal may well create a special incentive for them to do their worst."[56]

The Americans, in fact, did not know the extent of the Viscount conspiracy, but they were aware of the continuing difficulty presented by the presence of American-controlled goods aboard British aircraft. Confronted with a growing number of news reports heralding the proximity of a new aircraft deal with Beijing, American diplomats once more tried to warn London off the sale. "We are not presently aware of any component of the Comets which would raise problems involving our own Foreign Assets Control Regulations," Foggy Bottom reminded the British embassy. "However, our experience in the case of the Viscounts suggests that there is a danger here of an open conflict between national policies, which we should seek to avoid."[57]

This ambiguous warning set off alarm bells in Whitehall that ultimately put an end to the Comet deal. "These cryptic remarks about Viscounts combined with the complete silence since we reported to COCOM seem to indicate that the State Department may be prepared to turn a blind eye to the Viscounts," Ambassador Ormsby-Gore warned his superiors in London. It was more likely, however, "that they are putting us on notice, initially in friendly terms and at a low level, that they would not be so tolerant over Comets." Washington had perhaps been fooled once. They were unlikely to be so easily deceived, or so tolerant, a second time.[58]

Once more Britain's aerial hopes came down to questions of sovereignty and matters of power. London longed for the freedom to export at will, but lacked the ability to outfit its aircraft on its own. The fly in the ointment of the Comet sale to China thus brought into sharp relief what the Viscount sale had only recently brought to light: the realization that future British trade would, owing to the greater complexity of British machines and their ensuing prevalence of American components, prove ever more subject to Washington's export controls. Following rationalization, British manufacturers had outsourced much of their supply of avionics and communications equipment. This was the nature of high-tech manufacturing in an increasingly global economy. Viscounts manufactured in 1961 carried more American goods than a first-generation Comet, while Tridents or Comet 4s produced in 1964 used more than Viscounts. Future British planes, including the heralded Concorde, would use a greater percentage still. They could not manufacture their own avionics at a reasonable cost, what ministers termed "anglicizing" the aircraft. The veto that Washington held over the Viscount sale in 1961 would therefore prove a minor bump compared to the giant roadblock American-licensed goods posed to Britain's future hopes of monopolizing the China market.[59]

Fear and a depressing recognition of powerlessness ultimately drove Britain from this market: fear of American and Indian reprisals; fear of the future consequences of the Viscount conspiracy; and ultimately, the fearful implications of America's growing technological dominance. A host of British manufacturers far beyond the aviation field relied upon American goods and investment, and limitations imposed on either could potentially cripple British industry. Islamabad had been able to ignore American threats over the use of American-licensed goods in China. After committing the first abuse over the Viscount, London could not afford to play with fire again. They had nowhere else to turn for aid and commerce than across the Atlantic. China was alluring; collaboration with Europe was intriguing; and the Soviets were ever eager for further trade. But the Anglo-American relationship formed the bedrock of British diplomacy and economy. What British policymakers really feared was Washington's ability to stifle the flow of American technology and investment as punishment for transgressing the Pax Americana.

These fears ultimately played out in the cabinet. Deliberations pitted the Board of Trade and the Ministry of Aviation, which favored the sale of Comets and other aircraft to China despite such concerns, against the Foreign Office, which believed it better to sacrifice prospective sales than to damage Britain's special relationship with either Washington or New Delhi. The debate raged behind closed doors throughout 1964 ("a most involved and tiresome Whitehall process," one minister noted), and Board of Trade president Douglas Jay nearly carried the day in November with his persuasive argument that "China must be one of the few major markets for long-range aircraft which is unlikely to be dominated by the Americans." It was not to be. The cabinet initially allowed negotiations to continue with Beijing even as it debated their merits, reasoning that no sale could be consummated without the government's explicit consent. Eventually it became clear that the temptation of a nearly finalized sale would be impossible to withstand, so negotiations were halted lest London find itself with a question it preferred not to answer. Better to nip potential sales in the bud in the cool light of day, the cabinet finally reasoned, lest anguished media reports or angry unemployed workers force the government's hand as the clock struck midnight. "If I had to take up a position at this moment I would be inclined to discourage the sale of any Comets to China," Foreign Secretary Patrick Gordon Walker wrote Jay in December 1964. "I am impressed by the implications of the deepening American involvement in Indo-China and am most anxious not to lay us open to a charge, however ill-founded, of supplying China with the sinews of war."[60]

Whether the Chinese could have been convinced to buy British in 1964 remains an open question. They lacked easy access to the hard currency required to complete such a sale, and they refused to negotiate final details of any agreement without preapproval from Whitehall. Indeed, it is impossible to conclude if Britain might have come to dominate this market in the ensuing years if freed from its political burdens. With one eye fixed firmly on the future and the other on the indignities of the past, Beijing assiduously strove to avoid becoming anyone's monopoly. When Comet negotiations stalled, for example, they turned to French Caravelles instead, though more on that momentarily.[61]

We will never know if British firms might have turned their initial foothold in China into an aviation monopoly, because fears of foreign pressure prompted London to reel in its aviation sales teams. Not a single British policymaker of the period ever argued against exploitation of their aviation lead in China purely in military or even technological terms in 1963 or after. Each believed Britain would benefit from the trade. American policymakers opposed Chinese penetration of developing lands and lamented Beijing's growing nuclear threat. Their Indian counterparts feared growth of Chinese airlift capacity. The Foreign Office, in turn, feared heated reactions from both India and Washington, and even the Board of Trade recognized the potential economic consequences of American reprisals. British manufacturers still hoped to crack America's bountiful aircraft market, especially with the British Aircraft Corporation's 111 jetliner even then making the rounds of American airlines. "Any company that does business with China can expect its business prospects in the USA to suffer," the Washington embassy warned, "and long-range aircraft would invite a far more violent reaction than buses."[62]

British policymakers never opposed sale of long-range jet aircraft to China on the sale's own merits. On the contrary, such sales gave voice to their dreams. British strategists wanted China to engage the world, to prosper and grow while enjoying everything they believed aviation offered. They surely still longed for the international power a vibrant aircraft industry might bring for Britain, though such dreams were by the 1960s but wisps of what they had once been. They instead let their own hopes of developing this fruitful market die on the rocks of their fears, because of what they had done to enter that market in the first place, and because of what they feared would come to light if they went any further. Britain began the long search for aviation dominance and great-power status in 1942. Its policymakers throughout that decade and the next believed geopolitical independence would arrive on wings. By the late 1960s, they no longer spoke of aviation in such terms. The thin nature of their production base and their dependence upon American supply made the United States the true great power. London lacked even the strength to make this one last gasp at aviation greatness through conquest of the China market, a market wholly off-limits to American competition and entirely eager to buy British, because they could not afford to supply Chinese sales if they won.

The tragic irony of London's failure to make good on its aerial head start in China is that Washington appeared to have been completely unaware of the Viscount deception. The Kennedy and Johnson administrations knew some substitute for the American parts in question had been found. They even suspected that Vickers had located some supply of parts already purchased from American manufacturers. They did not know the truth. "According to its latest information on this matter," Foggy Bottom informed its European embassies in 1964, "the US knows of no parts or equipment on the Viscounts to China which are of US origin or made under license from American firms, or that are otherwise subject to US controls." The Americans fully believed their hardball diplomacy had worked, and that subsequent hard tactics might thwart Western aircraft sales to Beijing should the issue arise again. This was the threat they held out when news of budding Comet and Britannia sales leaked, and the same threat worked to great effect when France announced plans to sell its own jet airliner to Beijing in the spring of 1964.[63]

France, too, lost out on the China market during this period because of American regulations and the long reach of American power. Their mid-range Caravelle jetliners also used components manufactured in the United States, and Washington left no doubt that it would enforce its regulations to the hilt to keep China from obtaining advanced French planes. They had made the British remove their American parts from the Viscounts, American embassy officials warned the French Foreign Ministry in February 1964, and "our approach on Caravelles would be no different in scope or severity." Officials in Paris investigated the costs of substituting homegrown or at least non-American components, and they warned the State Department that once stripped of its links to American firms, French aviation would never again return as customers. They even explored selling the Caravelles to a third party before their final export to Beijing as a way around American restraints. Each of these plans ended with the same conclusion: the political and financial costs involved in "de-Americanizing" the planes for the sake of a single sale would be prohibitive. The potential costs to French industry would have been even greater.[64]

French policymakers ultimately canceled the Caravelle contract rather than face American reprisals. "They are no longer interested in sale to China," American ambassador Charles Bohlen reported in July 1964. The "few planes involved do not justify heavy expenditure needed to replace US equipment." French officials complained bitterly in COCOM that Washington's unilateralism undermined the concept of multilateral controls. "The Caravelles are not embargoed," Paris's COCOM representative said. The "French can sell them. But then, part of the equipment on them is of US origin . . . The Sud-Aviation company tries to equip the planes with non-US equipment so that the aircraft can be sold freely." After what he called "a large number of hours of work and millions in cost," the firm reluctantly concluded it had no such solution. That the planes could be exportable through supranational COCOM but not in relation to one nation's wishes seemed to him hardly "rational." By "agreeing to sale of Caravelles but not sale of equipment in them," the French negotiator privately told his American counterpart, "Americans give with one hand, and take away with [the] other."[65]

Appearances mattered less than success in Washington, where the overriding goal of isolating China proved remarkably successful. It is testament to both the reach of American subcontractors and the breadth of American power during these years that neither London nor Paris simply defied the White House in order to sell their planes. In contrast to their struggle with Pakistan, American diplomats never explicitly outlined the potential consequences of Comet or Caravelle sales. Their best threats were left unstated. Paris and London each correctly perceived that American policymakers would prove unyielding in their opposition to Asian Communism—more so as the Vietnam War progressed with every day—and unsympathetic toward any ally that helped Beijing increase its capabilities at home and abroad. They could not afford to sell planes to China without American parts aboard, and they could not afford the cost of selling planes to China with those American parts, either. Surreptitious efforts such as required to export the Viscounts had worked once. But only once.

The same pattern reappeared in 1965. Promising negotiations in Beijing for VC-10 and Trident jetliners collapsed once more when policymakers back in London refused to grant an export license for their sale. As before, British strategists were not moved by concerns of their own. They wanted the sale; their employees wanted the work; and they wanted China to gain the benefits new planes might bring. Board of Trade president Douglas Jay verily pleaded with his cabinet colleagues to endorse the deal. "The Chinese market must be potentially a large one," and was "one of the very few in which we are not subject to American competition." Tens of millions of pounds were at stake, and "other very big contracts [were] in the offing" as well, including "a major coal-fired power station . . . valued at £30–40 million, which UK firms have at least a 50/50 chance of getting." Having learned to be wary of British sales teams that seemed incapable of finalizing contracts, Chinese officials seemed prepared to shut down subsequent trade if the aircraft negotiations fell through. The British claimed to be willing to sell to everyone, they argued, just not, in the end, to Beijing. "Another snub over aircraft would certainly worsen" Britain's odds of ever succeeding in the market, Jay warned.[66]

Jay's Whitehall counterparts proved far less able to stomach the risk of offending either Washington or New Delhi. "We have already told the Indians that the second Chinese nuclear explosion is expected soon, and that it will probably be an air drop," the secretary of state for commonwealth relations noted in March 1965. "This would be a particularly unfortunate time therefore in Indian eyes for us to sell aircraft to China which could be adapted to a nuclear role." Diplomats based in Washington offered a different worry. The Americans were becoming more deeply embroiled in Vietnam with every passing month. President Johnson ordered two combat divisions of U.S. Marines to the country in April, a crucial step on the long road toward Americanizing the war. In July, he raised the total American troop commitment from 75,000 to 125,000. He would have more than 160,000 troops in the country by December. "Over this war—and all Asia," Johnson said, "lay the deepening shadow of Communist China," which "is helping the forces of violence in almost every continent."[67]

Fearing a supercharged American response in such an atmosphere, the cabinet once more vetoed a prospective British sale. American diplomats never threatened an end to trade if an aircraft sale went through. They never warned of an end to military aid, cessation of intelligence sharing, cancellation of contracts, or removal of American bases from British soil. Indeed, none of these dramatic steps seemed plausible retribution for British deals in Beijing. Yet the cabinet could not risk reprisals, or risk offending its closest global partner for the sake of salvaging a dying industry, no matter how dear to British hearts. Aviation Minister Roy Jenkins made the formal announcement in October 1965. There would be no subsequent British aircraft sale to China. Sino-Indian tensions made the sale problematic; Vietnam made it impractical; the necessity of strong Anglo-American ties made it impossible. "Should China want aircraft," the *Financial Times* concluded, "the application would be considered only on its merits, which, at present, are nil." The newspaper reported that government spokesmen were unable to list any other countries to which Britain categorically refused to sell aircraft. The cabinet's decision, though frustrating, seemed by this point merely part of a pattern. "Whenever the Chinese have shown an interest in a particular type of British aircraft," Denis Healey, secretary of state for defense, sadly concluded in December 1965, "Ministers have found some reason or another (not connected with COCOM strategic embargo) why a sale should be frustrated." The Johnson administration had not threatened or cajoled. It had not even brought up the history of the Viscount. Rather, by 1965 the centrality of the special relationship made potential threats so readily apparent as to not even require mention. "The Americans would likely downgrade us in the league table of dependable allies" if the deal went through,

Britain's ambassador to the United States cautioned. Even the Germans would seem "more reliable."[68]

When the cabinet once more ruled against authorizing a Trident sale the following year for the same set of reasons, Britain at least managed to get something out of its adherence to an American line. Talmudic scholars teach that the highest form of charity is given anonymously. There is no such premium on nameless charity in international relations. Having forfeited much-needed sales to American and Indian concerns, Prime Minister Harold Wilson personally informed Johnson and Indian prime minister Lal Bahadur Shastri of his country's deep sacrifice. "We have just had to take a most difficult decision on whether or not to allow the sale of a number of Trident aircraft to China," Wilson wrote. "We have decided not to permit the sale." His country needed the exports, and it surely did not want the Soviets or French to encroach on the budding Chinese market in Britain's absence. "[But in the end] I decided that we must be prepared to sacrifice these clear commercial advantages mainly because of the present situation in Vietnam and the inevitable reactions in India to such a sale."[69]

Wilson's denial of sales was no bit of anonymous charity. It was instead coldly calculated. "Our need of United States economic help has increased," his Washington embassy lamented, and Wilson asked Johnson to "look sympathetically on our efforts to secure sales of British aircraft in the United States" as a result of sacrifices in China. His note was not subtle, but it was clearly the truth. Britain did need help and technologies only the United States could supply, and thus it renounced commercial opportunities in Asia for the good of the special relationship. It may have proved impossible to anglicize the aircraft in question in the first place, and even this follow-on sale to the Viscount deal might not have solidified Britain's position as Beijing's aircraft supplier of choice. But whatever chance Britain had for a Chinese monopoly its leaders gave up because they feared the diplomatic response would far outweigh any potential profit. "So far as we could," Edward Boland, head of the Foreign Office's Far Eastern department, explained at the close of the affair, "we tried to set up an economic balance sheet setting the advantages of selling Tridents against the economic consequences of American displeasure. The economic arguments came out fairly evenly balanced. The decisive factors in the final decision were the political effect which a sale would have on our relationship with the US and India at a time when the former is so deeply involved in Vietnam and the latter particularly sensitive to imagined British 'treachery.'"[70]

With this decision, Britain's dreams of independent aviation power, of great-power status won through flight, and of technological mastery of the developing world carried on the most prestigious of products, came to an end. The Concorde remained, but this was European more than British. Aviation would no longer provide a counter to American dominance of the international system. Kennedy's policymakers had begun the decade with dreams of using aviation to make their dominance of that system a further reality. Their plans had not gone as they had hoped, surely not with the impact their quagmire in Vietnam played. Yet they achieved dominance nonetheless.

Conclusion

Britain never did win its long-sought aerial monopoly in China. Its follow-on sale to the Viscount did not occur until 1971, a decade after the initial breakthrough. Beijing agreed to purchase six Tridents that August, worth $48 million, nearly double the value of Britain's exports to China during the preceding six months. The following year, amid ceremonies marking the handoff of the first Trident, China's ambassador to Britain announced plans to purchase eight more. Beijing even placed a conditional order for three supersonic Concordes, though these were never delivered. By the start of 1972, China was no longer isolated, and Britain was, at least temporarily, its supplier of choice.[1]

It would never be China's sole supplier, however. The 1971 deal was not even China's first acquisition of Tridents. Pakistan International Airways, which had done so much to frustrate Washington's wall around the mainland regime throughout the 1960s, sold Beijing three used Tridents in 1970. These were the planes purchased by China in 1964 following Washington's reluctance to authorize a sale of Boeing 727s. PIA was never satisfied with their British machines, spurring its desire to upgrade to larger 707s. It required an influx of cash to do so, and China once more proved a willing buyer.[2]

Following what was by now a well-worn tradition, the Nixon administration initially reacted with fury to news of PIA's plans. "We have a potential crisis in US-Pak relations on our hands," America's ambassador in Islamabad cabled home. With State Department authorization, he threatened "termination of all United States Government assistance" if the sale went through. His arguments were familiar. The planes carried American components still barred from use in China; they could further aid Beijing's airlift capacity and ability to exploit instability abroad; and Washington was yet again unlikely to approve any export license for replacements. Pakistan could sell the planes, he warned, but in doing so it risked shutting off the spigot of American supply.[3]

And then, upon further reflection, the Nixon administration withdrew its formal opposition to the deal. Islamabad was undeterred by American bluff and bluster, and PIA fully intended to pursue its aviation agenda, confident that Washington would never make good on its threats. Its strategic location had not changed in the years since its first aircraft sale to China, and thus neither had its inherent leverage over American policymakers keen to maximize their influence in a vital and volatile region. Of even greater significance, the airline also pledged to use the proceeds of the Trident sale to purchase from Boeing. Nearly a decade after their first thwarted effort to supply the Pakistanis, the company desperately needed the deal, as did Seattle and the entire Pacific Northwest, where Boeing was by far the largest employer. Unlike the heady days of the 1950s, American aviation had suffered through an unprecedented post–World War II slump in the last years of the 1960s. Instability in international financial markets triggered a broad slowdown in global aviation and a corresponding reduction in demand for aircraft. Boeing went more than eighteen months without making a single airliner sale overseas, by far its longest such drought since the Great Depression. Massive layoffs proved unavoidable as assembly lines ground to a halt, leading to a mass exodus of the region's suddenly unemployed as the thousands of firms that depended upon Boeing workers found themselves without customers, and without prospects. The flood of refugees from the city became so rampant by 1969 that signs along Interstate 5 pointedly asked that "the last person in Seattle please turn out the lights."[4]

The Nixon administration permitted Boeing to sell PIA replacements for its Tridents in 1969, just as Johnson's White House had done in December 1963, because the company desperately needed the sale. The three 707s in question were not enough on their own to save the firm, but every sale helped the bottom line, and the last thing American aircraftmakers needed in the midst of a worldwide aviation slump was a renewed reputation for complicated export restrictions. The last thing the Nixon administration wanted, in turn, was blame for further Boeing layoffs, especially if word leaked that PIA once more chose a foreign supplier when it really wanted to buy American. Commerce again trumped security in American thinking, and by the close of 1970 China had its first, albeit secondhand, Western jetliner.[5]

This privileging of sales over security continued. The White House did not even lodge a formal protest with Islamabad when, in January 1972, PIA lost a 707 on an icy Chinese runway where it had flown at the height of the Indian-Pakistani war to pick up arms and ammunition in direct violation of the airline's lease agreement with an American firm, World Airways. Owners of purchased planes are fully free to do with them as they wished, as we have seen. Those who fly leased planes, however, are typically barred from dangerous activities such as picking up contraband for delivery to a war zone. The 707 in question was not only explicitly prohibited from such activities, it was also banned by American controls from ferrying Chinese arms for use against a third party! Such niceties mattered little to Pakistani leaders in the midst of a war for national survival. They mattered quite a lot to American policymakers, who had not only authorized lease of the 707 in question but also financed the deal through Export-Import Bank credits. Most American taxpayers would not have approved of their dollars being used to support Chinese arms sales. Uninterested in hindering Boeing's prospects as it moved slowly toward recovery, however, and generally supportive of Pakistan during the conflict, Nixon's officials not only swept such legal difficulties under the rug, they also approved sale of a replacement 707 the following year lest PIA be forced to operate a plane short. Such actions directly violated American laws. For the White House of Watergate, such details proved less important than sales and geopolitics.[6]

The Nixon years thus saw the culmination of Washington's conversion to a British line on aviation favoring commerce over security. Beijing appeared no less belligerent in 1969 than in 1963. American perceptions of the threat posed by its acquisition of jet aircraft was just as great as before. In both instances, however, Boeing needed the sale. In 1963 the fate of Asian aviation markets seemed at stake. In 1969 Boeing's existence seemed at risk. Neither period seemed a good time to forgo sales and jobs on principle. British policymakers had reached the same conclusion in 1945 when they authorized expansion of the Open List, in 1946 when they approved jet sales to the Soviet Union, and then in 1952 when they chose widespread Comet exports over American homeland security. On each occasion they chose commercial opportunities over perfect security for themselves or, more importantly, over perfect security for Washington. In each case they chose great-power dreams and the prospect of independent power within a special relationship of equals over the Anglo-American reality wherein Washington invariably ruled as the stronger partner.

This was not the case a decade later. Following their successful Viscount sale (and Viscount deception), British policymakers abandoned potential sales to China, and the jobs they would have provided, out of fear of American reprisals. Washington had not threatened retribution. Indeed, the risks to British interests in absolute terms seemed no greater during the 1960s than before. Why the change in British action? The answer lies in the gradual loss over the generation since 1945 of British great-power aspirations. The men who led the country immediately after World War II, Labour and Conservative alike, believed in Britain's central place in the world and took actions and risks accordingly. British leaders after 1963 understood their true role: they were an American vassal, and lesser powers who sought to remain on special terms with their betters did not seek to offend. Following Suez, Skybolt, and the Viscount, British strategists in the 1960s were more perceptive of their own relative strength than their predecessors had been, and the enduring nature of the special relationship that remains to this day is their legacy. But they were undoubtedly less brave (or perhaps less foolhardy) than those that came before. As for Washington, the change in policy from the unflinching anticommunism of the era before Vietnam to the shift toward commerce, first revealed in 1963 and then reinforced in subsequent years, can be attributed to sheer economics. Jobs were on the line, and if jobs were lost, the politicians in power would be blamed.

Triangular diplomacy was also in Washington's sights. President Richard Nixon and Henry Kissinger, his primary foreign policy adviser, sought a new relationship with China based on mutual interest rather than continued isolation. Both sides hoped to use the other as a counterweight to Moscow, and they began the long process of normalizing relations. In July 1969, only weeks after Pakistan first disclosed its plans to sell secondhand Tridents to Beijing, the White House lifted its ban on American travel to China. Further, it allowed Americans to import up to a hundred dollars' worth of Chinese goods and approved limited grain shipments to China. The two countries held their first direct talks since the 1940s in December 1969. "These measures," Kissinger later recorded, "though insignificant in themselves, were designed to convey America's new approach." That approach was one of tepid but sincere reconciliation based on mutual need. For both countries, self-interest proved stronger than altruism, and self-interest led them to each other.[7]

Larger steps soon followed, culminating in Nixon's world-altering voyage to Beijing in 1972. Formal diplomatic relations would not be finalized until

1979, but trade improved at a speedier pace. Once more aviation led the way. In August 1971, EDO Commercial Corporation, the leading producer of the LORAN navigation system employed by seventy-six airliners world-wide (including Aeroflot) applied to become the first American firm since 1949 to showcase its wares on Chinese soil. The White House approved their request in November, in time for participation in a Beijing trade fair the following April. RCA beat them to the punch, however, becoming in February 1972 the first American firm to win a major technology contract in China with their $2.9 million deal to supply ground equipment for satellite communications. In the preceding era of active economic warfare it would have been unthinkable for an American firm to so gleefully upgrade Chinese technology.[8]

Boeing would not be far behind. Company officials viewed British achievements in China with great trepidation. PIA's Trident deal exemplified not only Beijing's desire for Western aircraft but also the Nixon administration's tacit approval of American-built equipment in China. American strategists knew the British would use this opening to their best advantage, and they did not have long to wait. When pressed to decide if British firms could pursue sales opportunities in China in 1970, Prime Minister Edward Heath told American secretary of state William Rodgers that the "security question seems to have been settled." PIA had broken all the old barriers, and after all, "it seemed better to have Peking buy future spares from Britain than to be dependent on the Soviet Union." Boeing and other American firms consequently feared being frozen out of this budding market should Beijing's aviation officials hold a grudge. "Things are getting late as far as our penetrating that People's Republic of China market," Boeing's director of international affairs told the Senate Commerce Committee in February 1972. "They [the Chinese] are probably reluctant to depend on the Soviet Union but they are also very reluctant to depend on us, because they know our predilection for cutting off supplies by use of our export controls whenever something happens." The company predicted a near-term Chinese appetite for up to one hundred foreign aircraft. With a population approaching one billion, its appetite for aviation in the 1980s and beyond might eventually know no bounds.[9]

Boeing entered the market four months later. Company officials attended the Beijing trade show in April that featured EDO's LORAN navigation system, and immediately entered negotiations for 707s. In July, China initialed an agreement with Boeing for ten of the long-range planes, six designed for cargo or passengers, four strictly for passenger use. The deal, worth nearly

$150 million, marked Beijing's largest foreign purchase to date. It also of-
fered new hope for thousands of Boeing workers. "The 10 plane order
would at least keep the lagging 707 line from completely drying up," the
New York Times reported, "and officials had already begun discussions for sale
of 747s, 727s, and 737s."[10]

The opening of China's aviation market to American producers could not
have come a moment too soon for either side. Chinese officials desperately
sought foreign planes and an expanded aerial service in keeping with their
blossoming international role, and American firms welcomed any new customer. In July 1972, McDonnell Douglas sought and received permission
to sell its own long-range DC-10s to China, as Beijing once more made
preapproval of an export license a condition of commencing negotiations.
Before the year was out, the Chinese would sign deals for more than an additional $100 million in British, American, and Soviet aircraft. American
aviation diplomacy would never be the same. When Aerospatiale president
Henri Ziegler was asked in July 1972 if the American ban on trade of strategic materials with China would create any problems for his pending Concorde sale, he offered the last word on an era of American export controls.
"When you see Boeing negotiating with the Chinese that means the situation is completely changed. It is a matter of routine now."[11]

Today such sales are more than routine. They are vital to the entire international aircraft market. One in seven planes that rolled off Boeing's assembly lines in the 1990s went to China. In less than a generation, the country
that had once struggled to finance six aging turboprop Viscounts from Britain developed into the third-largest aircraft market in the world, trailing
only the United States and Japan. Taking an even broader perspective, by
the year 2000 more than 30 percent of American aircraft were sold to Asian
buyers. Boeing learned to sell in these markets despite Britain's head start.
Indeed, Boeing came to lean on China in particular. "China is our life's blood
these days," conceded Dean Thorton, president of the company's commercial planes division, in 1993. By the end of the 1990s, Washington even authorized the company to begin manufacture of tail assemblies and other aircraft sections on Chinese soil, a condition demanded by the Chinese (and
eagerly met by Europe's Airbus) in hopes of improving their own manufacturing base. Thus the same American government that had once banned inclusion of even the smallest electronic components on another country's aircraft bound for China only a generation later authorized high-technology
manufacturing beyond the Great Wall. Clearly, times had changed.[12]

The Atlantic competition in aviation had not. Boeing produced aircraft sections in China by the early 1990s. Airbus went one better, becoming the first Western company to construct whole jetliners on Chinese soil in 1997 in a deal worth more than $1.5 billion. Europe's willingness to support aircraft production while sidestepping issues of technology transfer made international analysts take notice. "We have almost the manufacturing level to produce one whole aircraft at the level of a Boeing 737," an official of the Xian Aircraft Company (which produced Boeing tail assemblies) announced in March 1997. Such technological proficiency—and the geopolitical independence it carried—seemed Beijing's ultimate goal. President Bill Clinton seemed more concerned with China's effect on American jobs than its ability to produce planes, however. After assuming office in 1993, Clinton made one of his first destinations Seattle, where he was confronted by Boeing workers desperately worried for their future, and with good reason. More than twenty-eight thousand had been laid off in the months before, and company officials promised further cutbacks if foreign buyers were not quickly found. "Most of these layoffs, maybe not all . . . but a lot of these layoffs would not have been announced had it not been for the $26 billion that the United States sat by and let Europe plow into Airbus over the last several years," Clinton said. "So we're going to change the rules of the game." Those rules had bothered American policymakers and manufacturers less during the Cold War when Pentagon spending more than offset Whitehall and European subsidies. Their Cold War victory meant American manufacturers faced a new world of competition without such unbridled support from their military-industrial complex, a prospect that did not appeal in the least.[13]

By the 1990s, commerce drove American export considerations in the commercial aerospace field, where once security had been Washington's sole concern. In this way American technology control policies for aerospace came to resemble Britain's of a generation before. Washington's larger strategic justification for this trade also shadowed an earlier British incarnation. Gone by the 1990s were American economic warfare plans for China. With them went American hopes for a China beset by internal difficulties, crumbling from the inside as a result of outside pressure. In its place was a new American commitment to Chinese prosperity, which Americans believed would be a precursor to liberalization, democracy, and peace. Such dreams cut across party lines. In renewing China's Most Favored Nation trading status in October 2000, Clinton reminded reporters that "the more China opens its markets the more it unleashes the power of economic freedom, and the more likely it will be to more fully liberate the human potential of its people." Conservatives such as President George W. Bush echoed this line. "I believe trade will encourage more freedom, particularly when it comes to individual liberties," Bush stated in April 2001. "I believe the marketplace promotes values," because "when people get a taste of freedom in the marketplace, they tend to demand other freedoms in their societies."[14]

These American proclamations of trade's liberalizing effects, and concurrent support of the idea that the West's best hope for China (and for totalitarian regimes more broadly) lay in promotion of a politically active and prosperous middle class, sound downright British. They speak to a fundamental transformation in Washington's understanding of economic warfare and of trade in technology that coincided with the final decades of the Cold War. Pinpointing the precise moment of this shift is at present impossible. It happened sometime after Boeing sold $150 million worth of aircraft to a regime that only months before had no formal trade with the United States. It happened a full generation after Foreign Secretary Ernest Bevin pleaded with Washington to "keep its foot in the door" in China, and after Winston Churchill had urged greater East-West trade in the hope that engagement might temper Communism's harsher tendencies. "The more trade there is between Great Britain and Soviet Russia and the satellites," Churchill said, "the better still will be the chances of our living together in increasing comfort." Neither Truman nor Eisenhower, Dulles nor Rusk, Radford nor McNamara would ever have uttered such words. These American leaders were all, to use Komer's phrase once again, "in the anticommunist business."[15]

To paraphrase A. D. Neale's 1950s thesis, nearly everyone of note in the special relationship wanted a fat China by the 1990s. A race was on, pitting the expanding power and ensuing potentially confrontational growth in self-esteem of a developing China against its desire to enjoy the fruits of its prosperity. Competing as well was the specter of internal strife spurred by a growing divide between China's rich and poor. Which future would win, whether unrest, hegemony, or peaceful relations, remains to be seen.

Anglo-American aviation diplomacy during the Cold War reveals more than just the radical transformation of American economic warfare ideals. The consistency of American Cold War zeal across the conflict's first half, and the corresponding fear and consternation this zeal caused among Washington's closest Cold War allies, Britain most especially, are equally evident. Washington simply feared the red menace more than the British did, for geographic and ideological reasons, as we have seen, and rigidly controlled its aviation exports accordingly lest the communist foe grow in strength through access to Western know-how. In comparison, as we have also seen, Britain consistently downplayed security threats when sales were at stake, and British analysts were relatively unconcerned about the strategic dangers in communists acquiring aviation technologies. Fearing Communism less, and needing sales more, British policymakers adopted less stringent aviation controls. Fearing Communism more and requiring sales less, their counterparts across the Atlantic became far more doctrinaire in their air policies, and in their broader Cold War policies.

But a crude calculus of sales versus security in which profits mattered most of all would not do justice to the complexity of this story. Power instead lies at its heart, and calculations of power grow from one's worldview. Matters of geography and history cannot be ignored in this comparison of the two allies' relative fear of Communism and ensuing zeal for export controls. The British, who feared Communism less, also knew aviation's destructive power far better. They knew that no export controls could save their land from atomic annihilation if war came once more. Their carpe diem approach to aviation restraints was developed to maximize profits, when no benefit could be gained from hindering sales. Conversely, American policymakers before 1945 had neither personal nor collective memory of aerial bombing. Their homes had been safe, their families secure. Such mental security was a thing of the past after 1945. American strategists saw what their own planes did to the Axis powers, to places as far removed as Dresden from Hiroshima, and they feared what future enemies might do to American cities. Long-range aviation coupled with the atomic bomb made America's future unsure for the first time in the nation's young history. British troops burned the White House in 1814 but could not destroy the country whole. Soviet Cold War flyers threatened to turn every American city of note to ash. Rigid defense based on the simple barbarity of mutual destruction offered one response. But hope lingered that such horrors might also be avoided if communist technological advancement might be kept at bay. Draconian export restraints resulted. This sense of palpable fear led in turn to aviation restraints even when homeland security was surely not at stake, as in the rigid controls imposed on China, an enemy viscerally despised beyond the Soviets for reasons of race and history too complex to be fully described here. A victory for Communism anywhere was a loss to the free world, such Cold War thinking ran. A free-world loss in Asia reeked of betrayal. European leaders made quixotic pleas for parity within their relationship with Washington as part of their mutual anti-Soviet fight. Such was never the case regarding Asia, where American leaders declared their intent to lead in a tone that did not invite questioning. Thus in their minds any communist victory along the Pacific moved America one day closer to losing its struggle for the Pax Americana, one day closer to the destruction of Washington's self-proclaimed fight for freedom, and one day closer to the day when America would truly be a reachable target.

In Britain and in America, export controls mimicked economic needs. Britain needed aviation exports for profit as much as for power. Washington wanted such sales, but its survival did not immediately depend upon them. Economics thus followed strategic concerns for both countries. Both pushed for sales when denial of commerce threatened its own perception of its great-power standing. For Britain, that moment came in 1942, when policymakers first articulated a path to international power leading to a modicum of parity within the special relationship forged through a vibrant and competitive aviation industry. America's crisis of great-power status did not come until the late 1960s, when the trials of Vietnam and the slow but steady breakup of the post-1945 Bretton Woods economic system (developed through American leadership and largely at American insistence) led to fears that Washington's time at the center of the international system had come and gone. Faced with unemployment and the loss of power should vital Cold War institutions such as Boeing fail, American policymakers chose sales over unflinching anticommunism. There can be no doubt that they would have opened relations with China without the push from Boeing. But that they eagerly equated aviation with power—and sales with aviation's survival—we can be sure with equal certainty. Both paths led to China. Manichean morality, the idea that right and wrong are immediately knowable and perhaps more importantly imposable, is, it would seem, the privilege of the wealthy and powerful. Needs, be they economic or political, make salespeople of us all.

This pattern of export controls echoed throughout British and American considerations of economic warfare. Britain remained consistently opposed to rigid economic restraints during the Cold War, believing that trade was better than isolation for dealing with communist states, and believing that communist prosperity offered its own hope for peace and détente. This was never the case among American thinkers, at least regarding China, until sales proved politically possible. American thinking changed, and not coincidentally, once the lure of the China market proved unavoidable and Chinese power proved desirable. American political and business leaders thereafter wanted trade with Mao's regime, just as they wanted China to develop. A prosperous China would purchase more from abroad, after all, and they wanted to sell aircraft to Beijing. None of these changes in American thinking would have been possible without a newfound need for sales.

Aircraft had been the bellwether of national policies throughout the first half of the Cold War, but by the early 1970s their central role had been replaced by newer technologies. In 1946, aircraft epitomized the modern age, its unparalleled freedoms and unimaginable fears. Ballistic missiles and computers ultimately assumed this role. The former brought humanity to the moon in 1969, the latter brought computational and then creative power previously inconceivable. Policymakers throughout Washington and Whitehall proved more concerned by the mid-1960s with constraining computer exports, in COCOM and unilaterally, than they did in containing aviation. Aviation played the central part in formulating export controls to that point. It was clearly the precedent-setting export during the first half of the Cold War, showing American morality at play in the international arena against a British ability to justify dangerous acts in terms of economic considerations, thereby, in truth, using great-power calculations. By the 1960s, planes put on display American technological strength and the flaws in Britain's own grand design for achieving international power through technological prowess. This was always a story about power. In the end, Britain lacked the power to stand alone.

What then does the study of Anglo-American aviation diplomacy tell us about the vaunted special relationship between Britain and America? Paradoxically, despite highlighting consistent differences in each nation's aviation policies and repeated divisions within their relationship in turn, this story proves the enduring strength of their alliance. The two sides bickered over plane sales, yet shared atomic secrets. They argued when Skybolt demonstrated Britain's dependence on American supply, but retained the ability to transfer nuclear technologies and to share nuclear submarine bases. They reached different conclusions about Soviet and Chinese aeronautical capabilities, but shared intelligence assessments in the process. Lastly, they fundamentally disagreed over the purpose and extent of trade and economic warfare with the communist world, yet throughout the Cold War they remained each other's most important trading partner outside their home hemispheres. They remained, as well, geopolitical intimates and political counselors, their private disputes notwithstanding. We knew so little about their disputes because they worked so hard to keep their most bitter fights behind closed doors. Only recent declassification of documents by both sides, many given up only grudgingly after persistent requests, brings their aviation strains to light. Indeed, Britain's 1953 decision to export the Comet 2 despite its clear implications for American homeland security might more than any other aviation case have ruptured the special relationship. The very implication of Washington's most trusted ally risking acquisition by its darkest enemy of the means of America's destruction is mind-boggling to ponder. Also awe-inspiring would have been the political calamity had Washington's fears and consequent inexorable pressure quashed the very crown jewel of Britain's postwar development program just at its moment of triumph. We will never know what the consequences of this debate and potential break in relations would have meant had the Comet not met with such tragedy. Churchill, as we have seen, believed that the risk and affront of worldwide Comet sales were capable of fostering a complete reorientation of American strategic policy toward Europe. Yet in the end, the two sides never broke off communications over the matter. They never lost the ability to discuss their differences. They read the same books. They shared the same heroes and the same enemies. The world looked different depending on whether it was viewed from the Thames or from the Potomac. But their basic perception of that world, so long as enemies threatened, during the Cold War and after, remained the bedrock of their alliance. Those enemies were perceived differently in the two capitals; their identities were not.

Then again, France faced this same threat, and Franco-American relations did not so thoroughly withstand Cold War strains. For those who might think Anglo-American relations impenetrable, it is worth remembering that the impossible can occur. Twice saved by American troops in the first half of the century, Paris still rejected American power in the latter half. French leaders owed their national survival to American blood—just as Lafayette's debt took centuries to repay—yet still demanded withdrawal of American troops in the 1960s. With their own nuclear deterrent in place, they faced the Cold War largely in search of their own defense. Once-intimate alliances can break. It is hard to claim that Washington's relationship with France was ever in the twentieth century as strong as its relations with the United Kingdom, and in this sense the comparison of Franco-American with Anglo-American relations, while useful, is of necessity unsatisfying. The French seemed to fear American hegemony both earlier and with greater passion.

With the Concorde and then with the Airbus, Britain and France would leave the twentieth century allied, in the air at least, against the true hegemon across the Atlantic. It is hard to imagine Britain ever breaking from the United States in the twenty-first century. Yet one might also have been surprised to learn that British leaders half a century before knowingly risked American homeland security for the sake of aircraft sales. Or that they knowingly violated American laws in order to surreptitiously sell in China. Or that they led the charge, time and again, against America's Cold War leadership in secretive though powerful organizations such as COCOM. It is hard to imagine what might yet strain the special relationship past the breaking point. But clearly, in the future search for a counter to American hegemony in which Britain's Cold War effort to present a solitary alternative to American power may well be replaced by a European collective, we would do well to consider outcomes that presently appear impossible. Republican theorists of the eighteenth century who constructed the ideology of liberalism and of the American Revolution, and later the French Revolution, feared power. They believed that power, by nature, encroaches; that those with power always desire more; and that those without power forever long for their share. What little stability could be found in human relations came only through overlapping restraints on power and its use, lest unconstrained power lead to corruption, oppression, and tyranny.

The modern international system is no different. Powerful states long for hegemony, those less powerful long for independence. They do not do so for power's sake, a complexity international relations realists too frequently fail to grasp. Rather, they strive for power because their vision of the world demands it. Britain wanted to be a great power after 1945. Its leaders longed for prosperity in keeping with their perceived birthright and as repayment for their sacrifices made in the name of freedom. They fought to play some major part in the international system accordingly, not because they were jealous of others or merely because glory is alluring. They strove for power lest their country be consumed by the growing fire of the conflict fought by each superpower in search of hegemony. Britain's way of life as they perceived it demanded such strength. This demanded control of the skies. Britain got neither.

American leaders looked to the world around them, a world in ruins, and sought to imprint their vision of security and stability, for their own sake and for the sake of civilization as they perceived it. They too sought power, not for power's sake, but because they—with good reason given the first half of the twentieth century—believed Europe's time in the sun had led only to war, destruction, turmoil, and hate. They envisioned something better and promised sacrifices of blood and treasure in order to lead the world into their pacific future, and could not for the life of them comprehend why others would not wish the same. During the first half of the Cold War, this struggle for power between the two principal members of the Western community played out in aviation. It was aviation that was considered key to military strength, commerce, politics, and status. How that battle will be fought in this new century, when once more America's closest allies and aspiring rivals perceive Washington's search for an imposed order as being as much a threat to their sovereignty as it is a chance for international stability, remains a question as yet unanswered.

Notes

305

Abbreviations

NARA		National Archives and Records Administration, College Park, Maryland
	RG 59	General Records of the Department of State
	RG 330	Records of the Secretary of Defense
	RG 334	Department of Defense, Office of Munitions Control Records
	RG 476	Bureau of International Commerce Records
	RG 489	Commerce Department Records
PRO		British Public Record Office, Kew, England
	AIR	Air Ministry Records
	AVIA	Ministry of Aviation (and its successor ministries)
	BT	Board of Trade Records
	CAB	Records of the Cabinet
	DEFE	Ministry of Defense Records
	DO	Dominions Office Records
	FO	Foreign Office Files
	PREM	Prime Minister's Files
	T	Treasury
FRUS		*Foreign Relations of the United States* (Washington, DC), multivolume series
Truman Library		Harry S. Truman Presidential Library, Independence, Missouri
Eisenhower Library		Dwight D. Eisenhower Presidential Library, Abilene, Kansas
Kennedy Library		John F. Kennedy Presidential Library, Boston, Massachusetts

Introduction

1. With apologies to neighbors north and south, I use the term *America* to refer to the United States. Paul Kennedy has argued that American strength at war's end was "artificially high," not entirely due to American strength, but rather only in

comparison to the recent wartime destruction of so many wartime competitors (*The Rise and Fall of the Great Powers* [New York, 1989], 357).

2. Kennedy, *Rise and Fall,* 360; Thomas McCormick, *America's Half-Century* (Baltimore, 1995), 28–33; Walter Isaacson and Evan Thomas, *Wise Men* (New York, 1986), 335.

3. Robert Skidelsky, *John Maynard Keynes: Fighting for Britain, 1937–1946* (London, 2000), 444.

4. NARA/RG59/611.41/5-350/May 3, 1950.

5. Alan Dobson, "Informally Special? The Churchill-Truman Talks of January 1952 and the State of Anglo-American Relations," *Review of International Studies* 23 (1997): 40–41.

6. Avi Schlaim et al., *British Foreign Secretaries since 1945* (London, 1977), 38; John Charmley, *Churchill's Grand Alliance* (New York, 1996), 89.

7. Frasier Harbutt, *The Iron Curtain* (New York, 1988), 63.

8. T. P. Wright, *Aviation's Place in Civilization* (Washington, 1945), 9.

9. Dave English, *Slipping the Surly Bonds* (New York, 1998), 79; *Vital Speeches of the Day* (New York, 1949), XV (12), 380–384.

10. PRO/FO371/84701/Jan. 6, 1950.

11. Matthew Josephson, *Empire of the Air* (New York, 1944), 3.

12. Correlli Barnett, *The Lost Victory* (London, 1995), 241.

13. PRO/FO371/99735/Dec. 1, 1952; David Edgerton, *England and the Aeroplane* (London, 1991), 101; PRO/CAB134/844/EA52(69)/May 23, 1952.

14. Hanson Baldwin, *The Price of Power* (New York, 1947), 19; Joseph Corn, *The Winged Gospel* (New York, 1983), 66.

15. Anthony Sampson, *Empires of the Sky* (New York, 1984), 63; Eugene Emme, *The Impact of Air Power* (New York, 1959), 300.

16. Harold Mansfield, *Vision* (New York, 1956), 279–280.

17. Alfred Gollin, *No Longer an Island* (Palo Alto, 1984); and Emme, *Impact of Air Power,* 5. For British aviation, see Keith Hayward, *The British Aircraft Industry* (New York, 1989) and *Government and British Civil Aerospace* (New York, 1983); Ely Devons, "The Aircraft Industry," in Duncan Burn, *The Structure of British Industry* (Cambridge, 1958); Edgerton, *England and the Aeroplane,* 83–108; and Barnett, *Lost Victory,* 228–249. For American aviation, see Charles Bright, *The Jet Makers* (Lawrence, 1978); T. Heppenheimer, *Turbulent Skies* (New York, 1995); Philip Jarrett, *Modern Air Transport* (London, 2000); Carl Solberg, *Conquest of the Skies* (Boston, 1979); Henry Smith, *Airways Abroad* (Washington, 1991); Alan Dobson, *Peaceful Air Warfare* (New York, 1991); Frank Kofsky, *Harry S. Truman and the War Scare of 1948* (New York, 1995); Michael Sherry, *The Rise of American Airpower* (New Haven, 1987); and Tami Biddle, *Rhetoric and Reality of Air Warfare* (Princeton, 2002).

18. George Kenney, "Survival in the Air Age," *Air Affairs* 3 (Dec. 1950): 453–458.

19. Mansfield, *Vision,* 320; John Newhouse, *The Sporty Game* (New York, 1982), 3–28.

20. Gregg Herken, *Counsels of War* (New York, 1985), 26–38.

21. J. Parker Van Zandt, *The Geography of World Air Transport* (Menasha, 1944), iii; Ronald Miller and David Sawers, *The Technical Development of Modern Aviation* (London, 1968). For "dual-use," see Michael Mastanduno, "Strategies of Economic Containment: U.S. Trade Relations with the Soviet Union," *World Politics* 37(4) (Spring 1985): 503–551.

22. Von Hardesty, "Made in the USSR," *Air & Space,* Feb.–Mar. 2001; Truman Library/Truman Papers/257/O.R.E. 1949/Apr. 6, 1950; *Vital Speeches of the Day* (New York, 1949), XV (18), 567–570.

23. NARA/RG59/LOT59D473/Box7/MLR1545/July 21, 1953.

24. Jacob Vander Meulen, *The Politics of Aircraft* (Lawrence, 1991); Mary Kaldor, *The Baroque Arsenal* (London, 1981); Doug Carroll, "Threat from Airbus," *USA Today,* Feb. 24, 1993, Money, 1; James Toedtman, "Battles over U.S. Trade Fought Across 1,000 Fronts," *Newsday,* Apr. 23, 1997, 45; Washington State Archives, Papers of Warren Magnusson/3181–4/217/18/Statement on H. R. 6649.

25. Jordan Schwarz, *Liberal* (New York, 1987), 224.

1. The Arsenal of Democracy versus British Planning

1. Roy Jenkins, *Churchill* (London, 2001), 645.

2. Russell Weigley, *The American Way of War* (Bloomington, 1977), 317; Robert Dallek, *Franklin D. Roosevelt and American Foreign Policy* (New York, 1995), 257; Churchill speech to the Commons, Aug. 20, 1940; Richard Overy, *Why the Allies Won* (London, 1995), 180.

3. Eugene Emme, *The Impact of Airpower* (Princeton, 1959), 69–72; Doris Kearns Goodwin, *No Ordinary Time* (New York, 1995), 44–45; Michael Sherry, *The Rise of American Air Power* (New Haven, 1987), 91–92; and Irving Holley, *Buying Aircraft* (Washington, 1964), 221–228.

4. John Wilson, "The Shape of Things to Come: The Military Impact of World War II on Civil Aviation," *Aerospace Historian* 28(4) (1981): 265; Goodwin, *No Ordinary Time,* 259–260; Yale University Archives, Robert Lovett Papers, 8/88/July 1940; Ed Cray, *General of the Army* (New York, 1990), 166.

5. Cray, *General of the Army,* 131, 192; Dallek, *Franklin D. Roosevelt,* 172–173.

6. Goodwin, *No Ordinary Time,* 45; Alec Cairncross, *Planning in Wartime* (New York, 1991), 171; Wayne Biddle, *Barons of the Sky* (New York, 1991), 271.

7. Goodwin, *No Ordinary Time,* 260; Keith Hayward, *British Aircraft Industry* (New York, 1989), 25; Overy, *Why the Allies Won,* 196.

8. John Slessor, *The Central Blue* (New York, 1957), 307. Historians differ on the RAF's actual strength; see Jenkins, *Churchill,* 632.

9. Hayward, *British Aircraft Industry,* 22–29; David Edgerton, *England and the Aeroplane* (London, 1991), 68–71; Ely Devons, *Planning in Practice* (Cambridge, 1950); A. J. P. Taylor, *Beaverbrook* (London, 1972), 412–467; Winston Churchill, *Their Finest Hour* (Boston, 1949), 674.

10. Jenkins, *Churchill,* 633; Arthur Reed, *Britain's Aircraft Industry* (London, 1973), 237.

11. Cairncross, *Planning in Wartime*, 13.

12. Slessor, *Central Blue*, 308; Hayward, *British Aircraft Industry*, 42.

13. PRO/PREM11/2213/Aug. 28, 1957; Cairncross, *Planning in Wartime*, 7–41.

14. Steven Fielding, "The Good War," in Nick Tiratsoo, ed., *From Blitz to Blair* (London, 1997), 31; Paul Addison, *The Road to 1945* (London, 1982), 103–190; Correlli Barnett, *The Audit of War* (London, 1986), 50; Reed, *Britain's Aircraft Industry*, 24.

15. John Moore-Brabazon, *The Brabazon Story* (London, 1956), 202.

16. Emme, *Impact of Airpower*, 222.

17. *American Heritage History of World War II* (New York, 1966), 147; H. Spector, *Eagle against the Sun* (New York, 1985), 128; Emme, *Impact of Airpower*, 300.

18. Alfred Gollin, *No Longer an Island* (Palo Alto, 1984); Edgerton, *England and the Aeroplane*, 1–18; Joseph Corn, *The Winged Gospel* (New York, 1983), 45; Sherry, *Rise of American Air Power*, 8–9; H. G. Wells, *War in the Air* (New York, 1967), 242; H. G. Wells, *Things to Come* (London, 1935); Emme, *Impact of Airpower*, 8; David Reynolds, *Britannia Overruled* (London, 2000), 116; Sherry, *Rise of American Air Power*, 74; Emme, *Impact of Airpower*, 3.

19. Jon Meacham, *Franklin and Winston* (New York, 2003), 6; Fraser Harbutt, *Iron Curtain* (New York, 1986), 76; Churchill, *Their Finest Hour*, 579; Emme, *Impact of Airpower*, 8, 344; M. J. Armitage and R. A. Mason, *Air Power in the Nuclear Age* (Urbana, 1985), 185.

20. Moore-Brabazon, *The Brabazon Story*, 202.

21. Barnett, *Audit of War*, 145–146; Edgerton, *England and the Aeroplane*, 72; Hayward, *British Aircraft Industry*, 42–43.

22. Overy, *Why the Allies Won*, 101.

23. PRO/CAB134/58/Mar. 6, 1947; "The Outlook," *Flight and Aircraft Engineer*, May 24, 1945; PRO/AIR2/7882/Oct. 9, 1944; John Stroud, "Airliner Evolution in the Postwar Era," in Philip Jarrett, ed., *Modern Air Transport* (London, 2000), 19–22.

24. PRO/AIR8/1370/Sept. 29, 1942; Reynolds, *Britannia Overruled*, 145.

25. Slessor, *Central Blue*, 420.

26. Ian Gould, "The Modern Jet Airliner—the Trailblazers," in Jarret, *Modern Air Transport*, 161; PRO/AIR8/1370/"British Requirements."

27. Donald Pattillo, *Pushing the Envelope* (Ann Arbor, 1998), 105–127; Biddle, *Barons of the Sky*, 232–288.

28. PRO/AIR8/1370/"British Requirements." The Arnold-Powers agreement is a source of some historical dispute. Alan Dobson (*Peaceful Air Warfare* [Oxford, 1991], 128) refers to this accord as part of the Lyttleton agreement, referencing Britain's Oliver Lyttleton, who negotiated a series of production schedules with the Americans in October 1942. Dobson cites the edited writings of Sir Richard Clarke (*Anglo-American Economic Collaboration in War and Peace* [Oxford, 1982]) as evidence, but he cites a page without specific mention of aircraft production. Anthony Sampson, *Empires of the Sky* (London, 1984), 64, refers to Britain's rejection of transport production, but without a specific reference. Keith Hayward (*British Aircraft Industry*, 38) refers to the British production decision without ref-

erence to an Anglo-American agreement, but his *Government and British Civil Aerospace* does not mention an accord. Jordan Schwarz refers to an Anglo-American "understanding" on production (*Liberal* [New York, 1987], 220). Arnold makes little reference to such production negotiations in his memoirs, *Global Mission* (New York, 1949), 313–319; Slessor mentions them in his own memoirs (*Central Blue*, 397–432), referring to the "Arnold-Portal-Towers" agreement, Towers being American rear admiral Jack Towers. Some claim the agreement did not exist (R. E. G. Davies and Philip Birtles, *De Havilland Comet* [McLean, 1999], 8), while Arthur Reed (*Britain's Aircraft Industry*, 22) cites Peter Masefield's reference to an explicit agreement as "a canard." These critics, their jingoistic defense of British civil transport aside, are clearly incorrect. The agreement most certainly did exist. See PRO/CAB134/58/Mar. 6, 1947; PRO/CAB128/6/CP46(317)/Aug. 2, 1946; PRO/CAB130/89/Dec. 17, 1953.

29. PRO/AIR8/1370/"British Requirements"; Slessor, *Central Blue*, 410.

30. Edgerton, *England and the Aeroplane*, 71–72; Frank Kofsky, *Harry S. Truman and the War Scare of 1948* (New York, 1995), 13–14; Pattillo, *Pushing the Envelope*, 133.

31. Aaron Friedberg, *In the Shadow of the Garrison State* (Princeton, 2000), 205; Roger Bilstein, *The American Aerospace Industry* (New York, 1996), 77.

32. Lovett Papers, 33/461/June 15, 1978, and 32/458/Feb. 13, 1959, p. 29.

33. Peter Young, ed., *The World Almanac Book of World War II* (New York, 1981), 516–518. Holley (*Buying Aircraft*, 29) notes five years of growth in American aviation preceding World War II.

34. PRO/AIR2/7882/Oct. 9, 1944; Barnett, *The Lost Victory* (London, 1995), 230. By 1946 the ministers of supply and aircraft production were describing American postwar dominance as "inevitable" (PRO/CAB128/6/CP46(317)/Aug. 2, 1946). "This arrangement, to which we had reluctantly to agree," Slessor concluded, "did affect adversely our position in the field of commercial air transport after the war" (*Central Blue*, 410).

35. Cairncross, *Planning in Wartime*, 177.

36. Edgerton, *England and the Aeroplane*, 80; Hayward, *British Aircraft Industry*, 27; Goodwin, *No Ordinary Time*, 363. Britain's aircraft productivity has spawned a pocket historiographical industry. All agree that British efficiency paled in comparison to American; no two critics can agree on just how wide was the divide. See Barnett's polemical *Audit of War* (143–158) and *Lost Victory* (228–248); Hayward (*British Aircraft Industry*, 22–29) dissents. Edgerton (*England and the Aeroplane*, 79–82) critiques Barnett in an attempt to settle the matter conclusively. See also Jonathan Zeitlin, "Flexibility and Mass Production at War: Aircraft Manufacture in Britain, the United States, and Germany, 1939–1945," *Technology and Culture* 36(1): 46–79; Erik Lund, "The Industrial History of Strategy: Reevaluating the Wartime Record of the British Aviation Industry in Comparative Perspective, 1919–1945," *Journal of Military History* 62(1): 75–99; Sebastian Ritchie, "The New Audit of War: The Productivity of Britain's Wartime Aircraft Industry Reconsidered," *War and Society* 12(1), 125–147; and David Edgerton, *Science, Technology, and the British Industrial "Decline"* (Cambridge, 1996), 3–24.

37. Hayward, *British Aircraft Industry*, 36–38, 63.

38. Keith Hayward, *Government and British Civil Aerospace* (New York, 1983), 13–19; Barnett, *Lost Victory*, 228–250; Dobson, *Peaceful Air Warfare*, 137; Davies and Birtles, *De Havilland Comet*, 8–9.

39. Hayward, *British Aircraft Industry*, 26.

40. Ibid., 29–36, 43; Virginia Dawson, "The American Turbojet Industry and British Competition," in William Leary, ed., *From Airships to Airbus* (Washington, 1992), 127–150, 128 for "magnitude."

41. Dawson, "American Turbojet Industry," 134–135.

42. Davies and Birtles, *De Havilland Comet*, 10; Barnett, *Lost Victory*, 231.

43. Hayward, *British Aircraft Industry*, 40.

44. PRO/AVIA2/2524/Oct. 13, 1944.

45. Yale University Archives, Adolph Berle Microfilm, reel 5, Nov. 18, 1944.

46. PRO/CAB128/6/CP46(317)/Aug. 2, 1946; Henry Smith, *Airways Abroad* (Washington, 1991), 112. For British Bible study, see PRO/BT217/2064/Apr. 3, 1946.

47. Sampson, *Empires of the Sky*, 77.

48. Marjorie Hunter, "House Committee Rescues a Mural by Rockwell Kent," *New York Times*, Nov. 19, 1978.

49. Mary Staniszewski, *The Power of Display* (Cambridge, 1998), 226–235; J. Van Zandt, *The Geography of World Air Transport* (Menasha, 1944), 4; Sampson, *Empires of the Sky*, 63.

50. Tom McCormick, *America's Half-Century* (Baltimore, 1995), 33; Berle Microfilm, reel 5, Nov. 2, 1944; Schwarz, *Liberal*, 222.

51. Travis Jacobs, *Navigating the Rapids* (New York, 1973), 499; Schwarz, *Liberal*, 216–219.

52. Pattillo, *Pushing the Envelope*, 120–127.

53. Ibid.; Kofsky, *Harry S. Truman*, 61.

54. Kofsky, *Harry S. Truman*, 34; John Morton Blum, *V was for Victory* (New York, 1976), 116; Friedberg, *In the Shadow*, 48–52; Biddle, *Barons of the Sky*, 279–300.

55. Kofsky, *Harry S. Truman*, 37; Biddle, *Barons of the Sky*, 279; Harold Mansfield, *Vision* (New York, 1956), 316.

56. Biddle, *Barons of the Sky*, 288–293.

57. Kofsky, *Harry S. Truman*, 27, 36; Sampson, *Empires of the Sky*, 77; Biddle, *Barons of the Sky*, 292.

58. Herken, *The Winning Weapon* (New York, 1980), 7–26; Peter Hugill, "Trading States, Territorial States, and Technology," in Brian W. Blouet, ed., *Global Geostrategy: Mackinder and the Defence of the West* (London, 2004), 121–122; Armitage and Mason, *Air Power*, 186.

59. Paul Boyer, *By the Bomb's Early Light* (Chapel Hill, 1994), 5, 14.

60. Corn, *Winged Gospel*, 38; Sherry, *Rise of American Air Power*, 30–37.

61. Armitage and Mason, *Air Power*, 16; "The 36 Hour War," *Life*, Nov. 19, 1945; Joseph Alsop and Stewart Alsop, "Your Flesh Should Creep," *Saturday Evening Post*, July 13, 1946, 49.

62. Boyer, *Bomb's Early Light*, 7.

63. H. W. Brands, "The Age of Vulnerability: Eisenhower and the National Insecurity State," *American Historical Review* 94(4) (1989): 963–989; Symington, "Our Air Force Policy," *Vital Speeches of the Day* (New York, 1949), July 1, 1949, 567–570; Paul Boyer, *Fallout* (Columbus, 1998), 38; Campbell Craig, *Destroying the Village* (New York, 1998), xv.

64. Michael Hunt, *Ideology and U.S. Foreign Policy* (New Haven, 1987), 19–45; Emme, *Impact of Airpower*, 101, 109; Symington, *Vital Speeches*, July 19, 1949, 567–570; *Congressional Record* 96(7): 8892–94, July 6, 1949.

65. Thomas Finletter, *Power and Policy* (New York, 1954).

66. PRO/AVIA2/2524/Oct. 13, 1944.

67. "CAB Proposes Jet Transport Subsidy Plan," *Aviation Week*, May 19, 1952, 12; Michael Hogan, *A Cross of Iron* (New York, 1998), 23–69, 184–206; Michael Sherry, *In the Shadow of War* (New Haven, 1995), 194; Francis Drake and Katharine Drake, "Our Next Pearl Harbor," *Atlantic Monthly*, Oct. 1947; Weigley, *American Way of War*, 377–379; Jeffrey Barlow, *The Revolt of the Admirals* (Washington, 1994); George Kenney, "Survival in the Air Age," *Air Affairs* 3 (Dec. 1950): 453–458.

68. Hogan, *A Cross of Iron*, 23–69; Alan Dobson, "Informally Special? The Churchill-Truman Talks of January 1952 and the State of Anglo-American Relations," *Review of International Studies* 23 (1997): 40–41.

2. Selling Jets to Stalin

1. PRO/CAB128/6/CP46(317)/Aug. 2, 1946; CAB128/6/CP47(134)/Apr. 21, 1947; and CAB128/9/CM38(47)/Apr. 22, 1947.

2. Correlli Barnett, *The Lost Victory* (London, 1995), 42; Robert Skidelsky, *John Maynard Keynes: Fighting for Britain, 1937–1946* (London, 2000), 451.

3. Skidelsky, *John Maynard Keynes*, 397.

4. PRO/CAB78/37/Oct. 18, 1945; Barnett, *Lost Victory*, 40–43.

5. Barnett, *Lost Victory*, 30, 40–43.

6. PRO/BT217/2064/May 8, 1946; PRO/PREM8/766/Mar. 25, 1947.

7. The following section is gleaned from PRO/AIR20/2612 and 20/2613; PREM11/806; PREM8/345; and FO371/86790, including internal "histories" of the Rolls sales to the Soviet Union. For "doubt," see AIR20/2612/May 24, 1946; "Our Latest on Show," *Flight and Aircraft Engineer*, Nov. 1, 1945, 469.

8. Ibid.

9. PRO/PREM11/806/May 19, 1952.

10. PRO/FO371/56922/Oct. 2 and Sept. 23, 1946.

11. PRO/PREM11/806/May 19, 1952; AIR20/2612/May 24, 1946.

12. PRO/FO371/86790/Apr. 14, 1950; AIR20/2612/May 24, 1946.

13. PRO/AIR20/2612/July 25, 1946.

14. Frank Kofsky, *Harry S. Truman and the War Scare of 1948* (New York, 1995), 27–36.

15. NARA/RG59/LOTFiles/MLR1494/52/Mar. 8, 1946.

16. *FRUS,* 1946, 11:278–282; NARA/RG59/810.20/7-1646 and 810.20/3-1247; PRO/PREM8/766/Feb. 8 and Mar. 22, 1947; PRO/CAB128/9/CM47(38)/Apr. 22, 1947.

17. PRO/PREM8/766/Mar. 22, 1947; NARA/RG59/835.796/2-1346/Feb. 13, 1946; PRO/PREM8/766/Mar. 25, 1947; PRO/FO371/81211/July 6, 1950.

18. PRO/FO800/442/Mar. 27, 1946.

19. Ibid.

20. PRO/FO800/442/Mar. 21, 1946.

21. John Crider, "New Delay Faces British Loan Vote," *New York Times,* May 2, 1946; *Congressional Record* 92 (Feb. 26, 1946): 4080.

22. PRO/FO800/442/Mar. 21, 1946.

23. PRO/FO800/442/Mar. 27, 1946.

24. PRO/AIR20/2612/July 25, 1946.

25. Ibid.

26. PRO/AIR20/2612/June 19, 1946.

27. PRO/PREM11/806/May 19, 1952; Truman Library/NSC Records/19/"Some Aspects of the British Sales of Aircraft and Engines"/Sept. 8, 1947.

28. PRO/AIR20/2612/May 24, 1946.

29. PRO/FO371/56922/Sept. 23, 1946.

30. PRO/AIR20/2612/May 24, 1946.

31. PRO/FO371/56922/Sept. 23, 1946; AIR20/2612/May 24, 1946. France was not the only country lambasted for security flaws. "I can think of nothing more idiotic," a British diplomat wrote, than sale of a manufacturing license to Ankara. "If we sell them manufacturing rights, Rolls Royce will no doubt get a nice lump sum in foreign exchange . . . but I cannot believe the Turks will make any efficient engines for some time, and the possibility of leakage of manufacturing knowledge or of individual turbine blades to Russia will be very much increased by the contract" (PRO/FO371/56922/Sept. 20, 1946).

32. PRO/AIR20/2612/Aug. 1, 1946.

33. PRO/AIR20/2612/Aug. 9, 1946; Truman Library/NSC Records/19/Air Intelligence Division Study #173/Sept. 8, 1947; PRO/FO371/56922/Sept. 23, 1946.

34. PRO/FO371/56922/Sept. 20, 1946.

35. Roy Hattersley, *Fifty Years On: A Prejudiced History of Britain since the War* (London, 1998), 20–21; PRO/FO371/56922/Sept. 23, 1946.

36. PRO/AIR20/2612/Sept. 26, 1946.

37. PRO/FO371/56922/Oct. 24, 1946 (two).

38. PRO/PREM8/345/Oct. 1, 1946.

39. Ibid.

40. PRO/AIR20/2612/Dec. 18, 1946; PRO/BT11/2835/July 18, 1947.

41. PRO/AIR20/2612/Feb. 21 and July 18, 1947.

42. PRO/AIR20/2612/Feb. 5 and July 18 (two), 1947.

43. PRO/FO953/10606 /June 6, 1951.

44. PRO/AIR20/2612/June 26 and July 14, 1947.

45. PRO/AIR20/2612/July 14, 1947.

46. NARA/RG59/810.20/7-3146/July 31, 1946; PRO/PREM8/766/Feb. 8, 1947; Apr. 4, 1948; Mar. 22 and 25, 1947; Apr. 20, 1947; *FRUS*, 1947, 8:171, 220.

47. PRO/FO371/61138/Jan. 29, 1947; PREM8/766/Feb. 8, 1947; NARA/RG59/ 835.34/5-2047/May 20, 1947.

48. PRO/PREM8/766/May 18, 1947.

49. Ibid.

50. PRO/PREM8/766/May 18, 19, and 22, 1947.

51. PRO/PREM8/766/May 19, 1947; NARA/RG59/810.20/5-2147/May 21, 1947.

52. PRO/PREM8/766/May 22 and June 26, 1947.

53. Truman Library/NSC Records/19/Air Intelligence Division Study #173/Sept. 8 and Oct. 10, 1947.

54. Ibid., Air Intelligence Division Study.

55. PRO/AIR20/2612/Nov. 1, 1947.

56. Truman Library/Symington Papers/Box 4/1946–1950/Oct. 27 and 31, 1947; Box 9/Memoranda of Meetings/Oct. 13, 1947; and Box 11/Spaatz/Aug. 17, 1947.

57. PRO/AIR20/2613/Jan. 14, 1948; FO953/1060/June 6, 1951; and Truman Library/Naval Aid Files/21/State Department Briefs, Sept.–Dec. 1947/Nov. 10, 1947.

58. PRO/FO800/502/Nov. 24, 1947.

59. PRO/AIR20/2612/Oct. 10, 1947.

60. PRO/AIR20/2613/Nov. 26 and Dec. 11, 1947; Dickson to Goddard (undated); Goddard to Dickson, Dec. 22, 1947; PRO/FO371/86790/Apr. 14, 1950.

61. PRO/FO953/1060/June 6, 1951; PRO/PREM11/806/May 19, 1952; PRO/AIR20/ 2613/Dec. 22, 1947.

62. PRO/AIR20/2613/Dec. 22, 1947.

63. PRO/FO371/70106/Jan. 23, 1948.

64. Ibid.; also Jan. 14, 1948; Nov. 27, 1948; Mar. 10 and Mar. 30, 1948.

65. Ibid., Mar. 10, 1948.

3. Death by Nene

1. Walter LaFeber, *The American Age* (New York, 1994), 484; David McCullough, *Truman* (New York, 1992), 630.

2. Melvyn Leffler, *The Specter of Communism* (New York, 1994), 92; LaFeber, *The American Age*, 484; Walter Isaacson and Evan Thomas, *The Wise Men* (New York, 1986), 497.

3. David Reynolds, *Britannia Overruled* (London, 2000), 175.

4. Michael Hogan, *The Marshall Plan* (New York, 1989), 88–101; J. A. Engel, "'Every Cent from America's Working Man': Fiscal Conservatism and the Politics of International Aid after World War II," *New England Journal of History* 58(1) (2001): 20–60.

5. *Washington Times Herald,* Apr. 28, 1948, 12; PRO/BT11/2835/Apr. 28, 1948.

6. *Washington Times Herald,* Apr. 28, 1948, 13; *Foreign Relations of the United States (FRUS) Microfiche Publication*/Memoranda of Conversation, 1947–1952/Doc. 521.

7. "Wartime Engines Shipped to Russians, Truman Ban Near," *New York Times,*

March 25, 1948, p. 1; "State, Justice Agencies Let Planes Go to Russia," *New York Times,* Mar. 26, 1948, p. 1; and "No Arms for Russia," *New York Times,* Mar. 27, 1948, p. 12; Truman Library/President's Secretary's Files/204/NSC Meetings July 14, 1948/Report to the National Security Council by the Department of State on US Civil Aviation Policy toward the USSR and Its Satellites, July 12, 1948 (hereafter cited as NSC-15/1).

8. NSC-15/1, 2.

9. A. Berle and Travis Jacobs, *Navigating the Rapids* (New York, 1973), 501.

10. Alan Dobson, *Peaceful Air Warfare* (New York, 1991), 150; David Mackenzie, "An 'Ambitious Dream': The Chicago Conference and the Quest for Multilateralism in International Air Transport," *Diplomacy and Statecraft* 2(2) (1991): 270–293.

11. John Schwarz, *Liberal* (New York, 1987), 248.

12. Berle and Jacobs, *Navigating the Rapids,* 495; Schwarz, *Liberal,* 241.

13. *FRUS,* 1948, 4:437–438; NARA/RG59/711.4027/1-1248 and NSC-15/1, 1–2.

14. NSC-15/1; PRO/FO371/70106, Jan. 23, 1948.

15. PRO/FO371/70106, Jan. 23, 1948.

16. *FRUS,* 1948, 4:448–451; NSC-15/1, 1–4; NARA/RG59/711.4027/7-2648/July 19, 1948.

17. NARA/RG59/740.0027/1-2248 and 856.79664/4-1348/Deak to State/Apr. 13, 1948.

18. Ibid.; NARA/RG59/856.79664/6-848 (emphasis mine); RG59/711.4027/7-2648; RG59/711.4027/11-1148.

19. NARA/RG59.711.4027/10-148/Oct. 1, 1948, and Bohlen to Kennan/Nov. 11, 1948.

20. PRO/FO371/65555, Apr. 1, 1947; FO371/70106, Oct. 1, 1948, and Note for Ministers, Sept. 22, 1948.

21. NARA/RG59/711.4027/10-148/Oct. 1, 1948.

22. Ibid.; NARA/RG59/711.4027/6-649/Minutes of May 5, 1949.

23. Ibid.

24. Ibid.; see also Eisenhower Library/NSC Staff Files/Disaster File/6/Aviation 1/ June 1 and July 20, 1949.

25. Eisenhower Library/NSC Staff Files/Disaster Files/6/Aviation (2); *FRUS,* 1950, 4:26, Feb. 16, 1950.

26. *FRUS,* 1950, 4:26, Feb. 16, 1950.

27. Eisenhower Library/NSC Staff Files/Disaster File/6/June 1, 1949.

28. Gordon Chang, *Friends and Enemies* (Palo Alto, 1990), 43; Nancy Tucker, *Patterns in the Dust* (New York, 1983); William Stueck, *The Road to Confrontation* (Chapel Hill, 1981); Victor Kaufman, *Confronting Communism* (Columbia, MO, 2001), 1–22.

29. Chang, *Friends and Enemies,* 47–48; Ronald McGlothlen, *Controlling the Waves* (New York, 1993).

30. William Leary, *Perilous Missions* (Birmingham, AL, 1984), 90–99; William Leary and William Stueck, "The Chennault Plan to Save China," *Diplomatic History* 8(4) (Fall 1984): 349–364; William Leary, "Aircraft and Anti-Communists: CAT in Action," *China Quarterly* 52 (Oct.–Dec. 1972): 654–670; and Victor Kaufman,

"The United States, Britain, and the CAT Controversy, 1949–1952," in author's possession.

31. Leary, "Aircraft and Anti-Communists," 656.

32. Ibid.

33. William Leary, "Portrait of a Cold War Warrior: Whiting Willauer and Civil Air Transport," *Modern Asian Studies* 5(4): 373–388. Also Xu Guangqui, "Americans and Nationalist Chinese Military Aviation, 1929–1949," *American Aviation Historical Society Journal* 44(1): 16–27; Xu Guangqui, "The Chinese Air Force with American Wings," *War and Society* 16(1): 61–81; Leary, "Aircraft and Anti-Communists," 655–656; Leary, *Perilous Missions,* 96.

34. NARA/RG59/893.796/Nov. 16, 1949; Kaufman, "CAT Controversy," 7; Kaufman, *Confronting Communism,* 21.

35. Leary, "Aircraft and Anti-Communists," 659.

36. PRO/FO371/84782/Jan. 6, 1950; NARA/RG59/893.796/Dec. 16, 1949; Alexander Grantham, *Via Ports* (Hong Kong, 1965), 162.

37. PRO/FO371/84782/Dec. 31, 1949, and Jan. 5 and Jan. 7, 1950. Holmes told Sir Strang, "Anyone who was acquainted with him would know that he is a difficult man to curb" (ibid., Jan. 7, 1950).

38. PRO/FO371/84782/Dec. 31, 1950. See also PRO/PREM8/1139/CP50(74)/Apr. 12, 1950, esp. Annex C, Apr. 19, 1950.

39. Ibid., Dec. 31, 1949, and Jan. 1, 1950.

40. Ibid., Jan. 7, 1950.

41. PRO/FO371/84782/Jan. 3 and Jan. 6, 1950.

42. PRO/FO371/83302/Feb. 2, 1950; Kaufman, "CAT Controversy," 13; Leary, "Aircraft and Anti-Communists," 660; NARA/RG59/711.5622/2-1450/Feb. 14, 1950.

43. Kaufman, "CAT Controversy," 9–12; Leary, "Aircraft and Anti-Communists," 660.

44. Leary, *Perilous Missions,* 97; *Congressional Record* 81(2): 233.

45. Truman Library/Acheson Papers/75/Mar. 27, 1950.

46. Roy Hattersley, *Fifty Years On* (London, 1998), 8; and Winston Churchill, *Their Finest Hour* (Boston, 1949), 78; Correlli Barnett, *The Lost Victory* (London, 1995), 174.

47. PRO/FO800/517/Mar. 8, 1950.

48. NARA/RG59/611.41/2-2750/Feb. 27, 1950 (emphasis mine), 611.41/1-2450/Jan. 24, 1950, and 611.41/3-750/Mar. 7, 1950.

49. Grantham, *Via Ports,* 162.

50. Leary, "Aircraft and Anti-Communists," 662; Brian Porter, *Britain and the Rise of Communist China* (London, 1967), 40.

51. "British See Delay on Chinese Planes," *New York Times,* May 31, 1950, 3; and "New Soviet Jets in China," *New York Times,* June 1, 1950, 11.

52. Kaufman, "CAT Controversy," 18; "US Doubts British Will Yield Planes," *New York Times,* May 31, 1950, 3.

53. Kaufman, *Confronting Communism,* 55.

54. Leary, "Aircraft and Anti-Communists," 665.

55. Lewis Purifoy, *Harry Truman's China Legacy* (New York, 1976), 259; Truman Library/Acheson Papers/65/Truman-Attlee Talks, Dec. 4, 1950.

56. PRO/FO371/86790/Apr. 14, 1950; PREM11/806/May 19, 1952; Robert Futrell et al., *The United States Air Force in Korea, 1950–1953* (Washington, 2000), 244; Rosemary Foot, *The Wrong War* (Ithaca, 1985), 173. Kenneth Whiting (*Soviet Air Power* [Boulder, 1986], 37) dates the first MiG-15 test-flight at December 30, 1947; Robert Jackson (*The Red Falcons* [London, 1970], 163) states the Soviets took a year to copy their Nenes.

57. PRO/PREM11/806/May 19, 1952; PREM8/1357/Cabinet Meeting of Nov. 23, 1950.

58. PRO/PREM8/1357/Nov. 17 and Nov. 23, 1950.

59. PRO/PREM8/1357/Nov. 17 and Nov. 22, 1950; PRO/AIR77/39/July 20, 1950; PRO/C51/23, Nov. 21, 1951.

60. Futrell et al., *United States Air Force in Korea*, 244; Conrad Crane, *American Airpower Strategy in Korea* (Lawrence, 2000); Jennie Chancey and William Forstchen, *Hot Shots* (New York, 2000); Hanson Baldwin, "Challenge of the MiG—and the Answer," *New York Times*, Dec. 9, 1951, 195; and "Soviet Progress in Air," *New York Times*, July 17, 1951, 9. See also A. W. Jessup, "MiG-15 Dims USAF's A-Bomb Hopes," *Aviation Week*, Feb. 4, 1952, 16.

61. Crane, *American Airpower Strategy*, 104.

62. Information gleaned from interviews and correspondence with Korean War pilots Richard Becker, Steve Bettinger, John Bolt, Guy Bordelon, Randall Cunningham, Francis Gabreski, James Low, and Chuck Yeager. For the F-86 and MiG, see Crane, *American Airpower Strategy*, 195. See also Alpheus Jessup, "Better Planes Needed to Match MiGs," *Aviation Week*, Nov. 19, 1951, and Alpheus Jessup, "Vandenberg: Red Jets Better," *Aviation Week*, June 4, 1951, 17.

63. "MiGs Top Sabres, US Jet Ace Says," *New York Times*, June 2, 1951, 2; "Soviet MiG-15 Wins Respect of US Ace," *New York Times*, June 13, 1951, 5. *Aviation Week*, June 11, 1951, 17; and "New Russian Planes," unsigned editorial, *New York Times*, July 11, 1951, 22; "Red Fighters on Film," *New York Times*, Jan. 3, 1951, 2; "Russians Can Make Good Planes," *Aviation Week*, Feb. 19, 1951; Austin Stevens, "Deterrent to War Cited by Finletter," *New York Times*, Jan. 30, 1951, 7. For *Look*, see "Helping Reds Keep Their Secrets," *Aviation Week*, Apr. 14, 1952, 98; Crane, *American Airpower Strategy*, 83.

64. PRO/FO953/1060/June 6 and June 27, 1951; *Times* (London), Apr. 26 and June 21, 1951. See also "AF Bares Secrets of MiG Engine," *Aviation Week*, June 11, 1951, 16.

65. PRO/FO953/1060/June 6, 1951.

66. *New York Times*, May 29, 1951, 4.

67. PRO/FO953/1060/June 6, 1951.

4. Comet Dreams

1. Alan P. Dobson, *The Politics of the Anglo-American Economic Special Relationship, 1940–1987* (New York, 1988), 125–146; Melvyn Leffler, *A Preponderance of Power:*

National Security, the Truman Administration, and the Cold War (Palo Alto, 1992), 446–463; PRO/FO800/836/Jan. 7, 1952; PRO/FO800/837/July 5, 1952.

2. Alan Dobson, "Informally Special? The Churchill-Truman Talks of January 1952 and the State of Anglo-American Relations," *Review of International Studies* 23 (1997), 33.

3. Dobson, "Informally Special," 25–33; PRO/FO800/836/Mar. 10, 1952; Peter Boyle, "Britain, America and the Transition from Economic to Military Assistance, 1948–1951," *Journal of Contemporary History* 22 (1987): 521–538; Martin Walker, *The Cold War* (New York, 1993), 86.

4. Dobson, "Informally Special," 25–33.

5. Thomas J. McCormick, *America's Half-Century,* 2nd ed. (Baltimore, 1995), 105; Iwan Morgan, *Deficit Government* (Chicago, 1995), 56–57.

6. Eugene Rodgers, *Flying High: The Story of Boeing and the Rise of the Jetliner Industry* (New York, 1996), 111; Richard Kirkendall, "Two Senators and the Boeing Company," *Columbia* 11(4): 38–43.

7. NARA/RG59/MLR1548/2/MDAP—United Kingdom/Dec. 18, 1951.

8. PRO/CAB128/24/CC52(4)/Jan. 17, 1952.

9. PRO/FO800/836/Jan. 25 and Mar. 10, 1952.

10. Keith Hayward, *British Aircraft Industry* (New York, 1989), 59–63; PRO/CAB129/48/C51/28/Nov. 26, 1951.

11. PRO/FO371/99735/Dec. 12, 1952, and Jan. 2, 1953; CAB134/844/EA52(69)/May 23, 1952; and AVIA55/126/Mar. 27, 1952.

12. PRO/CAB134/844/EA52(69)/May 23, 1952; *Flight and Aircraft Engineer,* Apr. 18, 1952. The plane pictured carries French colors, but the image from Britain's leading aviation magazine represents British technological prowess.

13. PRO/CAB134/844/EA52(69)/May 23, 1952.

14. PRO/PREM11/105/Jan. 29 and Feb. 28, 1952.

15. PRO/AVIA55/126/Feb. 29, 1952.

16. PRO/AVIA55/126/Feb. 29, Apr. 4, and Mar. 27, 1952; PREM11/105/Apr. 10, 1952.

17. PRO/AVIA54/856/July 30, 1952.

18. Derek Dempster, *The Tale of the Comet* (New York, 1958), 85; R. G. Davies and Philip Birtles, *De Havilland Comet* (McLean, 1999); Geoffrey de Havilland, *Sky Fever* (London, 1961), 169–191; John Golley, *John "Cat's Eye" Cunningham* (London, 1999); and author interview with Cunningham, Oct. 27, 1998. The April 18, 1952, edition of Britain's *Flight and Aircraft Engineer* is devoted to the plane.

19. John Stuart, "1952 Now Looms as Critical Year for U.S. Air Transport Industry," *New York Times,* May 4, 1952, 1; "British Jet Airliner Sets Mark to Africa," *New York Times,* May 4, 1952, 1.

20. *Aviation Week,* Oct. 19, 1953, 13; Rodgers, *Flying High,* 222–242; Charles Bright, *The Jet Makers* (Lawrence, 1978), 77–103; John Rae, *Climb to Greatness* (Cambridge, 1968), 173–205; and Carl Solberg, *Conquest of the Skies* (Boston, 1979), 391.

21. Truman Library/Truman Papers/Official File/Box 855/249/Feb. 29, 1952; Solberg, *Conquest of the Skies,* 389.

22. Stuart, "1952 Now Looms," May 4, 1; Dempster, *Tale of the Comet*, 20–21.

23. PRO/CAB134/845/EA52(111)/July 29, 1952; Stuart, "1952 Now Looms"; Dempster, *Tale of the Comet*, 94.

24. PRO/AVIA55/126/Mar. 12, 1952; *Flight and Aircraft Engineer*, Apr. 18, 1952.

25. T. A. Heppenheimer, *Turbulent Skies: The History of Commercial Aviation* (New York, 1995), 156; author interview with Cunningham, Oct. 27, 1998.

26. PRO/FO371/99735/June 23, 1952; CAB195/53/C52(245)/July 16, 1952.

27. PRO/CAB134/845/EA52(111)/July 29, 1952; CAB129/55/C52(331)/Oct. 13, 1952.

28. Davies and Birtles, *De Havilland Comet*, 16; Ronald Miller and David Sawers, *The Technical Development of Modern Aviation* (London, 1968), 160.

29. Author interview with John Cunningham, Oct. 27, 1998.

30. Truman Library/Truman Papers/Box 257/ORE 1949/"Estimate of the Effects of the Soviet Possession of the Atomic Bomb. . . "/Apr. 6, 1950.

31. PRO/DEFE7/2061/May 21, 1952.

32. PRO/FO371/98956/May 22, 1952.

33. PRO/PREM11/806/May 19, 1952.

34. PRO/DEFE7/2061/May 21, 1952; FO371/98956/May 22, 1952.

35. PRO/DEFE7/2061/May 21, 1952.

36. NARA/RG59/611.41/2-650/Feb. 6, 1950; John Bayliss, *Anglo-American Defense Relations, 1939–1984* (New York, 1984), 56–87.

37. PRO/DEFE7/2061/Aug. 20, 1952.

38. PRO/DEFE7/2061/Nov. 19, 1952.

39. PRO/DEFE7/2061/Nov. 19, 1952; NARA/RG59/441.1184/11-1054/Nov. 10, 1954; RG59/741.5622/9-652/Sept. 6 and Sept. 10, 1952.

40. PRO/DEFE7/2061, May 27, 1952; PRO/DEFE7/2061, Nov. 25, 1952; and NARA/RG59/441.1184/11-1054/Nov. 10, 1954.

41. PRO/DEFE7/2061/Powell to Elliott/Nov. 25, 1952.

42. PRO/DEFE7/2061/Dec. 8, 1952

43. PRO/FO371/98957/Dec. 6, 1952.

44. PRO/FO371/98957/Washington to FO, Dec. 2 and Dec. 6, 1952; DEFE7/2061/ Dec. 3, 1952.

45. PRO/DEFE7/2061/Washington to FO, Dec. 9, 1952 (emphasis mine), and Feb. 2, 1953.

46. PRO/FO800/837/Nov. 21, 1952; FO800/838/Feb. 7, 1953.

47. PRO/FO371/104995/Feb. 7, 1953; DEFE7/2061/Mar. 18, 1953.

48. PRO/DEFE7/693/Nov. 20, 1953; PRO/T225/274/Apr. 23, 1953.

49. PRO/T225/274/May 5 and May 15, 1953.

50. PRO/FO371/104996/Sept. 22, 1953; FO371/110134/Mar. 8, 1954.

51. PRO/FO371/104995/Apr. 23 and Apr. 30, 1953; DEFE7/2061/Mar. 18, 1953.

52. NARA/RG59/Miscellaneous Files of the Office of Munitions Control 1934–1959/ LOT59D473/SCA/MC/7/MLR1545/Jet Engines/July 21, 1953; RG334/4/337 State-Defense Military Information Control Committee/Agreed Record of London Discussions/Aug. 17–21, 1953 (hereafter cited as SDMICC).

53. PRO/FO371/104995/Apr. 23, 1953; SDMICC/Appendix G.

54. SDMICC/Appendix G.

55. SDMICC/Appendix G; PRO/T225/274/Apr. 23, 1953.

56. PRO/T225/274/May 15, May 18, and May 26, 1953, and undated (document 29 in series).

57. PRO/FO371/104996/Sept. 22, 1953; NARA/RG59/LOT59D473/7/Jet Engine Question/Dec. 2, 1953.

58. PRO/FO371/104997/Oct. 3, 1953.

59. PRO/FO371/104996/Sept. 22, 1953.

60. Ibid.

61. Ibid.

5. A Lead Lost

1. PRO/FO371/104996/Sept. 22, 1953; AIR8/2358/Oct. 2, Oct. 11, Nov. 11, Nov. 13, 1953; DEFE7/693/Oct. 13 and Oct. 23, 1953; FO371/104997/Oct. 27, 1953.

2. PRO/FO371/104997/Minutes of Anglo-American Talks of Aug. 1953; NARA/ RG59/LOT59D473/MLR1545/7/Jet Engine/Aug. 17, 1954; John Prados, *The Soviet Estimate* (New York, 1982); George Washington University/National Security Archive/"The Soviet Estimate"/SNIE 11.7.54/"Soviet Gross Capabilities for Attacks on the US and Key Overseas Installations through 1 July 1957."

3. NARA/RG334/4/337/Agreed Record of London Discussions/Aug. 17–21, 1953; RG59/LOT59D473/7/MLR1545/Jet Engine Question/Oct. 5, 1953.

4. PRO/FO371/104996/Sept. 22, 1953; FO371/104997/Oct. 3 1953; and AIR8/ 2358/Oct. 28, 1953.

5. PRO/AIR8/2358/Oct. 28 and Nov. 11, 1953; DEFE7/693/Nov. 13, 1953.

6. PRO/FO371/104997/Nov. 10 and Dec. 3, 1957; AIR8/2358/Oct. 28 and Nov. 11, 1953.

7. NARA/RG59/Records Relating to the Mutual Security Assistance Program/Military Assistance Coordination Division/Western European Country Files/2/ MLR1548/3/MDAP—UK Aircraft Program (June 1953–June 1954)/May 14, 1953; RG59/Office of Munitions Control/LOT59D473/7/MLR1545/July 21, 1953.

8. PRO/FO371/104997/Nov. 10, 1953; NARA/RG59/LOT59D473/7/MLR1545/Jet Engine/Oct. 7 and Dec. 2, 1953.

9. NARA/RG59/LOT59D473/7/ML1545/Jet Engine/Oct. 7 and Dec. 2, 1953.

10. NARA/RG59/LOT59D473/7/MLR1545/Jet Engine/Oct. 5 and 7, 1953.

11. PRO/DEFE7/693/Oct. 26, 1953.

12. PRO/AIR8/2358/Nov. 11, 1953; FO371/104997/Dec. 3, 1953.

13. PRO/DEFE 7/2061/Dec. 9, 1952.

14. PRO/FO800/841/Mar. 13, 1954; DEFE7/693/Mar. 29 and 30, 1954.

15. Eisenhower Library/Dulles Papers/Chronological Series/1/Mar. 1–17, 1953 (Telephone Calls)/Mar. 7, 1953; PRO/FO800/766/Feb. 9, 1954; Christina Klein, *Cold War Orientalism* (Berkeley, 2003), 47.

16. PRO/FO800/766/Mar. 1 and Mar. 2, 1954.

17. As of June 15, 2003, www.cia.gov/cia/public_affairs/press_release/archives/1997/pr122997.html.
18. PRO/DEFE7/693/Nov. 20, 1953.
19. Ibid.
20. Ibid.
21. PRO/AIR8/2358/Apr. 3, 1954.
22. Eisenhower Library/Dulles Papers/Chronological Files/7/12/May 10, 1954, and 16/May 21, 1954; "Challenge and Response in United States Policy," *Department of State Bulletin,* Oct. 1957, 574–578.
23. PRO/DEFE7/2036/Apr. 28, 1954; NARA/RG59/LOT59D473/SCA/MC/7/MLR1545/Apr. 15, 1954; University of Missouri/Western Manuscript Collection/Stuart Symington Papers/4017; PRO/FO800/841/Apr. 19, 1954.
24. Derek Dempster, *The Tale of the Comet* (New York, 1958); T. A. Heppenheimer, *Turbulent Skies: The History of Commercial Aviation* (New York, 1995), 156–157; and R. G. Davies and Philip Birtles, *De Havilland Comet* (McLean, 1999).
25. Ibid.
26. Keith Hayward, *British Aircraft Industry* (New York, 1989), 55; PRO/PREM11/2597/July 9, 1959.
27. NARA/RG59/LOT59D473/MLR1545/7/Jet Engine/Aug. 17, 1954.
28. PRO/DEFE7/2036/May 11 and 19, 1954; *Vital Speeches of the Day* (New York, 1949), Sept. 15, 1954, 711–716.
29. PRO/DEFE7/2036/May 4, 1954.
30. PRO/DEFE7/2036/Honi to Hudson, undated, May 20, May 21, Aug. 13, 1954.
31. NARA/RG59/MLR1548/2/MDAP UK–Aircraft Program (July–Dec. 1954)/July 21, 1954.
32. NARA/RG59/MLR1545/7/Jet Engines/Oct. 12, 1954.
33. Alan Wright, *Boeing 707* (Shepperton, 1990), 19–39; Eugene Rodgers, *Flying High* (New York, 1996), 89–121.
34. NARA/RG59/811.3333/9-254/Sept. 2, 1954.
35. NARA/RG59/Office of Munitions Control 1934–1959/MLR1545/7/Jet Engines/Oct. 12, 1954.
36. NARA/RG59/441.1184/11-1054/Oct. 22, 1954; RG59/MLR1545/7/Jet Engines/Oct. 12, 1954.
37. NARA/RG59/441.1184/11-1054/Foster to Beale/Nov. 10, 1954.
38. Ibid.
39. PRO/T225/274/May 6, 1953.
40. NARA/RG/59/611.41/7-2054/July 20, 1954.
41. PRO/FO800/843/June 18, 1954; NARA/RG59/611.41/6-254/June 2, 1954.
42. PRO/DEFE7/172/Dec. 10 1954; DEFE7/1293/Apr. 10, 1956.
43. PRO/FO371/109146/June 18 and 21, 1954.

6. Approaching China

1. Eugene Rodgers, *Flying High* (New York, 1996), 198.
2. Derek Wood, *Project Cancelled* (Indianapolis, 1975); Keith Hayward, *Government*

and British Civil Aerospace (New York, 1983), 57–58; Keith Hayward, *British Aircraft Industry* (New York, 1989), 22–27.

3. Wood, *Project Cancelled,* 98; Hayward, *British Aircraft Industry,* 24–27.

4. Peter Clarke, *Hope and Glory* (London, 1996), 265; Alan P. Dobson, *The Politics of the Anglo-American Economic Special Relationship, 1940–1987* (New York, 1988), 174; Robert Hathaway, *Great Britain and the United States* (Boston, 1990), 52; C. Bartlett, *British Foreign Policy in the Twentieth Century* (New York, 1989), 99; Ritchie Overdale, *Anglo-American Relations in the Twentieth Century* (New York, 1998), 121–122; David Nunnerley, *President Kennedy and Britain* (New York, 1972), 117.

5. Hayward, *British Aircraft Industry,* 67–73; PRO/CAB134/1371/Sept. 20, 1957; "Why Should the Aircraft Industry Be Given More Financial Help. . .," Nov. 1957; CAB128/31/CC57(50)/July 9, 1957; CAB129/88/C57(155)/July 1/1957 and C57(159)/July 5, 1957; Hayward, *British Aircraft Industry,* 67, 79; K. Hartley, "The Mergers in the UK Aircraft Industry, 1957–1960," *Journal of the Royal Aeronautical Society* 69 (Dec. 1965): 848–851.

6. PRO/CAB128/88/C57(154)/July 1, 1957.

7. Marilyn Bender, *The Chosen Instrument* (New York, 1982); PRO/CAB134/1371/ Sept. 20, 1957.

8. PRO/CAB134/1371/Sept. 20, 1957.

9. PRO/CAB128/88/C57(154)/July 1, 1957.

10. PRO/CAB129/99/C59(185)/Dec. 15, 1959; CAB128/33/CC59(64)/Dec. 17, 1959; PREM11/2597/Sept. 1, 1959.

11. PRO/CAB134/1371/Feb. 14, 1958; PREM11/3056/Mar. 23, 1960, and DO35/ 8333/Feb. 17, 1959.

12. COCOM awaits its definitive historian. See Michael Mastanduno, *Economic Containment* (Ithaca, 1992); Alan Dobson, *US Economic Statecraft for Survival, 1933– 1991* (New York, 2002); Ian Jackson, *The Economic Cold War* (New York, 2001); Tor Forland, "'Economic Warfare' and 'Strategic Goods': A Conceptual Framework for Analyzing COCOM," *Journal of Peace Research* 28 (May 1991): 191–204; Tor Forland, "'Selling Firearms to the Indians': Eisenhower's Export Control Policy, 1953–54," *Diplomatic History* 15 (Spring 1991): 221–244; Philip Funigiello, *American-Soviet Trade in the Cold War* (Chapel Hill, 1988); and Frank Cain, "Exporting the Cold War: British Responses to the USA's Establishment of COCOM, 1947–51," *Journal of Contemporary History* 29 (July 1994): 501–522.

13. PRO/FO371/133430/Jan. 12 and 22, 1958.

14. Eisenhower Library/OSANA/NSC Series/Policy Papers Subseries/NSC-5726/1/ Nov. 22, 1957 (hereafter cited as NSC-5726); Whitman File/9/NSC Meeting, Dec. 5, 1957; Whitman File/9/NSC Staff Files/Disaster Files/52/Eastern Europe Civil Aviation/Progress Report on NSC-15/3/May 21, 1956 (hereafter cited as Progress Report); Whitman File/9/White House Central Files/Confidential Files/ Subject Series, Box 64/Russia (28)/July 10, 1960.

15. Eisenhower Library/NSC Staff Files/Disaster Files/52/Eastern Europe—Civil Aviation/June 13, 1956.

16. NSC-5726, Appendix A, 4.

17. Progress Report/II/2.
18. Ibid.
19. Eisenhower Library/Whitman File/9/NSC Meeting/Dec. 5, 1957.
20. PRO/FO371/133430/Jan. 22, 1958; FO371/133187/Feb. 4, 1958.
21. For the literature on Sino-American trade relations, see Jeffrey A. Engel, "Of Fat and Thin Communists: Diplomacy and Philosophy in Western Economic Warfare Strategies toward China (and Tyrants, Broadly)," *Diplomatic History* 29(3) (June 2005): 445–474.
22. *FRUS*, 1951, 7, 1907.
23. Cain, "Exporting the Cold War," 48; Victor Kaufman, *Confronting Communism: US and British Policies toward China* (Columbia, MO, 2001), 104; *FRUS*, 1955–1967, 12:266–267.
24. Rosemary Foote, *The Practice of Power* (New York, 1995), 61; Qing Simei, "The Eisenhower Administration and Changes in Western Embargo Policy against China," in Warren Cohen and Akira Iriye, eds., *The Great Powers in East Asia, 1953–1960* (New York: 1990), 193.
25. Eisenhower Library/Whitman File/7/NSC Meeting/Dec. 9, 1955; Shu Guang Zhang, *Economic Cold War* (Palo Alto, 2001), 194; John Lewis Gaddis, *The Long Peace* (New York, 1987), 179.
26. NARA/RG59/LOT58D209/2/Chincom 1957/The Case for Maintaining a Meaningful China Trade Control Differential/Dec. 1956; Eisenhower Library/DDE Diary Series/12/Feb. 1956 Diary.
27. Truman Library/President's Secretary's Files/Subject File 159/Secretary of State (2)/Feb. 10, 1951; NARA/RG330/125/Letters for S/D to Service Secretaries/Dec. 26, 1952.
28. Zhang, *Economic Cold War*, 217.
29. Cain, "Exporting the Cold War," 42; Eisenhower Library/OSANSA/NSC Series/Policy Papers Subseries/20/US Economic Defense Policy (2)/June 13, 1957; NARA/RG59/Current Economic Developments/Master File 1945–1957/LOT70D467/MLR1579/6/Feb. 21, 1956.
30. NARA/RG59/Current Economic Developments/Master File 1945–1957/LOT70D467/Apr. 12, 1955.
31. Eisenhower Library/Whitman Files/International Series/19/President–Churchill, Jan. 1–June 30/1954(7)/Mar. 24, 1954.
32. PRO/PREM11/2131/Oct. 21, 1957.
33. Eisenhower Library/DDE Diary Series/12/Feb. 1956 Phone Calls/Feb. 1, 1956; Kaufman, *Confronting Communism*, 110.
34. PRO/PREM11/2529/May 20, May 29, 1957; Eisenhower Library/Whitman Files/International Series/23/Macmillan May 29, 1957, to Nov. 30, 1957(1)/May 29 and June 12, 1957.
35. Mark Spaulding, "Eisenhower and Export Controls: A Reply to Tor Forland," *Society of Historians of American Foreign Relations Newsletter* 25 (Spring 1994): 9–16; NARA/RG59/611.41/2-758/Feb. 7, 1958.
36. PRO/PREM11/4021/Aug. 1 and 2, 1962. See also PRO/CAB134/2508/Jan. 22,

1958; RG59/LOT67D469/50/MLR1597/FT—Foreign Trade 6/Mar. 4, 1963; Kennedy Library/Personal Papers of Luther Hodges/Reel 11/Statement of Dean Rusk, Oct. 25, 1961. For Kennedy economic warfare, see NARA/RG59/Bureau of European Affairs Office of Eastern European Affairs/Records Relating to Economic Affairs, 1943–1963/1/MLR3087/FT1 General Policies, Plans, Practices (East-West Trade) US/Aug. 2, 1963.

37. PRO/FO371/134427/Jan. 16 and 27, 1958; FO371/134429/Mar. 27 and 28, 1958

38. PRO/FO371/133430/Jan. 12 and 22, 1958.

39. NARA/Eisenhower Library/NSC Staff Files/Disaster Files/52/Easter Europe—Civil Aviation/June 13, 1956.

40. Ibid.

41. PRO/FO371/141306/Mar. 28 and May 14, 1959.

42. PRO/FO371/133430/Apr. 22, 1958.

43. PRO/FO371/134430/May 19, 1958 (emphasis mine).

44. PRO/FO371/134429/Mar. 21, 27, and 28, 1958

45. Ibid.

46. PRO/FO371/134430/July 7, 1958.

47. PRO/FO371/142451/Feb. 6, 1959. These COCOM negotiations are documented in FO371/142450–51.

48. PRO/FO371/133430/Dec. 2, 1958.

49. PRO/FO371/150433/Aug. 26 and Sept. 6, 1960.

50. PRO/FO371/150433/Aug. 11 and 16, and Sept. 14, 1960.

51. PRO/F0371/150433/Aug. 1, 1960; FO371/158087/Aug. 12 (two), 1961.

7. The Viscount Conspiracy

1. Keith Hayward, *British Aircraft Industry* (New York, 1989), 63–83; Keith Hayward, *Government and British Civil Aerospace* (New York, 1983), 27–49; David Edgerton, *England and the Aeroplane: An Essay on a Militant and Technological Nation* (London, 1991), 71–105; PRO/CAB129/106/C61(150)/Oct. 6, 1961.

2. PRO/CAB129/106/C61(150)/Oct. 6, 1961; PRO/CAB129/107/C61(159)/Oct. 11, 1961; Peter Clarke, *Hope and Glory* (London, 1996), 277–278; Alan P. Dobson, *The Politics of the Anglo-American Economic Special Relationship* (New York, 1988), 180–187.

3. Nigel Ashton, *Kennedy, Macmillan and the Cold War* (London, 2002), 161–162.

4. Robert Hathaway, *Great Britain and the United States* (Boston, 1990), 62; C. Bartlett, *British Foreign Policy in the Twentieth Century* (New York, 1989), 99; Hayward, *British Aircraft Industry,* 83–86; Alan P. Dobson, *Anglo-American Relations in the Twentieth Century* (New York, 1995), 128–131; Peter Roman, *Eisenhower and the Missile Gap* (Ithaca, 1995), 142–146, 161–163; David Nunnerly, *President Kennedy and Britain* (New York, 1972), 127–151; Richard Neustadt, *Report to JFK* (Ithaca, 1999).

5. Roy Hattersley, *Fifty Years On* (London, 1998), 141; Hathaway, *Great Britain and the United States*, 63.

6. Ashton, *Kennedy, Macmillan and the Cold War*, 155; PRO/CAB21/4979/Oct. 26, 1960.

7. Ashton, *Kennedy, Macmillan and the Cold War*, 156.

8. Neustadt, *Report to JFK*, 29; Nunnerly, *President Kennedy and Britain*, 147.

9. Hathaway, *Great Britain and the United States*, 64.

10. Nunnerly, *President Kennedy and Britain*, 141; PRO/AIR19/1096/July 4, 1960.

11. Hayward, *British Civil Aerospace*, 29–31; Eugene Rodgers, *Flying High* (New York, 1996), 207–216; PRO/CAB129/107/C61(159)/Oct. 11, 1961.

12. PRO/FO371/158087/Nov. 10, 1961; FO371/158424/Aug. 31, 1961. The full extent of British efforts for the Viscount, secret and otherwise, are best revealed in PRO/FO371/158087–89 and 170700–03.

13. PRO/CAB134/1698/EA63(32)/Feb. 25, 1963.

14. PRO/FO371/158073/Apr. 13, 1961.

15. PRO/FO371/158087/Aug. 12, 1961.

16. PRO/FO371/134429/Mar. 26, 1958; Victor Kaufman, *Confronting Communism* (Columbia, MO, 2001), 149–151; Rosemary Foote, *The Practice of Power* (New York, 1995), 97; PRO/FO371/158073/Dec. 30, 1960.

17. PRO/FO371/158424/Aug. 18, 1961; FO371/158087/Aug. 18, 1961.

18. Culled from PRO/FO371/158087.

19. PRO/FO371/158087/Aug. 12, 1961.

20. PRO/FO371/158424/Aug. 24 and 28, 1961.

21. PRO/FO371/158087/Oct. 5 and 6, 1961; FO371/158424/Aug. 24, 1961.

22. Michael Mastanduno, *Economic Containment* (Ithaca, NY, 1992), 110.

23. PRO/FO371/158073/Feb. 28, 1961.

24. Culled from PRO/FO371/158424 and FO371/158087; FO371/158087/Oct. 6, 1961.

25. Ibid.

26. NARA/RG59/993.7211/7-1560/3115/Sept. 1 and Oct. 3, 1961; PRO/FO371/158087/Oct. 14, 1961.

27. PRO/FO371/158087/Oct. 18 and 23, 1961.

28. PRO/FO371/158087/Oct. 25, 26, 27, and 30, 1961.

29. PRO/FO371/158087/"Secret Bid to Sell British Jet Liners to China," *Daily Express*, Oct. 28, 1961; Angus MacPherson, "China to Buy British Air Fleet," *Daily Mail*, Oct. 28, 1961.

30. "A Disservice to Free World," *Oakland Tribune*, Oct. 31, 1961.

31. PRO/FO371/158087/Oct. 31, 1961.

32. NARA/RG59/993.7211/7-1560/Nov. 9, 1961; RG59/Bureau of Far Eastern Affairs/10/Communist China, July–Dec. 1961/Nov. 3, 1961.

33. PRO/FO371/158087/Oct. 31, 1961, and Peggie to Fielding (undated, late October).

34. PRO/FO371/158087/Nov. 6, 1961.

35. PRO/FO371/158087/Nov. 10 (two), 1961.

36. Ibid.

37. PRO/FO371/158087/Nov. 10, 1961.

38. PRO/FO371/158087/Nov. 10, 1961; FO371/158088/Nov. 30, 1961.

39. PRO/FO371/158087/Nov. 15 and 17, 1961.

40. PRO/PREM11/4542/June 16 and Nov. 20, 1961; FO371/134428/Mar. 6, 1958.

41. PRO/FO371/158087/Nov. 13 (two), Nov. 14, and Nov. 20, 1961.

42. PRO/FO371/158088/Nov. 16, 1961.

43. PRO/FO371/158087/Nov. 18, 1961.

44. PRO/BT11/5834/Nov. 30 and Dec. 1, 1961.

45. Kennedy Library/NSC Files/170/12/1/61-12/10/61/Dec. 1, 1961; ibid./410/ China (CPR) 1961–1963 [3 of 3]/Dec. 7, 1961.

46. PRO/FO371/158087/Nov. 15, 1961.

47. Ibid.

48. NARA/RG59/Bureau of Far Eastern Affairs/Subject Personal Name and Country Files, 1960–1963/10/Communist China, July–Dec. 1961/Dec. 6, 1961; PRO/ FO371/158089/Dec. 4, 1961.

49. PRO/FO371/158089/Dec. 7, 1961.

50. PRO/FO371/158089/Dec. 22, 1961.

51. "Viscount Airliner: Red China Chooses," *Economist,* Dec. 9, 1961.

52. PRO/FO371/158089/Dec. 8, 1961; Kennedy Library/NSC Files/Box 170/UK General, 12/1/61-12/10/61/Dec. 7, 1961; "US Tried to Bar Jet Sale," *New York Herald Tribune,* Dec. 8, 1961.

53. PRO/FO371/158089/Dec. 9, 1961; Kennedy Library/NSC Files/Box 410/China (CPR) 1961–1963 [3 of 3]/Komer to Bundy, Dec. 11, 1961.

54. NARA/RG59/Bureau of Far Eastern Affairs/Subject Personal Name and Country File, 1960–1963/9/British Sale of "Viscount" Aircraft to Communist China/Dec. 16, 1961.

55. Kennedy Library/NSC Files/170/12/1/61-12/10/61/Dec. 4, 1961, and File: 2/22/ 62-3/21/62/Mar. 7, 1962; NARA/RG59/993.7211/7-1560/Jan. 30, 1962.

56. PRO/FO371/158426/Dec. 18, 1961; CAB134/1694/EA62(39)/Mar. 9, 1962; CAB134/1693/EA62(9)/Mar. 14, 1962.

57. PRO/CAB134/1694/EA63(39)/Mar. 9, 1962. See also PRO/CAB134/1693/Annex to EA62.39/"Position of British Electronics Firms Controlled by US Companies in Relation to US Export Controls."

58. PRO/CAB134/1694/EA63(39)/Mar. 9, 1962.

59. NARA/RG59/Records of the Policy Planning Staff/1962/LOT69D121/216/June 24, 1962.

60. NARA/Kennedy Library/NSC Files/170/UK General, 2/22/62-3/21/62/Mar. 7, 1962.

61. NARA/Kennedy Library/NSC Files/170A/12/11/62-12/31/62/Dec. 13, 1962; RG59/993.7211/7-1560/Jan. 17, 1963; RG59/611.41/9-1862/"Briefing Notes on the Check List of United States–Great Britain Bilateral Problems"; RG59/ 993.7211/7-1560/Dec. 4, 1962.

62. PRO/CAB134/1694/EA62(39)/Mar. 9, 1962; CAB134/1693/EA62(9)/Mar. 14, 1962.

63. PRO/FO371/172432/Feb. 28, 1963.

64. NARA/RG59/Alpha-Numeric Series/Box 3635/STR Chicom/STR CHICOM-A/ Mar. 8, 1963.
65. NARA/RG59/Central Foreign Policy Files/3342/Aviation (Civil)/Mar. 29, 1963, and ibid./AV12-2/Apr. 12 and Aug. 23, 1963.
66. NARA/RG59/3342/AV-Aviation (Civil) Chicom/Mar. 14 and Aug. 28, 1963; Kennedy Library/NSC Files/286/Department of State 4/7/63 to 4/22/63/Memorandum for Bundy, undated.
67. NARA/RG59/AV-Aviation (Civil) 2-1/Weekly Civil Air Summary #64/8/Feb. 9–15, 1964.
68. NARA/Kennedy Library/Hodges Personal Papers/East West Trade Reports 3/64-5/64/Mar. 16, 1964.
69. PRO/FO371/172432/Feb. 28, 1963.
70. PRO/FO371/172432/May 28, 1963.
71. PRO/FO371/172432/May 27, 1963.
72. PRO/FO371/172432/June 5 and 19, 1963; PRO/FO371/170701/June 6, 1963.
73. PRO/FO371/172432/June 13 and 20, 1963.
74. PRO/FO371/170702/Sept. 23, 1963.
75. PRO/FO371/170703/Sept. 23 (two), 1963; CAB129/112/C63(13)/Feb. 4, 1963.

8. Aviation on the New Frontier

1. *Public papers of the Presidents: John F. Kennedy, 1963* (Washington, D.C., 1964), June 14, 1963.
2. NARA/RG59/LOT64D452/2/Aviation (Civil)/June 28, 1963; Eisenhower Library/White House Central Files/Confidential Files/Subject Series/64/Russia (28)/July 10, 1960.
3. Kennedy Library/Najeeb Halaby Oral History/Sept. 2, 1964. These numbers do not include Soviets on official business.
4. Eisenhower Library/White House Central Files/Confidential Files/Subject Series/64/Russia (28)/July 10, 1960.
5. Ibid.
6. Kennedy Library/National Security Files/284/Dept. of State General, 3/6/61-3/31/61/Mar. 27, 1961; ibid./314/21/May 9, 1962.
7. Kennedy Library/Halaby Oral History/Sept. 2, 1964; Walter LaFeber, *The American Age* (New York, 1994), 596.
8. Kennedy Library/Halaby Oral History/Sept. 2, 1964.
9. Public papers of President Kennedy, June 10, 1963; Kennedy Library/President's Office Files/88A/State 2/63-3/63/Mar. 26, 1963.
10. NARA/RG59/1963 Alpha-Numeric Series/3343/AV Aviation (Civil) Com Bloc/May 14, 1963.
11. Eisenhower Library/Whitman Files/9/Minutes of the NSC Meeting/Dec. 5, 1957.
12. Ibid.; Eisenhower Library/OSANSA/OCB Series/Subject Subseries/2/Economic Defense Policy/Mar. 27, 1959, and OCB Series/Administration Subseries/4/OCB Minutes of Meetings 1959(3)/June 17, 1959; RG59/Records of Component

Offices of the Bureau of Economic Affairs, 1941–1963/LOT64D452/2/1/June 28, 1963. See also copy of State Department report in PRO/FO371/165223/Sept. 17, 1962, and British discussion, May 18, 1962.

13. Ron Davies, *A History of the World's Airlines* (London, 1982); Philip Jarrett, *Modern Air Transport* (London, 2000); John Newhouse, *The Sporty Game* (New York, 1982), 3–27; Thomas J. McCormick, *America's Half-Century,* 2nd ed. (Baltimore, 1995), 136; Victor Kaufman, *Confronting Communism* (Columbia, MO, 2001), 147–154; Gordon Chang, *Friends and Enemies* (Stanford, 1990), 217–252.

14. NARA/RG59/LOT64D452/2/1/Aviation (civil)/Staff Note #1/June 28 and July 2, 1963; PRO/FO371/16223/Sept. 17, 1962.

15. NARA/RG59/LOT64D452/2/1/Aviation (civil)/Staff Note #1/June 28 and July 2, 1963.

16. Chang, *Friends and Enemies,* 229; NARA/RG59/1963 Alpha-Numeric Files/3343/AV (Civil) Com Bloc/May 14, 1963.

17. NARA/RG 59/1964–1965 Alpha-Numeric Files/618/Aviation (civil) AV 10 Rates and Charges Can-US 1/64 to AV 6 Airlines Chile 1/1/64/Feb. 7, 1964; ibid./Box598/AV-Aviation 20-1 Civil Air Weekly Summaries #65/39/Oct. 4–8, 1965.

18. Kennedy Library/National Security Files/410/China, 1961–1963 [1 of 3]/Aug. 16 and Feb. 1, 1963; ibid./314/10/NSC Meetings/July 31, 1963.

19. NARA/RG59/1964–1965 Alpha-Numeric Series/AV-Aviation (Civil) 2-1 Air Weekly Summaries 1/1/64 #64/8/Feb. 9–15, 1964.

20. For background, see Robert McMahon, *The Cold War on the Periphery* (New York, 1994), and Andrew Rotter, *Comrades at Odds* (Ithaca, 2000). NARA/RG59/1963 Alpha-Numeric Files/3342/AV-Aviation (Civil) Chicom/June 3, 1963.

21. NARA/RG59/1963 Alpha-Numeric Files/3342/Aviation (Civil) Chicom/May 29, 1963.

22. Ibid./3336/Aviation (Civil) #63/22/June 2–8, 1963.

23. Myron Smith Jr., *The Airline Bibliography* (West Cornwall, CT, 1988), 327–329; www.piac.com.pk/inside_pia/history/pia_history.htm (accessed 12/15/03).

24. Tillman Durdin, "China's Shiny Airports Await Planes," *New York Times,* May 12, 1971, 4.

25. NARA/RG59/1963 Alpha-Numeric Files/3635/STR CHICOM-A/June 8, 1963; ibid./3342/AV-Aviation (Civil) Chicom/June 17, 1963.

26. NARA/RG59/1963 Alpha-Numeric Files/3342/AV-Aviation (Civil) Chicom/June 19, 1963; Kennedy Library/National Security Files/India Series/110/India, General/June 10–19, 1963.

27. Ibid.

28. David Mayers, "John F. Kennedy and His Advisers," paper presented to the Society of Historians of American Foreign Relations 2000 Conference, manuscript in author's possession; Kennedy Library/Papers of John Kenneth Galbraith/34/Jan. 28, 1960; NARA/RG59/1963 Alpha-Numeric Series/3342/AV-Aviation (Civil) Chicom/June 24, 1963.

29. NARA/RG59/1963 Alpha-Numeric Series/3342/AV-Aviation (Civil) Chicom/June 25, July 1 and July 9, 1963.

30. Kennedy Library/President's Office Files/123/Pakistan Security 1963/July 7, 1963.

31. Ibid., July 8 and Oct. 8, 1963 (emphasis in original).

32. NARA/RG59/Bureau of Far Eastern Affairs, Subject, Name, Country File, 1960–1963/22/Pol-7 Visits and Meetings/Undersecretary Ball's Visit to Pakistan, Aug. 1963/Aug. 12, 1963; ibid./1963 Alpha-Numeric Files/3350/AV-Aviation (Civil) Pakistan/July 25, 1963; ibid./Office of the Assistant Secretary/Subject Files, 1964/1/POL July–Sept. 1964/Aug. 14, 1964.

33. NARA/RG59/Bureau of Far Eastern Affairs, Subject, Name, Country File, 1960–1963/22/Pol-7 Visits and Meetings/Undersecretary Ball's Visit to Pakistan, Aug. 1963/Aug. 12, 1963. Publicly, Khan offered a conciliatory line, stating, "No objections have been conveyed to us" ("Air Pact with China Signed by Pakistan," *New York Times*, Aug. 30, 1963, 3); "Chinese Arrive in Pakistan to Sign Air-Link Agreement," *New York Times*, Aug. 15, 1963, 2.

34. Kennedy Library/President's Office Files/123/Pakistan Security 1963/Oct. 8, 1963.

35. Chang, *Friends and Enemies*, 228–252; "JFK, China, and the Bomb," *Journal of American History* 74(2): 1287–1310; NARA/RG59/Bureau of Far Eastern Affairs, Subject, Name, Country Files 1960–1963/21/Aug. 13, 1963.

36. NARA/RG59/1963 Alpha-Numeric Files/3347/AV-Aviation (Civil) Jap(an)/July 16, 1963.

37. Ibid., July 11, 1963.

38. Ibid./3350/Av-Aviation (Civil) Pakistan/July 29, 1963.

39. Ibid./Box3342/AV-Aviation (Civil) Chicom-A/Sept. 2, 1963.

40. Ibid./Oct. 24 and 31, 1963.

41. Ibid.; author interview with John Cunningham, Oct. 14, 1999; NARA/RG59/1963 Alpha-Numeric Files/3347/Aviation (Civil) Japan/Nov. 5, 1963.

42. NARA/RG59/1963 Alpha-Numeric Files/3342/AV-Aviation (Civil) Pakistan/Oct. 7 and 24, 1963.

43. Ibid./3350/Av-Aviation (Civil) Pakistan/Nov. 5 and Dec. 19, 1963; ibid./3347/AV-Aviation (Civil) Jap(an)/July 11, 1963.

44. NARA/RG59/Bureau of Far Eastern Affairs, Subject, Name, Country Files 1960–1963/21/DEF1963/Dec. 7, 1963; NARA/RG59/1963 Alpha-Numeric Files/3347/AV-Aviation (Civil) Jap(an)/Oct. 10, 1963.

45. NARA/RG59/1963 Alpha-Numeric Files/3347/Nov. 29, 1963; ibid./3342/AV-Aviation (Civil) Chicom/Dec. 6, 1963.

46. Ibid./3635/STR Chicom-A/Dec. 12, 1963; Boeing Company Archives/Allen Collection/Commercial Contacts—Government/Contracts "USAF/Government Officials" 7/63-6/64/Dec. 17, 1963; ibid./"Contracts" 1/7/60-12/67/Dec. 12, 1963.

47. NARA/RG59/1963 Alpha-Numeric Files/3336/Aviation (civil) AV 2-1/Weekly Civil Air Summary #63/49/Dec. 8–14, 1963; Smith, *Airline Bibliography*, 328; "China's Air Links Stirs U.S. Concern," *New York Times*, May 1, 1964, 3.

48. Kennedy Library/President's Office Files/123/Pakistan Security 1963/Oct. 8, 1963; "Pakistan to Store U.S. Parts in China," *New York Times*, Apr. 25, 1964, 58.

49. NARA/RG59/1964–1965 Alpha-Numeric Series/Box 1424/STR CHICOM 1/1/64/Jan. 14 and 27, 1964; "Pakistan Buys Jet Airliners in Britain Rather Than in U.S.," *New York Times*, Jan. 27, 1964, 46.

50. "Air Lines Discuss Routes to China," *New York Times*, Mar. 1, 1964, S17; Durdin, "China's Shiny Airports," 4; "Peking May Widen Air Links Abroad," *New York Times*, Jan. 26, 1971, 65.

51. NARA/RG/59/1964–1966 Alpha-Numeric Files/1417/STR 14-3 4/1/66/May 4, 1966; PRO/FO371/183448/Mar. 12 and Nov. 22, 1965.

52. Ibid./650/AV1 General Policy Plans, UK 1/1/64/Jan. 15, 1965; Keith Hayward, *Government and British Civil Aerospace* (New York, 1983), 70.

53. PRO/FO371/172432/Jan. 23, 1963.

54. NARA/RG59/1963 Alpha-Numeric Files/3635/STR CHICOM-A, MemCon/Nov. 21, 1963; Hanson Baldwin, "Peking Has Delivery System at Hand for Nuclear Attacks on Asian Points," *New York Times*, Oct. 26, 1964, 5; PRO/FO371/BT11/6222/Nov. 11, 1964.

55. PRO/FO371/170702/Aug. 27, 1963; DO196/254 for this topic.

56. PRO/FO371/170703/Sept. 30, 1963.

57. NARA/RG59/1963 Alpha-Numeric Files/3635/STR CHICOM-A/MemCon/Nov. 21, 1963.

58. PRO/FO371/170703/Nov. 23, 1963.

59. PRO/CAB129/112/C63(13)/Feb. 4, 1963; FO371/170702/Sept. 18 and 23, 1963; FO371/175496/Feb. 12, 1964.

60. PRO/FO371/175946/Feb. 12, Nov. 11, and Dec. 15, 1964.

61. PRO/FO371/164422/Nov. 30, 1962.

62. PRO/FO371/187023/Jan. 8, 1966.

63. NARA/RG59/1964–1966 Alpha Numeric Files/1423/STR Strategic Trade Control CHICOM A/Jan. 1, 1964.

64. NARA/RG59/1964–1966 Alpha-Numeric Files/599/AV-Aviation (Civil) 2-1/Air Weekly Summaries 1/1/64/Feb. 9–15, 1964; PRO/BT11/6222/Jan. 6, 1966.

65. NARA/RG/59/1964–1966 Alpha-Numeric Files/1423/STR9-1 CHICOM 3/1/66 to STR CHICOM-J 1/1/64/July 1, 1964; ibid./1963 Alpha-Numeric Files/3632/14-3 List Review/Dec. 27, 1963.

66. PRO/FO371/181017/Apr. 8, 1965; PREM13/759/Jan. 4, 1966.

67. PRO/FO371/181017/Mar. 19, 1965; LaFeber, *The American Age*, 611.

68. "NO VC10s for China," *Financial Times*, Oct. 7, 1965; PRO/BT11/6222/Note attached to Dec. 16, 1965; FO371/187023/Jan 8, 1966.

69. PRO/PREM13/759/Feb. 17 and 18, 1966.

70. Ibid.; PRO/FO371/187023/Jan. 8 and Feb. 18, 1966.

Conclusion

1. "China Will Purchase 6 British Jetliners in $48-Million Deal," *New York Times*, Aug. 25, 1971; "Chinese Team Is Named for Tour Here," *New York Times*, Mar. 20, 1972, 53.

2. "Long Trip by Chou Expected," *New York Times*, Aug. 18, 1970, 5.

3. NARA/RG59/1967–1969 Alpha-Numeric Series/550/AV 9-Pak/July 2 and Sept. 19, 1969; ibid./1970–1973 Alpha-Numeric Series/1538/STR: Chicom-P/Dec. 21, 1970 and Mar. 5, 1971; ibid./STR 12-3 Chicom/June 8, 1970.

4. "Seattle Braces for Boeing Slump," *Chicago Tribune,* Mar. 21, 1993, M9.

5. NARA/RG59/1970–1973 Subject Numeric Files/657/STR 12-3 Chicom-Pak/ June 29 and Dec. 4, 1970.

6. NARA/RG59/1970–1973 Subject Numeric Files/Box 657/AV-6-Pak 1/1/72/Aug. 19, 20, and 24, 1971, and Jan. 12, 1972; Raymond Rasenberger, "Letter to the Editor," *Washington Post,* Aug. 28, 1971.

7. Henry Kissinger, *Diplomacy* (New York, 1994), 723.

8. Bernard Gwertzman, "American Concern, with US Approval, Plans to Show Aerial Navigation Equipment in Peking in April," *New York Times,* Dec. 3, 1971, 15.

9. NARA/RG59/1970–1973 Alpha-Numeric Files/627/AV 12-2 CHICOM 1/1/70/ Dec. 18, 1970; "Chinese Airline Is Said to Get Soviet Jets," *New York Times,* Feb. 9, 1972, 4.

10. Richard Witkin, "US Grants Boeing License to Sell 10 707s to China," *New York Times,* July 6, 1972, 1.

11. NARA/RG 59/1970–1973 Alpha-Numeric Files/627/AV 12-2 1/1/72 Chicom/ July 24, 1972.

12. David Einstein, "Boeing Gives Seattle Stake in Asia/Pac Rim," *San Francisco Chronicle,* Nov. 17, 1993, 1; Edward Epstein, "Summit Notebook," *San Francisco Chronicle,* Nov. 20, 1993, A11; William Greider, "The Real Chinese Threat," *New York Times,* Mar. 5, 1997, A19.

13. Greider, "Real Chinese Threat," A19; Craig Smith, "Airbus Gets $1.5 Billion Order from China, a Boost in Duel with Boeing," *Wall Street Journal,* Apr. 16, 1997, A15; Tony Walker, "France Forges Ahead in Trade with China," *Financial Times,* May 16, 1997, 7; Gwen Ifill, "Clinton to Fight Foreign Subsidies," *New York Times,* Feb. 23, 1993, A1.

14. "Clinton Signs China Trade Bill," *New York Times,* Oct. 10, 2000, A1; "Remarks by the President at American Society of Newspaper Editors Annual Convention," Apr. 5, 2001, White House News Release.

15. Chang, *Friends and Enemies,* 43; Michael Mastanduno, *Economic Containment* (Ithaca, NY, 1992), 93; Kennedy Library/President's Office Files/123/Pakistan Security 1963/Oct. 8, 1963.

Archives, Manuscripts, and Private Interviews

Boeing Company Archives, Reston, Washington
    Papers of William Allen
British Public Record Office, Kew, England
    Air Ministry Files
    Board of Trade Files, BT 11
    Cabinet Records, CAB 134, CAB 21, CAB 130
    Defense Records, DEFE 7
    Dominions Office Records, DO 164
    Foreign Office Files, FO 371
    Foreign Office Files, Papers of the Foreign Secretary (Bevin and Eden), FO 800
    Ministry of Civil Aviation Files
    Ministry of Supply Files
    Prime Minister's Files, PREM 11 and PREM 13
Dwight D. Eisenhower Library, Abilene, Kansas
    Administration Series
    Ann Whitman File
    Cabinet Series
    D. D. Eisenhower Diary Series
    National Security Council Staff Papers
    Papers of Christian A. Herter
    Papers of Donald Quarles
    Papers of Elwood Quesada
    Papers of James C. Hagerty
    Papers of John Foster Dulles
    Papers of the President's Commission on Foreign Economic Policy

Papers of the White House Office, Office of the Staff Secretary
White House Central Files
Gelman Library, George Washington University, Washington, D.C.
National Security Archive
John F. Kennedy Library, Boston, Massachusetts
Bureau of International Commerce
Department of Commerce
National Security File
Oral History Files
Papers of Dean Rusk
Papers of George Ball
Papers of Jack Behrman
Papers of James C. Thomson
Papers of John K. Galbraith
Papers of Lincoln Gordon
Papers of Luther Hodges
Papers of Robert Murphy
Papers of Roger Hilsman
President's Office File
Presidential Papers
Records of the Department of Commerce
Records of the President's Boeing Aerospace Board
Records of the United States Civil Aeronautics Board
Records of the United States Office of Science and Technology
White House Staff Files
Library of Congress, Washington, D.C.
Papers of Robert Taft
Papers of W. Averell Harriman
George Meany Labor Archive, Silver Spring, Maryland
American Federation of Labor Correspondence Files
Mudd Library, Princeton University, Princeton, N.J.
Papers of John Foster Dulles
National Archives and Records Administration, College Park, Maryland
Bureau of International Commerce, Record Group 476
Commerce Department Records, Record Group 489
Defense Department Records, Office of Munitions Control, Record
Group 334
General Records of the Department of State, Record Group 59
Records of the Secretary of Defense, Record Group 330

Harry S. Truman Library, Independence, Missouri
    Clayton-Thorpe Papers
    Naval Aide Files
    Office Files: Records of the National Security Council
    Papers of Clark Clifford
    Papers of Dean Acheson
    Papers of George Elsey
    Papers of Stuart Symington
    Papers of Thomas Finletter
    President's Air Policy Commission
    President's Secretary's Files
    Records Relating to the Korean War
University of Washington Archives, Seattle, Washington
    Closed Papers of Warren Magnusson
    Papers of Brock Adams
    Papers of Henry Jackson
    Papers of Lloyd Meeds
    Papers of Thomas Pelley
    Papers of Warren Magnusson
Western Manuscript Collection, University of Missouri, Columbia
    Papers of Stuart Symington
Yale University Archives
    Papers of Robert Lovett
    Papers of Adolf Berle, Microfilm Collection
Private Correspondence and Interviews
    Richard Becker
    Steve Bettinger
    Guy Bordelon
    John C. Cunningham
    Randall Cunningham
    Cecil Foster
    Francis Gabreski
    Carl Kaysen
    Donald Lopez
    James Low
    W. Walter Rostow
    Charles "Chuck" Yeager

Acknowledgments

I have incurred numerous debts in pursuing this study. Most I will never adequately repay, at least until I might begin returning the favor to the next generation. Till then, I hope it will suffice if I merely mention the most glaring of those to whom credit is due. Financial support was provided by the Andrew W. Mellon Foundation, the University of Wisconsin's Vilas Fellowship Program, and the University of Wisconsin–Madison's History Department. A Daniel and Florence Guggenheim Fellowship of the National Air and Space Museum provided for sixteen months of study and research in that unrivaled institution. Grants from the Truman Presidential Library, the Eisenhower World Affairs Council, and the Kennedy Presidential Library made research possible. Archivists and their support staff at each of these archives made such work a pleasure, as did those at the National Archives in Maryland and the British Public Record Office in Kew. Each deserves special thanks for helping to declassify some of the best material for this study. The staffs at the University of Washington Library and the Boeing Company archive also went beyond the call of duty, and not only by providing Mariners tickets. I also thank the University of Pennsylvania's International Relations Program, where I served as a Lecturer while revising this manuscript, Yale University's superb International Security Studies center for a John M. Olin Postdoctoral Fellowship, and Texas A&M University's Bush School of Government & Public Service, where this peripatetic historian found a welcoming intellectual home and talented colleagues devoted to expanding the boundaries of service and scholarship. Dick Chilcoat, Chuck Hermann, and the Bush School have our undying gratitude for bringing us to the heart of Texas. The omnipresent Mine Hill Road Development Fund filled in the gaps of the above support.

Special thanks must go to Professor Richard Immerman and his Center for the Study of Force and Diplomacy at Temple University, who offered me an academic home when I needed one most. Though perpetually overburdened, Richard also greatly improved this book through his careful reading of the manuscript, and remains a fount of advice. He is a true mensch.

I also thank the many friends and colleagues who helped make this study a reality. Kathleen McDermott believed in this project from our first meeting. Gordon Baldwin, Tim Borstelmann, Ted Bromund, John Cooper, Ann Drier, Kathi Drummy, John Gaddis, Ian Jackson, Scott Kaufman, Paul Kennedy, Hiroshi Kitamura, Constance and Ben Kim-Gervey, Richard Kirkendall, Jennifer Logan, Wendy Nelson, Luis Rodrigues, the three Schlosses, the Simaneks, Jeremi Suri, Charlie Witham, and Tom Zeiler all contributed to this study in ways large and small. Geoff and Melissa French provided friendship, a shared home, and my beautiful goddaughter. Andrew Preston proved the best friend a fellowship ever brought; Walter LaFeber's unfailing support provided a standard of excellence; Alan Dobson opened numerous doors despite my suspicion that he did not believe even one of my interpretations; while Tom McCormick, my mentor, taught me more about life than history—and he taught me quite a bit of history at that. Special thanks must go to Elizabeth Webster and Luke Gerwe for their eleventh-hour editing, and Sydney Woodington organized the images and performed forensic accounting to secure permission for their use.

My family deserves thanks as well. Grandma Lovey's support, and Josh and Ben's examples of excellence, helped in ways they'll never know. Ben also applied his writer's eye to the entire manuscript at a crucial moment. My other brother, Ron, has been ever faithful. Adam, Trish, Miyoko, David, and the rest of the extended Huddell clan offered open hearts and Cougar Cheese. Special thanks to my father who explained all things of value, and the reason his son should go to Texas, through the gentle reminder of Jackie Robinson, the greatest American of all.

For my parents, and Katie, words can never suffice. Without the former I never would have achieved my goals. Without the latter, accomplishment would not have been worthwhile. I hope to become as good a parent and teacher as they were to me. I hope too, one day, to be as good a historian as she. That said, it is traditional as a concluding gesture to acknowledge that without the intellectual support of the preceding masses this study would not have been possible, though its mistakes I must bear as my own. In the past I ran contrary to this tradition by publicly blaming Katie for mistakes one might find in the text. Yet even if I alone found this funny, I must in good conscience blame her for one more thing as well: she is responsible for everything good in my world, including and especially for Marshall, whose smile reminds me to make the world a better place.

Index

Acheson, Dean, 91, 99, 102, 111; China trade and, 104, 105, 110, 112, 114, 116, 202

Aeroflot (Soviet airline), 195, 254, 255

Airbus, 6, 296, 302

aircraft industry: British and American compared, 7, 17; post-WWII, 6–7, 31, 39–45; workers in, 28, 32, 33, 279. *See also* Brabazon plan; *specific manufacturers*

Aircraft Industry Working Party (Britain), 191–192

Aircraft War Production Council (AWPC), 41–42

Air France, 137, 138

Air Intelligence Division study, 81

Air Ministry (Great Britain), 55, 65, 73–74, 88, 197; Comet sales and, 133, 174; export controls and, 143; Open List and, 56–57; sales to Soviets and, 66, 68, 118; Soviet air capability and, 141, 142. *See also* Ministry of Aviation (Great Britain)

Air Policy Commission, 49

airpower, 5–6, 8–9; as function of manufacturing might, 17; nuclear weapons and, 45–46, 48; Soviet display of, 174–175; strategic importance of, in World War II, 19–20, 24, 26; strategic importance of, postwar, 39–40; vs. manpower, for strategists, 26

"Airways to Peace" (exhibition), 39–40

Alexander, Harold, 142, 157, 158, 175;

axial-flow exports and, 150, 151–152, 154, 155–156

Allen, William, 43, 128, 135, 274–275

Allies, in World War II, 18–19. *See also* World War II

All Nippon Airways (Japan), 270, 273–275

Alsop, Joseph and Stewart, 47

American aviation coordination: Arnold-Powers agreement, 30, 31–32; aversion to government influence in, 40–43, 44, 50, 60; BOAC Comet and, 135–136; influence of Pentagon spending on, 43, 45, 49; line production in, 32; manufacturing plan of 1940, 19–20; "open skies" policy, 41, 95–97; Proclamation 2776 and, 94–95. *See also* Boeing Company; *specific manufacturers*

Amery, Julian, 216–217

Anglo-American competition, 29, 33, 51–52, 59; American market dominance and, 188–193; axial-flow driven jets and, 144, 146; Brabazon plan and, 34–35, 37; Comet success and, 135–136, 139, 155; export controls and, 60–61, 155, 178–79; post-WWII, 6–7, 40–41; sales to Soviets, 71; supersonic transport, 216–217; as zero-sum game, 65, 100, 132, 161, 185, 251, 277

Anglo-American relations, 11, 185–186, 300–302; anticommunism and, 92; Arnold-Powers agreement, 30, 31–32, 33, 35, 53; aviation diplomacy and, 16;